The Soviet Russian State

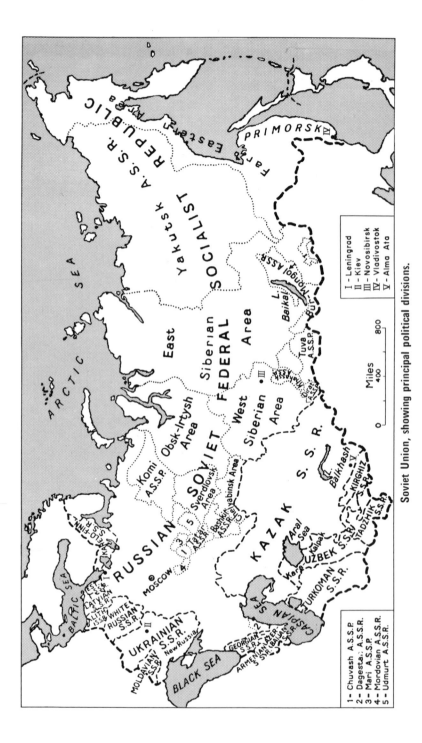

Soviet Union, showing principal political divisions.

Legend (upper):
I – Leningrad
II – Kiev
III – Novosibirsk
IV – Vladivostok
V – Alma Ata

Legend (lower):
1 – Chuvash A.S.S.R.
2 – Dagestan A.S.S.R.
3 – Mari A.S.S.R.
4 – Mordovian A.S.S.R.
5 – Udmurt A.S.S.R.

Map labels:
ARCTIC SEA
Far Eastern Region
YAKUTSK A.S.S.R.
SOCIALIST FEDERAL SOVIET REPUBLIC
East Siberian Area
West Siberian Area
RUSSIAN
Komi A.S.S.R.
Obsk-Irtysh Area
Sverdlovsk Area
Chelyabinsk Area
Bashkir A.S.S.R.
Tuva A.S.S.R.
Mongol A.S.S.R.
L. Baikal
PRIMORSK
KAZAK S.S.R.
L. Balkhash
KIRGHIZ S.S.R.
TADZHIK S.S.R.
Aral Sea
UZBEK S.S.R.
TURKOMAN S.S.R.
Kara Kalpak
CASPIAN SEA
MOSCOW
UKRAINIAN S.S.R.
New Russia
MOLDAVIAN S.S.R.
BLACK SEA
WHITE RUSSIAN S.S.R.
LITH. S.S.R.
LATVIAN S.S.R.
EST. S.S.R.
KARELO-FIN. S.S.R.
BALTIC SEA
GEORGIAN S.S.R.
ARMENIAN S.S.R.
AZERBAIJAN S.S.R.

Scale:
Miles
0   400   800

The Soviet Russian State

Robert G. Wesson

UNIVERSITY OF CALIFORNIA, SANTA BARBARA

John Wiley & Sons, Inc.

New York   London   Sydney   Toronto

Front Cover Photo: Marc Riboud, Magnum

Copyright © 1972, by John Wiley & Sons, Inc.

Library of Congress Cataloging in Publication Data
Wesson, Robert G.
  The Soviet Russian State

  1. Russia—Politics and government—1917-
I. Title.
JN6515 1972.W47   320.9′47′084   70–39013
ISBN 0–471–93380–5

Printed in the United States of America

10 9 8 7 6 5 4 3 2 1

Preface

Two major difficulties stand in the way of understanding of the Soviet system. One is that the subject is too large and complicated for our view. Books on Soviet politics inevitably differ markedly in the angle from which they look at the huge subject, the sides on which they focus and those which are left to the obscurity of the background. As observers grope toward understanding, the Soviet system is comparable to the elephant of the old story: one blind man thought it was like a wall, another like a tree, another like a rope, according to which part he laid hands on. The Soviet Union may be regarded primarily as a power-hungry dictatorship, as a polity of modernization, as an apparatus of bureaucratic rule, as an ideological-revolutionary state, or as a refurbished prolongation of the Russian empire. Each view has its share of truth, but no one can claim to present the whole truth. At the risk of neglect of some aspects, it is the hope of this book to offer a reasonably full and systematic outline of the entire Soviet political system and its functioning. This has required touching, albeit briefly, upon virtually all aspects of Soviet life, from strictly governmental institutions to problems of religion and literary creativity, from elements of historical continuity to current-day trends.

The other chief difficulty of Soviet studies arises from the fact that the Soviet leadership does little to facilitate analysis of their state. The Soviet political reality is as shrouded as the giant squid, only bits and pieces of which ever come to the surface of the ocean. This book claims no special gift of perception and attempts no Kremlinological analyses. Two broad ideas, however, have seemed most illuminating and helpful for understanding. One is the multinational character which sets the Soviet realm apart from all others and particularly the nation-states of the West. No other great power has a comparable problem of unity, and a strong case can be made for the thesis that much of Marxism-Leninism and the party-state with all its accompaniments derives from this fact. The other basic reality is that the Soviet Union has largely outgrown or outworn the revolutionary impulses and the social transformation of its birth and has become a settled authoritarian state. This also has very large implications, some of which are briefly explored here.

An effort has been made to draw upon Soviet sources and to let them speak for themselves. Most of this work, however, has inevitably been based on secondary works. It is unnecessary to apologize for making use of the laboriously gathered information and the judgment of numerous writers; but indebtedness to them, those indicated in footnotes and lists of readings and many others, is gratefully acknowledged. Thanks are also due to the editors of *Soviet Studies* and *Russian Review*, who have kindly given permission for use of material which originally appeared in their pages. Among those who have made comments and suggestions regarding the manuscript, Prof. Donald Carlisle was especially helpful. Much is owed to the encouragement and cooperation of the editor, Mr. Carl E. Beers. And deepest gratitude goes to Deborah Wesson, who not only typed thousands of pages but helped in many other ways to bring the work to completion.

Santa Barbara, California   Robert G. Wesson

Contents

x   **Contents**

The Soviet Russian State

Introduction

The importance of understanding the Soviet political system is apparent. Only the U.S.A. and the U.S.S.R. are superpowers, with global capacities and responsibilities. Although both have seen some weakening of their authority since the time, up to about 1960, when the world seemed truly bipolar, and their share of world industry has diminished with the upsurge of Western Europe and Japan, no challenge to their military might is on the horizon. The future of international relations in the nuclear age depends primarily upon their policies and outlooks.

It is hardly less important that Russia is the ideological leader of a substantial sector of the world's population and the political inspiration of others, including to some extent those which have broken away from it, as the People's Republic of China; and it is influential in many countries struggling to find means of integration and modernization. For much of the world's population, the Soviet model represents the alternative to the more traditional Western way. There are two great sign-posts to the future, the Western-American and the Soviet-Russian, the "capitalist" and the "socialist" (to use these misshapen terms), the looser individualistic and the more organized collectivist. The ideological dichotomy has weakened in recent years, as state regulation becomes more pervasive in the economies of Western lands, the Soviet Union becomes more conservative, and new problems of industrialization press on all modern societies. Yet, if the Soviet Union has lost revolutionary vocation, it has reasserted ideological fundamentals; and decay of political elan has been compensated by the growth of power, as the Soviets have brought themselves militarily level with the United States and have so gained new confidence and freedom of action abroad.

Not only those who subscribe to the Soviet doctrines and positions are influenced by them. Many of the non-Communist Left have taken something of vocabulary, goals and political mentality, consciously or unconsciously, from the Soviets—more from their words than from their actions. Many violent anti-Communists have also borrowed from the mentality and methods of the Bolsheviks, more from their actions than from their pretenses. Fascism was in a large part an imitation of the communism which it abhorred. All one-party regimes, whose numbers are legion, owe much to Lenin; the authoritarian state controlled by a mass-based mobilizing party has been the tremendous political innovation of our century. Tensions and opportunities for mass communication in relatively backward communities prone to despotic rule might have brought about something like the party-state, even if there had never been a Russian Revolution. But Lenin's party inaugurated that form, which, in full intensity in Russia or China or in diluted form in many African states, stands over the life of half of humanity. From this point of view, the Russian Revolution has been infinitely more successful than the event most comparable to it, the French Revolution. Without accepting the Marxist-Leninist vision of history, we can well agree that the Bolshevik seizure of power and establishment of the Soviet state was possibly the most important planned political event of all history and truly ushered in a new political era.

Yet the study of the Soviet experiment was long slighted. The initial reaction of the West to the seizure of power in the world's largest state by a band of internationalist fanatics was skepticism; the Leninists' claims seemed too wild to be taken seriously. When they won the civil war, they had to be taken into account; but it was still assumed, especially when seeds of restored capitalism seemed to sprout in the Russia of the early and middle 1920's, that their extremism was only a passing revolutionary fever. A few Western intellectuals were curious about bolshevism, but there was very little study of the system. The Stalinist "Second Revolution" of collectivization of agriculture and forced-draft industrialization under the five-year plans stirred wider interest and aroused the sympathies of many intellectuals; but only when the United States unexpectedly found the Soviet Union its most powerful ally, did that country become a major object of study in the universities. Admiration gave way to hostility in the cold war, but popular and scholarly attention to the Soviet system swelled. Nothing in history has been so thoroughly researched as the antecedents of the Russian Revolution.

Nonetheless, understanding of the Soviet Union remains difficult, as is evidenced both by the contradictoriness of interpretations and the frequency with which seemingly expert opinion has erred. One reason is that it is impossible to be quite dispassionate about something which is in one way or another so important to everyone. The Soviet Union represents one side in the world's greatest contest; and its ostensible purposes challenge, for better or worse, the economic, social and political order of the non-Communist world. Moreover, the question of whether or how we can get along with the Russians is practically a question of life or death. This disposes to irrationality in various modes, one or more of which probably enters the perceptions of practically everyone: to see the Soviet Union mostly as a threat and so to emphasize its unpleasant aspects; to see it primarily as an alternative to less admirable aspects of our own society; to see it as mild and unthreatening so that it not be taken as an excuse for militaristic development of our society; to seek reasons to hope that the differences between Soviet and American society and hence the likelihood of conflict are diminishing.[1] Western interpretations have fluctuated between tendencies to believe the best, or at least point to the positive aspects, and tendencies to believe the worst and to ignore real achievements, much as Soviet military power has been at times over and at times underestimated. It is truly a challenge to perceive reality without gross preconceptions, uninfluenced by emotional or political interests.

Deficiencies of information contribute to the difficulties. Much is published about various areas of Soviet life; but the more interesting something may be for the political scientist, the more likely it is to be shrouded in secrecy. The curtain is drawn closely over all important political processes; we are informed only partially of decisions taken. We most miss critical writing of informed Russians about their own system. Such glimpses of the inner workings as were vouchsafed in Khrushchev's day have not been repeated under his successors. Foreign visitors bring back interesting but usually rather superficial impressions about Soviet life and attitudes. Among the more informative are accounts of students who have remained for an extended period and mingled closely with their Soviet counterparts.[2] Some memoirs have appeared in recent years, but they have generally conformed to political expectations.[3] Refugees carry some useful information with them; but no highly placed Soviet leader has ever defected to shed light on the recesses of the apparatus. Attitudes and impressions of those who have turned their backs on their society and are constrained to justify that which is to their government a crime are properly suspect. Stalin's daughter, Svetlana Alliluyeva, offered interesting comments in her two books; but she saw little of the political process.

Study of Soviet politics also suffers from the fact that familiar concepts are applied to an alien field. Russian ways are measured by American standards, whereas it should be recognized that a very different society has different strengths and weaknesses. That Soviet political values are different from American should not be obscured by the fact that the Russians use Western terminology. "Party" in the Soviet context means not a political organization striving for political, especially electoral advantage, a "part" of the electorate, but means a tightly organized revolutionary group before the Revolution or the governing corporation today. Correspondingly, for the Soviets, "government" means little more than the administrative apparatus. "Democracy" means a certain deference to forms of popular sovereignty plus widespread public

---

[1] For a survey of attitudes toward the Soviet Union, see Walter Laqueur, *The Fate of the Revolution, Interpretations of Soviet History* (Weidenfeld and Nicolson), London, 1970.

[2] See, for example, William Taubman, *The View from the Lenin Hills* (Coward-McCann Inc.), New York, 1967.

[3] As of this writing, the authenticity of *Khrushchev Remembers* is disputed; it is in any case discreetly silent regarding recent developments.

participation in the carrying out of programs and a commitment to social justice. Such terms as "elections," "parliament," and "socialist" have such different meanings as applied by the Russians that their use in a book like this is excusable only because we lack substitutes.

The subject of political inquiry is also different from that to which the eye has become trained on the Western scene. The marked divergence of formal and overt aspects of government from the less formal power structure requires compensatory evaluation. Politics, understood as the contest for power, does not exist openly nor, so far as we know, in any organized way at all. Political struggle goes on behind the stage, but it seems to involve individuals and very loose followings much more than organizations or institutions. Yet many more matters than in more open societies are politically important and subject to political decision. State power makes itself felt in and draws upon almost every field of human endeavor. The student thus finds himself passing rapidly over the actions of the "legislature" but drawn to consider the management of industry, agriculture, education. literature, and art. He is called upon to understand an entire huge and involved society, with all the complexity of the modern industrial state plus such additional complications as the multinational character of the Soviet Union.

There is not much systematic method in the study of Soviet politics. For the most part, writers are guided less by coherent theories than by general knowledge of political behavior, human nature, and educated intuition, as they take the facts available[4] and try to assess them. However, students are apt to think to some extent in terms of one of two conceptual models emphasizing antithetical sides of the Soviet experiment. One may be called the totalitarian approach, although the adjective is dubiously descriptive. This stresses the aspect of power, the authoritarian leadership which varies in intensity from Lenin to Stalin's successors but which remains at all times determined to maintain maximum control of the entire society, holds economic progress secondary to political rule, and uses manipulatively the vaunted Marxist goals of ultimate liberation and equality. The other major tendency, which might be called the social democratic, stresses rather the development of the Soviet Union as an industrial state. In this view, the leadership seeks control not for its own sake but mostly to foster economic progress, which is making the harsher and more rigid methods of rule obsolete; and its ostensible utopian purposes are to be considered fairly genuine. There are correspondingly differing estimates of the capacity of the Communist Party to make effective a single will for the entire society and of the ability of subordinate organizations to protect vested interests and make themselves into effective although subordinate power centers. These

---

[4] Much of the most informative of Soviet writing is readily available in translation in *Current Digest of the Soviet Press,* and *Soviet and East European Abstract Series* (abbreviated ABSEES).

are perhaps the most crucial questions of sovietology, and much of this book will deal with them.

There have been some efforts to apply newer, more or less quantitative methods to the study of Soviet affairs; and, although it can hardly be claimed that they have furnished great enlightenment thus far, they may well become important for the future. However, if numerical data are often elusive in open Western societies, they are infinitely more so in the Soviet case. Limitations of Soviet statistics, both in coverage and reliability, are severe. Western scholars cannot conduct public opinion polls or questionnaires of representative samples in Moscow or Tbilisi. The Russians themselves have published some poll results, but there are doubts as to methodology, and Russian polls are mostly utilitarian, designed to learn such things as how workers may be made more satisfied or how leisure may be better organized. Those few which have political significance, usually also have political purpose. Thus the Komsomol, the party's youth section, polled young people on "Why do you like Lenin?", not, "Who is your favorite hero?". Content analysis of Soviet publications has brought out some interesting trends, but it suffers from the fact that one can seldom feel sure how much content of publications represents the writers' sentiments. The promise of elite studies is similarly qualified by the fact that we know little about the elites except what they desire us to know.

Various theoretical approaches suffer parallel handicaps. Political culture is obviously as important in the Soviet Union as elsewhere, but it is harder to define there, and we lack means of assessing it except in the most impressionistic fashion. Not only do popular attitudes and expectations contribute to the shaping of the government and limit what it can undertake, but the government to the best of its ability makes the political culture; cause is confounded with effect. Another approach more suited to the Western than Soviet politics is group theory. One can gather hints of independent views of various sectors of Soviet society, but it is not clear how far they have real independent influence on policy at the center. Perhaps the party simply consults them so far as convenient, and study of groups in the Soviet Union seems more descriptive than explanatory. Closely related input-output theory would like to see the political process as resultant of the demand-inputs which are aggregated and adjusted by the government to give rise to decision-outputs and allocations of resources. It is a truism that something of this must occur in every state, and we would like to know much more of it in the Soviet Union. But the Communist Party does not see itself as mediator of society. It has its own drives and purposes, which are not given by any other recognizable group. Neo-Marxist inquiry into what class interests are served by the political system is difficult, as ownership of means of production is not easily defined and differences of "classes" are obscure. Structural-functional analysis is more promising, at least if one thinks in terms not only of the economic functions normally emphasized in the West but in terms of political functions. Political institutions in the Soviet Union are consciously and apparently with much sophistication designed for their purposes, and understanding can be improved in this light.

In general, approaches tailored for the study of politics in Western lands can be usefully applied to the Soviet Union only if account is taken of the greater importance for the latter of political rulership as a force per se. Whatever the subsidiary autonomy, present or potential, of other groups, as industrial managers or the military, they all function in the force-field of the party, while it remains to be proved whether or how far the party is influenced by groups external to it.

This fact, however, compensates for some of the difficulties of studying the Soviet state. If the United States has an indefinite number of centers pulling in different directions, the Soviet Union is overwhelmingly dominated by a single one, which largely dictates the conditions in which others operate and the forms in which they may strive to make themselves felt. Although the latter is by no means so monolithic as it would present itself, unity of decision-making is incomparably greater than in Western societies. The power of the single leadership also imposes a simplifying uniformity. The institutions of party rule seem, like Soviet newspapers, to be practically the same, with only accidental local variations, over all the immense land, and even beyond it in satellites as Mongolia and Bulgaria.

We also enjoy the advantage that the Soviet regime seems to have come into a period of relative stability. Not only the Revolution but the transformations of Stalin's day are far behind and accepted as permanent facts; and the experimentation of Khrushchev has passed. There are perhaps growing pressures below, but inertia, if not equilibrium, prevails as never before in Soviet history. The element of caprice so prominent in Khrushchev's rule seems also to have largely disappeared. Stalin in his last major pronouncement could propose such an impracticality as that farmers should directly barter their produce for industrial goods, and Khrushchev was able to have corn planted on a large scale in near-arctic regions. But the present directorate seems cautious, impersonal, systematic, at least fairly well informed, and hence more predictable. This time of relative calm may be favorable for taking stock of the Soviet system, and perhaps for placing it in historical context as an understandable and integral part of world history and of the condition of modern civilization, even though we do not expect to learn much of its inner workings.

This book seeks only to present realities without drawing moral conclusions. This does not mean necessarily avoiding words which carry strong connotations or refusing to make appraisals. Thus, if democracy is taken in its etymological and traditional sense, one need not apologize for lack of objectivity in stating that the Soviet Union is less democratic than Denmark, or indeed than any country where political parties can freely promote their candidates and programs and can hope for success in uncontrolled elections. It can be fairly recognized that pluralism and diversity are much less in Soviet than in Western societies, hence that freedom as usually understood is less in the former, while order is greater. It is a matter of individual preference if one assesses more highly discipline and centrally directed purposefulness or perhaps anarchic freedom. Soviet vices and virtues are different from those of the "bourgeois" West, and the virtues may be other than those claimed. The Soviet system, being different, should be recognized as uncongenial to many Western values; this does not mean that it may not have values of its own.

But if the Soviet state is, for better or worse, deeply different from traditional Western political ways, it is part of mankind. So far as it has improved life in the present and shows promises of making a better life for the future, this should be cause for satisfaction. So far as it has failed, this is part of the broader failure of humanity, which has yet to solve the problem of government.

READINGS

L. G. Churchward, *Contemporary Soviet Government* (American Elsevier Publishing Co.), New York, 1968.

Merle Fainsod, *How Russia is Ruled* (Harvard University Press), Cambridge, Mass., 1963.

Richard C. Gripp, *Patterns of Soviet Politics*, 2nd. ed. (The Dorsey Press), Homewood, Ill., 1967.

John N. Hazard, *The Soviet System of Government*, 4th ed. (University of Chicago Press), Chicago, Ill., 1968.

David Lane, *Politics and Society in the USSR* (Random House), New York, 1971.

Alfred G. Meyer, *The Soviet Political System*, (Random House), New York, 1965.

John S. Reshetar, *The Soviet Polity* (Dodd, Mead & Co., Inc.), New York, 1971.

Derek J. R. Scott, *Russian Political Institutions* (Praeger), New York, 1966.

Recent works giving a sampling of sociological-behavior, quantitative, and empirically-oriented approaches include Roger E. Kanet, ed., *The Behavioral Revolution and Communist Studies* (The Free Press), New York, 1970; and Frederic J. Fleron, Jr., ed., *Communist Studies and the Social Sciences* (Rand-McNally & Co.), Chicago, Ill., 1969.

An over-all chronology is: George J. Prypic, *A Century of World Communism* (Barron's Educational Series), New York, 1970.

1. Old Regime

Lenin is hailed as the founder of the Soviet state, but in 1917 he saw himself as beginning a movement of world-historical renovation not to reform the state but to abolish it. The evil and exploitative institutions should be smashed, not replaced, and all nations fused in a new community. But, within a few months, the Bolsheviks found themselves constrained to make peace with Germany in order to save their infant regime from destruction by German armies. Because world revolution hung fire, it was necessary to build up an army and a state apparatus to protect the revolutionary movement where it had prevailed on the former Russian empire. For several years, however, the Soviet position was that this was only a temporary expedient pending the inevitable triumph of socialism everywhere, and when the Soviet Union was formally established in 1923 this was presented as a step toward a world Soviet state. But the temporary accommodations gradually became permanent. Stalin acknowledged the "temporary stabilization of capitalism" and proclaimed the building (although not the completion) of "socialism in one country". He subsequently repressed the Marxist theory of the withering away of the state and restored Russian history and patriotism to respectability. For several decades the idea that the Soviet state is eventually to be dissolved in a global Communist community has become ever more tenuous.

The Soviet polity has thus matured from apocalyptic movement to a state much like others, and it has become easier to see the state of the rather conservative bureaucrats of today as a continuation of the historical Russian empire, much as the France of Robespierre and Napoleon was a continuation of the France of Louis XIV. Soviet Russia occupies very nearly the same territory and is inhabited by the same peoples as tsarist Russia. The political culture of

9

tsardom inevitably went into the building of the new regime, and the Soviet state has inherited the geographical situation of the old empire, straddling Eastern Europe and Northern Asia, and many of its fundamental problems.

The character of the old Russian state was deeply influenced by its geographical situation, stretching across a vast plain open to both the European and the Asiatic world. At first, however, Russia seemed to belong thoroughly to Europe. Kievan Russia of the eleventh and twelfth centuries was a collection of small principalities and trading towns not greatly different from those rising all over Europe. But warriors from the faraway Mongolian plains flooded over the steppes in the thirteenth century, and they held nearly all the Russian lands in bondage for some two centuries. This subjection, which is played down in the Soviet writing of history, gave birth to and shaped the Russian state of modern times. The long period of near-isolation from Western civilization set Russia culturally far back. Coming out from under the Mongol yoke, Russia found itself handicapped by a technical-cultural lag which, despite some spurts, it has never been able fully to overcome. Russia was also set apart from Western political tradition, because the new Muscovite Russia took practical lessons in rulership from the Mongols, who taught their Russian subjects the arts of tax-gathering, census-taking, conscription, and postal communication. They introduced the death penalty, judicial torture, and the idea that the sovereign was owner of the state to whom all owed service; they furnished the model of a huge, absolutist, and effectively taxed empire quite unlike anything in Western Europe since the Roman empire.

The Mongols also opened the way to indefinite expansion of Russia across Asia, because the decay of their enormous state left a corresponding area of weakness. Rising at first by service to the Khans who ruled the Russias indirectly, the prince of Moscow was able to gather larger and larger territories under his own aegis, to weaken and then cast off the Mongol yoke, and to unite the Russian lands in a campaign of liberation against the alien and heathen forces of the Golden Horde. At about the same time, the Byzantine empire, with which the old Russia had had close ties, was finally liquidated by the Turks. The rulers of Russia now regarded themselves as the upholders of the Orthodox faith in the world, and successors of the Caesars of Byzantium and of Rome, who had claimed rightful dominion of the universe. Liberation merged into conquest; the unification of Russia continued into rapid expansion over alien lands. Russia became the heir ideally of the Byzantine empire and practically of the Mongol.

The Russian empire, taking shape in the latter part of the fifteenth century, went forward for many generations, mostly by slow pressure, with the benefit of few spectacular campaigns or glorious victories, sometimes halting but rarely retreating from any land once claimed. Like the overseas empires of Western European states—Portugal, Spain, Holland, etc.—being formed concurrently, it was made possible by technological superiority. Despite its own relative inferiority, Russia was close enough to the West, geographically and culturally, to borrow fairly readily instruments of modern warfare and rulership, while most of its neighbors remained much more backward; it was the only semi-European power with a backyard stretching indefinitely into Asia. Most gains were consequently made in Asia with little difficulty; smaller acquisitions on the Western frontiers were usually far more costly.

The growth of the Russian empire differed from that of the overseas European empires in its primarily political motivation. It was a continuation of the conflict with the Mongols, which knew no stopping point on the endless plains; mixed with love of glory and power was the lingering fear that the Asiatic warriors might return to the attack. It was a crusade of Orthodoxy against heathens or heretics on the frontiers. It was a movement into thinly settled territories, wherein peasant settlers often preceded soldiers and administrators. It was a civilizing mission to less civilized lands. Frequently, the Russians put down rebellions and moved to eliminate threats on the frontiers, and in so doing pushed their power into new lands, to which there were new threats to be dealt with in turn. Everywhere they strode forth as bearers of justice, peace, and righteousness, and protectors of the people, an interpretation continued by Soviet historians. The chief purpose was to build strength; expansion meant greatness and security, the glory of the rulers and security against the ever present threat of a technologically superior West.

Expansion was continuous and unending; even as tsardom was coming under great strains in its last decades, the court was dreaming of new lands in Manchuria, Iran, the Balkans, and Eastern Europe. Boundaries were not fixed and traditional, as Russian rule extended where it was strong enough to do so. Unlike contemporary overseas empires, it was contiguous; the few non-contiguous acquisitions, as Alaska, were readily relinquished. This meant that the new lands were not held as colonies but were incorporated into the Russian state, becoming integral and inseparable parts of the sacred body. For a nation as France, imperial possessions were attractive but not vital; for Russia, they came to seem indispensable for greatness and even survival.

Russia thus became a multinational continental empire, a polity very different from the nation-states of the West. As early as Ivan the Terrible (1547–1584), it had engulfed large numbers of Finns and Tatars; to them were added Ukrainians, various Siberian peoples, Turks and others of Central Asia, the great and small nationalities of the Caucasus, Balts, Poles, etc. All formed a supranational conglomerate, a medley of races and cultures, cemented by force, bureaucracy, loyalty to the tsar, and to some extent Orthodoxy, with the Russian core comprising much less than half of the total. The aristocracy was multinational, too, as local magnates who were willing to serve the tsar were rewarded with high office; only a small fraction of the nobility was of wholly Russian origin. The royal family itself became non-Russian, mostly German by ancestry. There was little prejudice, and those who accepted the empire and its faith were generally received as equals. The government of the many peoples was rather successful (except chiefly in Poland, where crude coercion antagonized a proud people) and russification progressed well, at least until forces of nationalism began making themselves felt in the latter part of the nineteenth century.

This composite state so much grander than ordinary nations was—and is—extremely impressive. The Russians have drawn far-reaching conclusions from the infinitude of their space. As Gogol wrote, "What does this limitless space prophesy? Is not limitless thought to be born here, when thou art limitless? Is not here a land for the great . . .?" Russians like to call their country "boundless" ("bezbrezhnaia"). The signature of Moscow radio has long been "Broad is my native land" ("Shiroka strana moia rodnaia"). In wartime, the Russians have made much of the size of their land, the token of its invincibility. "One has but to look at a map of the world to be filled with holy awe at the future destinies of Russia," wrote a Russian publicist in 1831.[1]

In view of its size and catholicity, it was natural that Russia should dream of mastery of the globe, which seemed its appointed destiny. In the infancy of the empire, pious Russians regarded their tsar as more than an ordinary monarch; at the end of the fifteenth century, a monk wrote to Ivan III, "All kingdoms of the Orthodox Christian faith are merged into thy kingdom. Thou alone, in all that is under heaven, art a Christian tsar . . . two Romes have fallen, but the Third stands, and there will be no fourth."[2] Russia should then, as ever, be the center of the believing world. Belief that Russia, or the Russian ideal, should rule indefinitely continued through the nineteenth century, finding eloquent expression in such writers as Danilevsky and Dostoievsky. The latter saw the Russians as a peculiarly universal people, called upon to overcome the divisions of mankind by the "all-uniting Russian soul."[3]

There was in this no sense of aggressivity but enormous self-righteousness. Danilevsky, eager for territorial and cultural expansion, found Russia uniquely free from greed for power; and Dostoievsky saw the empire as based on the thirst for brotherly unity. In conquering and civilizing, the Russians felt themselves fulfilling a noble duty for peace and unity, even suffering for the redemption of mankind. Radicals opposed to the power of the tsar were hardly

---

[1] Luigi Villari, *Russia under the Great Shadow* (T. Fisher Unwin), London, 1905, p. 138.

[2] There is a curious parallel to the Soviet eschatology whereby, after the fall of feudalism and capitalism, Moscow stands forth as the bearer of the new order of socialism.

[3] "The curious fact is that if one substitutes communism for [Dostoievsky's] conception of the mission of the Orthodox faith and world revolution for his notion of a Pan-Slavic war against Europe, the identity of his whole position with that of the modern Soviet Russia would be striking." Ernest J. Simmons, *Dostoievsky, the Making of a Novelist* (Oxford University Press), New York, 1940, pp. 327-328.

less impressed with the vocation of the Russian people to lead the brotherhood of humanity.

AUTOCRATIC STATE

Immensity also made autocracy inevitable. The huge realm elevated the rulership and submerged the individual, and called for a symbol of unity and a firm center of control to secure the coherence of the whole. There was no room in the imperial scheme for autonomous rights of any province or group; no division should compromise its unity. The tsar claimed, and his subjects believed, that the defense of the realm and its integrity, if not its sublime mission, required a single unquestioned authority. The principle of the Russian world, from the fifteenth century to the present, has been union, in antithesis to the divisiveness—anarchy, as it has seemed to Russians—of the West.

Ivan III, who first set the Muscovite state on a firm foundation and greatly expanded its area, borrowed the forms of Byzantine rulership and set himself up as autocrat. Ivan IV (the Terrible), who also greatly enlarged Russian dominions, made autocracy into despotism. He regarded all his subjects, high and low, as his slaves and executed many of the old nobility who were insufficiently humble. Peter the Great, who went to great lengths to modernize and westernize his land, had no idea of introducing Western notions of constitutionalism. Instead, he terrorized, hardened the enserfment of the peasants and the obligations of the gentry, and proclaimed his absolutism juridically. Despite infiltration of Western ideas in the following two centuries, the tsar's autocratic power continued to be upheld as necessary for the empire. His will was legally supreme. Although admittedly mortal in body, he was divine in authority; and the realm in theory belonged to him as his estate. Defeats, first in the Crimean War and then in the war against Japan, led to some relaxation of absolutism, and the half-revolution of 1905 forced the tsar to concede a half-constitution. But as the dynasty neared its downfall, Nicholas II was thinking of doing away with this blemish on the monarchic power.

Important aspects of tsarist government, society, and culture, some of which have continued in modified form into the Soviet state, are directly or indirectly outgrowths of the vocation and burdens of the continental empire. Great imperial states, as dynastic China, the old Turkish empire, the Roman empire, the Persian, even that of the Incas on a more primitive level, have been basically similar political systems with much in common under varied appearances.[4] This is understandable, as their common preoccupation is the preserva-

---

[4] For a detailed treatment of the ways of empires, see: Robert G. Wesson, *The Imperial Order* (University of California Press), Berkeley, Calif., 1967.

tion of the integrity of a huge domain. The Russian empire was hardly different from other universal or semi-universal empires except in terms of relations with the outside world. The classic empires, of which the Chinese and Roman are the best examples, could practically ignore the external world except for the necessity of occasionally warding off barbarian incursions. The Russian empire had always to compete with and learn from dynamic states on its western frontiers.

It is presumably for this reason that Russia has not seen the degradation of despotism that came over other empires. The concentration of authority in the person of the ruler was, however, far more than that which ordinary European kings could boast. According to the fundamental law of the empire, obedience to his command was ordained by God, and there were no legal limitations to his command in any sphere. The adjective "holy" was freely applied both to Russia and to its ruler; subjects eager to please a forceful character like Peter the Great equated him with God. The old Russian vision was that a wonderfully benevolent Father of his Country, like a Chinese sage-emperor, should bring happiness to the people. These were convinced that only their immediate oppressors were evil and that the distant tsar only wished to help them.

It was the tsar, however, who conferred all authority. There were no real institutions apart from his office, only instruments and extensions of it. Justice and legality had meaning only in relation to his sovereign will, and a person was important so far as he enjoyed the favor of the ruler. The tsar's councils were appointed and advisory, to make suggestions and to register his decrees. There was no ministry or prime minister until the monarchy was shaken by the semi-revolution of 1905. Ministers reported independently to the tsar even after a ministry of sorts was established, lest they should form a solid front and so acquire some authority of their own.

So far as there was pressure for a constitution, it was because of Western influences and examples. When the regime was weakened in the troubles of the first half of the seventeenth century, a sort of proto-parliament like feudal estates of Western Europe met a few times, but it was no longer convoked after the monarchy was restabilized. Russia was too big for a national assembly to be practical, and the tsar had no need to secure the concurrence of a burgher class for his taxes. After Peter, a group of nobles tried to impose a constitution on the accession of Ann, in order to enhance their own privileges, but she literally tore it up. In the nineteenth century, various tsars mulled over constitutional schemes which would have supposedly broadened participation in the government and so given it a sounder basis without appreciably restricting the will of the autocrat. Nothing came of such schemes; and conservatives remained convinced that a constitution would be the ruin of Russia, even as liberals began demanding constitutional government as essential to catching up with the West.

Without a constitution, there was not much of a legal order; laws were less respected as they proliferated abundantly and were often neglected or modified by administrative action or set aside. Right conduct was the loyal carrying out of the wishes of the sovereign, not conformity to any legality. The tangle of rules benefitted chiefly the bureaucrats who interpreted and applied them.

The bureaucracy ruled in the name of the autocrat. The administrators and the military held the empire together, and they formed the ruling classes. They might be called a single class, as the military and bureaucratic ladders were parallel, with equivalent ranks, and men readily shifted from one to the other. Promotion was theoretically by merit but mostly by seniority or favor; it became more dependent on intrigue as one approached the summit, where cliques competed for the ear of the tsar and he played them off one against another for the fullness of his own authority. Russian literature abounds in satires on the ignorance, indolence, and especially the venality of lower officials; but the apparatus managed to fulfill its necessary functions.

Despite its immensity and diversity, the state was highly centralized and left minimal scope for local autonomy. The empire was divided into some fifty "governments," each under a governor who was servant of the tsar but himself a little tsar to those below. The territorial divisions were drawn independently of history or nationality. Many parts of the empire, as the Ukraine, Poland, and Baltic states, had a special status for a time after they were acquired; but the tendency was nearly always toward full incorporation and administrative equality. It was feared that any concessions to local separatism would only raise demands for more. In imitation of Western institutions, Catherine II established self-governing bodies of cities and of local nobility, but they were endowed with no real powers and became lifeless organs of administration. So extreme was centralization that no public buildings could be built except on plans approved by the capital, and a permit was required for the erection of any house with more than five windows.

To make effective the will of the tsar and his administrative apparatus, a large police force, regular and political, was necessary; and there were manifold although ordinarily ineffective controls over all potentially dangerous activities. Unauthorized associations, theoretically even informal discussion groups, were banned by law; and societies were to be set up only in officially approved form. By the passport system (which was anathema to revolutionaries, including Lenin, but which Stalin reinstated) everyone needed a passport to travel away from his place of residence. Travellers had to register with police, and a permit was required for a change of residence. Police agents were everywhere; porters, for example, informed police of arrivals and departures and other suspicious events. At a time when international movement in most of Europe was very casual, Russia had strict controls of exit and entry.

Although bars were somewhat lowered after 1860, it was long difficult for nonofficial Russians to leave their country. Foreigners, if not excluded, were treated with much suspicion, often watched by the police, and at times isolated from the people.

In outward mildness, tsarist Russia had a death penalty only for political crimes. But flogging and other corporal punishments were common, and banishment to Siberia was widely used. After a modern court system was established, the police retained powers of administrative exile. The village commune, too, had the authority to exile delinquent members;[5] the popular justice which Khrushchev introduced as progress toward communism included authorization for neighborhoods similarly to cast out "parasitic" individuals.

The political police first became prominent when the *Oprichnina* of Ivan the Terrible carried around a dog's head and broom as symbols of sniffing out treason and sweeping it away. Peter reorganized and strengthened this department, as he did most aspects of autocracy, and gave it full powers to execute its decisions. Such agencies grow slack in time and require reorganization to restore effectiveness; in 1825 Nicholas I set up the "Third Section" to promote political tranquility. It was not only to persecute dissent but to forestall it by benevolent and welfare programs, but the latter aspect was soon neglected. The Third Section, or Okhrana ("Guard"), as it came to be called, became more active as the revolutionary movement grew in the latter decades of the nineteenth century. Dabbling in revolutionary intrigue, it was a political power in its own right, sometimes conniving in political assassinations. About one-tenth of the membership of revolutionary parties in 1912 were police agents.

Assertive tsars such as Ivan the Terrible and Peter were ready to kill tens of thousands to eliminate those suspected of evil intentions and cow the remainder. Paul, at the end of the eighteenth century, struck down thousands. It was probably a sign of decreasing self-confidence that subsequent tsars shrank from mass slaughter even when threatened by real and violent revolutionary movements. Only in the aftermath of the near-overthrow of the government in 1905 were a few thousands executed.

Peter the Great introduced censorship along with printing; with greater or less stringency, it has continued in effect ever since (except briefly in revolutionary breakdowns, 1905 and 1917). In the latter decades of tsardom, however, it lost much of its effectiveness. Contacts with the West eroded it, and private ownership of a growing press enabled publishers and journalists to pit their wits freely against the censors. The tsarist state, not greatly concerned with public opinion and lacking a dynamic ideology, did not greatly exert itself to mould the minds of the people. Writers were prevented from publishing materials deemed seditious, but there was little effort to give them positive

[5] Sergei Puskarev, *The Emergence of Modern Russia* (Holt, Rinehart and Winston), New York, 1963, p. 144.

instructions. In the nineteenth century, the official ideology, summarizing the bases of the regime as "Orthodoxy, Autocracy, Nationality," carried only mild conviction. S. S. Uvarov, who formulated it for the good of the state, had personally the opposite convictions: he was a skeptic, liberal, and cosmopolitan.[6]

The church was an auxiliary of the state. Its roots were in Byzantium, traditional center of caesaropapism; but its real loss of independence came with the expulsion of the Mongols and the establishment of the autocracy. Rulers of premodern Western Europe tolerated an independent church not because they approved of it but because they lacked power to subdue it; Russian rulers had such power. The subjection of the Orthodox Church to the state was practically completed by Peter, who declined to appoint a new patriarch but placed the church under a synod of bishops named by himself and headed by a lay official, the Over-Procurator. Subsequently, the church became practically a department of the state apparatus and shared its rot.

Although the church had some direct political functions, as keeping records of the population and reporting suspicious persons, its chief function was to bless the social and political order, stressing respect for the government, obedience to the tsar, and the duty of paying his taxes. Religious instruction was mandatory in schools, and adherence to Orthodoxy was a mark of belonging to the political community. Alien peoples were encouraged to join, although not forced to do so; and no one was permitted officially to leave the church.

Russia experienced no reinvigorating Reformation because it lacked independent political centers which made the Reformation possible. Lacking stimulation for independent thought, the Orthodox Church became extremely conservative, dogmatic, and formalistic. Exalting faith over reason, it seemed to many to stand for ignorance and sloth. The consequent weakness of religious faith in an atmosphere of intense religious emotion helped to nourish revolutionary utopianism.

Like the church, the Russian nobility was denied any autonomy faintly comparable to that of its counterparts in the West. As the Russian state was growing, well before Ivan the Terrible, the hereditary nobles were becoming highly dependent on the tsar's favor. Ivan nonetheless extirpated them as dangerously independent and largely replaced them with a new nobility of conditional landholding and service to himself. Even the highest called themselves the tsar's slaves. Peter ennobled thousands of commoners over the old families, and he regularized the scheme of rankings by position. In theory anyone could enter as a youth at the bottom of the ladder and rise according to loyalty and ability alone. Adopting Western patterns, eighteenth-century rulers relieved the nobility of the obligation of state service, but birth gave little status

---

[6] S. V. Utechin, *Russian Political Thought* (Frederick A. Praeger), New York, 1963, p. 72.

compared with rank in the army or bureaucracy. There was little class feeling or sense of nobles' honor. Such class organizations as the nobility had were imitations of the West, lacked vitality, and mostly amounted to agencies of administration. Without primogeniture, estates were divided and titles cheapened by passing to all children; Russia was overrun with princes and princesses.

The theory that status depended only on service was ineffective, as the road to the top was short for those born to wealth and official connections and was nearly impossible for the vast majority of the population. But social mobility was probably higher than in many Western countries. From Boris Godunov down to leading generals in the forces of the last tsar (and chiefs of the White armies in the civil war), many a man rose from poverty to the highest standing. Nor was race a barrier; Turks or Tatars (if russified) had a fair chance. As in imperial China, education opened the door to advancement, if a poor boy managed to obtain it. Any one with a university degree could step onto the civil service ladder; and there was some feeling that, having been educated by the state, he was duty-bound to do so. Military boarding schools also offered some poor boys a way to indefinite advancement.

Behind the notion of rank by service there was an ethos of the equality of all beneath the all-powerful tsar, who was in turn devoted to the welfare of his charges. It was held excellent to be a slave, as all together were, of the master of the universe. Standing above classes, he was guardian of a kind of democracy, which in the tsarist as in the Soviet context meant not civil liberties or any positive power for the people but mostly social justice and equality. By the theory of autocracy, the greatness of the empire rested on the close union of tsar and people. "We are all in state service," said Nicholas I, a martinet autocrat who boasted of the popular election of his dynasty. Autocracy was supposed to protect the humble and prevent the exploitation of man by man; and in some places as in Poland, the tsars did take the part of the lower classes against the upper. Russians dreamed of a great collectivist state based on the loyal masses and the loving ruler.

Soviet history tends to regard the tsar as protector of the people from rapacious nobles, at least in premodern times. In reality, the peasants, comprising the overwhelming mass of the population (nearly four-fifths as late as the Revolution) were enserfed from the sixteenth century until well into the nineteenth, their condition worsening to virtual slavery at the same time that serfdom was coming to an end in Western Europe. Their obligations of service to the landholder were supposed to correspond to the latter's to the state; but when the gentry was released from obligations, the serfs remained in bondage. The emancipation of 1861 failed to improve their lot greatly because of its onerous conditions. The government then strengthened the peasant village commune as a means of control and taxation. Often driven to the edge of starvation by the taxgatherer, they were vulnerable to extortion in a variety of modes, subject to conscription which was not unlike a long penal servitude, and usually regarded practically as cattle by haughty bureaucrats. They lived in practically a different world and certainly another century from that of the privileged and educated. Their accumulated rage came occasionally to the fore in jacqueries, when they would burn the manor house and chase away or perhaps murder the gentry family. When the tsar ceased to rule in 1917, their alienation surged into unrestrainable violence, without which the Bolsheviks could never have climbed to power.

An equalitarian feature of the peasant commune, which many radicals much admired and of which Karl Marx approved, was the periodic redivision of cropland. Cultivation was done by individual families, but there was a good deal of communalism within the commune, and ideas of individual property were weak. This was not, however, merely peasant mentality; the sanctity of property rights was generally much less in Russia than in the West. In line with the theory that all Russia was the estate of the ruler, private ownership was theoretically always conditional, although in practice reasonably secure; and there was a feeling that powerful private interests were incompatible with the dignity of the state. The idea of an aristocracy of wealth or a bourgeois political order was abhorrent. The ethos of the tsarist empire, like other comparable empires, was profoundly anticapitalistic.[7]

Commerce was held in low esteem, the merchant class being regarded for the most part as loathsome rascals. Commerce was hence largely in the hands of Jews and other non-Russians, Germans, Poles, Armenians, etc., whether because they were more adept at it or because it was beneath Russian dignity. Foreign capital owned a large part of industry and mining, somewhat as in Latin America today. Xenophobia was added to hatred of the bourgeoisie to produce a climate for Marxist radicalism.

The Russian middle and industrial classes were the weaker because much of the economy was government-owned or controlled. A large fraction of the land, employing millions of peasants, belonged to the state or crown. The government built the railroads and largely managed foreign trade, at one time an official monopoly. Forced-draft industrialization under Peter and again in the last decades of the nineteenth century was sponsored by the state primarily for military needs. At the end of the nineteenth century, many large enterprises were state-owned, and most of the rest depended upon state orders or official protection. Nationalization of industry by the Leninists represented no transcendent change.

The state-dominated economy was inefficient; and Russia was much poorer than such countries as England, France, or Germany, despite abundance of land and raw materials. There are many accounts of the peasants sharing

[7] Cf. Wesson, *The Imperial Order*, pp. 93-95.

one-room huts with the cow, industrial workers living in barracks like sheepfolds, and the like; Russia was a semi-undeveloped country. This was not simply a matter of overcoming the backwardness inflicted by the Mongol dominion. From the sixteenth century, the tsarist state was fostering the importation of Western technology, at least so far as relevant to military needs. Around the beginning of the eighteenth century, Peter the Great strove to modernize in all ways, even requiring his subjects to shave and smoke. No Western nation ever made such a mighty official effort to raise its level of civilization; and Peter successfully imported much technology, and established many industries. Russia remained thereafter definitely a member of the European state system, and Peter's successors were fond of Western fashions; the court and aristocracy even became French-speaking. But they became complacent; and from the first part of the eighteenth century until the last decades of the nineteenth, Russia tended to fall farther behind.

The lag became greater after Western economic progress began to accelerate in the industrial revolution, which began in England in the latter part of the eighteenth century and gradually spread to the Continent. For example, Russia in the eighteenth century had one of the world's largest iron industries, based on an abundant raw material, charcoal. When coal came to be used for smelting iron and steel, Russia could not keep pace, despite excellent coal deposits; and its output hardly grew while that of England and other countries multiplied many fold. The worst time of stagnation was the reign of Nicholas I (1825–1855), when the government, confident of its strength in the memory of the victories of the Napoleonic wars and fearful of liberal contagion, closed off the country for a generation as it had not been since the time of Peter.

The Crimean War in 1854, when Russia was unable to cope with a small Anglo-French force on Russian soil, thousands of miles from bases of the Western powers, showed the results. The safety of the empire clearly demanded reinvigoration; and a series of liberalizing reforms, most importantly emancipation of the serfs, was followed by an economic upswing. Under the leadership of an energetic finance minister, Count Witte, the currency was strengthened, many railway lines were constructed, and a substantial industrial plant was swiftly built up. There was considerable progress toward catching up with the industrializing countries of the West, although these were also growing rapidly. But Witte's policies were widely unpopular, and he was removed when his work was only well begun. Tsardom's last decade, after defeat by Japan and the convulsion of 1905, saw a new surge of industrial progress, which now owed less to the government. But the world war again revealed grave backwardness and inefficiency.

When it felt pressed, or when galvanized by a strong will not overly frightened of alien ideas, the tsarist state could industrialize fairly competently. But there was little autonomous drive to material progress. Why this was so is a question beyond the scope of this book. It is entangled with the whole problem of why less developed parts of the world have remained less developed despite ample opportunities in many areas to learn the latest modes of production for decades or generations. It is also related to the opposite question of why some countries have been elected to lead scientific-industrial revolution. But it is clear that the Russian system was devised and directed primarily toward assuring political control, and economic considerations were sacrificed to political. For this reason and because there was no organized opposition force to check officials' instincts for power and desire for gain, Russian society was, from the point of view of economic development, over- (and ill-) governed and over-taxed, controls and taxation lying most heavily on producers. Competition was seen as evil in principle. There were few incentives for improvement of production; political favor was the way to get ahead. Commercial morality and work habits were poor; the typical Russian was traditionally unmethodical, unpunctual, and lacking in thoroughness and other "bourgeois" virtues.

Such were some features of the tsarist state. The raw materials of the Soviet state are the same as those of its predecessor, with allowance for changes time has brought to civilization, and so are its main political problems. If it is true that the kind of problems a regime is called upon to meet is a principal determinant of its character, one might logically expect to encounter much in the Soviet Union reminiscent of tsarist practices.

TROUBLED STATE

The Russian situation spanning Europe and Asia made it possible to use Western technology to subdue much of the East and to draw strength from empire to resist the West, but it raised a host of problems which have plagued the Russian state and society to this day. Russian greatness rested on two somewhat contrary things, imperial rulership and the ability to adopt the technological civilization developed by looser Western societies. There has always been tension between the two. Progress was necessary, yet progress was subversive—at one time, censorship forbad mention of the word. It always caused cleavages between government and masses, when the former sought to push modernization vigorously, or between government and the educated as the latter wished more political changes than the government could countenance. The rulership wished to admit only that which would strengthen itself, but it has never been able to devise a perfect sieve to let pass necessary technical knowledge while excluding social and political ideas, or to take over large parts of Western culture without accepting their implications.

By geography, the concentration of population in the Western part of the empire, by race and religious and general cultural background, Russia has always been close to the West. Russians travelled in increasingly large numbers to western Europe. They measured themselves by European standards and, since their country always lagged behind, they were the more troubled by their perennial sense of inferiority. The consequent urge to follow Western ways and ideas led Peter to demand that his nobles dress in Western styles and inspired upper-class ladies of the nineteenth century to speak French and become ecstatic over French romances. As the penchant for Western things and ideas grew, the government answered with official xenophobia. Educated Russians became alienated from their background and from Russian political values.

The clash of purposes and outlooks goes back at least to Ivan the Terrible, who imported Western technicians while crushing vestiges of independence among his servitors, some of whom longed for the freedom and constitutionalism of then-great Poland. It became far more acute under Peter. A disastrous defeat at the hands of Swedes at Narva taught him the necessity of rapid development of military industry, and he went on to westernization on a broad front, even while tightening the grip of autocracy. He sought, with some success, to build up the economy by fiat, commanding managers and merchants like administrators. In his fondness for Western rationalism, he despised the conservative, ritualistic Orthodox Church and parodied its patriarch, yet he used it as a political instrument.

As Peter's successors coasted on the momentum he had given to the state, Russia began evolving from a simple society of rulers and serfs toward a complex pluralism, with the beginnings of middle and professional classes. A few writers and thinkers began playing with libertarian ideas, and the idea of a constitution was mooted. This type of discontent was superficial; but the separation of elite from masses deepened, as the former took on imported fashions while the latter remained backward and depressed. The government was shaken by rebellious peasants, who mounted a serious uprising under Pugachev, not by revolutionary intellectuals. The prevailing form in the West was "enlightened despotism"; and Catherine II welcomed French philosophers without thought of danger to her state, until the French Revolution shed a new light on relations between rationalistic-libertarian thought and the stability of monarchy.

The exposure of large numbers of Russian officers to Western society in the Napoleonic wars created new problems. Liberalism became something of an intellectual fad in the upper classes, and Alexander I himself gave thought to a constitution. On his death in December, 1825, a group of French-influenced officers attempted to impose a constitution by mutiny, an event later hallowed as the beginning of revolutionary action in Russia. Some of the Decembrists, as they were called, wanted a constitutional monarchy, others an authoritarian republic; but their ideas were so alien to the popular political culture that they had to tell their own troops that they stood merely for the legitimacy of the succession. The government did not take them very seriously, as only five persons were hanged and 120 exiled for the attempted overthrow of the regime. The abortive coup of 1825, however, gave the tsarist government a fear of imported ideas. Nicholas' answer was to exclude them so far as possible while keeping tight the reins at home. He thus kept Russia rather quiet for three decades at the cost of stagnation.

The response to defeat in the Crimean War was a series of liberalizing measures to patch up the old order. The freeing of the peasants from semislavery in 1861 was called for not only for humanitarian reasons but because grain exports required more productive agriculture and incipient industrialization needed free labor. It had been long on the agenda and long desired by the serfs, but the peasants were deprived of part of the land and were burdened with heavy "redemption" payments. Unrest in the countryside soon revived.

Another reform was the institution of an independent court system, with jury trials, on the most advanced Western model. This enlightened move backfired when the courts showed themselves unwilling to convict political offenders; and the police resorted to arbitrary administrative powers, including the right freely to exile anyone to remote localities in Siberia.

More promising was the institution of local self-government organs, the zemstvos. It was widely expected that this was a step toward some sort of national parliament, but it was a halting step. Elections to the zemstvos were so managed that they were practically organs of the local nobility, yet the government did not trust them and soon began whittling down their limited powers. They usually met only a few days yearly, and they could function only in innocuous areas such as roads, education, and public health, for which their financial resources were very meager. However, they showed the broad aspirations for improvement of the upper classes; and they educated a class of liberal political leaders who might, in different circumstances, have figured prominently in Russia's destiny.

Despite such measures, the situation of the government continued to deteriorate, and strains accumulated as Russia strove to keep up with the accelerating progress of the West. The industrialization program was fairly successful in providing the indispensable foundation for modern military strength. From 1860 to 1913 industrial production grew 5% yearly, a very respectable rate near which the Soviet growth rate seems to be settling. The growth of heavy industrial production was especially impressive. But there was much waste from bureaucratic incompetence, accentuating the abuses commonly encountered in early stages of industrialization. The prominence of foreign capital, controlling about four-fifths of the important industries, helped to make the whole program unpopular. Resentment of it tended to turn the nobility against the government, and the intelligentsia was generally hostile to industrialization. The still feeble industrial class was itself unfriendly to autocracy. Commerce and industry were inherently subversive of the tsarist order and alien to its mentality, and monetary values were rising at the expense of the traditional.

The conflict of values was felt most strongly by the small but rapidly growing urban working class. The peasants who came to town broke away from their traditional place in society and often left behind the church as well. Because of the shortage of housing, they were commonly put in barracks, the ideal situation for radical agitation. They carried with them their peasants' hatred against the owners, and they were freer to raise demands in the city than in the village. Yet the tsarist state offered them little. They had no political participation, not even the limited management of their own affairs which the peasant commune enjoyed. The government more or less effectively prohibited strikes and unions in the interests of industrialization; although there was some factory legislation against the worst abuses in the 1880's and afterwards, it was slackly enforced. In the early 1900's, the regime experimented with police-organized unions. When they got out of control and caused difficulties for factory owners, they were abandoned; but they taught the workers to organize. As Lenin recognized, the small Russian working class, concentrated in large plants in the main cities, was a disproportionately potent force for revolution.

The workers were discontented, although their earnings were rising fairly rapidly; the peasants were discontented without the benefit of material improvement. The burdens of industrialization fell on the latter, somewhat as they were to in Soviet times. They were unfairly taxed; and although per capita grain production declined, more was exported to finance imports. The grain export policy caused famines from time to time; and the tsarist government, like the Soviet, neglected investment in agriculture. Average landholdings decreased with the natural increase of population. New industry competed with hand-crafts and deprived the peasants of a secondary income. Old patterns of life were tending to break up. With the growth of commercial values and of contacts with the city, expectations of material improvement were filtering down even to the peasants.

The class structure of Russia was also changing. The nobility, the class upon which the regime saw itself resting, was increasingly demoralized. Unprepared for commercial agriculture and disposed to sell land to maintain the accustomed standard of living, no longer so important in the government in an age of growing specialization, the nobility was becoming self-consciously useless. It, too, was increasingly critical of the autocracy; and not a few of its offspring became revolutionaries. At the same time, the more liberally-inclined classes were rising. These included not only the small but growing numbers of business managers, merchants, bankers, and the like. Equally or more important was the multiplication of nonbureaucratic professionals, lawyers, scientists, doctors, engineers, journalists, and teachers. Unlike landlords, bureaucrats, police, and soldiers, these people were not instruments of domination but resistant to it.

Potentially independent-minded, they were some half million strong at the close of the nineteenth century; and they were the most important leaven of tsarist society.

The ideological foundations of the autocracy were also crumbling. The old messianism, with its universal vocation for Russia and her tsar, was becoming obsolete as decades wore on and Russia found itself playing the game of power politics on a level with other states and none too successfully. The failure to achieve the gains hoped from the Russo-Turkish War of 1878 contributed to disillusionment, and defeat by Japan in 1904 was much worse. There could be no great feeling of military superiority; and it was ironic that Russia was a great power by courtesy of Western financing. The ideas of autocracy, orthodoxy, and nationality were equally eroded. Loyalty to a ruling house, particularly one which had produced no very inspiring personality since Alexander I, was no longer an adequate bond of imperial unity. The doctrinally weak Orthodox Church was mystically backward and bureaucratically run, and it shared the corruption of the government. The seminaries produced not only priests but many revolutionaries, of whom Stalin was one. The use of the church to support the state led to cynicism and atheism and aroused resentment in the large non-Orthodox minorities.

The last element of the triad, nationality, was equally ineffectual. The multinational empire required a supranational or universalist basis; but nationalism, the basis of western European states, could not be excluded. The Russians began thinking of the empire less as a universal entity and more as a Russian possession. Beginning in the 1880's, russification, often harsh and crudely managed, became official policy. Pressures were directed especially against Poles, Ukrainians, and Jews, peoples who were more resentful as they felt themselves culturally superior to Russians. The minorities were becoming infected with ideals of national liberation flooding across Eastern Europe; the effort to squeeze them into Russian ways only alienated them further. By the end of the empire, some were dreaming of autonomy, others of independence.

The increasingly although somewhat superficially westernized educated sectors were almost unanimously desirous of great change and critical of a standpat regime lacking an ideal basis. They were ashamed of the poverty of the peasants and the backwardness of the government. They were frustrated by nonparticipation and inability to make the contribution which many longed to make to their society. Suffering from inferiority to the West abroad and from their lack of status, if not uselessness at home, many of them became passionately negative, rejecting the past and present of Russia even while moved by a great idealism for its renovation.

The regime was consequently subjected in the latter part of the nineteenth century to a rising tide of intellectual and literary criticism reminiscent of that which pounded the Bourbon regime prior to the French

Revolution. If the tsarist government had permitted full freedom of the press, it would probably have been swamped by a mass of irresponsible and extremist attacks from the alienated intelligentsia. Censorship was, however, considerably relaxed in 1865. Writers could usually transmit their message, and readers learned to get "Aesopian" meanings, which the censorship made more interesting and exciting. The progress of journalism made many more channels of expression and increased the problems of the censors. The expansion of higher education, required by the needs of bureaucracy and favored by the interests of the privileged classes, swelled the ranks of the unemployed or underemployed intellectuals. Great efforts were made to check radicalism at universities, as police kept students under surveillance and inspectors had stern disciplinary powers; but they were largely counterproductive, increasing the hatred of students for the regime.[8] Students expelled for radicalism, like Lenin, formed the mainstay of revolutionary organizations.

The main concern of the intelligentsia was the meaning and purpose of Russia in the world—Russian culture has always been somewhat narcissistic—and their preoccupation was with relations with the West. These relations became more painful with rapidly growing communications and travel; the intellectuals as never before belonged to two worlds. Since Russian backwardness was becoming more glaring and was less compensated for by military power, it was more than ever necessary to learn from the West and to admire it; yet this was a grievous humiliation for an empire with such an obvious claim to greatness. Some drew a logical conclusion and became westernizers, although it was not easy to see how Russia could really westernize and remain Russia. The majority took the psychologically more attractive course of disparaging the West while seeking to overtake it by borrowing its achievements, claiming spiritual superiority in compensation for technical inferiority. The West, as writers like Danilevsky saw it, was basically hostile, cheating Russia and profiting by its innocence. This feeling merged into native Russian anticapitalism and the low opinion of merchants and commerce: the West was bourgeois, materialistic in values, and therefore to be despised. The prevalence of non-Russians and foreign capital in Russian industry and trade enabled the writers to mix their scorn for the foreigner with their dislike for the antagonists of their state. They turned to immoderate revilement of the bourgeois West, which they accepted materially but rejected morally; Russia was poor but virtuous.

The compensation for inferiority was admiration of the Russian soul, the worth of which could be asserted without fear of disproof. Deep spiritual values were hardly to be found in the government and political institutions, but they were perceived in the peasant and his immemorial socialism. This came to be the main theme of the Slavophils, subsequently of the

---

[8] Bernard Pares, *Russia and Reform* (Archibald and Constable), London, 1907, p. 67.

Populists, and in this century of the Socialist-Revolutionaries. This stream of thinking owed a great deal to Western popular-democratic ideals, but it was turned against the West: Russia should be like a big family, perhaps under a good tsar, guided by moral-religious or communal feelings, in opposition to the supposedly anarchic, legalistic, materialistic West. In the view of the Slavophils, this meant that Russian backwardness was really a blessing, an idea employed later in a slightly different form by Trotsky. Having had to take lessons so long from the West, the Russians were disposed to see themselves as teachers; and the peculiar virtues of their natively socialist country were taken as giving it a mission of order and harmony, of moral if not political redemption of the capitalist West.

There were various strains of such thinking among the intellectuals of the latter nineteenth century, who seldom agreed for long on anything except their dislike for existent institutions and confidence in their own moral superiority. There were elements of irrationality; many, in escaping the unacceptable present reality, drifted to fantasy and indulged in imbalanced and immature criticism and in daydreams of the perfect society and how they would make it. Nihilism was for a time a fashion; in a semi-hysterical reaction against futility, bright young men and women talked about scrapping the old world without any clear idea of what they would put in its place. Poverty was praised, although they would relieve it; and Western standards were decried, although it was these which made Russians aware of suffering. It was the confusion of people who knew that their country had to be great yet saw it becoming weaker and more dependent, who felt that they should be doing something great yet did not know what to do.

How weak the moral foundations of the regime had become under several decades of intellectual attack was shown by its near-collapse in 1905. The regime entered an unpopular war against Japan in hopes of helping itself by military victory. Rapid and humiliating defeats brought popular protests, strikes, and demands for reform. After the massacre of about a thousand petitioners before the tsar's palace in January, 1905, discontent snowballed, with business leaders and professional men joining workers in demonstrations and strikes, while peasants looted and burned, until by October the country was paralyzed. Shame for Russia's political backwardness and disgust at the inadequacy of the regime left it with few supporters even among the upper classes. It was a signal change from half a century earlier when defeat in the Crimean War had caused no popular manifestations at all, a demonstration of the fragility which was to prove fatal in new defeats a few years later.

In the emergency, the tsar felt compelled to issue his October Manifesto, promising an elected legislative body and extensive civil rights, similar to those later enshrined in the Soviet constitution, freedom of speech and assembly, freedom from arbitrary arrest, and universal suffrage. This was a tactical success, as it appeased the moderates, while the extremists sought to continue violent action. In December, an uprising in Moscow, led by an assembly (Russian, "Soviet") of workers' representatives joined by various radicals, lasted for a week; but this was the last serious threat to the regime. The armed forces remained generally loyal, and in 1906 the government began a campaign of repression and reconsolidation. The peasants were subdued, the strike movement was broken, and many leaders of discontent were driven abroad, exiled to Siberia, or executed. The radical movements and parties were nearly liquidated, and tranquility reigned as it had not for years past.

The constitutional reform was less successful. Although the Duma, as the parliamentary body was called, was elected under a law designed to favor the conservatives, there was no possibility of agreement between it and the government. The Duma wanted a limited monarchy and radical reforms; the court was willing to concede practically no power and regarded the idea of a popular assembly with horror. As the Dowager Empress commented on the first session, "They looked at us as upon their enemies, and I could not make myself stop looking at certain faces, so much did they seem to reflect an incomprehensible hatred of all of us."[9]

The conflict led the government to dissolve the First Duma after a little over two months. It went no better with the Second Duma, which had a larger representation of the extreme Left, including parties which had boycotted the first. After it, too, was dissolved, the electoral law was changed by monarchic fiat to make representation of the different classes extremely disproportionate, and elections were rigged. Subsequent Dumas were sufficiently conservative and passive enough to cause the government no great concern. They were also constitutionally impotent. The Duma could neither control the ministries nor draw up legislation; it had only limited powers over the budget; its actions were subject to the veto of an appointive upper chamber. Yet it could question and criticize, and it provided for the first time a recognized forum for public debate. Despite overrepresentation of the nobility, even the Bolsheviks had a few deputies and through them could reach a broader audience. The Duma informed public opinion, gave some idea of parliamentary politics, and formed a focus for responsible political parties.

The modest success of the later Dumas helped the reformist parties and the liberal currents in Russian society. In general, the last peacetime years of the tsarist government were a time of increasing freedom, increasing spirit of legality, individualism, a maturing, semifree critical press,[10]

---

[9] Vladimir N. Kokovstov, *Out of My Past* (Stanford University Press), Stanford, Calif., 1935.

[10] Newspapers multiplied from 123 in 1898 to 1158 in 1913. T. Riha in Theofanis G. Stavrou, ed., *Russia under the Last Tsar* (University of Minnesota Press), St. Paul, 1969.

and flourishing literature. Education was progressing rapidly. Appropriations for primary schools were quadrupled, 1907–1913. In 1914 there were schools for about half the children, and it was contemplated that primary education would be nearly universal by 1920.[11]

With the rapid expansion of the liberal classes the old class structure was being left behind. Although in office at the pleasure of the monarch, ministers were learning to look to public opinion to support their policies. There seemed some prospects that the Duma would gradually achieve more authority, just as Western European parliaments had done in their historical evolution. There was a growing inclination to accept Russia's place as a member of the European state system instead of maker of universal order. The intellectuals were turning away from idealistic radicalism and apocalyptic visions to tackle practical problems or to seek the enjoyments of the day.

One reason for the decline of intellectual radicalism was that the peasant commune, mainstay of Populist thought, lost its cast of ideal virtue. In view of the magnitude of peasant disorders in 1905, the government gave up its old faith in the commune as stabilizer of the countryside. For this reason and because it stood in the way of modernization of agriculture, the premier, Stolypin, launched an attack on the commune in 1906. It was made possible for peasants to demand separation of their holdings from the commune and so to become independent farmers. Many of them hastened to do so, to the marked betterment of agriculture. A small-owner class was growing up as the world war began.

Industrial development also resumed, with a larger role for private ownership; and there was a marked buildup of heavy industry for military purposes as the international situation grew more tense. It is easily—although perhaps unfairly—calculated that if Russia could have kept up the growth rate of these years it would by now be at least as advanced as the Soviet Union after its series of five-year plans.

However, if tsarist Russia seemed on the eve of the world war to be clearly going the way of the West, the political problem was by no means solved. The traditional autocracy was patently obsolete, and there was no apparent way it could be reformed or replaced. The growing business and working classes were certain to demand a place which tsarist prerogative could not allow. There was growing social disorganization in the conflict of old and new values, a crudity of undigested change and uncertainty of direction akin to that seen in many less developed countries today. To educate was to raise a host of demands that traditional autocracy could not satisfy. The break-up of the village commune, however desirable agriculturally, meant loosening the social fabric. While some

[11] Michael T. Florinsky, *The End of the Russian Empire* (Yale University Press), New Haven, 1931, p. 13.

peasants became independent farmers, others became a new rural proletariat or joined the floating mass in the cities. It was not a fancy of the conservatives that the fixity of the commune was a foundation for the regime.

Yet the tsarist leaders were unable to consider basic reforms. Change would have meant curtailment of their power; and, in the weakness of their position, they feared to make concessions. The entourage of the tsar regarded the Duma as something extorted in a moment of weakness, a nuisance to be gotten rid of whenever feasible. There was never any theoretical retreat from the principle of absolutism. The government, whose only real supporters were the most conservative bureaucrats who dominated it, was becoming more and more isolated.

In this isolation and the unreal atmosphere of the court, accidents of personality—the modest intelligence and feebleness of Nicholas, the narrowness and neuroticism of the empress, the hemophilia of the heir, and the sinister powers of the unscrupulous monk Rasputin—spelled disaster. It is arguable that but for them the dynasty might well have survived. But it was symptomatic of decay that Rasputin's vices began undermining the standing of the monarchy from about 1912, and that men of the highest nobility were ready to murder him in 1916.

The tsarist regime, unable to liberalize itself, also lacked the capacity to reaffirm forcibly its authority. The ideological basis which had served adequately as legitimation of rulership in the eighteenth century was a broken reed. Repression was ineffective because guards tended to sympathize with prisoners, there was no basis for indoctrination, and prisons became schools of revolution. Efforts to organize the workers in an approved and controlled fashion failed because the government had nothing to teach them. Political education was attempted in the army after the troubles of 1905 had shown the shakiness of discipline, but it had to be given up after a few years. The regime was driven to such expedients as antisemitism and pogroms to seek to enlist popular support, but they further alienated the intelligentsia and provided much Jewish leadership for the revolutionary movement.

Revolutionary change thus seems to have been unavoidable on the eve of the world war. For decades, a Russian revolution had been predicted on all sides, and the close call of 1905 seemed to confirm the expectations. The pressures building up against a stubbornly unrealistic monarchy resembled those in France before 1789 and made predictable the same result, a crash of the regime. Revolutions come not because people are poor and oppressed but because they begin to demand more, not from stagnation but because of breakdown of institutions and failure of adjustment. These were patent facts of 1913 Russia.

From 1911 there was a rising volume of strikes, mostly political. Antigovernment parties recovered strength, and unrest grew. Labor troubles surged in the first months of 1914 and down to the beginning of the war. Perhaps it was only a wave, due to recede in due course. But the government, hard pressed at home, felt that its prestige absolutely required a firm stand abroad. Yielding to the demands of nationalism and hoping to restore itself by victory and glorious expansion, it entered a war for which it was unprepared and from which it could hardly have emerged intact.

This does not mean bolshevism was in any sense inevitable. The very fact that radical revolution was widely foreseen made it less likely, and the 1905 semirevolution probably did not raise (as the Bolsheviks claimed) but lowered the readiness of the country for a violent attack on existing institutions. Then the army had saved the dynasty because it had remained loyal and had been prepared to fire on rioters. In future disturbances, it might permit the Romanovs to be overthrown, but it would surely halt any revolutionary movement far short of the extremism of the Leninists. For these to come to power, it was indispensable that the regular military forces be effectively destroyed, which could occur only in an unsuccessful major war.

On the other hand, there is no basis for the assumption that, but for the world war and bolshevism, the Russian empire must have ripened into some sort of democratic parliamentary state. The Russians were desirous of a constitution because it was a symbol of modernization and the autocracy was bankrupt, but had little idea what representative government meant. It was not easy for them to learn, as the fissures in Russian society were too many and too grave. Not only was there an almost unbridgeable gap between westernized upper classes and the "dark people"; democracy must have meant fragmentation of authority and dissolution of the empire. Parliamentary government requires fairly high standards of civic morality, willingness to compromise, mutual respect for rights, toleration of differences, and agreement on fundamentals, all of which were strikingly absent.

A democratic empire, which the liberals proposed, is a contradiction in terms; and the least tractable of the problems a parliamentary Russia would face was that of the differences of nationality, compounded by differences of religion. Of all the minorities, only the Germans, who enjoyed a privileged position in the Baltic states and were favored in the bureaucracy, supported the autocracy; others were to varying degrees disaffected and were becoming more so as national awareness spread. It is indicative of the difficulty of squaring multinationalism with representative government that zemstvos were not established in less Russian parts of the empire. Nationality questions caused much trouble in the first Dumas; it was felt necessary by the revised electoral law largely to eliminate minority representation.

The firmly rooted British parliamentary system was brought to the brink of disaster in 1914 by the Irish question. A Duma with dozens of parties representing dozens of nationalities, all desirous of more freedom, with a minority of Russians, could have produced only chaos. Federation or confederation was also an unlikely remedy. The Russian element was too strong for a balanced group. More important, it could hardly be an association of free choice. If they were to affiliate with someone, the Turkic peoples of Central Asia would prefer to join Turkey instead of Russia, the Balts would probably want a Scandinavian alignment, the Poles would want independence, etc. Even the Ukrainians, racially and linguistically close to the Great Russians, might well prefer ties with Western Europe instead of Moscow.

It was with reason that conservatives accused the liberals of proposing the dismemberment of the empire. The liberals had to base themselves on a false proposition, that Russia was basically like the West. If it were to follow the road to westernization to the end, it could only become a set of nation-states like those of the West, surrendering what the leaders of Russia had built up over four centuries. Then a liberal-democratic development would be conceivable. But such a loss was and remains an unthinkable proposition to nearly all Russians.

The obvious alternative would have been a convulsion of disorders, some turnover of elites followed by a reassertion of strengthened authority. Any modernized Russian state would probably look in many ways like the Soviet Union of today. It would probably search, also, for an ideological basis of authority and for organizational means of integrating disparate peoples. But it could hardly arrive at anything so strange to Russian tradition as Marxism-Leninism without the chain of events which led Lenin to rule the Kremlin.

READINGS

Anatole Leroy-Beaulieu: *The Empire of the Tsars and the Russians*, vol. II (G. P. Putnam's Sons), New York, 1903.

Nicholas Berdyaev: *The Origins of Russian Communism* (University of Michigan Press), Ann Arbor, 1960.

Cyril E. Black, ed.: *The Transformation of Soviet Society* (Harvard University Press), Cambridge, Mass., 1960.

Michael Cherniavsky: *Tsar and People* (Yale University Press), New Haven, Conn., 1961.

George Fischer: *Russian Liberalism* (Harvard University Press), Cambridge, Mass., 1958.

Hugh Seton-Watson: *The Russian Empire, 1801–1917* (Clarendon Press), Oxford, 1967.

Ernest J. Simmons, ed.: *Continuity and Change in Russian and Soviet Thought* (Harvard University Press), Cambridge, Mass., 1955.

Theofanis G. Stavrou: *Russia under the Last Tsar* (University of Minnesota Press), Minneapolis, Minn., 1969.

Nicolas Vakar: *The Taproot of Soviet Society* (Harper & Bros.), New York, 1962.

Jacob Walkin: *The Rise of Democracy in Pre-Revolutionary Russia* (Praeger), New York, 1962.

2. Revolution

REVOLUTIONARY MOVEMENT

The opposition which became articulate in Russia after the middle of the nineteenth century reflected the society against which it was a reaction. Keenly aware of the enormous gap between promise and realization in Russia, the radicals looked to the West for ideas and theories; but their attitudes and ideals were Russian even if, like the liberal Herzen, the anarchist Bakunin, or the Marxist Lenin, they spent much of their lives abroad. Frustrated, unable to find a place in tsarist society, often with more education than could be gainfully employed, the revolutionaries of the 1870's or 1880's were typically dramatic and emotional, disposed to reject objectivity and balance, leaving no room for compromise or middle ground. Living in a limbo between the backward government and the uncomprehending masses, Russian intellectuals liked to "set out in search of a single and all-embracing truth, which was to dominate the whole world . . . by the constant assertion of its own absoluteness."[1] With little hope of reforms and no means of legitimate expression, they let their thoughts roam to all manner of utopias, somehow to be realized by violent exercise of the will. Many of them were infatuated with science, seemingly the key to Western power, yet they had no sense of qualified validity or patient search for truth by weighing contrary ideas and evidence. Bitter, intoxicated with undigested philosophies, and impatient with gradual development, they insisted on an absolutist moral evaluation of politics.

The core of their morality was the equalitarianism which the empire proclaimed but failed to bring about. Their creed was hatred for the bureaucracy and worship of the common people, the peasants, and their virtues as the

---

[1] Pares, *Russia and Reform*, p. 343.

salvation of Russia if not of the world. The institution which they exalted was the peasant commune, a heritage to be restored to its pristine purity of selflessness. Somehow the peasants should assert themselves, sweep away bureaucratic incrustations and foreign decadence, and make a new, powerful, and perfect Russia. How this was to come about was not clear. But the unhappy intellectuals became convinced that their duty was to give the message to the countryside. In 1873–1874 thousands of young men and women, mostly students and of the privileged classes, undertook a unique pilgrimage to the people, a mission which gave the movement the name of Populists ("Narodniks," from "narod," "people"). This very Russian outpouring of faith and idealism was more educational for the intellectuals, however, than for the peasants. The latter were only puzzled by the strange ideas of these missionaries from another world, and instead of joining the cause, commonly denounced them to the police.

The peasant commune as idealized by the Populists was a perfect brotherly association, where all worked cooperatively and together enjoyed the fruits of their labors. This idea, conceived primarily as an urge to moral-political rather than material well-being, was by no means strange to the tsarist empire. This, in fact, was occasionally dubbed "communistic" by foreigners who were impressed by its emphasis on collectivity and equality, the fondness of Russians for the idea of socialism and the dislike of capitalism, the lack of sanctity of private property, the communalism of the peasant village and household (in which almost all property was jointly owned), and the power of the tsar over persons and things. "The whole spirit of the old regime was collectivist in character."[2] Alexander I even attempted to introduce communal living. Peasants were gathered into regimented settlements, where they lived in barracks and farmed collectively under orders. The experiment included some 307,000 men by the end of his reign. If it had been successful, it would presumably have been extended; but it was abandoned as both costly and unproductive.[3]

Russia was not exceptional in this regard; authoritarian empires have frequently generated demands for the sharing of material goods.[4] Their people feel cheated of promised equality and justice, and they see wealth as the product of corruption and rapacity of officials. Rights of private ownership are somewhat indistinct, while everything ultimately belongs to the god-like ruler, by implication to the whole body of the people. Private property is regarded as tainted with sin, a cause of envy and dissension. If the people should seize it for their use, they would be claiming what is really their own. With little idea of individualistic democracy or constitutional restrictions of power, moreover,

---

[2] Bernard Pares, *My Russian Memoirs* (J. Cape), London, 1931, p. 52.
[3] Avrahm Yarmolinsky, *Road to Revolution* (Cassell), London, 1957, p. 19.
[4] For a comparative treatment, see Wesson, *The Imperial Order*, pp. 425–442.

visionaries conceive not a free society in the Western sense but an ordered and integrated society of collectivist justice, equal duties and equal access to the goods of earth. They would not destroy the system but perfect it. As Herzen remarked a century ago, "Communism is Russian autocracy turned upside-down."

In the Russian popular culture there were recurrent tendencies to communism. Land was commonly regarded as belonging properly to the tsar, so to God, or to the people in general. Peasants ordinarily cultivated by households, but plowland was subject to periodic redistribution; hayfields and woodlots were held and used in common. The sharing of property was a widespread ideal, at least of the discontented; it was sometimes broadened even to abolition of the family and communal child-rearing. Various sectarian groups, of whom the Dukhobors are best known, renounced ownership as evil and lived in more or less full communism. Russian emigres abroad often formed little family-style communes. Lenin's party was less enthusiastic about this aspect of communism, as they focused attention on the prime questions of political power. But elemental popular drives for equal sharing, with bitter hatred of the privileged, provided emotional force behind the Bolshevik revolution and gave the strength necessary to win the civil war.

How society should be structured to assure virtuous equality and brotherly living was a question for which the revolutionaries had only the vaguest answers, so far as answers were felt necessary at all; when the old order was smashed, good will would suffice to build the new. They were not much exercised by the need of democracy and freedom in a Western sense, although they spoke often of popular rights and liberation. The concepts of equality and freedom clash frequently, as the sharing of work and goods requires encompassing controls; and the Russians were entirely enamored with equality to the neglect, if not distrust of freedom.

Some radicals looked to a strengthened autocracy as the instrument of their dreams. Overriding classes and groups, a strong tsar should embody the popular interest, redeem his people, and institute the utopian order of peace, justice, and equality among his children. For a long time, revolutionaries were reluctant to discard the institution of tsardom in their ideal state despite its obvious vices, perhaps largely because they had nothing to place in its stead. Even when they rejected the traditional rulership, their mentality was authoritarian. There was no place in their utopia for private associations. All was to be for and by the great community. The Populists saw constitutionalism as protector of wealth and privilege in the West. Even when they promised ultimate freedom, they were quite willing, as Lenin later was, to contemplate a rather indefinite dictatorial power to perfect the new order. They wanted freedom for themselves, not intellectual freedom in which their own theories should be contested.

After the failure of the campaign of enlightenment of the 1870's, the movement became more elitist. As the many remained loyal to orthodoxy and the state, the few decided that they knew what the many needed and should desire. As the majority did not support revolution, it should be made without them, against them if necessary; they would accept it afterwards. Much as the tsarist state was the abstract benefactor of all but in practice oppressor of most, the revolutionaries adored humanity but lost sight of humans. A leaflet of Moscow students in 1862 called for "rivers of blood" for the sake of revolution.

To make a new order, the elect had to be bound into a revolutionary organization. A pioneer in this direction and influential precursor of Lenin was Peter Tkachev, who stressed the need of a disciplined corps of intellectuals to guide the masses; for this purpose they must devote themselves utterly to the business of revolution. Another was the notorious Nechaev, who wanted a conspiratorial organization so morally or amorally strong that it was entitled to murder a member.

Unscrupulous violence was justified by the holiness of the cause and the worthlessness of its opponents. Because the effort of propaganda seemed so unavailing, revolutionaries turned to a program of terror. They naively calculated that picking off a few key members of the oppressor class would throw tsarist society into such confusion and fear that it would collapse or at least grant far-reaching demands of the terrorists. This campaign reached its climax of success and at the same time failure in the assassination of tsar Alexander II in 1881. The result was the advent of a new and less enlightened tsar, who inaugurated severe repressions.

Thereafter, the revolutionary movement divided and changed in character. The idea of raising the country by preaching and of coercing the government by terror seemed equally futile, and radical organizations were broken up or pushed into obscurity by police action. Many intellectuals were wearying of the whole frustrating business. The growth of industry was also undermining the anticapitalism of the Populists and their exclusive preoccupation with agrarian affairs. It ceased to be realistic to oppose railroads on principle, when peasants were becoming more dependent on distant markets. The peasant commune itself was obviously decadent and increasingly subject to capitalistic influences. A new intellectual influence from the West was also making itself felt in writings of a philosopher-economist not yet very influential in the West, Karl Marx. His influence was not entirely contrary to Populism, for he shared for a time the enthusiasm for the peasant commune as a means of bypassing capitalism to socialism. But Marxism introduced a profoundly engaging set of new ideas.

From the frustrations of the latter part of the nineteenth century there consequently emerged three main streams of radicalism. Some stayed faithful to the main directions of Populism although, chastened by failures, they retreated from its extremism. The peasants remained, after all, the large majority of the population and the most ill-used. The neo-Populists in 1904 founded the Socialist-Revolutionary party, the main proposal of which was no longer the enthronement of communalism but the "socialization" of the land. This was a fairly moderate proposal that those who actually worked the land should possess it. The party by no means renounced terror, however. Among its victims was the architect of official agrarian reform, Prime Minister Peter Stolypin, shot in 1911. The party prospered, and in 1917 it had many more adherents than the Bolsheviks; but it lacked unity and enough determination seriously to contest Lenin's bid for power.

Another and more radical current was anarchism, of which Bakunin had earlier been a violent exponent, but which attained much wider popularity after his disappearance. In theory rejecting all government, anarchism represented an emotional protest against the modernization which was severely eroding traditional ways and values. The anarchists hated the bourgeoisie with special fervor, and their battle cry was equality. They were too allergic to organization of any kind, even their own, ever to represent much of a positive political force. But anarchism ran deep in the Russian revolutionary tradition; and anarchists, waving black flags and shooting at the well-dressed folk, were conspicuous in Petrograd in 1917. They were a great help to the Bolsheviks in tearing down the Provisional Government, but after its fall they were an embarrassment to the new regime and were duly suppressed.

The Marxists represented a more moderate tendency. In the last decades of the tsarist government there was a marked retreat from the wilder ideas of the 1870's and 1880's to a recognition that change would probably not be apocalyptic but would depend upon the evolution of Russian society. The intellectuals were losing faith in peculiar Russian virtues and wished to see Russia more a part of the European world, sharing its values. In this situation, Marxism represented the most congenial train of Western thinking, and its influence rapidly expanded.

The appeals of Marxism were multiple. It gave a reason to accept the apparently inevitable capitalistic industrial development as a progressive stage of history, and it reconciled this acceptance with revolutionary spirit. It allowed radicals to look to the proletariat when the peasantry failed, and gave a promise, based on elaborate theory, that the proletariat could not fail. The first Marxist group in Russia was founded by a group of ex-Populists, led by Georgy Plekhanov, disgusted by peasant conservatism. They found the workers, a new and rootless group like themselves, more receptive than the peasants had been; and they felt that in turning from peasant to proletariat they were turning from past to future.

Marx gave radicalism a coherent doctrine instead of the nebulous theories of his predecessors. He enjoyed the advantage of having a doctrine of "scientific socialism," supposedly based on the latest scientific learning of the West, at a time when science had boundless prestige. That Marxism was materialistic and antireligious delighted the almost unanimously antichurch Russian intelligentsia, and its comprehensiveness satisfied the yearning for a single great answer to all questions. The Marxist could view himself as marching with the intellectual vanguard of humanity; and if Marxism was rejected by the West, the Russian who adopted it could feel himself the more progressive.

Marxism at the same time saved the long-suffering Russian self-respect. By its analysis, backwardness was no fault but only a stage of economic development certain to be overcome. The Russian Marxist could indulge, with more rational basis, the same scorn for the decadent West that the Slavophils had permitted themselves on mystic grounds in earlier decades. In the Marxist outlook, poverty was rather a virtue, as the Slavophils had told themselves, and wealth was the result of exploitation; if the West was rich, so much the worse for it. This is probably the chief reason Marxism has found a large following among the educated and half educated of countries irritated by contact with the technologically superior West down to the present time.

Marxism enjoyed another advantage in tsarist Russia; it was more or less legal and Marxist writings could be fairly easily circulated. Realistically, the regime saw it as relatively harmless. It did not propose or authorize immediate revolution, while consistent Marxists warned that a premature attempt to bring socialism · might only bring a new despotism. The Socialist-Revolutionaries accused the Marxist Social Democrats of serving capitalism, and poured scorn on their lack of militancy. The rather dry theorizing of Marxism was not likely to stir the masses, and if the intellectuals entertained themselves with disputes about the stages of history, so much the better. The Marxists also had the virtue of rejecting individual terrorism, however they might favor an eventual violent revolution; and present terrorism was much more of a nuisance than the chimera of putative proletarian uprisings. The regime was pleased, also, that the main thrust of Marxism was not anti-tsarist but anticapitalistic, to a degree anti-Western, a theme popular where much of the economy was foreign-dominated. One cannot say that the government was mistaken, although it was eventually replaced by a Marxist party. The Bolsheviks had little to do with its demise, however successfully they stepped into the breach.

Marxists who were involved in strikes and disturbances were subject to police action. But many, including so-called "Legal Marxists," were about as concerned with bringing Russia up to Western levels as with leaping ahead into socialism. Others, following the revisionism which was current in Europe in view of the failure of Marxist prophecies, turned to economic issues, the struggle of the workers for improvement. In Russia as elsewhere, at the beginning of this century, Marxism was a decreasingly radical creed of economic interpretation of history, subject to the erosion of a milieu in which capitalism was, as elsewhere, working fairly well and bringing material benefits to workers as well as to owners.

Among those who most bitterly fought against this tendency was the youngish Lenin, who polemicized at great length against all who would water down, as he saw it, the revolutionary force of Marxist doctrine. Without him, the Russian Marxist movement might well have gone down the path to revisionist moderation, like the Social Democratic parties of Western Europe. But when the activist leaders of Russian Marxism gathered to organize the Russian Social Democratic Party in 1903, first at Brussels and then in London, Lenin was determined to have a truly revolutionary party. Eventually he succeeded, but it was a long and at times doubtful struggle.

LENINISM

Vladimir Ilich Ulianov was born in Simbirsk, on the middle Volga, on April 22, 1870. His ancestry was mixed, Tatar and German with Russian. His background was nonproletarian; family affluence made it possible for him to spend his time ruminating on injustice and revolution. His maternal grandfather was a doctor and serf-owner who entered the nobility. His father rose from a humble station to become a science teacher and then district school inspector with a rank of hereditary nobility, equivalent to major general. Lenin is known to have designated himself as "nobleman" on an official application.[5] The traumatic event of his youth was the execution of his elder brother for participation in a plot to assassinate the tsar. He entered Kazan University to study law not long thereafter, but was shortly involved in student disorders, arrested, and expelled. He obtained his law degree by private study, but he was barred from the normal ladder of official employment by his record. Choosing Marxism over the Populism which had led his brother to destruction, he began writing polemical pamphlets and took part in organizing Marxist circles among workers.

In 1895, Ulianov was arrested and sent, after fourteen months in jail, to exile in a Siberian village. There he acquired the pseudonym "Lenin" (apparently from the Lena river); having an alias was *de rigueur* for revolutionaries, although it seldom fooled the police. He also acquired further political schooling. Tsarist exile practice was extremely ill-advised; it irritated the budding revolutionary yet had no real deterrent value. Freely receiving books and papers, Lenin spent his years of exile studying and writing. By the time of his return, in 1900, he seems to have come to his mature political outlook. This centered

[5] Louis Fischer, *The Life of Lenin* (Harper and Row), New York, 1964, p. 18.

around the conviction that, just as the peasantry was no real basis for a revolutionary movement, the proletariat left to itself tended to turn "petty bourgeois"; hence, socialism was to be brought by a revolutionary party.

From 1900 until 1905 and from 1907 until after the abdication of Nicholas II in 1917, Lenin remained abroad. His principal purpose in the first years was to combat the ameliorative approach toward which most intellectual leaders of Russian Marxism had drifted, or, as Lenin saw it, defected. Lenin recognized that it was necessary to adopt slogans popular with the workers, but he felt that any real effort to improve their living standards detracted from the basic political goal. The workers should be led to struggle only for the overriding purpose of establishing the new order. Lenin thus at one time opposed relief for famine-struck peasants on political principle.[6]

The workers, still mostly loyal to the tsar, were much more interested in rubles than revolution; to fill them with the proper class purpose, Lenin looked to a firmly organized party, wholly dedicated to revolution. The first step, in Lenin's view, was the establishment of a party newspaper. In 1900 he began publication, with a number of other Marxist intellectuals, of an irregular little sheet called *Iskra*, or "Spark," to set Russia aflame. This was smuggled to the Marxist groups being formed inside Russia. With the emphasis his party has always placed on organized propaganda Lenin hoped thus to assure centralized direction of the movement. The next step was the organization of the party. Lenin directed himself to this theme in his seminal work, *What is to Be Done*, written in 1901–1902, in which he characteristically elaborated not the beauties of socialism but the necessity of a cohesive party to guide the proletariat.

Lenin's chance to put his ideas into effect came with the Second Congress, actually founding Congress of the Russian Social Democratic Party, in 1903. (A First Congress on Russian territory in 1898 was negated by police action.) The congress, representing a few dozen Marxist groups in Russia, soon found that it was basically divided between those who were, with Lenin, most anxious to have revolution straightway, and those who were most concerned that it be socialistic. The split came in debate over conditions of membership. Lenin would have party membership contingent not only upon payment of dues and adherence to party principles but "personal participation in one of the party organizations," while Lenin's opponent, Martov, would require that a member "render regular personal cooperation under the direction of one of the party organs." The difference was outwardly slight; but, in the propensity of exile politicians and even more of Russian conspirators to squabble, tempers flared; and the issue was recognized as fundamental, the cleavage between hard-liners and moderates.

[6] Adam B. Ulam, *The Bolsheviks* (Macmillan Co.), New York, 1965, p. 107.

At first Lenin was defeated on the membership issue, but after some delegates withdrew, his faction became the majority and took the name of "Bolsheviks" (in Russian, "majorityites"), while their opponents were called "Mensheviks" ("minorityites"). This was a psychological advantage for the Leninists in succeeding years when they were more often than not actually in a minority. Lenin came out of the congress seemingly controlling the party organ, *Iskra*. But he was better able to push through a program than to keep his group together, and by vagaries of politics Lenin shortly found himself out of the *Iskra* board and nearly isolated.

Soon, however, events in Russia made exile politics seem irrelevant. The long-awaited revolutionary situation suddenly appeared. The Bolsheviks had had almost nothing to do with its coming—in 1904 they published only about a dozen leaflets and had only a few hundred agitators in all Russia—and they hardly knew what to do with it. Lenin, would-be architect of revolution, seems to have been indecisive and confused. He did not even return to Russia until November, 1905, ten months after the beginning of violence. He then played an insignificant part, although the government was so paralyzed that the St. Petersburg workers' council, or Soviet, was able to operate practically like a government for more than a month. Its last chairman was Leon Trotsky, a brilliant youth of twenty-six. His basic position was close to that of Lenin, but they were often opposed for reasons of personality, and Trotsky was not to join the Bolsheviks until 1917.

The disorders swelled the membership of the previously tiny Social Democratic Party to some hundreds of thousands. However, the Moscow uprising, for which the Bolsheviks claimed credit, was repressed; and Lenin and other leaders retreated again abroad as the revolution ebbed. The principal question facing the radicals was whether or not to cooperate with liberalism and constitutionalism by entering the Duma. Both Mensheviks and Bolsheviks boycotted the first Duma elections. The Mensheviks decided to participate in the second, and Lenin insisted that the Bolsheviks should do likewise. In this position, which was unpopular with his followers, he was moved not by moderation but by his pragmatism; the Bolsheviks could use the Duma forum to discredit parliamentarianism.

As the government recovered control, the radical parties were reduced to insignificance for several years. As frustrated political movements usually do, the Social Democratic Party divided and became somewhat demoralized. In a long series of bickerings and efforts to restore at least appearances of unity, Lenin was frequently able to keep with him only a minority of a minuscule party. He demanded above all firm unity, yet he could not keep his own narrow faction united, and again and again he cast out dissidents instead of admitting differences within the ranks. A self-proclaimed leader of what seemed little more than a pedantic sect with few and unreliable followers, he could have had no inkling how historians were laboriously to chronicle his acts and words of these years.

Lenin remained, however, leader of one wing of Russian Social Democracy. Although the split between Bolsheviks and Mensheviks was deep, they remained officially a single party until Lenin engineered a definitive separation in 1912. Then he summoned a rump congress which all the other intellectual leaders of Russian Marxism shunned. Their place was taken by faithful Leninists whose names were written large in later years, such as Kamenev, Zinoviev, and Stalin.

On almost every issue, Bolsheviks and Mensheviks diverged. The former wanted a narrow, conspiratorial party; the latter wanted to draw in more members of different shades of opinion and to work more openly. The former were willing to use funds acquired by banditry ("expropriations," some planned by Stalin); the latter were scandalized. The former damned the liberal bourgeoisie and preferred encouraging peasant violence; the latter worked with liberals against the autocracy. The former hoped for an early revolution; the latter thought that socialism could come only when Russia should be ripe for it and feared that premature revolutionizing would only lead to an authoritarian reaction.

The essence of the difference, in terms popular at the time, was "consciousness" versus "spontaneity." In other words, the Leninists wished to use Marxism for the making of revolution in Russia; their opponents wished to apply Marxism to the development of Russia to socialism. Any Marxist had to modify the theories of the master to inspire political action in Russia, a country for which they were not intended and whose conditions were quite different from those which Marx understood best. Marx himself was, as mentioned, flexibly willing to see socialism in the primitive commune. Lenin, although disposed to polemicize by quotations of Marx and Engels, prided himself on flexibility of method and admitted much more latitude in "creative Marxism" than his more theoretically minded rivals among the Mensheviks.

Concretely, he was ready to employ any opposition to the tsarist government for revolutionary purposes. This meant in the first instance the peasantry. Marx had paid very little attention to the peasants, who did not fit his general scheme. Russian Marxists, in reaction to the failures of Populism, turned away from them, but Lenin decried the neglect of their revolutionary potential. A peasant uprising was indispensable for the overthrow of the social order in an agrarian country; and the 1905 revolution confirmed the readiness of the peasant masses to turn on the possessing classes. To square this with Marxist theory, Lenin looked to the developing differentiation of the villages and found landless agricultural laborers and the poorest peasants to be a kind of growing proletariat, giving Russia a proletarian majority. Those who hired a few hands and owned several horses were placed among the capitalists, along with masters of industry. Lenin had difficulties with the agrarian question, however. As a Marxist, he had to favor nationalization of land; but this did not appeal to the peasants. On the other hand, he wanted no legal land reform. He consequently spoke mostly in terms of revolutionary seizure of land by the village poor and remained vague about nationalization.

Eager to harness any unrest to his purposes, Lenin, despite his atheism, made a great effort to appeal to dissenting religious groups. He also wished to make use of national discontent. For Marxists generally, nationalism was a negative, backward force, a hindrance to economic and political integration. Lenin entirely shared this view, but he saw the immense utility of enlisting the minorities of the Russian empire in his struggle. For this purpose he promised them, to the chagrin of many Social Democrats, complete independence. He had no desire, however, to permit this to become a reality, and so insisted that the party must be entirely centralized. The party, then, remained free to oppose the exercise of the theoretical right of secession; if a nationality, deceived by reactionary influences, asked for separation, the interests of socialism required that they be restrained. This ability to grant in form while denying the substance of independence helped the Bolsheviks to win the civil war. It later became the keystone of the nationality policy of the Soviet Union.

Lenin also had to devise a passably Marxist rationalization for the making of revolution in Russia. This country, although not comparable in underdevelopment to most of Asia and Africa, was only entering a capitalistic stage of development and was generations away from the overripe capitalism the breakdown of which should usher in the age of socialism. It was central to the Marxian understanding of history that a new form of society should be based on new means of production, not political action. Revolution should arrive when "material productive forces of society come into conflict with existing production relationships." According to *Capital*, "A form of society does not disappear until it has developed all the productive forces which it contains." The Mensheviks accepted the implications of this and saw themselves limited to helping to bring about the bourgeois revolution and influencing it toward maximum freedom and rights for workers. Lenin instead propounded that the proletariat, aided by the peasantry, should help to make the bourgeois revolution and then make its own proletarian revolution, practically skipping over the stage of capitalism.

This was somewhat contrary to Marxist logic, but Lenin sought to support it in several ways. One was the previously mentioned perception of capitalism in the countryside. Lenin also pointed to the large size of the few industrial plants. Marx had emphasized the growing concentration of capital; and Russian factories, something of an alien transplant, were on the average the largest of Europe. If Russian proletarians were few, they were gathered in large, politically mobilizable groups, strategically concentrated in the capital cities.

Lenin also justified revolution in Russia by a more basic revision of Marxism, one which greatly added to its appeal not only for Russia but for all less developed lands. By his theory of imperialism, latter-day capitalism saves itself from overproduction, crises, and class warfare by exporting surplus capital, exploiting colonial territories, and using part of the booty to bribe the native working class. This explained why the socialist revolution had failed to arrive in Europe as expected by Marx. More important, it put exploited countries almost in the place of an exploited proletariat. Although Russia, an underdeveloped importer of capital but a very expansionist state, was a living refutation of this theory, Lenin saw it as exploited victim of the foreign capital which figured so largely in its economy. Logically, then, Russia should be a good country in which to begin the world socialist revolution. Lenin, like Marx, believed that the revolution would have to be international; but Russia, as he put it, was the weakest link of world capitalism, and there the chain could be broken. This was the more appropriate as Lenin followed Marx and Engels in regarding Russia as the gendarme of Europe, a prime support of reaction everywhere. Lenin's argument might have been extended, of course, actually to preclude socialist revolution in the more advanced and ipso facto exploitative nations.

The politicizing of Marxism was fairly realistic. Lenin's goal, a dictatorship allegedly of the proletariat, was more easily attainable in a less advanced country accustomed to autocratic government and with weak middle classes. This meant that, in a reversal of Marxism, the correct degree of backwardness was an advantage for the building of something to be called socialism. But this required that the revolution be made not by an economic class but by a political organization. However much Lenin stressed the "dictatorship of the proletariat," he had not the slightest faith in the proletariat's knowing its own will. For Marx, the workers should develop class consciousness from their struggle and conditions; Lenin insisted they must be given it from the outside. Left to themselves, the workers generate only trade union consciousness, as he observed in *What is to Be Done*. The proletariat embodied truth but, "The party is the conscious advance stratum of a class, its vanguard," like the father who knows what his children need. To lead effectively in the difficult and violent class warfare, it must be a disciplined, secret, semimilitary organization of dedicated revolutionaries. Lenin's wife, Krupskaya, summarized the essence of *What is to Be Done* (and perhaps of Leninism): "It put forward a complete organizational plan in which everyone could find a place, in which everyone could become a cog in the revolutionary machine."[7]

This role of the party meant that workers were to be led to socialism not by men from their own ranks by by a self-appointed group of nonworking-class origins. It was very difficult for a genuine proletarian to find time to become a more or less full-time revolutionary worker, as a Bolshevik should be.

[7] Quoted by Ulam, *The Bolsheviks*, p. 181.

The party leadership of the Bolsheviks (and Mensheviks, including Trotsky) was of the middle or upper class background which made possible leisure and education. Few indeed were the outstanding Bolsheviks of humble birth; and these, like Stalin, took little part in party councils in exile. Leninism gave a mission to the discontented bourgeois intelligentsia. This, along with the theory of imperialism, accounts for much of its popularity in the less developed countries today.

As the party became something of a religious entity, deriving its authority not from consent but from its possession of truth, democracy was excluded. The Bolsheviks had to stand for minority rule in a land whose industrial proletariat was no more numerous than the nobility, and the enormity of the task of bringing a socialist revolution to a relatively backward peasant country justified strong rule overriding any considerations of majority will— which was as likely to be misguided as the urge of minority peoples to independence. Hence Lenin made much of the idea of dictatorship of the proletariat, a concept which Marx had used but had not elaborated. It was the duty of the party, representing the proletariat, to grasp power as best it could and retain it by the means necessary. In this prospect, there was no place of representative popular government in the traditional sense; this would allow the return of capitalistic oligarchy.

It was generally assumed, however, that there should be democracy within the party, with responsibility of leadership to the members. Lenin's apparently candid opinion was expressed in *What is to Be Done*: party democracy in Russian political conditions was only "a useless and harmful toy." He developed a face-saving compromise with his doctrine of "Democratic Centralism," under which free discussion should be allowed within the party but only until decisions were taken, and higher party bodies were to be elected but to have full authority over lower bodies. Lenin's party was (and continued to be after the Revolution) directed by the leadership with limited accountability to the membership; and the chief executive body, theoretically to be elected, was in fact coopted or simply named by Lenin.

Lenin's political ideas were part of his unusual personality. Intolerant of differences of opinion, he rushed to attack anything that smelled to him like doctrinal deviationism. Most of his writings from the first were directed not at the tsarist regime but against those who shared his professed goals but favored different approaches. He argued with ridicule and rude insult, impugning the motives of those who differed with him, and tried to forbid socializing of his followers with those of heretical views. One reason that he preferred a small party of the faithful may have been that arguments jarred his nerves. No important thinker stood with him through the exile years, and in 1908 he rejoiced that the bourgeois-tainted intellectuals were leaving his party.[8]

---

[8] Fischer, *Lenin*, pp. 62–63.

Lenin was more tactician than original thinker. His own works are drawn from many sources, often with much ingenuity; he especially liked to build arguments with well-chosen quotations from Marx. He vacillated a good deal in his formulations according to the needs of the day, but the unifying core of his thought was the need for revolution. In this emotion, he was undoubtedly a better Marxist than his more theory-minded rivals. Marx himself was ready to welcome a revolutionary situation whether or not it agreed with schematic expectations, as in agrarian Germany in 1848. The truth of Marxism, as Lenin saw it, was whatever advanced the cause. Thus in 1906 as in 1917 he approved of the workers' councils ("Soviets") when they seemed to be useful to the Bolsheviks and turned his back on them when they seemed less propitious. He instructed the Bolsheviks in 1905 and at other times to denounce the liberals yet to take advantage of cooperation with them. He was rather candid in demanding agitation for benefits for workers and peasants only to cultivate revolutionary sentiments, as in clamoring for universal suffrage while despising parliaments. So far as necessary, force was an acceptable means to the supreme end, if not actually preferable for its decisiveness; Lenin had no patience for any argument that socialism might be brought by gradual or peaceful action. The supreme strategy, of course, was the party organization, the means of spreading the influence of a few over the many. Lenin believed in free man only in a dim utopia; for the here and now he wanted organized, some might say regimented, men.

In some ways, Leninism amounted to reversion to more primitive Russian patterns, a sort of Marxist Populism. During his long stay abroad, Lenin lived spiritually in Russia and formed few associations and no friendships at all with Westerners. A great internationalist in theory, he was wholly preoccupied with the destiny of Russia. For him, as for Dostoievsky, Europe was decadent; Russia was to save it. He admired not only Marx and Engels, but Populists like Tkachev and Chernyshevsky, and the terrorists of the 1880's.

Lenin's ideas of political organization were also in the Russian Populist mode. There was some European precedent for an elite party, as in the Jacobins of French revolutionary times; but the ordinary political party in Western practice was a very loose and open affair, and it was taken for granted that Marxist Social-Democratic parties should be mass-based. Lenin's plausible excuse for secrecy and narrowness was the difficulty of operation under police repression. But the police had no difficulty in penetrating the Bolshevik, as the other antiregime organizations; for many years a member of Lenin's Central Committee was a police spy. In the freedom of 1905, he still continued to insist on the need for conspiratorial organization; and in 1917 and after, the ruling party retained its elitist conspiratorial style. Lenin's party was the oppositional image of the tsarist governing apparatus, with its own authoritarianism.

The mentality of Leninism was also close to that of many Populists in the urge to secrecy, in willingness to use violence (on a "class," instead of individual basis), in the conviction that the value of its goal sanctified practically any means, and in concern with a social aim, nominally of complete equality, over freedom. Lenin was also at one with the Populists in seeking an early socialist revolution. They wished to skip the capitalist stage by resorting to the peasant commune. Lenin wanted to abbreviate Russian capitalism to insignificance by revolutionizing the proletariat in alliance with the peasantry.

The tsarist state at the same time created favorable conditions for Bolshevism. Its repressiveness justified extremism and gave respectability to violence of language and program. The repression of trade unions and strikes was the best evidence for the Leninists' argument that the workers should look to political, not economic goals. On the other hand, the tsarist police did not do much to suppress Bolshevism. It was more alarmed by Socialist-Revolutionaries or Constitutional Democrats than by Marxist Social Democrats. And of Social Democrats, it preferred Bolsheviks to Mensheviks, as the former were the determined splitters of the movement.

Trends in the decade before the war were, however, unfavorable to the Leninist approach. Prosperity was eroding the morale of revolutionary parties. If socialist ideas were percolating to the growing working class, the intellectuals were turning away. Increased freedom of discussion within Russia further discouraged extremism. Bolshevism seemed to pertain more to the past than the future of Russia; in 1914 the party was pretty much a shambles.

But Lenin had displayed a powerful mind and an impressive personality, marked especially by formidable determination, singleness of purpose, and basic self-confidence that carried others along with him. The Bolshevik party was strictly his creation. Its great advantage derived from the fact that other parties were more or less loose coalitions; only Lenin's could focus effectively, thanks to its unity, on the conquest of power. Because of its narrowness, Lenin's party could not achieve much in normal conditions. But in a fluid and uncertain situation calling for leadership to impose order and direction, none was so well prepared to grasp the helm as Lenin and his adherents.

1917

Plagued by a rising tide of unrest, the Russian government was not much displeased to go to war in 1914. In the ensuing patriotic enthusiasm, strikes and clashes with police ceased immediately, and revolutionary parties were reduced to insignificance. But there had been well grounded apprehension. The Minister of the Interior, Durnovo, memorialized in February, 1914, as follows:

In the event of defeat . . . social revolution in its most extreme form is inevitable . . . beginning with the division of the land and succeeded by a division of all valuables and property. The defeated army, having lost its most dependable men, and carried away by the tide of primitive peasant desire for land, will find itself too demoralized to serve as a bulwark of law and order. The legislative institutions and the intellectual opposition parties, lacking real authority in the eyes of the people, will be powerless to stem the popular tide, aroused by themselves, and Russia will be flung into hopeless anarchy, the issue of which cannot be foreseen.[9]

The Russian army was severely battered by the Germans from the beginning of the war. Defeats discredited the autocracy, a *raison d'etre* of which was the maintenance of military strength. The reliable and well-trained officers and troops were decimated and replaced by increasingly unreliable recruits. Munitions ran short. Soldiers sent into battle against German planes and artillery sometimes without rifles began to blame the regime if not to suspect treason. A growing stream of deserters and draft dodgers filled the cities with outlaws who had the strongest interest in the downfall of the regime. They were joined by an embittered multitude of refugees, victims of scorched-earth tactics.

Cut off from Western suppliers, production and transportation deteriorated steadily. With galloping inflation, real earnings of industrial workers fell to less than half from 1914 to 1917.[10] Housing, fuel, and food grew increasingly scarce, but illegal fortunes were made even as the population hungered. Little more than a year after the beginning of the war, strikes began to multiply. By the beginning of 1917, Russian industry was in turmoil, and the police were increasingly unable to check violence.

In its hour of trial, the regime demonstrated astonishing incapacity. Nicholas lost touch with everyone but his own family. When the British ambassador in January, 1917, sought to urge on him the necessity of change, "the Emperor, drawing himself up, asked whether he was to regain the confidence of his people or whether they were to regain his confidence."[11] In September, 1915, he dutifully went off to the front to assume responsibility; but he was then blamed for defeats and the empress and Rasputin took charge in the capital. The Duma was prorogued, and a minister's wish to work in cooperation with them was cause for dismissal. The government showed itself more concerned with its monopoly of authority than with winning the war. Voluntary organizations for the production of badly needed military supplies were only restricted and harassed. But controls began breaking down; private criticism grew to public shouting. Rumor had it that the court was pro-German, and the conviction grew that it was an obstacle to victory.

[9] Frank A. Golder, ed., *Documents of Russian History, 1914–1917* (Century Co.), New York, 1927, pp. 21–22.

[10] Florinsky, *End of the Russian Empire*, p. 126.

[11] Bernard Pares, *The Fall of the Russian Monarchy* (Vintage Books), New York, 1961, p. 422.

In March, 1917, riots in the capital grew out of control of the police, and troops were called upon to suppress them. But they turned on their officers instead. The generals then decided that Nicholas must go, and he quietly bowed out. His brother Michael prudently declined the throne, and the dynasty was at an end.

With the age-old autocracy gone, it seemed that all of Russia's problems should be easily solved; there was a veritable intoxication of liberty undampened by appreciation of the enormous difficulties of building the new and more just state. The new Russia would find fresh strength for the war, as all joined in defense of their new freedom. Political prisoners were released and exiles were welcomed home; the new regime even insisted that Britain free extremists, like Trotsky, detained for antiwar propaganda. All parties came together in rare harmony. Even the Bolsheviks, much weaker than Mensheviks and Socialist-Revolutionaries, after initial hesitation lent half-hearted support to the new Provisional Government and its policy of carrying on the war.

But the self-designated Provisional Government was definitely provisional and was never an effective government. The autocrat had been the only national symbol and center of political power; without him, the situation was basically anarchic. The Duma had been dissolved by Nicholas in one of his last acts, and it had declined to try to continue in official session. To save the situation, a group of Duma leaders came together to form a sort of cabinet and carry on the business of the nation pending the election of a constituent assembly.

This unsubstantial government could act only with the acquiescence of the Petrograd Soviet (St. Petersburg having been Slavicized in the war). In a replay of 1905, this body sprang into existence with alacrity when the old authority vanished. At the insistence of some leftists and labor officials, Petrograd workers elected some 500 delegates who were joined by some two thousand men from the local garrison. The fact that it was in reality mostly representative of the army gave the Petrograd Soviet (and others like it arose rapidly all over Russia) special strength. Meeting in the Duma building, the Soviet immediately took over some functions of government, such as food distribution and the establishment of a militia; and its decrees were more persuasive for workers and soldiers than those of the recognized government. It particularly claimed a voice in military matters. Its celebrated Order No. 1 abolished saluting, provided that elected committees of soldiers should control arms, and claimed for the Soviet ultimate jurisdiction over the armed forces.

Despite this forwardness, the Socialist-Revolutionaries and Mensheviks who dominated the Soviet did not believe the day of socialism had dawned and refused to try to take over the government. Only the "bourgeoisie," they felt, could rule; but they set themselves the task of checking the Provisional Government, severely reducing its ability to construct a new order while carrying on the war. Thus for several months there were two independent and contrary political powers in the land, the one unprepared and the other unable to grapple with the pressing issues of the war, land reform, economic ruin, and the institution of a constitutional regime.

Into this fluid situation Lenin dropped as a catalyst of explosion. He had spent the war in Switzerland, talking and writing, uninformed about what was going on at home and with few hopes of action. He had been most exercised against the Social Democrats who had, as he saw it, betrayed Marxism by supporting the war effort of their respective governments; and he had endeavored with little success to enlist the international socialist movement to agitate not for peace but for "turning the imperialist war into a civil war," for the sake of revolution. He could not return immediately after the tsar's abdication because the Allied Powers were reluctant to facilitate the travel of an antiwar agitator; at length, arrangements were made for him, with a number of other socialists, to traverse Germany.

Arriving in Petrograd on April 16, Lenin was greeted as a fellow-socialist by the president of the Soviet, who expressed the hope that Lenin would join in the defense of newly-free Russia. Lenin instead turned to his own followers with a call for revolutionary action. Lenin was apparently determined to make up for his hesitancy in 1905. Already in Switzerland he had reiterated his opposition to the war and had called for the seizure of power by the Soviets. With hardly a look at the situation, Lenin promulgated his intransigently radical April Theses: all power to be exercised by the Soviets; police, army, and bureaucracy to be abolished; a national bank under the Soviets to control the economy; confiscation of private landholdings; etc. At first, the extremist position was rejected by a large majority of the Bolshevik leadership; and Lenin then and in subsequent months had great difficulty in convincing his own select band that Russia was ripe for socialist revolution. However, by force of will, conviction, and persuasiveness, Lenin rallied the party behind him and thereby sealed, or resealed, his personal ascendancy, never again to be challenged.

Lenin's propositions rapidly came to seem less wild as Russia drifted into chaos. Workers and peasants began claiming the benefits they had expected from the revolution. Aggressive unions sprang up, demanded higher wages than owners or managers would or could pay, and struck or often seized plants. Peasants grabbed more and more private land. Production continued to fall, and inflation accelerated. The country also found itself much less united than it had seemed in its euphoria. Friction increased between the Soviet and the Provisional Government, as the Provisional Government was unwilling to subordinate itself to a body representing only workers, soldiers, and leftist political leaders. There was a crisis over war aims, as the Petrograd masses were much less willing than the government to support the Western Allies. The cabinet was reorganized to include a number of moderate socialists. This temporarily reinforced the government but divided the non-Bolshevik socialists and drove many of the discontented into the Bolshevik ranks. Meanwhile, the Provisional Government could not bring itself to fill rapidly its legitimating function, the calling of an assembly to write a constitution.

The result was a startling growth of Lenin's party. From about 20,000 members at the time of the tsar's overthrow, it swelled to some 75,000 in little over a month and continued to expand precipitously; by May there were more Bolsheviks than Mensheviks or Socialist-Revolutionaries on the Petrograd streets. In June, the Bolsheviks had a majority in the workers' section of the Soviet, which was falling behind the mood of the masses. When Lenin proposed arresting the capitalists, the deputies laughed, but the mob applauded.[12] By the beginning of July, Petrograd street demonstrations were taking a strongly Bolshevik coloring.

In this situation, the Provisional Government, with moderate socialist Alexander Kerensky as war minister, tried to revive the spirits of the army and the nation by launching a grand offensive. The army had reacted joyfully at first to the revolution, but demoralization soon set in with conflict between soldiers and officers, who might be murdered if disrespectful of newly found rights. The vaunted July offensive, for which there could be no adequate preparation and support, turned into a disaster.

As the offensive floundered, popular anger rose and turned into confused anarchist and pro-Bolshevik riots in Petrograd. The government was momentarily helpless, but the Leninists were not yet well enough organized or sufficiently resolute to try to grasp power. The government was able to restore order, and in so doing it blamed the Bolsheviks for insurrection. Evidence was produced to show that Lenin was a German hireling, the party was partially suppressed, a number of leaders were arrested, and Lenin went into hiding.

This seeming victory gave the hard-pressed cabinet little respite. Because of defeat, lack of authority of the officers, and the urge of peasant soldiers to share in the land bonanza, the army practically fell apart. Those who swarmed into the cities were natural advocates of the Bolshevik line of a prompt peace and willing recruits for the party. This was set back only a little by the July failure, as the government was unable to do much to suppress it; Bolshevik membership and organizations continued to grow rapidly. The economy kept sliding downward, and Petrograd was finding that there was less to eat in freedom than there had been under the tsar.

Sharpening issues were splitting leftists and rightists and making both dissatisfied with the government which could please neither. The peasants were calling more loudly for land transfers or, as a peasant congress did in June, for the socialization of all land. The government alarmed conservatives by moves toward agrarian reform. It antagonized the peasantry—including most of the soldiers—by seeking to halt the agrarian revolution in the countryside in the

---

[12] Alexander Kerensky, *The Catastrophe* (D. Appleton), London, 1927, p. 215.

interests of food production as well as order, at least until it could be legalized. The government was also unable to find an answer for the problem of the minorities. In particular, it could not meet Ukrainian demands for autonomy without seeming to rightists to be surrendering the empire. The war was a burden beyond the strength of the feeble semiliberal regime. The leftists saw the government—now headed by the self-confident but rather volatile Kerensky—as unable to make peace; conservatives saw it unable to restore discipline and to win the war.

The reaction of conservatives was to look to military dictatorship. At the beginning of September, the front commander, General Kornilov, was encouraged to move on the capital, displace the Kerensky regime, and hang the Bolsheviks, with whom conservatives lumped socialists and leftists in general. Many moderates, desperate for restoration of order, sided with him. Kerensky, alarmed, called upon all socialists, including the Bolsheviks, to join in repulsing the attempted coup. Bolshevik leaders were released, and arms were given to their Red Guards. The railroad workers refused to cooperate with Kornilov and his soldiers to fight for him, and Kerensky was temporarily saved. But he could no longer control the mounting Bolshevik strength in the capital.

A few days after the Kornilov movement was crushed, the Petrograd and other major soviets, with their fluid membership, went over to the Bolsheviks. These, presenting themselves as saviors of the revolution and victors over the reaction, returned to the slogan, "All Power to the Soviets," although after the July fiasco, Lenin had dismissed the popular assemblies as "fig leaves of the counterrevolution." Lenin, fretting underground in Finland, began calling insistently on his party to seize power. The more cautious men of the Central Committee in Petrograd held back in fear that an attempted coup without broader support of the country could only lead to civil war if not reactionary military dictatorship. But Lenin kept demanding early action, lest the opportunity be missed; and the Committee agreed, in the middle of October, to authorize preparations for an uprising. Two of Lenin's longtime cohorts, Kamenev and Zinoviev, dissented so strongly that they attacked the decision in a non-Bolshevik paper, a sin to be held against them long afterward.

Meanwhile the Kerensky regime was collapsing. Anarchism, often not far from banditry, was burgeoning in city and countryside; beside the anarchists, the Bolsheviks seemed cultured moderates. Much of the Ukraine had slipped out of control, and numerous local soviets across the land asserted independence in September and afterwards, with or without a Bolshevik majority. Discipline in the army became still more tenuous, as men regarded officers, who were mostly supporters of Kornilov, as traitors and counter-revolutionaries. The government vainly tried various expedients to muster public support; frequent reshuffles further lowered its authority. The leftists became more alienated and readier to listen to endlessly repeated Bolshevik promises of "Peace, bread and land." Most persons of property and education, on the other hand, were becoming frightened and despaired of Kerensky restoring the country to what they regarded as good order. Liberalism in the eyes of many was discredited, and democracy promised only socialism and disorder. The generals, incredulous of the possibility of a Bolshevik regime, were not loath to see Lenin destroy Kerensky, thereby making it easier for them to step in.

The chief means of the Leninists to power was their influence with the soldiers, who, if disinclined to fight for bolshevism, were even less disposed to defend the barely legitimate Provisional Government. From the first days of the revolution, the Soviet had dispatched its representatives, or commissars, to the armed forces to coordinate policy and secure respect for Soviet decrees; and as the Bolsheviks gained majorities in soviets, these delegates became Bolshevik commissars. The Bolsheviks also dominated the military committees which were set up at the time of the Kornilov episode and which they refused to disband afterwards. The Red Guards, undisciplined and poorly armed but increasingly numerous, drilled and talked of fighting capitalists. And sailors of the Baltic fleet were the most reliable Bolshevik force of all.

In October, the military situation was worsening, and rumors were flying that the government was preparing to abandon Petrograd or that the garrison of the capital would be sent to the front. In this atmosphere, the Bolshevik-dominated Petrograd Soviet, with its Military Revolutionary Committee headed by Trotsky, asserted authority over the garrison of the city; and the soldiers acknowledged that authority on November 3–4. The insurrection was practically made thereby. On November 6, the government, seeking belatedly to strike back, tried to close Bolshevik newspapers, summon more reliable troops, and arrest Bolshevik leaders; but its orders had little effect. The Bolshevik leadership proceeded to carry out plans for occupation of strategic points and the seat of government, the tsars' old Winter Palace. There was little resistance or bloodshed; no one but a few cadets and a Women's Battalion was prepared to risk death for the Provisional Government.

The Bolsheviks probably did not have to make the insurrection in order to gain power. The Second Congress of Soviets was to meet on November 7. In it the Bolsheviks, who had only one-sixth of the delegates in the First Congress in June, could count on a majority. It was assumed that the congress would call for power to be transferred to itself, and Lenin could then have acted in the name of the Soviets with much less risk, and less divisively. Kerensky himself seems to have expected Lenin to wait.[13] In many provincial centers, power passed quite peaceably to Bolshevik-ruled soviets before as well as after November 7.

Lenin preferred a violent and dramatic overthrow, as called for by the ideology of class warfare and revolution, to make a clean break with the

---

[13] Alexander F. Kerensky, *The Crucifixion of Liberty* (John Day Co.), New York, 1934, p. 336.

past. Since then, the Soviet Union has made the events of those days part of the mythology of Leninism. The picture of armed workers storming the fortresses of the bourgeoisie made it possible to call the great Russian Revolution that of November, not that of March. It was equally significant that Lenin wanted the new era of history to be inaugurated not by the organization of the soviets but by his party. It was a party action, and although the party grandly presented power to the Congress of Soviets on the night of November 7, 1917, it has retained the reality of rule firmly in its own hands ever since.

WHY LENIN WON

Before November 7, few contemplated that the Bolsheviks could take power, much less hold it. For weeks or months, many in Russia, not to speak of the West, found it hard to take Lenin's crew seriously as a government; it was almost unbelievable to those with faith in constitutional order and democracy. Yet their conquest of power in the largest country of the world was surprisingly easy, much easier than they themselves had expected.

With advantage of retrospect it is not difficult to understand the advent of Leninism, even to paint it in colors of inevitability. In critical and difficult times, extremists usually come to the fore, and Russia in 1917 was in deepest confusion. Lenin's party was strong in its power orientation, self-confidence, and corresponding ruthlessness, while others fumbled hesitantly. Yet the Bolsheviks could make progress only in a society deeply troubled, disorganized, lacking and needing integrating leadership; and their organization could not have found support unless it corresponded to broad and deep Russian political urges.

Having stressed organization for years in exile, Lenin had the nucleus of a formidable political machine, while rival groups were more like debating societies. It meant much more to be a Bolshevik than to belong to a looser, less politically conscious Menshevik, Socialist-Revolutionary or other group. This accounted for a good deal of the Bolshevik ascendancy of September and October, when adherents of other parties tended to fall away in indifference and confusion. Bolshevik strength also derived from the fact that their organization was semimilitary in discipline and structure. No other party had its own militia in 1917, and they subsequently proved skilled in working with and organizing military forces.

Thanks to the organizational coherence of his party and its dedication to an overriding ideal, Lenin could be pragmatic and opportunistic without dividing and alienating his followers. He took over the slogans of land for the peasants and freedom for the minorities with little regard for what had seemed the imperatives of Marxism. He was quick also to perceive the utility of the soviets as a means through which Bolsheviks might first challenge the Provisional Government and then legitimize their own rule.

Part of Lenin's pragmatism was his ability to accept favors from anywhere. Before 1917, the Bolsheviks received funds not only from sundry capitalists but from "expropriations" of capitalist property. This facilitated the maintenance of an effective organization and an illegal press. In 1917, Lenin's party seems to have received substantial sums from German sources, and this may have been crucial for its success.[14] The Germans were intelligent enough to perceive the utility of Bolshevik propaganda to their cause. They had already in 1915–1916 used Lenin's writings in leaflets for the Russian army, and they were carrying on large-scale defeatist propaganda of their own in Russia (which incidentally served Bolshevik purposes). It is also clear that the Bolsheviks needed much more money than they were likely to get in contributions from their impecunious membership, while gifts from the conscience-stricken wealthy must have ceased after the downfall of the tsar. The Bolshevik press was large, and the papers were mostly given away. Funds were needed for arms and support for the Red Guards, and for the full-time staff which propagandized and organized.

There has been found no evidence that Lenin was ever a German agent in the sense of doing their bidding; and he may not have been directly involved in the receipt of German money, sent through intermediaries in Sweden. But his purposes corresponded with theirs, and there was no reason in his political philosophy to decline assistance from any source. Lenin seems, in any event, to have found Germany less repugnant than Britain and France, as his denunciations of the latter powers were more frequent and bitter. Perhaps this is because he admired German organizational efficiency, and the German political style was nearer his own.

Lenin's success, however, came at least as much from the failures of his opponents as from his own qualities, more from the weakness of Russian society than from the strength of the Bolshevik party. The Soviet version of the October Revolution ascribes its success both to Lenin's genius and to the massive upsurge of the working classes. It would be more realistic to say that the removal of tsarist authoritarianism left a political vacuum waiting to be filled by a new authoritarianism. Only Lenin seemed determined to rule. The monarchists and conservatives were discredited and demoralized after the fall of the tsar, the sole integrating institution of the government and symbol of authority. Even in the course of the civil war few were willing to ask that a new monarchy be set

---

[14] This question and the pertinent evidence are discussed in many accounts of the period, including Ulam, *The Bolsheviks*, p. 327; Leonard Schapiro, *The Communist Party of the Soviet Union* (Random House), New York, 1959, pp. 175–177; John S. Reshetar, Jr., *A Concise History of the Communist Party of the Soviet Union* (Praeger), 1959, p. 127.

up—the Romanov family was slain—and no one had a clear idea how a conservative order should be structured without a monarch.

The liberals, Constitutional Democrats and others, were too divided, insufficiently demagogic, and too scrupulous to bid strongly for power. Russia was hardly riper for a democratic than for a socialist state. The people had no understanding of or feeling for parliamentary government, and their initial enthusiasm quickly faded as life grew worse in the new freedom. The middle classes and independent forces of society, the foundations of constitutional government, hung impotently between the upper classes, which scorned the dirty multitude, and the lower classes, which snarled at the "bourgeois" and threatened to hang them.

The Provisional Government, a self-chosen body, pretended to rule while sailors and sundry extremists and rowdies marauded, but it could hardly give convincing reasons why anyone should fight for it. Unable either to secure agreement or to coerce, it could not grapple with the issues of peace, land, and a failing economy. It delayed the early convocation of a Constituent Assembly which might have undercut radicalism as it did in the disturbed Germany of 1918–1919. It failed even to act firmly in its own defense. It neither used what remained of the tsarist police and security forces nor established a political police of its own; all manner of subversives agitated in almost complete freedom.

The Socialist-Revolutionaries lacked a clear program, coherent organization, and a firm social base in the cities. The anarchists were anarchic. The Mensheviks, although they formed only a loose group, might have come to power thanks to their strength in the Soviet in the first months. But they held to the doctrinaire position, for which they had long argued, that it was their duty only to check the "bourgeois" government, not to try to cheat history by replacing it. Moreover, they were much afraid, with some reason, that if they took power they would not be able to hold it. In June, a Menshevik leader, Tseretelli, told a meeting that no party was prepared to take power; when Lenin rose and shouted that his Bolsheviks were indeed ready for this responsibility, it seemed rather ridiculous.

The Bolsheviks profited also from their label of socialists. Socialism was supposedly the opposite of tsardom. Autocracy in the name of socialism was hard to conceive, as none had been known to exist, although Lenin had given warning enough of the "dictatorship of the proletariat." Marxists, Mensheviks, and others saw reason to fear only class enemies or reactionaries. Most people were confident that the Bolsheviks were too impractical to form a government in any case. Probably not even Lenin was really aware of the potentialities of one-party government.

From a Marxist point of view, Bolshevik rule was ridiculous. The propertied classes, kulaks, landlords, merchants, managers, etc., were some 16% of the population, industrial workers only 2.5%. But Lenin did not hesitate. As he wrote in September, 1917, "If after the 1905 revolution Russia was ruled by 150,000 landowners, why then should Russia not now be ruled by 240,000 membership of the Bolshevik Party—ruled in the interests of the poor and against the rich?"[15]

Lenin triumphed because he was able to use Western ideas while turning his back on the West and ruling in a Russian way. His program coincided with broad Russian aspirations, emotions coming to the surface in a time of crisis. One of these was the urge of the peasants for land. They had repeatedly shown a disposition to rampage when controls were removed, as in 1905 and 1917. The socialization of landholding was demanded by peasant congresses in both revolutions, and it was a widespread expectation even before the fall of the dynasty.[16] The anger of the peasants was much greater than seems justified by the holdings of the gentry, which had shrunk since the emancipation of 1861 to less than a quarter as much as peasant holdings in 1914.[17] The average allotment of about 11 hectares in 1905 would seem tolerably adequate, except for the pressure of taxes; Soviet collective farmers today provide about half their food from household plots of less than half a hectare. But the peasants remembered the injustices and oppression of the past, and they sought social equality. In 1917 even small owners who had availed themselves of the Stolypin reforms to separate from the village commune were dispossessed.

The peasants turned factory workers or soldiers carried with them their urge for social justice and communalism. They wanted "socialism," by which they understood equality, dignity for the poor, expropriation of the wealthy, anticommercialism, and the abolition of all the old rights and privileges. All leftist parties favored some kind of workers' control or socialization of industry, an idea which came easier in view of the needs and controls of wartime. Here and there factories were taken over by workers' committees or local soviets well before the Bolsheviks came to power. However, the parties differed on how socialization was to be carried out, and only Lenin's party felt free to encourage the workers to assert themselves without concern for the effects on production, just as they were uninhibited in calling on the peasants to seize land.

The Bolshevik appeal to distrust for property and collectivism was mingled with and overshadowed by the appeal to end a war which was not only dangerous (especially in the shortage of munitions) but was presented as slaughter in the interests of landowners and capitalists or Western capitalist-imperialists. The war was the paramount question, and the effort to continue fighting (upon which the Western Allies were adamant) was fatal for the

---

[15] *Sochinenia*, 4th ed., vol. 26, Moscow, 1949, p. 87.
[16] Florinsky, *The End of the Russian Empire*, p. 143.
[17] G. T. Robinson, *Rural Russia under the Old Regime* (Macmillan), New York, 1949.

Kerensky government. Lenin's peace propaganda helped destroy the main force which might still have kept the Bolsheviks from power; they were lifted to the top by hordes of soldiers and ex-soldiers anxious not to be sent to the front. The Bolsheviks could excuse their attack on the defensive capacity of the Motherland and justify the promise of an early peace on the grounds that the German workers would soon overthrow their ruling classes.

Rejection of "bourgeois" values and antiwar agitation merged into antiwesternism and Russian messianism garbed in Marxism. In disorder and defeat, Lenin proclaimed a Russian world mission of overthrowing the old order and leading mankind into the new era of freedom, justice, and socialism in the name of the oppressed and suffering peoples. Russia, beaten in the war, undertook the more glorious task of ending all wars; bent in exhaustion, she should become teacher and savior of all. This comforting messianism was coupled with a utopianism as attractive as it was visionary. The new era of universal peace and justice should mean, in the Bolshevik message, the end of the hated institution of the state itself, eventually (in common belief, very soon) the end of money and the inauguration of brotherly community of goods. In his work written in hiding in Finland, *State and Revolution*, Lenin thus proposed immediate dissolution of the bureaucratic apparatus, full equality of wages, and government administration shared by all alike irrespective of training or qualifications. Perhaps Lenin saw this vision, more anarchist than Marxist in spirit, as politically useful; or he may have been infected by the mood of the day, when people were ready to hope for anything.

Leaving behind the Western liberal-rationalist tradition, the Leninists offered not a change of government but a dream, or something for many dreams: land for peasants, workers' control of industry, freedom for minorities, rule of the underprivileged, and above all peace. Their advent to power ushered in the contrary, long years of conflict and hardships beyond any Russia had known for centuries. But they gave Russia an effective government.

READINGS

Anthony Cash, *The Russian Revolution* (Ernest Benn Ltd.), London, 1967.

Louis Fischer, *The Life of Lenin* (Harper and Row), New York, 1964.

J. L. Talmon, *The Origins of Totalitarian Democracy* (Secker & Warburg), London, 1952.

Adam B. Ulam, *The Bolsheviks* (Macmillan & Co.), New York, 1965.

Franco Venturi, *Roots of Revolution* (Alfred A. Knopf), New York, 1960.

Theodore H. Von Laue, *Why Lenin? Why Stalin?* (J. B. Lippincott Co.), Philadelphia, 1964.

Bertram D. Wolfe, *Three Who Made a Revolution* (Dial Press), New York, 1964.

Collections of materials on the Revolution are:

Frank A. Golder, ed., *Documents of Russian History* (Century Co.), New York, 1927.

Dimitri von Mohrenschildt, *The Russian Revolution of 1917, Contemporary Accounts* (Oxford University Press), New York, 1971.

3. Making of the State 1917-1939

LENIN'S STATE

Toward Political Monopoly

With simple grandiloquence, Lenin announced to the assembled toilers of the Congress of Soviets, "We will now proceed to build the socialist order." No one then could say what a socialist order was or what Lenin's coup might mean to Russia, soon to be renamed Soviet Union. Nor could anyone have foreseen how long would be required to complete the Revolution. It was only after more than two decades that the Soviet state settled into the form given it by Stalin.

Those decades were eventful and complicated, but one theme runs through the political development of the whole period, the elimination of competition and dissent. When Lenin took hold of the reins in 1917, there were many freely operating political parties, and hardly anyone thought in terms of single-party government, much less one party's monopoly of political action. There was a free press. Local soviets did as they pleased. In 1917, even Lenin's party was accustomed to debate and differences of opinion; it would have seemed absurd to speculate that comrades one day might be penalized for slightly dissident views.

By the time Stalin had consolidated his power with the great purges of 1936–1938, not only was the press reduced to an echo of official policy; art and literature were brought to servility. Industry and agriculture had been centralized to an unprecedented extent. A breath of opposition to the will of the leader, sometimes even of lukewarmness, was an invitation to forced labor or

63

death at the hands of a political police which had grown to be one of the major powers in the state.

This political metamorphosis was related to and excused by the transformation of the country from a land of individual peasant farming and largely private economy to one of state–managed agriculture, industry, and trade. But the political development was steadier than the economic, and it continued even when socialization of the economy halted. Much of it depended upon such factors as the gradual acceptance by Russians of the idea of the party's omniscience and omnipotence, the party's own ripening view of its rights and duties, and the slow building up of an apparatus to make the will of the party (or of the leader) effective.

The first step was Lenin's decision to have the party overthrow Kerensky without waiting for the Congress of Soviets to sanction it. The next came in the formation of a new government. It was widely assumed that there should be a coalition of socialist parties. Mensheviks and Socialist-Revolutionaries warned that it could only lead to civil war if the Bolsheviks attempted to set up a one-party regime. Civil servants and the railwaymen's union threatened to boycott an all-Bolshevik government. Even most Bolsheviks agreed; only Lenin and a few next to him seem to have thought in terms of unshared Bolshevik power. There were futile negotiations with the other socialist parties, and a substantial minority of the Central Committee resigned in protest against Lenin's highhandedness. But Lenin had his way, and the dissenters returned to the fold as an all-Bolshevik Council of Commissars was set up—the word "commissar" being a tribute to the propensity of Russian revolutionaries to think of theirs as a sequel to the French Revolution.

The government was somewhat broadened in a few days, however, by the inclusion of Left Socialist-Revolutionaries. The old peasant party had split in November, and its leftist offshoot was close to the Bolsheviks in revolutionary philosophy. The non-Marxist Left S. R.'s were more acceptable to Lenin than the theoretically closer moderate Marxists. They were useful, moreover, because they had a strong basis in the countryside, where Bolshevik organization was and long remained extremely weak. There was never a question of real sharing of power, however; Left S. R.'s had only a small minority of seats in the Council of Commissars and in the Central Executive Committee, which legally held the powers of the Congress of Soviets in its absence. It was also clear that power was not to go to the soviets. The first decrees were passed practically without debate or opposition, and the Congress was sent home.

Setting up an administration was harder. The new commissars were experienced agitators, but they thought in terms of agitation and had hardly any notion of administration, and most government officials went on strike against the new masters. But they gradually resumed work, for lack of choice. Many of the educated and professional classes emigrated, but the bureaucrats had no skills useful elsewhere. They also found life under bolshevism not so bad as feared, as Lenin was quite willing to use bourgeois specialists for their skills and to pay them correspondingly. Consequently the new Soviet bureaucracy was to a large extent, perhaps in a substantial majority, simply a continuation of the old.

As the Bolsheviks became accustomed to ruling, their attitudes hardened. The day after the Revolution, Lenin promised to govern according to the will of the people and to accept the verdict of the forthcoming Constituent Assembly; and at the end of November, elections to that body were permitted (against Lenin's will) to go forward as planned. But in January, the Bolsheviks dissolved by bayonets the Assembly long and loudly demanded by all revolutionary parties. Since the elections were held only about three weeks after the Revolution, the Bolsheviks could do little toward influencing the results, at least in the countryside where the mass of peasants were indifferent to Marxism. Consequently the Socialist-Revolutionaries won over half the votes, while the Bolsheviks could count only a quarter, although these reflected Bolshevik predominance in the army and the big cities. The Constituent Assembly was prepared to support major Bolshevik policies but not to give Lenin's government blanket endorsement. After a one-day meeting, January 18, 1917, the largely Anarchist guard sent the delegates home. A few days later, a new, Bolshevik-controlled Congress of Soviets met and declared itself a permanent government.
[margin note: as opposed to Kerensky's Provisional Gov't.]

Lenin justified the suppression of the freely elected Assembly on the grounds that the split in the Socialist-Revolutionary party meant that the Left S. R.'s did not have a fair representation in the lists. On ideological grounds, he contended that the workers (and by extension their Bolshevik vanguard) were under no obligation to bow to a peasant majority in view of the class backwardness of the latter. Most remarkable, however, was the general indifference to something which had seemed so vital a few months earlier. The extremists of the left, the Anarchists, were enthusiastic to have it out of the way; the rightists were unmoved; the moderate socialists who had a stake in the Assembly which they dominated found the people indifferent now that Russia had a government. That Lenin did not bother to temporize or to permit an Assembly purged of anti-Bolsheviks to function is a testimony to his ability to ignore even appearances of conventional democracy.

The Bolsheviks began immediately to institute authoritarian controls. One of Lenin's first acts in power was to curb the press, closing non-socialist papers and subsequently socialist ones, a reversal of a long-held socialist position shocking to some of the more idealistic in Lenin's party. From the beginning the Bolsheviks also began closing, disrupting, or taking control of uncooperative organizations, including trade unions friendly to the Mensheviks. They did this by persuasion, mobilizing minorities, forming rump or competing organizations, or by coercion. Practically from the outset opposition was treated as sabotage and class betrayal.

In December, a secret police was formed, the Special Commission or Cheka, as it was known by its Russian initials. It took over not only the functions of the tsarist Okhrana but also part of its personnel; officials of the old organization went back to work for the Bolsheviks.[1] Within a few weeks it was arresting Menshevik and Socialist Revolutionary leaders, as well as more obvious class enemies. Although it legally had no right of judgment and execution, the Cheka soon instituted terrorism (at first on a small scale) and execution of "counterrevolutionaries."

REFORM

The Bolsheviks began rapidly also to reshape institutions, making the Revolution more and more difficult to reverse. One of the first (and most popular) moves was ending private property in land, in a sense returning to the old Muscovite system whereby all land was property of the ruler. There were only feeble efforts to socialize agriculture, but the forcible requisition of grain was begun in order to feed the cities without giving the peasants much in return, and a state monopoly of grain was instituted. Foreign trade was also put under a state monopoly. Banks were nationalized, a vital step not only in view of Lenin's estimate of the importance of finance capital but also a practical measure to deprive oppositionists of funds. Workers' control of factories was decreed, but this at first meant little more than a sanctioning of the workers' committees which had taken charge to settle disputes or to keep factories operating when managers fled. Formal nationalization of most plants was decreed in June, 1918, and the government gradually took over administration.

There was a cascade of social-political changes. The Orthodox Church was separated from the state and then deprived of the right to hold property and to conduct religious education. Marriage and family laws were loosened, although Lenin, a man of rather bourgeois manners, had no liking for the proposals of radical Bolsheviks that the family be dissolved altogether and children raised in common. Class relationships were inverted, as it became desirable to be a proletarian while those better off were reviled and penalized so far as they did not disappear.

The new regime did not at first take very seriously its responsibility for administration. It thought of itself as part of a universal revolutionary wave, and its business was the propagation of revolution, not the humdrum management of affairs. Publication of Marxist and Bolshevik writings was a main concern, and early decrees were more declarative and propagandistic than executive. Although the Revolution had spread over the country with remarkable ease—Moscow exceptionally saw about a week's fighting—the authority of the central government was tenuous. Local soviets thought the new freedom meant managing their own affairs, and in the general confusion no one

[1] A. T. Vassilyev, _The Ochrana, the Russian Secret Police_ (G. G. Harrap), London, 1930, p. 22.

could check them. The state itself should cease soon to exist, many thought, or be swallowed up in a world socialist community. Or else Soviet power was sure to be overthrown. No Marxist could imagine the socialist revolution enduring in Russia alone; Lenin is said to have leaped with joy when he noticed that his government had outlasted the seventy-one days of the Paris Commune.

The Bolsheviks turned seriously to the building of a new state only in March, 1918, when by accepting the Peace of Brest-Litovsk they in effect admitted that world revolution might be delayed. The German workers unaccountably lagged behind their Russian comrades, fraternization failed to dissolve German military might, and the Bolsheviks found themselves forced to contemplate standing alone for an extended and ultimately indefinite period. The Bolsheviks had continued after the Revolution to dissolve the army as a potential counterrevolutionary force; now they saw themselves constrained to build a new one.

The Brest-Litovsk decision was also a major landmark on the road to authoritarianism. A majority of Bolsheviks, not to speak of all other parties, were passionately opposed to acceptance of German conditions, which included separation of the Baltic area and the Ukraine. After the German advance had been renewed to threaten Petrograd, Lenin managed to swing the party to acceptance. The group of "Left Communists" headed by Bukharin, later an outstanding theorist of the party, were pardoned their defiant insistence on guerrilla warfare and allowed to return to their party posts; but they were the last such deviationists to be so gently treated. The Brest-Litovsk decision was also the last issue really subject to debate in the party. Until the latter 1920's, leaders could speak out in party congresses, but never again was the outcome in doubt. The debate over ratification in the Congress of Soviets was similarly the last genuine debate in the theoretically sovereign body.

The peace also saw the end of the coalition with the Left S. R.'s, who favored continued warfare by any means possible. This was more feasible for a peasant-based party than for the Bolsheviks, whose strength lay in the cities. The Left S. R.'s were also aggrieved at the brutal requisitioning of grain from the peasants. Consequently they left the Council of Commissars at this time, and all collaboration ended in July, when the Left S. R.'s tried to resume the war by assassinating the German ambassador and mounting an insurrection against Bolshevik rule.

At the time of Brest-Litovsk, Lenin took two other notable steps. The seat of government was moved from Petrograd to Moscow and its ancient Kremlin, as Petrograd was dangerously exposed to the German advance. The motive was strategic, but it seemed to symbolize a rejection of the Western orientation of Russia ever since Peter had acquired his window on the Baltic. Even today, Leningrad seems considerably more Western in outlook than Moscow. Lenin also changed the name of the party from "Social Democratic" to

"Communist," to differentiate his party from the allegedly revisionist Marxist parties of Western Europe, "social patriots," as he termed them.

IDEOLOGICAL ONENESS

After the crushing of the Left S. R. rising, the Bolshevik party monopoly was made absolute. Menshevik and Socialist-Revolutionaries had already been expelled from the soviets as antisoviet. Now Left S. R. deputies were arrested or in some cases executed. The Anarchists were broken, too. Some non-Bolshevik groups were allowed to function in the civil war so far as they cooperated and were even allowed nominal representation in some local soviets for two years more, but after July, 1918, political competition was outlawed. In August, Lenin was wounded by a would-be assassin, and the Cheka was loosed for the indiscriminate Red Terror against "class enemies."

Civil War

The insurrection of the Left S. R.'s brought to an end the "breathing space" Lenin pleaded in for the Brest-Litovsk debate and marked the beginning of a new period of conflict and turmoil lasting for some three years. The struggle was confused, complicated by interventionist efforts of Russia's former allies, an army of Czech ex-prisoners, the aspirations of minorities for independence from both Communist and anti-Communist Russians, and conflicts between democratic and monarchic factions of the latter. At times as many as twenty independent political authorities claimed the government of all or part of the former empire.

The advantages of the Whites included foreign support and the inheritance of military skills of the old army. Those of the Reds included antiforeignism—the limited and ineffective Western intervention was presented as the real villain of the war—the semimilitary discipline of the party, and possession of the main centers. The ranks of the party swelled as it called upon the patriotic idealism of Russians, and they served as a corps of reliable shock troops to rush in wherever need was direst. Lenin's and Trotsky's pragmatism also helped overcome the lack of Bolshevik officers. Just as they administered the country thanks to the loyal work of "bourgeois" bureaucrats and specialists, they built up a fairly effective new Red Army by hiring or drafting tsarist officers, next to whom Bolshevik commissars were placed to guard against disloyalty. Shortly after the Revolution a proletarian ensign was named to command the Soviet armed forces; but in 1919, a tsarist general was given the post. Disregarding class considerations made Bolshevik victory possible.

The anti-Bolsheviks included conservatives, moderates, and socialists; and they were often not on speaking terms. Efforts to promote a semi-democratic alternative attracted little support, and as the generals took charge many moderates saw little reason for choosing between left and right; the two sides were about equally violent, terroristic, and dictatorial. The Leninists were held together by purpose and ideology. The vision of world socialist revolution led by Russia was sufficiently intoxicating to seem plausible. The Bolsheviks promised a socialist paradise, while their opponents held out hopes of little more than a return to the past. The struggle against the exploiting classes was excuse enough for the delay in attainment of the perfect order of sharing, a promise reiterated by the Party Program of 1919. Meanwhile, the replacement of wages by rations, the worthlessness of money, the reduction of much of the economy to barter, theoretical state control of all industrial production, and equality in poverty for workers, officials, and managers were interpreted as movement toward the goal of communism.

The anticommunists had little to put in place of the Bolshevik answers to the grave questions of the hour, such as the organization of the economy and land tenure; peasants feared their victory would mean return of the landlords. They were especially handicapped in regard to the issue of the minorities of the Russian empire. The White leaders felt bound to uphold "Russia one and indivisible." This appeal to Russianism was anathema to minority peoples; and the Whites were operating from peripheral, or mostly minority areas of the empire. Minority nationalities, demanding independence, were at odds with the Russians and to some extent with one another.

Lenin's solution was a work of political genius. Immediately after the Revolution, he proclaimed the equal freedom of all peoples of the empire, including freedom of secession. At first he assumed, in accordance with his theory, that the peoples given freedom would no longer feel oppressed and so would not want to secede. When this was belied by a rush to independence of a dozen areas, the Bolsheviks insisted, so far as they were able, that all areas should have Soviet-style governments dominated by their party. Formal independence was granted while unity was saved. Along with nominal statehood minorities received freedom to develop their own culture and to use their own language. In most places, moreover, the non-Russians were of the lower classes and Russians were regarded as exploiters. Hence the message found resonance that the only liberation they needed was from capitalists, bureaucrats, and landlords.

Russia gained greatly in self-esteem by changing from master-nation of an empire into leader of the grand movement of supposedly free peoples, a higher unity in a glorious destiny. The fact that the Bolsheviks held the capital at all times, while they pointed to Allied assistance to anti-Bolshevik movements, White or nationalistic, in outlying regions, made their cause more convincing. Tsarist officers could see the Bolsheviks as the party capable of restoring the Russian empire; and many fought voluntarily for their cause, even against other tsarist officers in White forces. When Soviet Russia in 1920 fought newly independent Poland, tsarist officers joined with nationalistic enthusiasm. They were right; only a very strong creed such as bolshevism could have held together the old conglomerate of peoples. The Leninists, from the standpoint of Russian greatness, deserved to win.

Leninist Synthesis

The civil war plus the disturbances directly related to the Revolution and the world war were made more calamitous by an effort to implement total controls for which the regime was unprepared and by the loss of most of the former educated classes through war, emigration, terrorism, and hardship. Russia by 1921 was a shambles. Agricultural production was down to one-half and industrial production to one-fifth of prewar levels. Transportation was at a standstill. The hungry cities had lost half their population. The economy was set back to the level of the middle of the nineteenth century.

The Communist Party, on the other hand, came out of the ordeal hardened and strengthened, proud of having defeated alone the forces (as they saw it) of world capitalism. It had become a more militant and semimilitary body fond of military terminology, accustomed to sole command and vindicated in its authority.

Some, including Trotsky, thought that, having won the war by command, they could carry out reconstruction by drafted labor, but this rapidly proved a failure. The peasantry was in revolt against grain requisitions, now that there was no longer fear of the landowners' reclaiming their properties; and an uprising in March, 1921, of the Kronstadt sailors, successors of those who had once been the Bolsheviks' best supporters, showed a dangerous weakness. In the general misery, controls had so broken down that almost half the cities' food supply went through the black market. Lenin's answer, in the spring of 1921, was a sharp change of economic direction, the New Economic Policy (NEP). Peasants were no longer to be required to give up all their produce beyond subsistence but had to pay a fixed grain tax and could sell their surplus freely in the open market. By extension, retail trade in general was freed. To restore industry, private entrepreneurs were permitted to run small plants, and even foreign capital was invited, without much success, to enter on the basis of concessions. Control of nationalized industries was relaxed, and managers were instructed to try to make a profit. A new currency was introduced and stabilized. For predictability of relations, civil, land, and criminal codes were introduced, largely copied from German models with secondary place for "revolutionary consciousness." The private sector of industry never employed over one-fifth of the industrial workers, but it quickly provided increasing quantities of the most necessary consumer goods. Russia seemed for a few years to be successfully evolving a mixed economy.

Many thought that this meant the end of communism, but the Leninists had no intention of loosening the grip of the party. Instead, they stiffened its monopoly in defense against renascent capitalist influences. The industrial proletariat was half of the small numbers of 1913, and many of the workers who remained had switched loyalties to the Mensheviks. To have granted any degree of freedom would have been to surrender power. The last non-Bolshevik leftist organizations and publications were eliminated. The autonomy of local soviets, which had been much reduced during the civil conflict, was cut down; and the nominally independent Soviet nations, the Ukraine, Georgia with the other Caucasian republics, and others, were formally amalgamated, 1922–1923, into the Union of Soviet Socialist Republics.

Control within the party was hardened. In March, 1919, the five-member Politburo was formally established as a guiding nucleus within the Central Committee, with ordinary Central Committee members allowed to attend Politburo meetings. Six months later this was dropped; and at the Tenth Party Congress, March, 1921, meetings of the Central Committee were reduced from twice monthly to once in two months, thereby effectively removing this body from decision-making. The Tenth Congress was also a watershed in the suppression of dissent. A minority, expressing the workers' disillusionment, favored a greater role in management of industry for the trade unions, as representatives of the proletariat which was to exercise its dictatorship; they wanted something of a tripartite political structure of party, state, and unions. Another group, kindred in spirit, pleaded for more democracy in party affairs and freedom for local party bodies. Lenin made some concessions, mostly of form; he rejected the Trotsky-Bukharin thesis that unions should be merely agencies of the state and allowed them a role in protecting workers against abuses. But he got the obedient Congress to endorse a resolution sharply condemning the Workers' Opposition and another forbidding factionalism in general. Party members were to be free henceforth to discuss undecided questions and to make proposals but not to get together to promote them. "Factionalists" were made subject to expulsion from the Central Committee and even from the party. Subject to the broadest interpretation, this rule became later a powerful tool in Stalin's hands.

The Tenth Congress was followed by the first purge of the party. The excuse and to some extent the reason was that persons who had been admitted during the civil war (when joining the party was an act of dedication) lacked proper party devotion. About a quarter of the membership was stricken from the rolls, including some who had supported the Workers' Opposition. It was becoming regular policy to render disapproved leaders impotent by assigning them to distant posts. The party bureaucracy grew; a control commission set up to check bureaucratic practices itself became an instrument of centralization. Local party organizations were turned into administrative agencies. Power gravitated toward the center, from committees to secretaries, and especially to the Secretariat of the Central Committee, headed by Stalin from April, 1922.

The Cheka, set up to deal with counterrevolutionaries, received the power to arrest, although not yet supposedly to punish, party members.

The Soviet Russian state continued much of the underlying substance of the tsarist Russian state. The government which came out of the crucible of the Revolution and subsequent turmoil was strongly centralist, leaving no important decision-making to local authorities; it was executive-dominated, with no legislature or judiciary capable of checking the administrative power; it was elitist, concentrating authority in the hands of a very few persons around an exalted leader. Criticism of Lenin became as inadmissible as of Nicholas or Alexander.

The overall effect of the Russian Revolution, like that of the milder French Revolution, was to strengthen the state. If the middle and more independent sectors of society were weak before the Revolution, afterwards they were practically nonexistent. Some writers, scientists, teachers, and other professionals remained through the years of danger and hardship; but there were few persons of education in Lenin's government except the returned exiles, who formed a thin cap on the cruder mass. Lenin is said to have agreed with Clara Zetkin's comment that he should not object to illiteracy because it had helped to make the Revolution.[2] The upheaval brought into positions of authority, especially as party chairmen, men whose mentality was often premodern and uninfluenced by the West; in due course they became the basis of Stalin's power.

While Russian society was rendered more backward, the political system under Lenin's gifted leadership was modernized and made more effective. The political party was forged into a sort of civilian army, to control and staff the state apparatus. The party's ideological framework, the heart of which was the drive to unity, made possible an elitist equalitarianism whereby the Bolsheviks could identify themselves with the people and popular demands without subjecting themselves to checks by the people. They could hold elections (at this time by show of hands) and claim the assent of the multitude while doing as they saw fit. Lenin's party made its own the indignation of the people, their anti-Westernism and anticapitalism, and the yearning for release from tensions and divisions, from economic, political, and social inequality; and it promised fulfillment of immemorial yearnings. Yet at the same time the party was engineered to maintain and enlarge political power.

A leader can only give history a push in the direction it is prepared to go; but the Soviet synthesis was to a large extent the work of Lenin. He was a remarkable blend of doer and thinker, dogmatic in ideas but flexible in means, a utopian ready to compromise principles. His determination prodded the party into gambling on a revolution; his ascendancy held it together through the trials which followed. Only Lenin could have made it right in the civil war to hire

---

[2] Louis Fischer, *The Life of Lenin* (Harper and Row), New York, 1964, p. 490.

bourgeois specialists at high pay, when party men were not supposed to receive more than workers, and to revert to small scale capitalism when the communism of the war years had evidently failed.

Belief in the necessity of force was an integral part of his political philosophy. He freely approved of executions for moral effect of many persons only marginally guilty. He once remarked to the writer Gorky, "...it is necessary to beat people on the head, beat them pitilessly, although our ideal is opposed to all coercion...."[3] Opposition to his views roused him to fury. However, he had some willingness, especially in his first years in power, to listen to different viewpoints. In contrast to Stalin, he several times accepted opponents back into responsible positions when they repented.

COERCION

It can hardly be doubted that Lenin was moved by idealism. He was a man of culture, in touch with Western values. He was much impressed with modern technology as a means to political and moral improvement. The socialist society, he predicted, would be practically a technocracy, with politicians replaced by engineers and agronomists. He seems to have felt qualms about dictatorship, which he explained and justified repeatedly, as though in part to satisfy his own conscience. Whatever his ambitions, they were not for personal adulation and luxury. He was always modest in his ways even as his associates were beginning to delight in the fruits of power.

His better side came to the fore in his last months. In May, 1922, he suffered a stroke and remained more or less incapacitated until his death in January, 1924. In sickness, he reflected more deeply on his life's works. Observing how bureaucratic tyranny was coming back under Soviet forms and slogans, he became concerned that his state fulfill more of its promise of liberation. Anxious for the rights of the national minorities, he proposed that the powers of the central regime be limited to foreign affairs and defense. He came violently into conflict with Stalin over the latter's maltreatment of Georgia. Although he had found Stalin's political style acceptable during many years, Lenin in his political testament proposed that he be removed from the position of General Secretary and replaced by someone "more patient, more loyal, more polite and more attentive to comrades, less capricious, etc."

It might be contended, however, that Stalin stood closer than Lenin to the political reality of postrevolutionary Russia. Lenin belonged to the old semiwesternized elite. As long as the Leninists were in charge, the Bolshevik regime was not prepared to realize the potentialities of despotism of dewesternized Russia. This was left to Stalin, whose ascension to dictatorship began as Lenin and the other leaders of the party in exile began to lose their grip on Soviet affairs.

[3] Quoted by John Reshetar, *A Concise History of the Communist Party of the Soviet Union* (Praeger), New York, 1964, p. 143.

STALIN'S SECOND REVOLUTION

As *Pravda* wrote in 1969, "Ninety years have passed from the day of birth of Joseph Vissarionovich Stalin (Dzhugashvili).

"Stalin entered the revolutionary struggle as a youth. In 1898, he joined the Russian Social Democratic Workers Party and became very active in the Social Democratic organizations of the Transcaucasus. He came forward as a party organizer and publicist in defense of the Leninist line in the workers' movement against Menshevism and other opportunistic currents. . . .

"Released from exile after the February bourgeois democratic revolution, he returned to revolutionary Petrograd where he entered the Bureau of the Central Committee and the editorial board of the newspaper *Pravda*. He took part in the work of the Seventh (April) All-Russian Conference and the Sixth Congress of the Party. He presented reports to them and was elected to the Central Committee of the R.S.D.W.P. (Bolsheviks). At the historical sessions of the Central Committee in October, 1917, he became a member of the Military-Revolutionary Center, the party organ for guiding the armed uprising.

"After the victory of the Revolution, at the Second All-Russian Conference, J. V. Stalin was chosen commissar of Nationalities in the first Soviet government, which was headed by V. I. Lenin. In the years of foreign intervention and civil war, Stalin, under the orders of the Central Committee of the Party, fulfilled responsible tasks in Party, Soviet, and military organs; he was a member of the Military Revolutionary Council of the Republic and the Military Revolutionary Councils of a number of fronts. In 1919–1920, he was the head of the People's Commissariat of State Control and later he was People's Commissar of Workers' and Peasants' Inspection. In 1922, the Plenum of the Central Committee of the Russian Communist Party (Bolsheviks) chose J. V. Stalin General Secretary, and in this position he worked for more than thirty years.

"In its assessment of the work of Stalin, the Communist Party of the Soviet Union is guided by the well-known statement of the Central Committee of the KPSS of 30 June, 1956, entitled 'On Overcoming the Cult of Personality and its Consequences.'

"During the years when J. V. Stalin was General Secretary of the Central Committee, the Soviet people under the leadership of the Communist Party and its Central Committee, carried out a gigantic task of world historical significance and enormous difficulty, the socialist reconstruction of the country—industrialization, the collectivization of agriculture and the up-building of its culture. In those same years the Soviet people under the leadership of the party achieved immortal victory in the great patriotic war against fascist Germany.

"As an outstanding theoretician and organizer, J. V. Stalin, together with other leading activists of the Party, headed the struggle against Trotskyist rightist opportunists and bourgeois nationalists. In the ideological, political struggle with the enemies of Leninism, Stalin made an important contribution by his theoretical works and practical efforts.

"At the same time, Stalin committed theoretical and political errors which took on a grave character in the last part of his life. In the years when V. I. Lenin stood at the head of the Party and the principles of collective leadership were strictly observed, the errors of Stalin could not attain full development. Vladimir Ilich with his wonderful understanding of the leading cadres of the Party exercised a favorable influence upon them, brought out their best qualities, and subjected them to timely and principled criticism.

"In his well known 'Letter to the Congress,' Lenin well characterized a number of members of the Central Committee, including Stalin. Considering him one of the outstanding leaders of the party, Vladimir Ilich at the same time proposed considering the question of naming to the position of General Secretary of the Central Committee another comrade 'who is different from Comrade Stalin in one particular way, namely more patient, more loyal, more polite, more attentive to the comrades, less capricious, and so forth.' [Collected Works, Vol. 45, p. 346] The leader of the party underlined that these negative qualities might take on decisive significance as Stalin was concentrating great power in his own hands.

"At the thirteenth Congress of the Party, which met after the decease of Lenin, under conditions of marked sharpening of the struggle with Trotskyism, this letter was judged by the delegates. Considering the important role of Stalin in defeating attacks on Leninism, and his authority in the Party, and hoping that he would take account of the critical remarks of Lenin, the delegates favored leaving Stalin in his position of General Secretary of the Central Committee.

"In his first years of working without Lenin, Stalin took his criticism into account. However, thereafter he gradually began to deviate from the principles of collective leadership and norms of Party line; he overestimated his own merit in the successes of the Party and of the whole Soviet people, and came to believe in his own infallibility. As a result, there were committed acts of unjustifiable limitation of democracy and gross infringements of socialist legality, unwarranted repressions against important party, government, military leaders and other cadres.

"On the eve of the great patriotic war, J. V. Stalin, taking a leading role in the heightened activity of the party in strengthening the defensive potentiality of the country, was somewhat misled in his estimates of the time of a possible attack Hitlerite Germany on the USSR. As president of the State by

Committee of Defense and Supreme Commander, he was very active in the war in the leadership of Soviet military forces, the organization of the rear, the unification and mobilization of the whole people for the smashing of fascism. After the end of the war, when there arose before the country acute questions of reconstruction and development of the national economy, Stalin along with positive measures not rarely took decisions on his own responsibility, which did not correspond with the economic needs of the country.

"The mistakes and distortions connected with the cult of personality harmed the whole cause of the building of communism. However, they did not change and could not change the nature of socialist society, the theoretical, political and organizational bases of the activity of the CPSU. Socialism is the work of the whole party, the work of tens of millions of toilers; and its gradual development cannot be changed by any force, much less by a single personality. . . ."[4]

This assessment, published at a time when the post-Khrushchev leadership was restoring Stalin to respectability, was unexpectedly critical. Yet it gives a very pale notion, in mentioning "unwarranted repressions," of one of the greatest calamities ever to smite the Russian people. And while Lenin is everywhere, a semideified father figure, the debt of the Soviet system to Stalin is seldom acknowledged. Yet Stalin carried Leninism to its logical conclusions. Stalin's policies may be seen as implicit in the work of Lenin, yet in carrying them out Stalin wrought an enormous further transformation of state and society. Although the present-day Soviet rulership claims the ideological and political heritage of Lenin, it was Stalin who gave the party and state approximately the shape and stature which they have today.

Road to the Top

Joseph V. Stalin was born in 1879 in a small town of Georgia, son of a drunken cobbler. Far from the upper-middle class milieu of the cultured Ulianovs and the "repentant noble" types who composed the overwhelming majority of Bolshevik revolutionary leadership, Stalin's background was of ex-serfdom and deprivation. His mother was illiterate but she had sufficient ambition for her only surviving child (whose father died when he was eleven) to send him to the seminary at Tbilisi. Like Lenin, the young Stalin was a capable student; but he got into difficulties with the authorities, was expelled from school, and entered the revolutionary movement. However, while Lenin went on to an émigré existence in such intellectual centers as London and Geneva, Stalin

[4] *Pravda*, December, 21, 1969.

never left Georgia until age 25, when the police transported him to Siberia; and he subsequently made only brief stays abroad.

Stalin, unlike most of the Leninist leadership, had a genuine class grievance against tsarist society. As seen in the violence of his prerevolutionary writings, Stalin's hatred for the privileged seems to have been deeper, more like that of the anarchist sailors who in 1917 shot well-dressed men for sport. Unlike the exile politicians, his education was meager, and he knew no Western language. While the emigres discussed doctrine in the cafés, Stalin's activity was illegal and by the code of the day criminal. Lenin's world merged into that of Western socialist philosophy, Stalin's into that of banditry. It is hence understandable that Stalin, although ready to subordinate himself to Lenin as head of the "hard" faction of Russian Social Democracy, had deeply hostile feelings for the exile leaders and was glad eventually to destroy them.

It is possible that Stalin was involved not only with more or less criminal activities but with the police. The evidence[5] is not solid. But the spheres of criminality, revolutionary agitation, and police surveillance overlapped in tsarist Russia as elsewhere; and it would not be difficult for an opponent of the regime to accept some collaboration with the police as the price of semifreedom and ability to act and to rise in the revolutionary hierarchy as more principled fighters were picked off and removed from the scene. If Stalin had such a skeleton in his closet, this might account for some of the paranoia he displayed when his power became absolute.

Although lacking in human warmth—his biography is practically silent about friendships and personal relations—Stalin had organizational talent. He rose rapidly in the Caucasian revolutionary movement, won the confidence of Lenin, and was coopted into the Central Committee when Lenin wanted faithful adherents to staff the newly separated party. Under Lenin's direction he wrote in 1913 a passable treatise on the nationality problem, which became his specialty.

In 1917, as in the disturbances of 1905, Stalin played no conspicuous part, although an enormous effort was made in years of his absolutism to portray him as coleader of the Revolution. He was not an outstanding agitator; Trotsky, a brilliant speaker, termed him a "gray nonentity." His star began rising when organization of the new state became the Bolshevik task. Stalin was above all a party man, master of the levers of the apparatus, hard working and always faithful to the Leninist line. He was fairly prominent in the civil war and seems not to have been a bad military leader—perhaps then acquiring the overconfidence in his strategic abilities which proved disastrous in the Second World War.

[5] Presented by Edward E. Smith, *The Young Stalin* (Farrar, Strauss and Giroux), New York, 1967, passim.

Stalin's position as Commissar of Nationalities in the new government was important because of the urgency of securing the adherence of the minority peoples. He was also a member of the Politburo (or "Policy Bureau") of the Central Committee which became steadily more ascendant as the Central Committee itself became larger and met less often. At the same time there was set up the Orgburo (Organizational Bureau) to direct the party's organizational work; and after March, 1921, Stalin had the advantage of being the only person on these two leading party organs. Stalin also found his way into about a dozen other party or state offices, including the headship of the Workers-Peasants' Inspectorate, which conferred authority to reward and especially to punish. In April, 1922, he acquired the office that was to be his main base of power for thirty-one years when he was appointed General Secretary of the Central Committee, with two faithful adherents, Molotov and Kuibyshev, as deputies.

From this date, which nearly coincided with the incapacity of Lenin, Stalin was probably the most influential individual (after Lenin so far as he could function) in the Soviet government. The Secretaryship gave Stalin an unequalled handle on power. His rivals, men of words for the most part, seem to have been oblivious of its potentialities, perhaps because previous holders of the office had not made much use of it. But whoever drew up the agenda for the Politburo, transmitted orders and saw to their execution, above all the man who kept the files and could place his followers in strategic positions, was in a position to make himself supreme.

It is hence difficult to understand not that Stalin became dictator but that it took him so long. Perhaps Stalin also did not immediately grasp the full potentialities of his office. He did not rise very conspicuously during Lenin's illness. Stalin then displayed unaccustomed obtuseness in permitting himself to speak harshly to Lenin's wife, Krupskaya, and in failing to placate the ailing Lenin, who was trying rather frantically to keep in touch with affairs. Lenin's injunction that Stalin be replaced as General Secretary weakened his position, but the testament was read only to a few leading Communists, and the Politburo was not prepared to heed it against a man who seemed loyally to carry out its will.[6]   Lenin's other prescription to check the ambitions of Stalin was surprisingly naive, to enlarge the Central Committee from twenty-seven to "fifty or a hundred" by adding good proletarians. Stalin was glad to carry this out to the detriment of the party intellectuals and to his benefit.

Stalin used the channels of the party organization, intrigue, and bossism, to build a personal following. With patience for routine work, he was ready to take charge where there was a job to be done. At the time, he largely kept out of quarrels and so acquired a reputation for modesty and moderation. He kept calm and spoke little and usually only to make practical proposals. He

[6] Ulam, *The Bolsheviks*, p. 567, maintains that Stalin was acting for the Politburo in opposing Lenin.

always acted in the name of Lenin's party, to which he professed perfect loyalty when it was rapidly becoming Stalin's party. Stalin also built up the cult of Lenin, whose cadaver was placed on display in Red Square, before the Kremlin, where it lies today, in the Russian tradition of reverence for saints whose remains miraculously resist decomposition. Lenin was made to serve as a symbol of practically superhuman authority, and Stalin presented himself as the best and truest disciple in apostolic succession.

One of Stalin's means of honoring Lenin was to enroll many new Communists, mostly proletarians, nearly doubling the party membership. Then he brought about the expulsion of many less reliable members, and had a party much more amenable to his desires. He also called for the appointment of more men of working class background to party posts. Marxists could only applaud these measures, which meant bringing in persons of mentality closer to Stalin's than to that of the exile politicians. The makers of the Revolution were yielding to the cruder, homebred type, who saw Stalin as one of their own and who owed their advancement to him.

Stalin had paid little attention to ideology prior to the demise of Lenin. It was necessary, however, that a high party leader have a claim to doctrinal authority, and Stalin published in 1924 a major work, *Foundations of Leninism*. In this he set forth a simplified Leninism, with emphasis on organization, unity, and the authority of the party. Shortly after this, however, he came upon the idea (specifically negated in *Foundations of Leninism*) of "Socialism in One Country." This thesis that the Soviet regime and its progress toward socialism could go forward without assistance from world revolution had a quick and powerful appeal for Communists weary of waiting for the laggard German proletariat. It reversed the original priorities and subordinated the universal to the Russian cause. And it was an admirable weapon with which to cut down the emigre leadership.

The idea of Socialism in One Country was most effective against Trotsky, high priest of the internationalist revolutionary cause and Stalin's rival in the civil war. Trotsky was a greater hero of the Revolution and of the civil war than Stalin and was Commissar of War, commander of the armed forces. But Trotsky was a poor contestant for top leadership. Brilliant but arrogant, he was Stalin's opposite, except in sharing his ruthlessness. He was something of an outsider among the old Bolsheviks, having joined only in 1917, and the party leaders were much more afraid of Trotsky than of the less conspicuous Stalin. Obsessed with precedents of the French Revolution, they were especially fearful of a Bonapartist takeover. Stalin was hence able to join with Kamenev and Zinoviev—who led the attack—and isolate Trotsky. The latter was inhibited by his acceptance that the party was always in the right by ideological definition ("I know one cannot be right against the party"). He denounced bureaucracy in the party, but bureaucrats ran it.

By 1925, Trotsky had been sufficiently weakened that Stalin could turn on Kamenev and Zinoviev. The latter favored a leftist policy of squeezing the wealthier peasants and forcing the pace of industrialization, questions already coming to the fore. Against them Stalin used both the unpopularity of this program and their history of disagreements with Lenin. Now allied with obvious inferiors in party standing, as Bukharin and Rykov, Stalin easily mobilized party majorities to condemn them in the name of party unity and the Leninist no-fraction rule. The last important display of opposition within the party came at the Fourteenth Congress, in December, 1925, when Stalinists shouted down the Leningrad delegation, still faithful to Zinoviev.

The next year, Kamenev and Zinoviev tried to save themselves by alliance with their old foe, Trotsky. It was too late; all three were compelled publicly to confess their sins. In the fall of 1927, they desperately tried to rouse the people against the danger of a Stalinist-bureaucratic tyranny, as though they had believed in rights of the people against the party. Trotsky was banished to Central Asia and later exiled, a mistake Stalin would not repeat. Most oppositionists were expelled from the party. They might recant, but if they were allowed to come back degraded, it was only on sufferance of the boss, who in due course had them all executed. After 1927, it was no longer possible to contest party elections or to appeal to the party as a whole, and the last more or less independent organizations were banned. The party, by now enlarged to over a million members, was composed of, or at least staffed by, careerists who knew that their prosperity depended upon pleasing the powers at the center.

In 1928–1929, no longer having allies but only subordinates, Stalin turned on those who had recently helped him defeat the leftists, Bukharin and the other "moderates," and expelled them or compelled them to surrender. After 1930, only Stalinists remained in the Politburo, and even when Stalin's position was shaken by economic difficulties and unrest of the peasants, there was no concerted move against him. There were still a few with sufficient independence of mind to oppose some of Stalin's excesses, especially in regard to the purges; Stalin was not personally absolute until these men had been disposed of in the latter 1930's. But from 1929, Stalin was the new autocrat of all the Russias, the cult of whose personality blossomed with his fiftieth birthday, December 21, 1929.

The promise of Lenin's concept was thus fulfilled. If the party could take the place of the proletariat, the same reasoning applied within the party. As Trotsky stated long before the Revolution with a better appreciation at twenty-four than he was to show in middle age, "the organization of the party takes the place of the party itself; the Central Committee takes the place of the organization; and finally, the dictator takes the place of the Central Committee."[7] Very few Communists in the 1920's wanted freedom and democracy for all, however much they clamored for a hearing for themselves when in the minority. Stalin could always point out that his opponents had used strong arm methods, if not arbitrary terror, and all were for discipline when they were in charge. All agreed that the party had the right to impose its will on society, and they could not conceive the legitimacy of an opposition party. With no right outside of and against the party, it was impossible to sustain rights within the leadership. It is a tribute to the old mentality—the émigré, non-Stalinist mentality—that something of free speech within the party lasted a decade.

Planned Industrialization

Having made himself absolute, Stalin moved to transform Soviet society and economy through industrialization under party-state direction and the collectivization of the peasantry. The Soviet economy had done remarkably well under the mixed regimen of Lenin's New Economic Policy, industrial production in 1928 having surpassed the prewar level. However, the growth rate, very high as long as the country could go forward by repairing and restoring old facilities, was visibly slowing. There was a mounting problem how to push further.

The principal answer was governmental planning of the economy, which had always been on the Soviet agenda. The unworkable controls of War Communism proved a failure and were largely given up in the relaxation of the NEP. But the planning agency, Gosplan, which had originally been formed to forward electrification, continued to try to guide the economy. Its projections were little more than estimates of what might be expected until in 1928 it was given directives to lay out an economic blueprint for the coming five years.

Stalin demanded that the planners set targets far above those which economists could justify. Then, as a grand campaign was launched for storming heights of production, targets were again and again raised to levels of fantasy, in the style of Mao's Great Leap Forward. In an atmosphere of genuine excitement, enthusiasm, and a revival of revolutionary spirit, the wildest expectations were created, as though the utopia which had not come from political action was to be brought by economic miracle. By a few years of hard work, Russia would be industrialized and modernized in communist abundance.

By great sacrifices, the bases of heavy industry, especially coal, iron and steel production, were greatly expanded in the First Five-Year Plan. The

[7] Quoted by Merle Fainsod, *How Russia is Ruled* (Harvard University Press), Cambridge, Mass., 1963, p. 42.

Second, beginning in 1933, was more rational, less overambitious, better organized, and more successful. The first two plans raised the national product by perhaps 7–9% yearly—estimates vary according to weights and prices. Rate of investment, perhaps the chief key to growth, was doubled to about a quarter of national income, near which level it has remained. Not least, the plans gave the Soviet Union the foundations of an armaments industry to carry it through the Second World War.

But lack of experience and inefficient mechanisms of planning and control caused enormous confusion and waste. Imported machines rusted or were wrecked by ignorant peasants drafted into factories. Factories were built in the wrong places, supplies were uncoordinated, etc. While the First Five-Year Plan was building up heavy industry, it destroyed much light industry and artisan production, shortfalls and mistakes being made up by diverting resources from less favored sectors. Contrary to glowing promises, consumer goods production and the standard of living fell sharply until 1934. Inflation and shortages necessitated rationing of nearly everything. Real incomes of workers in 1932 were less than two-thirds of the 1928 level, which was not reattained until 1952.

The distortion of the five-year plans was not only away from consumer to producer goods but from smaller to larger scale industry. Probably in large part because the ministerial apparatus could more easily oversee big plants than little ones, partly because of the idea that bigness was modern, there was an inordinate penchant for giantism. Through political will, the Soviet Union should immediately build the hugest plants in the world, testifying to the omnipotence of the regime as the pyramids bespoke the greatness of the Pharaohs. An example of possibly inspiring but otherwise uneconomic display was the Moscow subway, built deep underground with palatial stations at a cost which for several years was larger than the total investment in light industry.

More productive was the stimulus given to education. Soviet education had been rather general, with slack discipline. Stalin turned it to purposeful study, the acquisition of knowledge, and the development of useful skills. Soviet institutes began turning out a rapidly growing number of technicians, especially engineers for industry. Stalinist Russia became the first country to put education purposefully at the service of economic growth and national strength.

The new engineers and managers rose rapidly in the maturing industrial society. The equalitarianism of the civil war had given way to some differentiation in the NEP period, and this was followed by some levelling in the first ideologically enthusiastic years of the five-year plan. But Stalin by 1931 was branding equalitarianism as deviationist and petty-bourgeois. Inequality of pay under socialism was Marxist, he claimed, so far as it corresponded to productivity. But the Stalinists paid not only on a piecework basis but at multiple rates for overquota production, and created castes of privileged skills and professions. If wage differentials in industry were about 1:3 in 1928, by 1940 they were 1:40. One means of pressure on the ordinary workers was the Stakhanovite campaign of the middle 1930's, whereby heroes of production, enormously exceeding norms (under artificially favorable conditions), were given both high honors and material rewards and were used as an excuse for raising quotas of all. The high elite, meanwhile, was coming into royal luxuries far from the austerity of the early Bolsheviks.[8]

Stalinist industrialization also required discipline of labor, which was at first very fluid because of difficulties of adjustment and shortages of housing and other facilities. In 1930, there were issued the first decrees limiting workers' freedom of movement. Subsequently internal passports were introduced along with more and more controls and penalties until in 1940 workers were strictly frozen to their jobs. The trade unions were also turned into what some had wished to make them in 1921, practically agencies of the state. Their head, Tomsky, who wished them to defend workers' interests, was ousted in 1929; and the Stalinists left the unions little function but that of cooperating in the fulfillment of the plan. Stalin, unlike the tsars, could harness unions instead of having to suppress them.

By compulsion, incentives, and persuasion, Stalin thus engineered a westernization of Russia far more drastic than that of Peter. Its basic purpose was the same, strength. The backwardness of Russian industry had been a major factor in defeat in the First World War; and Russia was relatively farther behind in 1928 than it had been in 1913. In 1931, Stalin stated that Russia would be beaten again as in the past unless it caught up in the next ten years.[9] It can hardly be laid to insight that attack did come in just ten years, because the enemy envisaged in 1931 was England. For years there had been no threat from Western powers, and Germany was a good friend. But Stalin was determined to have an industrial basis of greatness. The drive for rapid industrialization was also rationalized on the thesis that heavy industry would make it possible subsequently to produce the abundance of consumer goods prerequisite for the communist society. But consumer goods production has always remained the stepchild of planning.

Political motives also figured. The Bolsheviks envisioned ruling an industrial, not an agrarian society. They were still extremely weak in the

[8] Picturesque details are given by David J. Dallin, *The New Soviet Empire* (Yale University Press), New Haven, 1951, Chapter 9.

[9] "One feature of the history of old Russia was the continual beatings she suffered for falling behind, for her backwardness. She was beaten by the Mongol Khans . . . Swedish feudal lords . . . Polish and Lithuanian gentry . . . British and French capitalists . . . Japanese barons. . . . We are fifty to a hundred years behind the advanced countries. We must make good this distance in ten years." (*Leninism* [International Publishers], New York, 1942, p. 200.) He did not mention the Germans, then useful friends. Russia in fact beat all the enumerated enemies, or at least secured their withdrawal from Russian territory.

countryside, and they have always been more successful in the management of industry than in agriculture. Radical change of strategy was not dictated by a failure of Lenin's New Economic Policy, even though it may have been imperative to take measures to increase the rate of investment. But the country had recovered sufficiently by 1928 so that a more ideological-political approach seemed possible.

A few months before embarking on his super-leftist course of industrialization, Stalin had taken a position of moderation to discredit his leftist opponents. The reason for his subsequent turn must have been that he rather suddenly saw himself freed of any encumbering opposition, able to move to place the economy under control. The methods used were dictated less by the desire for rapid economic growth than by Stalin's modes of political action. The plans themselves hardly amounted to economic calculation or rational efforts to coordinate production, but they were vehicles of political mobilization and centralization.

Collectivization

The storm of industrialization in the cities was mild compared to the tempest of collectivization which struck the villages at the same time. The worker found himself hungrier, shabbier, and more cramped; but he was tolerably respected and could look forward to improvement in a few years. The peasants, hit by the most massive transformation ever inflicted on Russia, were by millions driven from their homes and deported or deprived of grain stocks and left to starve. They were put to farm largely for the grain collectors, and there was little amelioration until after the death of Stalin.

The rationalization of collectivization was economic, to secure for the state more grain to feed the growing cities and to export in order to purchase equipment for the five-year plan. The Soviet grain surplus was much less than that of tsarist Russia, although production had recovered to prewar levels. Under the old regime, marketed grain had come from the estates and larger peasant holdings; the middle and poorer peasants consumed their own or purchased on the market (paying by craft production or hiring themselves out). The Revolution eliminated the larger holdings. Taxes on the peasantry were much less than they had been, and the shortage of consumer goods induced the peasant to convert grain into eggs, meat, and milk, or home brew, rather than to sell.

The extent of the shortfall of deliveries is not clear, but Stalin argued (misusing statistics[10]) that peasants, led by their richer brethren, were withholding grain from the market. Brushing aside the argument of Bukharin

[10] Jerzy F. Karcz, "Thoughts on the Grain Problem," *Soviet Studies*, vol. 18, no. 4, April, 1967.

and the "rightists" in the party that the peasants should be given incentives to produce more, Stalin contended that it was indispensable to socialize agriculture. He was encouraged in this view by the fact that a few voluntary collective farms, which produced about 2% of the grain in 1926–1927, sold over four times as large a proportion of their output as the individual peasants. This was possible only because they received special favors and were ideologically motivated. But it was easy for Stalin to conclude that he had only to get the rest of the peasants into collectives where their produce would be subject to control and removal.

Collectivization was argued on ideological grounds, but Marx and Engels did not try to scheme the future of agriculture, and Lenin before the Revolution apparently did not propose collectivization. Marxism could easily be squared with free peasant farming, loose cooperatives, or state farms. Socialist countries as Poland and Yugoslavia have lived for decades with individual peasant agriculture.[11] Somewhat paradoxically, when Stalin insisted on general collectivization he did away with the few truly communistic groups, the agricultural communes.

The "ideological" demand for collectivization covered a political drive. Lenin had regarded with greatest misgivings the emergence of prosperous peasants;[12] those who had risen to a modest prosperity in the years of some economic freedom represented the chief non-Communist force in the country. Bolsheviks were still few in the villages, and the Soviet government had no counterpart for the gentry as outposts of authority in the countryside.

At least equally convincing for Stalin must have been the fact that the peasantry formed the principal backing for the last important non-Stalinist sector of the party, the "rightists" or moderates, whose most effective spokesman was Bukharin, a few years earlier leader of the ultra–left. They earned peasant gratitude by a go-slow approach; Bukharin even suggested that it would not be bad if farmers got (relatively) rich by producing more, in the same way that Stolypin twenty years earlier had tried to stabilize the countryside by laying his wager on the strong and efficient. When Stalin got the better of the "rightists" at the top of the party, he turned almost immediately to liquidating their basis of support.

Stalin could claim, however, that collectivization was party policy. Lenin wanted to turn estates into collective or state farms, but it was usually not practicable to do so. In the first years of the NEP, the party quite lost interest in the collectives; the few which had been established declined in numbers and membership. But about the time agriculture reattained prewar levels, in 1925, the party began holding up the collective farms, or kolkhozes, as a good thing

[11] A small proportion of their land is farmed by collectives, which, as in the Soviet Union before 1929, contribute disproportionately to market supplies.

[12] Fischer, *Life of Lenin*, p. 454.

and giving them incentives and encouragement. In 1927, the Party Congress underlined the formation of collectives as a basic task. But less than 3% of the peasantry had joined by the spring of 1929.

In November, 1929, Stalin spoke of "the year of the great change" and called for a rapid speedup in the establishment of collective and state farms. If the regime had judged that it was necessary to choose between collectivization and large-scale capitalist farming, it might reasonably have opted for the former. However, this would indicate a policy of gradually increasing the number of collective farms as equipment became available to make them remunerative, and of fostering cooperatives among the peasants to bring them as voluntarily as possible to change their way of life. Stalin's procedure was the contrary, the same violence and haste which he applied to industrialization. Peasants were bludgeoned *en masse* into full collectives wherein they gave up not only their land holdings but equipment, draft animals, and for a time even single cows and pigs. By veritable warfare, well over half of peasant households were thus collectivized, at least on paper, by March, 1930. This was coupled, as though to underline its political nature, with a violent campaign against the church.

The excesses of stupidity and cruelty brought the peasant masses to the edge of revolt. Stalin called a halt, blamed overzealous subordinates for departures from the voluntary principle, decried attacks on the church, and said that collective farms should permit households a small plot of land and a limited amount of livestock. He also proclaimed the freedom of peasants to leave the newly created collectives, and most of those who had nominally joined promptly did so, although they had to leave behind their tools and cattle. But in a few months the campaign was resumed more systematically and with more judicious use of force. By the middle of the following year, the majority of Russia's peasants were collective farmers; and by 1934, collectivization was basically accomplished. Thereafter, remaining individual peasants were gradually squeezed to the vanishing point.

All who might be assumed to be against collectivization were removed. Consequently, the collectivization campaign ran into "the liquidation of the kulaks as a class." In the old Russian village, "kulaks," or wealthier peasants, apt to be money-lenders, were regarded as grasping and exploitative. Now the term was applied to any more prosperous peasants, who were attacked as wreckers and class enemies. They, along with many ordinary peasants, were ruthlessly deported. Probably well over five million died from harsh treatment and in the famine brought about by seizure of grain stocks.[13]

An economic plus was the flow of labor to the cities, both as better-off peasants were driven out and as the kolkhozes were required to supply

[13] Philip Hanson, *The Consumer in the Soviet Economy* (Northwestern University Press), 1968, p. 36.

labor under recruitment contracts. But agriculture continued long to suffer a grave loss of human resources, as the more successful farmers were removed. After 1934, the peasants gradually became more or less resigned to working for the collective which turned over most of its production to the state; but there was a heritage of alienation that could fade only with the rise of a new generation. Half of Russia's livestock was lost. For about five years, production was much reduced, and thereafter it rose quite slowly. Stalin paid little attention to agriculture—according to Khrushchev, he never visited a village but saw peasant life only in propagandistic movies—and devoted scanty investment to it; but from it was extracted the basic capital for industrialization.

Collectivization was an economic calamity despite which and not because of which industrialization proceeded.[14] Taxation would have been a much more practical means of raising capital than herding peasants into chaotic and unequipped collectives. If the regime could destroy the kulaks, or wealthier peasants, it could have compelled them to surrender grain. The argument that collectivization was necessary for mechanization was specious; the government had hardly any machinery to offer. It was, however, a political victory, which continues to be celebrated as one of Stalin's achievements. It destroyed the traditional village organization and brought all the peasants into an organization commanded by a chairman chosen by the party, usually a city Communist in the early years. Collectivization made the countryside much more governable and exploitable in the Soviet manner, while creating hundreds of thousands of controlling positions. The Nazis occupying Russian territories recognized the utility of the kolkhozes, to which they were ideologically opposed, for grain collections and political control.

Purges

Stalin's third great measure for the remaking of Soviet society was the purge, cleansing the population of political independence. The terror, however, was no more Stalin's invention than planned industrialization and collectivization; it began practically with the Revolution. ◄─── ?

Under Lenin, Bolsheviks might be forgiven serious political sins if they repented; and the idea of murdering comrades for differences of personal affiliation would have seemed madness. However, Lenin set a precedent in the show trial of Socialist-Revolutionaries sentenced to death in 1922. Reprisals against errant Bolsheviks grew after opposition from other parties was eliminated and the political struggle, so far as it continued, became factionalism within the party. Measures taken against dissidents in 1921 suggested further possibilities; and in 1923, police were used to enforce party discipline. From 1928, there

---

[14] A view supported by James R. Millar, "Soviet Rapid Development and the Agricultural Surplus Hypothesis," *Soviet Studies*, vol. XXII, no. 1, July, 1970, p. 93.

were more show trials for alleged espionage and counterrevolutionary activities. During the First Five-Year Plan, despite the dire need for technicians, two to three thousand engineers and specialists were arrested for alleged wrecking and sabotage.

The liquidation of the kulaks was a long step toward the institutionalization of terror. Its massive inhumanity strengthened the habit of using force for political ends and showed that large scale violence could be employed with impunity. It demonstrated the possibilities of forced labor, which became an important resource of the economy. It also evoked an enlarged police organization given to coercion and the exploitation of prisoners.

The party still shrank, however, from the murder of its own leaders. In 1932, a Politburo majority led by Sergei Kirov was able to restrain Stalin from the execution of a minor party figure who circulated an anti-Stalin manifesto. In 1934, the police organization, then known as the OGPU, was reorganized, supposedly restricted, and reincorporated as the NKVD (People's Commissariat of the Interior). Some of Stalin's old antagonists were allowed to address the Seventeenth Party Congress, dubbed "The Congress of Victors" in a mood of conciliatory self-congratulation that the worst was over on both the industrial and the agricultural fronts.

The Great Terror began with the assassination of Kirov in December, 1934. A relatively popular and intelligent Stalinist, Kirov may have posed some threat to Stalin's monopoly of power. He was shot under circumstances indicating complicity of Stalinists if not of Stalin. But his murder was held up as a frightful example of the cost of slackness toward the enemy in order to overcome the reluctance of Bolsheviks to shed Bolshevik blood. Moving with dispatch that suggested previous preparation, Stalin set the machinery in motion. The NKVD was given powers of judgment and execution. Not only was everyone conceivably connected with the assassination executed; hundreds of persons with no relation to it were massacred and thousands were arrested and sentenced to forced labor.[15]

The purge which rolled on through 1935 was mild only by comparison with what was to follow. A screening of party membership brought many expulsions in 1935–1936. In August, 1936, Kamenev, Zinoviev, and fourteen associates were publicly charged with organizing, in complicity with arch-villain Trotsky, a terrorist gang. To the amazement of the world, they publicly confessed. Hundreds of thousands followed them to prison or to the grave. Another great show trial of ex-oppositionists of the second rank was held in January, 1937, with emphasis shifted to wrecking, espionage, and planned overthrow of socialism on behalf of foreign powers. In March, some three thousand NKVD were executed. In June, the armed forces were hit; leading

[15] For a full account of the purges, see Robert Conquest, *The Great Terror* (Macmillan Co.), New York, 1968.

generals and then officers of lower ranks were struck down. In March, 1938, another group of prominent Bolsheviks, including Bukharin, several other ex-members of the Politburo, and Yagoda, head of the NKVD until September, 1936, had their turn at the dock, to tell the world how they had been secret enemies of the Soviet state. The public trials were the signal for mass terror, which hit every sphere of Soviet life from mid-1936 to the latter part of 1938. Then the chief purger, N. Yezhov (after whom the period is known as the "Yezhovshchina") was purged, along with many of his subordinates, and a slightly less cruel man, Lavrenty Beria, took charge. The worst was over, although in the remainder of Stalin's life hundreds of thousands were arrested and thousands were executed yearly.

The more responsible a person's position, the poorer his chances of escaping, except Stalin's immediate coterie. About half of the membership of the party was removed. Nearest to immune were members of the tsarist intelligentsia and churchmen, persons of no possible political potential. Worst struck were generals and party bosses. Of 121 regional first secretaries, 118 were shot, Khrushchev, Zhdanov and Beria being the sole escapees. Of the six persons named by Lenin's testament as the most important in the party, of the seven members of the Politburo of 1924, of Lenin's fifteen-man government, only Stalin survived. Of 1966 delegates to the "Congress of Victors" of 1934, 1108 were shot; only 35 returned to the March, 1939, congress. About half the officer corps of the army was shot, the percentage increasing to nearly 100% at the top; only those who had been with Stalin in the civil war had good chances of escaping. All military district and corps commanders, and almost all brigade, division, and fleet commanders were killed. One reason for severity with the army may have been rivalry of the NKVD as a paramilitary organization. However, many in the police forces were taken, too. Provocateurs whose confessions were used to lend plausibility to show trials were subject to execution.

Old Bolsheviks of the intelligentsia were nearly wiped out except for a few women. Layers of management were removed, replaced, and the replacements taken in turn, even three or four times. Leaders in minority regions were suspect; of 102 members and candidates of the Ukrainian Central Committee three survived, and other Soviet republics fared similarly. Persons with any foreign connection, including stamp collectors or those who chanced to receive a letter from abroad, were in gravest danger. Many foreign Communists were liquidated, particularly members of the once-potent German party who had found refuge from Hitlerism. The leadership of the Polish party was obliterated, and others fared nearly as badly.

Linguists or mathematicians might be caught up for some remark or real or alleged deviation. The Central Statistical Bureau was purged for allegedly falsifying the 1937 census, which was suppressed. One might be arrested because he was denounced by someone else who was forced to implicate supposed accomplices or because of some other relation to someone arrested, because of a slip of the tongue, or because he had suffered in the past and was assumed hostile. It might be enough to have received an endorsement from a purged general or to have served in the same unit with him. Wives and children of the executed were often imprisoned. Savage brutality was mixed with bureaucratic stupidity; a diplomat was sentenced for "anti-German views" in September, 1941, three months after the German assault.[16]

Public trials, for the benefit of the press and world opinion, were the privilege of a few outstanding figures. There was much speculation why ex-revolutionary fighters would accuse themselves publicly of horrendous and implausible sins, and psychological motives have been adduced. For one, confession was a last service to the party, outside of which the dedicated Bolshevik had few values. A prosecutor urged an accused man who had been his longtime friend to confess: "I do not doubt your innocence. We are both fulfilling our duty to the party."[17] However, the NKVD was officially permitted to torture prisoners, and by all accounts it did so very freely. Victims were also induced to cooperate by promises of mercy for themselves and their families. Accused and accusers would then go to considerable effort to fabricate more or less plausible plots. In some cases, men were killed unofficially, as probably the writer Maxim Gorky, or driven to suicide. In this case, their reputation was not besmirched.

A large majority of the sentences were not death but forced labor. Men were sent to camps in intemperate regions and employed on construction, mining, lumbering, or other projects; about eight million were so engaged in 1938.[18] There was little hope of release until Stalin's death; even if one survived to the end of his sentence, he was usually held or rearrested. A large majority succumbed to cold, overwork, or undernourishment; less than 10%, according to one estimate, regained freedom.[19] Their unpaid labor, although basically inefficient, seems to have been an important part of the planned economy. Large areas of the north of the USSR were practically NKVD "autonomous republics."

One can search in vain for a rational explanation of the madness of the purges. There was no excuse of crisis or danger. The damage inflicted on the army reflects indifference to needs of defense; if the Nazis had struck in 1939, they would have encountered a crippled Red Army, the reconstruction of which really began only after the war with Finland. In the war, generals were taken out

[16] Conquest, *The Great Terror*, p. 488.

[17] According to the Soviet underground publication, *Khronika tekushchikh sobytii*, no. 10, October, 1969, p. 21.

[18] Conquest, *The Great Terror*, pp. 333–335.

[19] Andrei D. Sakharov, *Peace, Coexistence, and Intellectual Freedom* (W. W. Norton and Co.), New York, 1968, p. 55.

of prison camps and placed in command. There was no social purpose, such as that which supposedly justified the liquidation of the kulaks. There was no rationale in Marxist ideology, in the light of which it would be inconceivable that a large number of beneficiaries of the socialist order should be conspiring to destroy it. Perhaps the insanity of the purges should be attributed to psychosis on the part of Stalin, yet there is ample testimony to his sanity on the part of Westerners who dealt with him during the world war.[20]

[margin note: psychological view of Stalin]

The purges had, however, some political sense. In part, their extensiveness was due to bureaucratic stupidity made possible by indifference to human values. Prisoners provided cheap although inefficient labor; and the NKVD, given free rein, built a little empire. It even had plans and quotas for arrests to keep departments from going slack. The obtaining of confessions had a snowball effect, as one accused person implicated others. Suspicion fed upon itself; the chief qualification of a good Bolshevik became vigilance, and the way to save oneself was to ferret out and denounce hidden oppositionists and enemy agents.

A broader political purpose was to find scapegoats for failures in agriculture and industry. Stalin may well have believed that shortfalls were caused largely by malevolence of his enemies. Since he could not err (and no one was going to suggest that he had erred) troubles should be due to treason. Hence all manner of faults were ascribed to "wrecking," from industrial accidents and production of shoddy goods to the prevalence of weeds in the fields and ticks on cows.

The primary motive, however, seems to have been the desire to extirpate every vestige of opposition at the cost of however many lives. Stalin was inordinately suspicious and apparently felt insecure in his power, as illegitimate ruler of all the Russias. There was some opposition to Stalin in 1934 on the part of Stalinists who wished not to oust him but to restrain him. Again in 1936 and into the beginning of 1937 many on the top level were opposed to extension of the purges. Such opposition as existed was scattered, without a program, without even a coherent will to resist destruction; but Stalin apparently believed it was dangerous. When the prosecutor accused Bolsheviks of scheming to deliver the Ukraine or other territories to Nazi Germany, this may have been suggested by minority peoples' discontent, just as the charge that the Czechs were surrendering their country to West Germany in 1968 was an exaggeration of the fact that they wanted better relations with that country. Harping on connections with Trotsky reflected a fear that the exiled leader, who

---

[20] Stalin could show a sense of humor. When Ilya Ehrenburg was trying in 1941 to secure publication of his novel, *The Fall of Paris*, he managed to get the manuscript to Stalin's attention. The latter liked it and telephoned Ehrenburg, "Just go on writing, you and I will try to push it through [censorship]." Ilya Ehrenburg, *Memoirs* (World Publishing Co.), Cleveland, 1953, p. 505.

tried to maintain contacts with the homeland, was still inordinately influential. But the obvious purpose of terror is to terrorize. Stalin pounded out of the Russian people for many years any willfulness or independent spirit and made them, high and low, passive and servile. Up to 1936, Russians were not much afraid of expressing themselves privately; afterwards, as long as Stalin lived, dissent was silenced. The very magnitude of the horror evoked awe and in a sense sanctified the system. Institutionalized anxiety may be rational in the value-system of an autocrat. Hordes of new officials knew all too well that their positions and lives depended upon pleasing the master, who used insecurity balanced by material rewards to maximize his authority. It is hard to avoid the conclusion, however, that Stalin enjoyed exercising the ultimate power, that of annihilating his fellows.

The cost included about thirteen million lives through executions and deaths in labor camps. Because of loss of manpower and disorganization, previously rapid industrial growth halted and the economy stagnated, 1936–1941. The standard of living, which had begun to recover in 1934, declined.[21] Only the energetic training of new specialists averted economic disaster. The damage to the armed forces was reflected in the lack of success of the Red Army against Finland in the first months of the 1939–1940 war. Finally, Stalin lost many loyal and valuable assistants, whose fault was what was most needed, intelligence and initiative.

Mature Stalinism

As Lenin moved beyond Marx, Stalin went beyond Lenin to the extreme implications of his doctrines and political philosophy, stressing politics over economics and power over welfare. He destroyed not only competing parties but all independent forces in the land. Industry and agriculture were placed under centralized control so far as mechanically feasible. Labor was strictly regimented and trade unions were, like the party and soviets, turned into "transmission belts," as Stalin expressed it. Art, literature, and music were harnessed to the needs of the state in the tightening of the 1930's; artists were no longer told what they might not do but were instructed what they must do for the party and the leader in the name of "Socialist Realism." For example, Stalin had some 200 plays written to glorify the Moscow-Volga Canal. The schools were made authoritarian agencies of indoctrination and the imparting of useful skills. Soviet philosophy, economics, and history were purged of independent thinking; there was to be a single way and a single truth dictated from on high. Uniformity was pressed on the land; building styles were almost identical from the Baltic to the Pacific. Stalin, who had wanted a centralized state when the Soviet Union was created in 1922, annulled the feeble autonomy

[21] Hanson, *Soviet Consumer,* p. 30.

STALINISM = CENTRALISATION (2.)
            NATIONALLISTIC

enjoyed by the legally sovereign Soviet republics and centralized the Russian realm as never before; the Georgian was the prince of russifiers. The church was cowed, and religion was crushed to insignificance. There was no politics in the ordinary sense but only a covert struggle of individuals or at most cliques for influence with higher powers.

Socialism for Stalin was full command of society, and the Stalinist state emerging from the purges had achieved this. It remained not to change but to rule. Stalin brought to an end the revolutionary mentality. For purposes of rule, he needed Marxism-Leninism, but he renounced world revolutionary purposes. The Soviet Union became a basically conservative state, and earlier ideas of social transformation were decreed to be "petty-bourgeois." Interest in utopia gave way to interest in order and obedience, and the idea of the withering away of the state was banned. There was a return to Russian patriotism and nationalism, and old tsars were restored to respectability. Equalitarianism was decried, and privileged groups were created, whose interests lay not with the masses but with the rulers. The Soviet became a layered society, replete with ranks, much more status-conscious than "bourgeois" countries. Not only were ranks restored in the army but officers were instructed in dancing and etiquette.[22] Revolutionary Russia found the family backward; Stalinist Russia turned back to it as keeper of order. Divorce was made difficult, and abortion illegal; mothers were rewarded for numerous children; a new puritanism covered public behavior.

The bureaucratized autocracy of Stalin reverted to prerevolutionary patterns and to more primitive ones, to the Muscovite despotism of ruler and slaves of the sixteenth century. It was easy for Russia to relapse to ways and attitudes of earlier times because of the destruction or loss, 1917–1922, of most of the westernized layers of society; additionally, education was largely in abeyance from 1918 to 1924, and a generation of Stalinists grew up with little schooling. Stalin, who was often and rightly called a Red Tsar, regarded himself as successor of Peter and especially of Ivan the Terrible, whom he criticized only for not having liquidated enough boyars.

As rulers of great empires have been wont, Stalin was practically deified as embodiment of truth and power, symbol of the union of the peoples. His pronouncements were taken as divine truth not only on political and economic affairs but on history, linguistics, or genetics. He was high priest, expressing Marxist-Leninist ideas in suitably simple terms, and his thought and person were supposed to be the inspiration of those blessed by his leadership.

Stalin's mystique was furthered by his aloofness in the Kremlin; Muscovites glimpsed a curtained black limousine speeding along guarded roads. Secrecy became the rule of the state. In the 1920's, the Soviet Union published a

---

[22] Raymond L. Garthoff, *Soviet Military Policy* (Praeger), New York, 1966, p. 36.

great deal of economic and other data, but this was cut down in the 1930's to practically no solid information. Secrecy, in Russia as elsewhere, fostered corruption and falsification. The present was gilded; and the past was shrouded and remade, with events and persons inconvenient to the leader obliterated while his own image was haloed.

Behind the screen, power flowed in Byzantine channels. The police, the party apparatus, to a lesser extent the military, the regular bureaucracy and economic managers, exerted obscure and unassessable influence. Power gravitated from the Secretariat of the party, which Stalin headed, to the Secretariat of the General Secretary, composed of men totally invisible to the public. Stalin's chief bodyguard took it upon himself to dictate to the arts on the basis of his knowledge of the leader's tastes. Stalin himself could not really control such influence-groups; he had great difficulty even getting an accounting of his household expenses.[23]

In an arbitrary government, wherein fortune was determined by favor, fear was a prime principle of government. Initiative was in theory demanded, but fear caused bureaucrats to refer everything possible to superiors and so to exaggerate centralization. Everything was to serve the leader's will; information was desired not to check but to confirm policy. Hence countless warnings of impending attack in 1941 were disregarded.

In the fear of deviant ideas and distrust for all that could not be controlled, Stalinist Russia had to isolate itself from the outside world. It became almost impossible for Soviet citizens to cross the borders, and unofficial contacts with the outside world were banned. The few diplomats and officials posted abroad were most carefully screened for conformity, left families behind as hostages, and were kept secluded in their foreign stations. Despite the fact that the country could by no means fill all its needs, foreign trade was discouraged and greatly reduced after an early surge of importing equipment for industrialization.

Stalinism had obvious points of resemblance to another modern despotism, that of Hitler's Germany, of which it was for a time verbal antagonist, then half-ally, and finally military enemy. Both made the select but mass party a main political instrument, with an ideology more revolutionary in pretense than reality. The Nazis glorified force more and had a more military ethos, but the difference was one of degree. The sweep of the NKVD was much broader than that of the Gestapo; in Nazi Germany insiders were nearly immune, while in Stalin's Russia they were most vulnerable. Adulation of the leader was more pervasive in the Soviet Union, although it conflicted with the spirit of Marxism-Leninism and the "Führerprinzip" was the heart of Nazi ideology.

---

[23] Svetlana Alliluyeva, *Twenty Letters to a Friend* (Harper and Row), New York, 1967, pp. 126, 210.

Planning of the economy was much more effective in the Soviet Union, as was the mobilization of literature and art, but Nazi Germany followed some of the same patterns. Anti-semitism came to the fore in Stalinism only after the war and was never explicit.

Nazism and Stalinism were concurrent, both maturing in the latter 1930's. The Nazi flag, party organization, and methods of propaganda and control were influenced by Bolshevik originals. Stalin, on the other hand, reverted to Russian nationalism as the Nazi success in the exploitation of German nationalism was becoming apparent. He embarked on the purges of the party just a few months after Hitler's successful blood purge in June, 1934. Stalin came nearer trusting Hitler than any other foreign statesman. In the months after August, 1939, the Soviet Union seemed a better and more willing friend of Nazi Germany than it has ever been of any other non-Communist country in peacetime.

The two totalitarianisms also showed differences. The Nazis had a narrow racial instead of an internationalist creed and were antiequalitarian in theory as well as practice. The Nazis were past-oriented and less favorable to education; Stalinism had its mission of modernization and industrialization. This factor has made Soviet authoritarianism less repugnant to many intellectuals than fascism and has given it an appeal to the many states, from Kemal Ataturk's Turkey to African dictatorships, which have taken it on themselves to drive out barbarism by barbarian means. Industrialization requires subordination, specialization, and bureaucracy, as well as education; and it can be advanced by governmental action. Stalinism presented itself as a remedy for Russian backwardness. Collectivization shook up the countryside; forced-draft industrialization was not very rational economically, but might be considered necessary to initiate rapid progress in backward Russia.

Leftist and equalitarian ideology proved little handicap to Stalin's drive for total power. By bringing in proletarians whom he could more easily manipulate he swamped the revolutionary intellectuals. Advancing to despotic power, Stalin introduced impressive democratic reforms. In 1936, he announced the end of legal class distinctions, which had come down from revolutionary discriminations; the franchise was henceforth to be equal and universal. The superficially democratic constitution of 1936 also provided for direct elections by secret ballot to all soviets, from top to bottom, and gave these ample paper powers. In 1939, Stalin ended class discrimination in admission of new members of the party. He also introduced secret balloting into the party elections which are less unimportant than the soviet elections. Most of all he satisfied aspirations of the masses by opening all careers to talents, making peasants' sons and serfs' grandsons into engineers and managers, commissars, and party bosses. But if peasants become kulaks in the old days could be usurious and selfish, peasants turned party secretary could be demanding masters and unscrupulous careerists.

For this reason, as well as because of lack of criticism from an independent press and independent groups within society, Stalinist Russia was vastly more self-righteous in its use of force than tsarist Russia had been.

The steady advance of the Soviet system to the absolutism, or totalitarianism, of full Stalinism makes the process seem inevitable. It is unlikely that Stalin in 1922, when he grasped the levers of supreme power as General Secretary, had any idea of the road ahead. But he used every opportunity to enhance his own position. When he found that terrorism against Bolsheviks raised his own standing, he went on until he had removed everyone conceivably inconvenient to himself.

Stalin was able to do this despite lack of personal charm or charisma. He was a dull speaker and writer, repetitious and given to clichés, although he could state neo-Marxist positions effectively. No one ever credited him with the ability to hypnotize an audience or to dominate those with whom he spoke as Hitler could. Nor can it be contended that he had any great understanding of the economic and political needs of his country. His victory was entirely of the organization, won through manipulation and management of men. By virtue of organizational superiority and ideological monopoly backed by force, a very few could work their will on the many.

READINGS

The most important writings of Joseph Stalin are gathered in his *Leninism*, or *Problems of Leninism*, many editions.

Svetlana Alliluyeva, *Twenty Letters to a Friend* (Harper & Row), New York, 1967.

John A. Armstrong, *The Politics of Totalitarianism: The Communist Party of the Soviet Union from 1934 to the Present* (Random House), New York, 1961.

Seweryn Bialer, ed., *Stalin and His Generals* (Pegasus), New York, 1969.

Robert V. Daniels, *The Conscience of the Revolution* (Harvard University Press), Cambridge, Mass., 1960.

Isaac Deutscher, *Stalin, a Political Biography* (Oxford University Press), New York, 1967.

Merle Fainsod, *Smolensk under Soviet Rule* (Harvard University Press), Cambridge, Mass., 1958.

A. V. Gorbatov, *Years of My Life* (W. W. Norton), New York, 1964.

Leonard Schapiro, *The Origin of the Communist Autocracy* (Praeger), New York, 1965.

John Scott, *Behind the Urals* (Houghton Mifflin), Boston, 1942.

A. I. Solzhenitsyn, *One Day in the Life of Ivan Denisovich* (Praeger), New York, 1963.

Boris Souvarine, *Stalin, a Critical Survey of Bolshevism* (Longmans, Green, and Co.), London, 1939.

Nicholas S. Timasheff, *The Great Retreat* (E. P. Dutton), New York, 1946.

4. Stalinism to Collective Leadership

SETTLED DICTATORSHIP

With the end of the mass purges in 1939, the Soviet Union entered its postrevolutionary period, and the following thirty-odd years brought less change than the previous decade. Crudities have been outgrown, the people and the ruling apparatus have become much more educated and sophisticated, arbitrary use of force has receded, and controls have become more regularized. But the party-state apparatus runs in the tracks on which Stalin set it.

The machinery of control of the economy was little changed as long as Stalin lived, and even thereafter it has been subjected only to tinkering or reshuffling. The sequence of five-year plans goes on. The collective farm statute of 1935 underwent only minor modification in 1969, although the farms are physically much changed. The constitution adopted in 1936 has undergone only minor amendment. The controls Stalin established over literature and the arts function with marginal relaxation; the official doctrine is still Socialist Realism. Collectivity of leadership after Stalin and after Khrushchev has brought less change than was to be expected.

The terror after 1939 was not disruptive and took few of the ruling group, which remained very stable until after Stalin's death. Of the Central Committee chosen in 1952, 61% were veterans of the Central Committee of 1939; and the Politburo suffered much less turnover than customary in Western cabinets. There were only a few policy innovations, as the institution in 1940 of a draft of youths for industrial work training, accompanied by fees (contrary to the Soviet constitution) for secondary and higher education, measures which remained in effect until 1956.

99

There was also further stiffening of labor discipline, with criminal liability for being more than twenty minutes late to work. This was related to the international situation and the drive to increase military strength. Military budgets began climbing in the mid 1930's; and Soviet concern with world politics rose with German rearmament, the Spanish civil war, and the failure of collective security. The end of mass purging in 1938 coincided with the obvious rise of international tension, as Hitler acquired Austria and prepared to deal with Czechoslovakia.

It is unnecessary to inquire how far the Soviet Union was moved by fear of attack and how far by the desire to profit from the disturbed condition of the world, which indicated an end to the "stabilization of capitalism" and promised opportunities for expansion. But attention was now directed outward; and negotiations were carried on in the spirit of power politics with both sides. By the Nazi-Soviet pact of August 23, 1939, Russia recovered most of the territories lost in the aftermath of the Revolution. These were sovietized in 1940 and added to the Soviet Union as four new republics, the former Baltic states and Moldavia (Bessarabia).

As Hitler overran most of Western Europe, Stalin further greatly increased military spending. In May, 1941, he assumed the premiership, remaining General Secretary of the party. Refusing to believe in the possibility of a German attack, he seems to have been dazed by the assault of June 22, 1941; he kept silent for eleven days, leaving others to speak for his regime. The government, too, was slow to react; six hours after the beginning of the invasion, Moscow radio was broadcasting its usual calisthenics and reports on the latest feats of labor.[1]

Despite large expenditures, the Soviet forces at the beginning of the war were badly equipped, incompetently led, and poorly disciplined. The early defeats were catastrophic and would have liquidated a country with less manpower and space to sacrifice. But in the mortal danger an extremely stringent mobilization of labor and resources was put into effect. Production of nonessentials and civilian goods was practically halted, and the Soviet people again experienced extreme deprivations. Munitions production rose rapidly to a level comparable with that of the United States. Enormous amounts of industrial equipment were shifted from threatened regions to set up new factories in the Urals and Siberia. The tightly organized, disciplined system was extremely effective when motivated by strong popular emotions.

As long as he lived, Stalin was given almost sole credit as architect of victory. But Khrushchev ridiculed his war role; and, although Soviet writers in recent years have portrayed him as a sensible generalissimo, he seems to have been a mediocre war leader. He visited the front only once and briefly. He must

[1] V. M. Berezhkov in Bialer, ed., *Stalin and His Generals*, p. 218.

bear much responsibility not only for refusal to heed warnings and unreadiness in 1941 but for encirclement of armies which he refused to allow to retreat. His answer to initial defeats was to execute commanders for treason, often naming party hacks to take their place. However, as realism prevailed, some capable generals were brought back from labor camps and others promoted from the ranks. The high command remained totally obedient to Stalin, whose complete domination of the government in war as in peacetime must be laid not only to his elimination of potential alternative leadership but to political astuteness and will.

It was Stalin's merit to bring out the patriotism of the Russian people. He addressed them as "Comrades, citizens, brothers and sisters," appealing not to Marxist-Leninist or class values but to the instincts of a threatened people. Some were at first prepared to welcome Hitler, but Nazi treatment of Slavs as subhuman soon convinced the Russians that they were fighting for survival. The regime correspondingly changed its style. Censorship was largely forgotten, and many inspiring patriotic works were produced. The government came to an understanding with the church, which in return gave moral and some material support for the war effort. Collective farm controls were relaxed and peasants were encouraged to produce however they could; although most of their manpower was taken away, they did so quite effectively. The party was opened to good fighters for the Fatherland with little regard for ideological conformity. The party grew, despite huge losses, from four million at the beginning of the war to nearly six million at its end. Old national themes stirred the people; even Panslavism, the imperial Russian ideal of brotherhood of Slavic peoples, was called upon to replace proletarian internationalism.

Feelings between people and government, joined in common purpose, became better than ever since the Revolution. The people felt that by immense sacrifices—hardly a family escaped loss of some of its men, about seven and one-half million soldiers and eleven million civilians having been killed, although estimates vary—they earned release from harsher demands and controls of Stalinism. There surely would be no more need for terrorism, and the truly popular government could hold free elections. Alliance with Britain and the United States seemed to signify a new departure for Russia. Consumer goods would be plentiful when Soviet industry no longer had to be devoted to armaments.

However, as soon as victory was assured, there began a return to the ideological-party approach. Political indoctrination was resumed in the army in February, 1944.[2] The guns were hardly silent before Soviet spokesmen were warning again of the dangers of "capitalist encirclement." Frictions with the

[2] Iu. P. Petrov, *Stroitelstvo politorganov, partiinykh i komsomolskikh organizatsii armii i flota* (Voennoe izd.), Moscow, 1968, p. 398.

Western powers rapidly grew toward Cold War. The direction of following years was set by the new five-year plan and Stalin's speech of February, 1946: the Soviet Union would continue to concentrate on military-industrial muscle. Repressions of deviants were resumed; and the most popular marshals, including Zhukov, were removed.

With the intensification of the Cold War in 1947, deeper chill descended on the Soviet Union. In a campaign for purification of the creative arts, one of Stalin's righthand men, Andrei Zhdanov, called upon writers, artists, even musicians, to recant. Only totally conformist works extolling the Soviet system, its glories, and its leader, were permitted; wartime productions which gave too much credit to the people instead of the party had to be rewritten. Xenophobia was pushed to new heights, with insistence on Soviet and Russian superiority in all things. Most useful inventions were found to have been made by Russians but stolen by the West. The strong Soviet Union of the latter 1940's seemed more fearful of Western influence than the land emerging from the ravages of the civil war a generation earlier. The extreme was reached in 1949, when the Soviet Union saw only satellites and unconditional adherents as friends, the economy was being remilitarized, and a purge, striking some two thousand functionaries, silently hit Leningrad. In December of that year, the deification of the leader reached its zenith in the celebrations of his seventieth birthday. *Pravda* was still publishing congratulations two and one-half years later.

In the last years of Stalin's life, the Soviet Union was showing signs of outgrowing Stalinism. His foreign policy was outworn, antagonizing even those who, like many leaders of the Third World, would have liked to see in the Soviet Union a friend. Although Stalin seems to have opposed any detente with the West, there were moves toward opening up foreign trade outside the bloc, which had shrunk to a trickle. More significant was the calling of the Nineteenth Congress of the Party in the fall of 1952. Stalin did not like large gatherings, even of handpicked supporters; and there had been no congress since 1939, although party rules required one every four years. At the congress, not Stalin but Malenkov made the principal presentation, and there were hints of differing views.

Stalin, whose mental powers were declining, seems to have felt his authority slipping. The death penalty, which had been revoked in 1947 (without halting executions), was restored for state crimes in 1950. There were a series of grim purge trials in Eastern Europe, and in 1952 Stalin's native Georgia was hard hit. According to Khrushchev's Secret Speech, Stalin no longer felt able to work with the twelve-man Politburo but used ad hoc committees. At the Nineteenth Congress, he enlarged the Politburo to a twenty-five man Presidium of the Central Committee, presumably because of distrust of the old oligarchs.

This may have been, again according to Khrushchev, prelude to the liquidation of the senior members. From the beginning of 1953, the Soviet press was calling for vigilance against enemy agents and wreckers. A number of Kremlin doctors, mostly Jewish, were arrested and accused of medical murder of Zhdanov and others and of plotting, with Zionist organizations and the American intelligence service, against leading Soviet generals (medical murder was a recurrent theme in the purges of the 1930's). No less sinister were charges of sabotage, espionage, and laxness on the part of the police. In an atmosphere of mounting apprehension, March 5, 1953, the dictator died, presumably of natural causes but under suggestive circumstances. People are said to have wept on the streets, mourning the genius of victory. But of his nearest collaborators, Malenkov, Beria, and Molotov, only the last, the most faithful Stalinist for over thirty years, mustered tears at Stalin's bier.

SUCCESSION

Those who took charge—no succession had been prepared—seem to have had little confidence in the stability of the regime, as they warned the people against "disorder and panic." But there was no visible stir, and the party leadership carried on as it had after Lenin's disappearance. There was not even a fairly open contest for leadership as occurred after Lenin. The struggle for predominance after Stalin was entirely among Stalinists whose political outlook had been almost indistinguishable, and it went on entirely in the shadows.

For a brief time, it seemed that Malenkov, apparently closest to Stalin, was moving into his place, as he occupied the key positions of secretary of the party and premier of the government, and the press for a week hailed him almost as a new dictator. But he lost his secretaryship and became merely a member, although perhaps the leading one, of the oligarchy. The Presidium was cut back from twenty-five to fifteen, on no legal basis but probably by virtue of the inner circle's control of the police in the capital. Marshal Zhukov was recalled from semibanishment and made Minister of Defense to assure the cooperation of the armed forces. Beria, who had been demoted as Stalin prepared a new purge, was restored to command of a reorganized police ministry.

As after Lenin's death, collective leadership was the order of the day, with calls for return to Leninist principles and denunciations of one-man decisions. The new regime dissociated itself from the worst of Stalinism. The extralegal sentencing of "socially dangerous" persons was ended. Criminal (but not political) prisoners were amnestied. The atmosphere of terror was lifted; Beria spoke of the need for socialist legality, and charges against the Kremlin doctors were dropped. There were sundry acts of relaxation. Compulsory deliveries from peasants' household plots were reduced. Regulations regarding divorce and abortion were eased. There was a little opening to the outside world, and emphasis was slightly shifted to consumer goods.

Despite removal from the Secretariat, Malenkov, whom Stalin's daughter called "clearly the most reasonable and sagacious member of the Politburo,"[3] remained the leading or at least most prominent personality. However, he was a party apparatus man of the purest water, and he seems to have been less effective as chief of the state administration. Beside him stood Beria, sinister boss of the police, whose cooperation was necessary in the organization of the regime. Behind them stood Khrushchev, like Stalin at an early stage more powerful than he appeared. He had spent a long time away from the center, in the Ukraine, having been brought back in 1949 apparently to offset the growing power of Malenkov and Beria. When Malenkov left the Secretariat, Khrushchev was the only man in both it and the Politburo. In September, 1953, he became First Secretary.[4]

Others of the old inner circle were less powerful. Molotov had apparently tied his personality too much to Stalin. Mikoyan, Armenian specialist in trade, had gained and kept a place in the top ranks by political dexterity but had no control of the party machinery. Kaganovich, last Jew in the leadership, was disqualified by his prominent role in the purges.

The first break in the collective leadership was the ouster of Beria from control of the police in June and his execution in December. The others could not feel secure as long as Beria was in charge of the police; he had demonstrated his potentialities by taking control of Moscow in the first days after Stalin's death. When he was weakened by the failure of the police in the Berlin riots of June, 1953, his enemies struck. With the help of leading generals, he was separated from his bodyguards and arrested. In the old style, he was accused of having always been a spy for the British; and a number of aides accompanied him in death. Leaders have not subsequently been so branded or physically liquidated, although executions of some of Beria's associates went on for several years.

Malenkov took up nonparty and popular causes. He inaugurated something of a detente in international relations, proposing, it seems, concessions at the expense of Soviet control of East Germany. He advocated developing light industry as rapidly as heavy, using aluminum for pans instead of airplanes, and aroused great expectations. To relieve overcentralization, he began to transfer thousands of plants to the jurisdiction of the separate republics.

---

[3] Alliluyeva, *Only One Year*, p. 415.

[4] The infighting of this period is well detailed by Robert Conquest, *Power and Policy in the USSR* (Macmillan and Co.), New York, 1961.

There was a thaw in literature, and a beginning was made in the rehabilitation of purge victims, mostly posthumously. Malenkov also favored some devolution of authority within the party apparatus.

All this was apparently alarming to party stalwarts and the military-industrial complex, whose spokesman Khrushchev made himself. Toward the end of 1954, the Soviet Union saw the first public semidebate for twenty years: the party organ, *Pravda*, decried and the government organ, *Izvestia*, defended the lowered priority for heavy and defense industry. In February, 1955, Malenkov resigned as premier, apologizing for "failures in agriculture." He remained in the Presidium.

The new head of administration was a somewhat ineffectual political soldier, Marshal Bulganin. For a few years there was an ostensible duumvirate of Khrushchev and Bulganin as heads of party and state apparatus, but the real power was clearly with the former. Khrushchev had once been more Stalinist than Stalin, and his rapid rise was apparently due to ability to anticipate the policies of the boss. No one was louder in praise of Stalin. In charge of sovietization of territories taken from Poland in 1939, he did a nasty job with apparent efficiency. However, his character may have been changed and ripened by his part in the war, which he, unlike most of the men near the top, experienced at close hand.[5] He was uneducated, a peasant at heart; but he had a lively intelligence, was willing to experiment, and aroused unaccustomed hopes of change.

Having associated himself with the military-conservative wing against Malenkov, Khrushchev proceeded in 1955 to follow his course. The armed forces were reduced, there was a serious approach to disarmament, the Soviet Union agreed to a treaty with Austria and withdrew from its zone of that country, and Khrushchev and Bulganin met Eisenhower at a summit conference in Geneva. Khrushchev also showed a different outlook from that of Stalin by his extensive travels (with Bulganin in tow) to England, to India and Burma, and to Belgrade to apologize to Tito, whom Stalin had excommunicated and anathematized eight years before.

Khrushchev also undertook, in 1955 and 1956, a series of ideological revisions to rationalize and modernize the official Soviet outlook. These dealt mostly with foreign affairs but had important implications for domestic politics. In the nuclear age, war was no longer to be considered inevitable, as Lenin had insisted, but "Peaceful Coexistence" must be accepted as normal. Socialism then could come not only by violent revolution but by peaceful development and by different roads according to specific conditions of different countries. The Stalinist thesis of the sharpening of the class struggle was repudiated. The

[5] This is the deduction of Edward Crankshaw, *Khrushchev, a Career* (Viking Press), New York, 1960, p. 138.

struggle between capitalism and socialism was to be turned into a peaceful contest of social systems, which the Soviet Union was sure to win by its capacity for economic and cultural growth.

This softening of ideology must have been painful to many of the old Stalinists. But their discomfiture at Peaceful Coexistence and its connotations was nothing compared to the effects of Khrushchev's denunciation of Stalin as incompetent and a criminal at the February, 1956, Twentieth Congress of the Party.

The opening shot was fired by Mikoyan, who attacked Stalin's "cult of the personality" in a public speech. This was followed by a sensational speech behind closed doors by Khrushchev, later read to party members throughout the Soviet Union. Leaked by foreign Communists and published by the American State Department, it has never been confirmed or denied by the Soviet government. In considerable detail, Khrushchev charged Stalin with inordinate self-glorification, with murdering good Communists, and with abuse of power in the latter years of his rule. Khrushchev took pains to deflate Stalin's reputation as a genius–commander, portraying him as a military nincompoop.

Khrushchev must have intended to cast off burdens of the past and to promote a moral revival in the party. Also, and perhaps this was a more important consideration, he was in effect attacking his chief contenders for power, Molotov, Malenkov, and associates, who had stood nearer to Stalin, while dissociating himself from the excesses of Stalinism. It was a risky venture, but Khrushchev was bold.

The gambit of de-Stalinization might have worked out well enough if only the Soviet Union were concerned; its peoples were passive in the face of a promise of liberalization as they were when menaced by terror. But Eastern Europeans, including Communist Party members, interpreted the dethronement of Stalin's image as an invitation to more independence. The Poles came near to forceful resistance in October, and the situation was saved only by a compromise permitting much more internal autonomy in return for Poland's cooperation in external and defense matters. In Hungary, the Communist Party fell apart in a resurgence of national feeling; and only Russian troops restored Soviet hegemony.

This threat to Russian dominion of Eastern Europe armed the opposition to Khrushchev, but it became strong enough to threaten him only after May, 1957, when he pushed through an economic decentralization plan dissolving ministries in Moscow and transferring staffs to provincial centers. This made economic sense and pleased regional bosses, but for many at the center being sent out of Moscow was banishment. In June, Malenkov, Molotov, and Kaganovich led a move to strip Khrushchev of his position as First Secretary. Although only two members stood consistently by him, Khrushchev fought in the Presidium for three days, during which he was able, with the help of the army, to bring in supporters from outside Moscow. In a constitutional innovation, Khrushchev appealed to the Central Committee, which had formally elected him. The Central Committee, dominated by Khrushchev's provincial followers, sustained him and expelled his chief antagonists from the Presidium. They were labelled the "Anti-Party Group"; but they were accused only of personal faults, not ideological sins as in past purges, and their punishment was demotion to minor posts.[6]

A largely new Presidium was named, including several of Khrushchev's colleagues in the Secretariat. Khrushchev was now fairly secure, but his victory was only partial and could be harvested only gradually. Bulganin, who had joined the opposition, remained as premier until March, 1958, when Khrushchev took that position. In 1961, at the Twenty-Second Congress, Khrushchev was still trying to secure condign punishment for men who opposed him in 1957. Khrushchev also had to reward Marshal Zhukov by making him the first military man to become full member of the Presidium. However, Khrushchev had reason to distrust a man who had shown his ability to intervene in a crisis. A few months later, Khrushchev took advantage of Zhukov's tripping in Albania to dismiss him.

Khrushchev thereby completed a rise to power distantly parallel to that of Stalin thirty years earlier. But he had no possibility of emulating the great dictator. He was fifty-nine when he became First Secretary compared to Stalin's forty-three at accession to General Secretary. Khrushchev does not seem to have desired bloodshed, and he was probably never strong enough to terrorize the party. There was no social transformation to justify mass repressions, or strong revolutionary-ideological feeling on which to base them. Finally, the fact that the Soviet Union had matured into a modern industrial power with a fairly high educational level impeded a Stalinesque dictatorship.

KHRUSHCHEV ALTERNATIVE

The new boss was a contradictory character. He was basically ignorant but shrewd and quick; with no liking for intellectuals, he yet permitted considerable latitude to writers and artists. He played on the theme of peace and seems to have been basically pacific, but he indulged in rocket-rattling and military threats far more than Stalin did. He was folksy and gregarious and at the same time a party manipulator. He ended political terror, but applied the death penalty for economic crimes. He was hard and could be deceitful, but he was

---

[6] For a full treatment of this episode, see Roger Pethybridge, *A Key to Soviet Politics* (Frederick A. Praeger, Inc.), New York, 1962.

more human and likable than his predecessors and successors. He showed no definite principles and few scruples, but he seems to have genuinely desired to improve the government of Russia and perhaps fell because he insisted on change.

A Soviet Union long stifled in the grip of Stalinist regimentation called for release and new departures, and Khrushchev wished to help the country enter a new era. He saw the Soviet way as the historically justified answer to the big problems of modernity, leading to the glorious future. Stalin's misdeeds were only distortions of true communism; Khrushchev proposed, then, to return to the ideals of Leninism and the Revolution.

Return to Leninism also meant revitalizing the Communist Party. Stalin had never ceased to act in the name of the party. However, while using it as his chief tool, he offset it by other organs, particularly the political police; and he exercised control over the governmental apparatus and the economy directly, through his private secretariat more than through the party mechanism. As First Secretary, Khrushchev had a personal interest in building up the role of the party while Malenkov headed the administration; and his victory over Malenkov sealed the renewed supremacy of the party apparatus. Khrushchev continued to stress the party's leadership in all fields, from education to the military. He wanted the party to have chief responsibility for industry and agriculture, for which purpose he gave it a more technical, less ideological orientation. One effect, perhaps the chief purpose, of his decentralization of 1957 was to give local party heads, the oblast secretaries, much more power over the economy.

Khrushchev increased the recruitment of workers and peasants into the party, which under Stalin had been increasingly dominated by white collars; and the party grew to be a truly mass organization, with 9.7 million members in 1961. He also sought to revive the party's political life. Under Stalin, intervals between congresses became successively longer, until it seemed a major concession that he permitted one in 1952. Khrushchev seemingly liked these huge conclaves of the faithful, as he summoned them oftener than required by party statute, in 1956, 1959, and 1961. They did not again become real forums of controversy, as they had been in Lenin's time, and votes were always unanimous, as under Stalin; but they heard some sharp and interesting speeches, particularly from Khrushchev himself. The Central Committee, which had almost lapsed under Stalin, also had frequent and at times lively meetings. Party members were given more freedom to criticize their superiors. Although he never contemplated any real weakening of central control, Khrushchev talked a good deal of democratic procedure within the party. To shake up local bosses, he instituted a plan for rotation of positions and limitation of length of service in one office.

The ideology was made more Marxist, with less emphasis than in Stalin's day upon nationalistic and Russian themes; tsarist history became again more a story of class conflict, less a tale of glory; and Ivan the Terrible ceased to be a hero. Antireligious propaganda was stepped up. Gross inequalities of income were cut down, and minimum wages were increased (to sixty rubles per month). Some effort was made to equalize educational opportunities. Nearly all students were required to spend two years at labor to become eligible for higher education, to the irritation of elite parents. Correspondence and evening schools were expanded, manual and vocational training was mixed with academic, and Khrushchev proposed that most or all children be given a good communist start in life in boarding schools. He reversed the Stalinist tendency to put people in uniform.

In agriculture, Khrushchev sought to bring the peasants into communities more suitable for a socialist society. In 1949, under Stalin, he undertook a program for amalgamating collective farms, supposedly in the interests of production but probably more for ideological-political considerations; this continued through his years in office until the kolkhozes had been reduced to one-fifth of their previous numbers and had correspondingly swollen to gigantic size, with thousands of acres and many hundred workers, comparable to the gigantic state farms or sovkhozes. This was accompanied by the changeover of many collective, theoretically private-cooperative farms to the "higher" form of state farms, wholly integrated into the controlled economic scheme. These were approaching half the cultivated acreage by the end of Khrushchev's power. He nourished a Marxist vision of urbanizing the country; in his "agrogorods" ex-peasants would live in apartment houses, enjoy all manner of communal services, and take a bus to work. He lacked resources to further this utopia, but he exerted pressure on the remnant of private enterprise in the countryside, the peasants' garden plots and their livestock holdings.

Khrushchev attempted to reinstitute the goal of an eventual utopian-communist society, in which money should disappear because goods would be abundant enough for free apportionment to all according to need, and the state should wither away to leave the citizens to manage their own affairs. Many expected such a paradise on the morrow of the Revolution, although it is not clear how seriously Lenin and other leading Bolsheviks took such dreams. Stalin discouraged the whole idea, although it was never explicitly renounced as a long-term goal. Khrushchev incorporated it in the revised program of the party (the first revision since 1919) promulgated by the Twenty-Second Party Congress (1961). This mapped out the road to a partial communistic society to be established by 1980, with an improved standard of living, many more nonpaid services, and transfer of some state functions to "social" organizations of various kinds, with no lessening, however, of the role of the party.

This was for the future, but some of Khrushchev's policies pointed in this direction, as the expansion of boarding schools and the fusion of collective farms and their conversion to state farms. It was made cheaper to have meals in public eating places than to prepare dinner in the private kitchen. To reduce the state apparatus at the local level, volunteer citizens' organizations took on some official functions. Volunteer groups, mostly of Komsomols (Young Communists) were called upon to patrol the streets. Neighborhood meetings were given power to banish social parasites, and semiofficial, rather informal "comrade courts," which had lapsed under Stalin, were revived to handle minor disputes and infractions.

Some of these measures seemed to the outside world to imply that communism meant something like an anthill (or a beehive, as Khrushchev once put it), wherein it would be small improvement if control were exercised more directly by the strictly political and ideologically directed Communist Party and less by governmental agencies. However, Khrushchev recognized the need for change which the party could not always anticipate and direct and was prepared to accept, if not always to welcome, some loosening of controls. This did not mean liberty; the party leadership never dropped the whip nor permitted questioning of fundamentals. The latitude granted to dissent widened and narrowed from time to time, as Khrushchev played "liberal" and "conservative" themes; but areas of freedom were broadened to an extent inconceivable in Stalin's latter years.

Xenophobia and secrecy were somewhat eased. Foreign trade expanded, and many cultural exchanges were instituted with Western and other countries. Growing numbers of tourists were admitted to what under Stalin was almost a forbidden kingdom, and numerous cities were opened. A street map of Moscow was put on sale in 1962; in that year also, a telephone directory was published. Russians lost their fear of contact with foreigners, and a few were even permitted to travel abroad. Khrushchev received many foreign visitors and conversed with them with an ease and openness that was to become a fading memory after he left office. The production of consumer goods was improved, although not to the detriment of the traditional priority on heavy industry. Such frivolities as lipstick became commonplace, and the Soviet Union began holding fashion shows. The canons of Socialist Realism were loosened sufficiently to permit some writing for mere entertainment.

Chief beneficiaries were perhaps the creative artists and intellectuals. Some literature very critical of Soviet faults, at least of the recent past, was published, accounts of concentration camp experiences and descriptions of life in the countryside. In 1961–1962, the liberals were able to gain ascendancy in the Union of Writers. Painters and musicians likewise were given a little freedom to create in their own way. Khrushchev might upbraid creative artists, even obscenely, but he did not have them arrested, was willing to talk with them almost as equals, and sometimes admitted that the writers were better judges of literature than the party. Foreign literature was made more accessible. University students were permitted more independence, and they took to questioning of doctrines as fears wore off.[7] Scientists gained some immunity from party interference. When the Academy of Sciences refused membership to a candidate favored by the leader, he only fumed and started an investigation. In the latter Khrushchev years, one could reasonably speak of differing schools of Soviet philosophy, with some contentions as to the true meaning of Marxism-Leninism. There was even opened up some discussion of international affairs, and scholars were permitted to treat the world as more complicated than the conventional class-struggle.

Khrushchev's claim that there were no political prisoners required a very narrow interpretation of the term, but legal procedures were regularized (except for the popular justice mentioned), and more attention was given to the rights of the accused. New law codes were produced in the republics, and law enforcement was partly devolved to them, the central Ministry of Justice being dissolved. Victims of Stalin's repressions were freed and rehabilitated, although the condemnations of such men as Trotsky, Kamenev, Zinoviev, Bukharin, and their fellows were not retracted.

Some latitude of discussion was permitted within the party, and at the 1961 congress someone seems to have made the heretical suggestion that factions should be allowed to state their views. To secure support for his policies, Khrushchev went outside the party elite, licensing rather wide-ranging discussion of such matters as economic decentralization and educational reforms. Such debates in the press were initiated by the top leadership and the conclusions were dictated by it, but it was an innovation that controversy was let come to the surface. Khrushchev proposed that major laws be passed by referendum, but this was never realized. He made a bow to the popular will by proclaiming that the "dictatorship of the proletariat" had after four decades ripened into the "state of the whole people."

Attacking economic problems, Khrushchev devoted more attention to agriculture, the weakest and most neglected sector of the economy. Here he came up with one panacea after another: the plowing of millions of acres of "Virgin Lands" of marginal rainfall in Kazakhstan, the planting of corn almost everywhere, the cultivation of grasslands, the "chemicalization" of agriculture. Most of all, however, he was disposed to reorganize, as though the motto were: when in trouble, reshuffle. Not only did he decree a major relocation of industrial management in the decentralization of 1957; economic planning was repeatedly shifted, divided, and rejoined in a confusion of state committees and councils. Rural administration was reorganized at least five times. Most drastic and most damaging was the move in 1962 to split the party and soviet system up to the provincial (oblast) level into agricultural and industrial sectors so that the

---

[7] Cf. Wm. Taubman, *The View from the Lenin Hills* (Coward-McCann, Inc.), New York, 1967, passim.

party could give full attention to each. Such innovations were regularly ill-prepared and overdone. Pushed with fanfare, they aroused hopes of an early solution to fundamental problems; but they cost, in confusion and misdirected resources, more than they gained. After all the panaceas, agriculture met such disaster in 1963 that massive grain imports were needed to prevent hunger. Khrushchev was weakened by personal identification (such as Stalin avoided) with many dubious projects; and countless party functionaries, high and low, could only be irritated by being shifted around.

De-Stalinization was the key issue of Khrushchev's reign. How far the regime was prepared to go in renouncing the image and ways of the dictator indicated how far it was willing to undertake basic reform. To favor de-Stalinization was to favor freedom for literature and art, international contacts and detente, economic reform and consumerism. To oppose it was to oppose all these and to favor ideological fundamentalism and strong control everywhere. It was reminiscent of the split between Mensheviks and Bolsheviks fifty years before, or between Westernizers and Slavophils a half century earlier still.

In this cleavage, Khrushchev, the great de-Stalinizer, could not or would not take a firm stand. At the 1956 congress he spoke confidentially, curiously seeking to keep such an important turn within the elite. Moreover, his account was far from complete. It blackened Stalin excessively in some ways, as in respect to his incapacity as wartime leader; but only the murder of leading cadres and good Stalinists was lamented. Not only did Khrushchev not criticize collectivization, he failed to utter a word against the extreme brutality with which it was carried through. Subsequently, as after the troubles in Eastern Europe in 1956, he reemphasized the qualities of Stalin as a good Communist. In following years, rehabilitations proceeded irregularly and cautiously, and Stalin was praised off and on. The climax of de-Stalinization came only with the 1961 congress, when Khrushchev coupled a new assault on Stalin with a renewed attack on Malenkov, Molotov, and company. Then, in published speeches, he sharpened his charges of criminality, including an implication of Stalin's complicity in the murder of Kirov that served as trigger for the purges. Stalin's body was removed from its place next to Lenin. In 1961–1962, hundreds of Soviet cities, factories, collective farms, and the like lost the name of Stalin; and hundreds of thousands of empty pedestals and a flurry of anti-Stalin writing brought de-Stalinization home to the Soviet people.

It was probably impossible for Khrushchev to carry it further without discrediting himself and his supporters, if not the whole party, unless he were prepared to preside over fundamental changes. Of the old leaders, only Mikoyan seems to have sided wholeheartedly with Khrushchev on the issue. It was not easy to uphold the unqualified superiority of a system while damning the man who had shaped it. Khrushchev contended that the party itself had really been in control and that the faults of the dictator were accidental and peripheral, caused by a quirk of personality. Leninism was brought forward as an alternative source of authority. Khrushchev only wanted to make party control more tolerable and so more effective.

This was not unsuccessful. De-Stalinization facilitated ideological renewal, and it hastened the rise to top rank of a new set of leaders, more or less beholden to Khrushchev. It pleased army commanders who remembered the purges. It was popular among millions of victims and their relatives. To the intellectuals it opened up vistas of unlimited improvement. Khrushchev seems to have felt that he could govern better and improve the Soviet system and the Soviet position in the world by placing himself toward the liberal end of the Soviet political spectrum, that he could get the country to move faster by slackening the reins a little.

But if de-Stalinization was helpful to the Soviet Union and in the short run to Khrushchev, in the longer run it was hurtful to his authority. There was always resistance to it in the party. Many ordinary citizens, conditioned by many years of indoctrination, felt that Stalin was slandered, especially in his war role. And criticism of Stalin logically implicated the present leaders; if he was an ogre, his protegés were hardly the worthiest of the worthy. Khrushchev claimed that he had opposed Stalin on occasion, but he thereby sanctioned opposition to himself. The defamation of other prominent men, as Molotov and Malenkov, further undermined Soviet legitimacy. If de-Stalinization helped Khrushchev against the old guard, it left him defenseless against the younger men coming up who were less associated than he with the evils of the dictatorship.

The party stalwarts also saw Khrushchev threatening their authority by going outside the inner circle. He reached out to base himself, in part at least, on specialists and administrators in various branches, frequently inviting outsiders, officials, journalists, or sundry experts, to speak in favor of his ideas in the Central Committee. He used public discussions in the press to advance measures, as the educational reform, which the insiders viewed with displeasure. The conservatives found his impulsiveness and openness to novelty distasteful and dangerous to the comfortable status quo. The infection of Western decadence seemed to grow menacingly, as the street corners and cafes of Moscow and Leningrad were overrun with supermodern youth aping the latest styles of England and America.

This was the more grievous for the ebullient Chairman as he was unable to find firm support outside. But he caused headshaking in the party without satisfying the liberals. He maintained controls and ideology, never really retreating from the basic view of two worlds in conflict. He relaxed tensions slightly in the world but brought no real detente. There was no concession to liberty in the sense of limitation of party power. If a few critical works were permitted, hundreds more were refused publication. Khrushchev expected the nonparty intelligentsia to cooperate gratefully in return for small blessings, but they wanted much more than he could give. They regarded him as a crude boor, but he was probably as easy a master as could be expected as long as the party remained the essential bond of the Soviet system.

Consequently, after Khrushchev had gotten rid of his former peers and had seen his day of glory with his new Party Program and revised Party Rules in 1961, his troubles piled up. He could not manage men he himself had elevated; a large majority of regional secretaries had been replaced in the preceding few years, and 60% of the Central Committee was new. He had difficulty in implementing economic reforms; and in March, 1962, he seems to have failed to secure approval of his consumer goods program. His proposal to raise his son-in-law, Adzhubei, to the party Secretariat was defeated.[8] Sundry initiatives in world affairs, from pressure on Berlin and the wooing of the underdeveloped world to missiles in Cuba, had been more or less costly failures. Eastern Europe was in ferment and Soviet dominion seemed potentially in question. The Communist movement was in disarray, and the Sino-Soviet split was deepening. Economic growth, instead of speeding up, had considerably decelerated; and gains after 1961 were modest. It was no longer obvious that the Soviet Union was soon going to catch up with the United States. Worst was the shortfall in agriculture, Khrushchev's specialty.

By 1964, a large number of high party leaders were unhappy with the policies of Khrushchev. However, he seems to have treated the Presidium rather cavalierly and pushed his own personality cult; his birthday in April filled eleven pages of *Pravda*. Hence, when he moved toward a major overhaul of policy, including reduction of armaments and emphasis on consumer goods, opposition in the Presidium seems to have become overwhelming. It only remained quietly to organize a coup.[9]

DICTATORSHIP SANS DICTATOR

On October 14, 1964, Radio Moscow, after some bulletins on production, informed that N. S. Khrushchev had resigned his high positions because of age and health. Within hours, his pictures were taken down and his works were being removed from bookstores. There were a few critical commentaries, eschewing the name but making their target clear, with vague

---

[8] For details of the complicated politics of this era, see especially Michel Tatu, *Power in the Kremlin, from Khrushchev to Kosygin* (Viking Press), New York, 1969.

[9] Events of these months are detailed by William Hyland and Richard W. Shryock, *The Fall of Khrushchev* (Funk and Wagnalls), New York, 1968.

accusations of foolish schemes, subjectivism, and nepotism. But since then his name has rarely been printed in the Soviet Union, and little explanation has been given for his deposition.[10] No ideological issue was raised, and Khrushchev was allowed to depart without self-blame like that imposed on Malenkov.

Khrushchev's ouster was a Kremlin coup in which the masses were considered to have little legitimate interest and to which they reacted entirely passively. Within the framework of the party rules, however, it was constitutional. Khrushchev was summoned back from a Crimean holiday to face a Presidium solidly against him. He appealed to the Central Committee as in 1957 but was voted down by a large majority. For the first time in Russian history, a ruler was removed from office by legal and nonviolent means. The nearest precedent was the forced resignation of the premiership by Malenkov in 1955; but Malenkov was never ruler in the sense that Khrushchev was. Khrushchev was given a good pension and apartment to ease his retirement.[11] His gentle treatment of the "Anti-Party Group," who were merely demoted to minor positions, served him in good stead.

Few persons shared in the leader's fall, only a handful of his immediate entourage, including his favored son-in-law. He was ousted by the leadership group as a whole, mostly former Khrushchevites. M. Suslov, who apparently led the plot, had heaped the most fulsome praise upon the boss a few months before. Those who worked at the center and managed the party apparatus seem to have feared that he was undermining the authority of the party, resented his seeking of support outside or behind the backs of the inner circle, disliked the ideological uncertainty which he permitted, and hated his repeated reorganizations—sins which they were to avoid in following years. Most of them represented a better-educated generation who probably felt themselves, as did Soviet intellectuals, superior to the bumbling oldster who used earthy language and banged his shoe on the desk at the United Nations. For the men of party-bureaucratic or technical qualifications who had been brought forward to manage the increasingly developed Soviet state, Khrushchev became unnecessary as soon as he ceased to be successful.

The top leaders were about ten years younger than Khrushchev and witnessed the Revolution and civil war as children only; they belonged to the generation of technicians and managers raised up by Stalin and advanced in the purges. Aleksei Kosygin, new Chairman of the Council of Ministers, or premier, born in 1904, was graduated from a textile institute and, exceptionally among Soviet leaders, rose in the less favored channels of light industry and finance. Nikolai Podgorny, who in 1965 succeeded Mokoyan as figurehead president and

[10] The official version has continued to be "age and health." *Istoria kommunisticheskoi partii sovetskogo soiuza* (Politizdat), Moscow, 1969, p. 628. His death in 1971 received a one-sentence notice in *Pravda* and *Izvestia* only.

[11] In 1970, he was reported whiling the days in abstract painting.

second in Soviet protocol, born in 1903, received his diploma from a food industry institute. Leonid Brezhnev, the new party leader, born in 1906, was graduated from a metallurgical institute but became strictly a party apparatchik, stepping mostly from one secretaryship to another. In the world war he was a political officer. In Stalin's last year, Brezhnev became a member of the Central Committee and one of its secretaries; under Khrushchev he became First Secretary in Kazakhstan, full member of the party Presidium, President of the Presidium of the Supreme Soviet, and heir apparent in Khrushchev's last year.

These and other members of the Politburo and Secretariat seem to have agreed, however, to avoid a new dictatorship; the most concrete measure was a Central Committee resolution that the Chairmanship of the Council of Ministers should be kept separate from the First Secretaryship of the party. Collectivity of leadership was sufficiently effective at first that the world could only guess who was particularly influential behind the screen of secrecy.[12] The dozen or so top leaders very seldom appeared in public except on formal occasions, as reviewing a holiday parade, and they hardly ever hinted a personal opinion; the best informed observers had few ideas as to who might be responsible for what.

Whatever differences of policy there may have been were evidently a matter of slant and shading only. Kosygin, who has struck foreign visitors as well-informed and business-like, obviously paid more attention to economic matters and seemed to favor consumer goods; he was perhaps supported by Shelepin and Mazurov. Brezhnev seemed to have a more party-ideological bent, as did Shelest and Kirilenko. These two groups may have corresponded roughly to the dichotomy of administrative-technical interests and party-apparatus power represented by Malenkov and Khrushchev long before. But there is no evidence of any clear-cut division, fixed alignments or definite personal followings within the Politburo, members of which seem to value stability and unity above considerations of policy.

Collective leadership is less decisive than single leadership and more subject to divisive pressures. It hence seemed quite expectable that in the absence of a strongman the anonymous committee regime would continue the opening of Soviet society inaugurated by Khrushchev. The new government dropped the Khrushchevian flamboyance and braggartry, took a quiet line in foreign affairs, and moved to an increase of consumer goods production and foreign trade. Economic planning became more modest and realistic, and there were no more grand schemes. Experts and specialists were allowed more autonomy in their work. The utopianism of the Party Program dropped from sight. There were more rehabilitations. In the first part of 1965, Soviet citizens were speaking out more freely than since the end of the 1920's. It was even

[12] See Sidney Ploss, "Soviet Politics in the Eve of the 24th Party Congress," *World Politics*, vol. XXIII, no. 1, October, 1970.

suggested that in due course there might be a choice of (party-approved) candidates in elections. In March, 1965, an anti-American demonstration was dispersed by force. The Soviet Union seemingly was moving toward an authoritarianism like that of the last tsars, with a government committed to legality and fairly broad freedom except for those who attacked the existing order.

From the spring of 1965, however, many measures pointed to a return to orthodoxy and a reduction of freedom of dissent. A series of editorials in *Pravda* hammered on the need for ideological improvement. In May, 1965, began the restoration of Stalin's image, especially in regard to his qualities as a leader in wartime. A series of generals' memoirs found him reasonable and accessible. In 1966, the Stalin Museum in Georgia was reopened, and by 1969 some writers were urging that he be put back on his pedestal. Denunciation of the "cult of personality" ceased, and de-Stalinization was found to hurt ideological education. In 1969, his birthday was observed, for the first time since 1956. In 1970, his grave was graced with a benign statue; by then, he was occasionally quoted as an ideologue. The party rehabilitated the long period dominated by Stalin; in 1969 the First Five-Year Plan was officially celebrated. The regime had no quarrel with any part of Stalin's doctrines. Many people seemed ready to welcome him back.

The limited ideological revisions of Khrushchev came under attack in the press. Peaceful Coexistence seemed half forgotten (unless defined as "a form of ideological struggle"), and the doctrine of "different roads to socialism," with its corollary of peaceful transition, was allowed to lapse. Khrushchev tended to single out "dogmatism" as the chief ideological danger; his successors warned against both "dogmatism" and "revisionism" with much more attention for the latter.[13] In 1968 and after came a stiffening of ideological terms, with a return to Stalinist positions: unequivocal presentation of the world as scene of titanic struggle of capitalism and socialism, and the thesis of intensifying class struggle as the victory of the workers approaches. Brezhnev personally sustained the necessity of the dictatorship of the proletariat along the whole road from capitalism to socialism. The Lenin cult became more exaggerated, especially in the two-year campaign of preparation for the supreme event, his hundredth birthday in April, 1970. Military-patriotic themes were inflated more than ever before in peacetime. The security forces were much glorified; they became knights of the safety of socialism and the people against insidious enemies.

From late summer 1965, there were arrests of "bourgeois national-ists," especially in the Ukraine. The writers came under pressure; the atmosphere changed radically with the arrest of two of them, Siniavsky and Daniel, late in that year and their subsequent sentencing to forced labor. Occasionally

---

[13] A small reversal was the rejection in October, 1965, of the suggestion put forward in January, that political science be introduced as an academic subject.

thereafter dissenters were imprisoned or consigned to mental hospitals. Political nonconformists were warned of unpleasant consequences of hostility to the system, including loss of employment, banishment to some remote area (probably in Siberia), or possibly forced labor. Repression continued to be much milder than under Stalin and was relatively rational; it was attempted to punish only those who really opposed the system. But the collective leadership was much less inhibited than Khrushchev had been from using force.

One purpose of intimidation was to discourage undesirable communication of Soviet citizens with foreigners; Western correspondents were more isolated than since Stalin. Although there was no return to Stalinist xenophobia, foreign contacts and exchanges were checked. Foreign travel was made more difficult, and the passport fee was raised to 400 rubles ($484). Areas open to foreign tourists remained restricted, including only three cities and a few specific points of interest in Siberia. Jamming of foreign broadcasts was resumed in August, 1968. Communication between leadership and people was also reduced. The blanket of secrecy over political affairs became dense as every effort was made to prevent indications of policy disagreements among the top leadership from coming to public view, and the rulers decreasingly felt impelled to inform of reasons for decisions. Their personalities and personal lives were wrapped in secrecy. Outsiders were no longer often brought into Central Committee meetings, and the practice of publishing accounts of sessions was discontinued after March, 1965. Debates over major policy questions were continued only in subdued and inconspicuous form.

More than ever, the party as an entity has been raised up as master of state, economy, and culture, as teacher of the peoples and guardian of ideology, responsible for discipline and unequivocal unity. Much more attention was given to indoctrination than ever before, and the people were called upon to exercise vigilance. Even physicists and composers were summoned to contribute to the war of ideas against the West. Power was drawn back to the center after the timorous previous steps to spread it out in the interests of efficiency. The administrative functions of the Soviet republics were cut down. The economic reform of September, 1965, seemed ambivalent, as discretionary authority of managers was broadened while the economic ministries were restored to Moscow; but the former aspect appeared, after a few years, much less effective than the latter. It was indicative that the number of candidates defeated in local soviet elections, which rose markedly under Khrushchev (to about one in seven thousand) shrank by 1971 to Stalinist proportions (about one in twenty thousand). The several changes made in party rules at the Twenty-Fourth Congress (April, 1971) were all in the direction of reducing consultation and giving the party apparatus more stability; periods between conferences and congresses were lengthened, and terms of office were extended.

Gone, however, was the revolutionary ethos. It had been taken for granted that social transformation, admittedly still incomplete, was a major goal of the Soviet leadership and accounted for much of their behavior. This no longer appears to be the case to any significant degree, as even the modest proposals of change of the Khrushchev era are forgotten. The entire structure has grown stiff; order is the rule. The bureaucratic principle of tenure seems prevalent. From 1952 to 1956, and again from 1956 to 1961, there was a turnover of about half in Central Committee membership, but of the 1961 Central Committee, nearly five-sixths were continued in 1966; of the 1966 Central Committee, four-fifths were continued in 1971. Many ministers have been in office for twenty years or more, some (as of Food Industry, Non-Ferrous Metallurgy, and Fisheries) for about thirty years. Andrei Gromyko was Deputy Foreign Minister since 1947, and has been Foreign Minister since 1957. The government by the same token is ripe in years; the average age of full members of the Central Committee has crept up from forty-nine in 1952 to sixty in 1970. Reforms are feeble and labored; changes have been mostly reversions. The project to replace the ("Stalin") constitution of 1936, begun in 1961, was forgotten. Soviet patterns, as in education, were more rigid than American. The equalitarian educational changes of Khrushchev, forwarding boarding schools, mixing work with academic training, and requiring labor experience as prerequisite for higher education, were undone. In conservative spirit, the Brezhnev-Kosygin regime greatly increased expenditures of scarce capital for the restoration of historical monuments, returning tsarist palaces to their dazzling splendor. A tsarist nobleman might be glorified for supporting the Soviet army in the Second World War.[14] The Soviet Union has thus swung away from a trend which has been taken for granted in the Western world in recent decades, toward fuller information for a better educated public, participation of broader circles in discussion (if not formulation) of policy, greater equality, and deeper skepticism of traditional values. The political and intellectual gulf between the Soviet Union and the Western world thus failed to continue to narrow, as it did under Khrushchev and as seemed expectable under the imperatives of modern industrial civilization.

In parallel with this trend, collectivity of leadership was gradually eroded by the accumulating authority of the General Secretary. In 1965, Brezhnev added an important post, chairmanship of the Russian Party Bureau of the Central Committee. At the very conformist Twenty-Third Party Congress, in April, 1966, Brezhnev received the title of General Secretary, Stalin's badge of authority. In 1965 and 1967, two potential rivals, Podgorny and Shelepin, were transferred out of the Secretariat. A two-volume collection of Brezhnev's

---

[14] *Pravda*, October 29, 1969, p. 3.

pronouncements was published in Russian and other languages of the Soviet Union, and he was the only member whose dicta were frequently cited as ideological verities. In May, 1970, he received about as many honorary nominations to the Supreme Soviet as all his colleagues together.

Later that year, his colleagues may have sought to check his rise. On July 3, 1970, he announced a party congress for that year; on July 14, a pronouncement in the name of the Central Committee called the congress for March, 1971; and Brezhnev's birthday, which had been shifted in Soviet calendars to place it on January 1, was put back to the correct December 16 date. By March, 1971, however, he had more than recovered, so that he alone (as no one since Stalin) signed the directive for the new five-year plan; and the Twenty-Fourth Party Congress, April, 1971, rang with praise for the General Secretary and cries of Glory! to his name. The four additions to the Politburo in April, 1971, Kunaev, Kulakov, Grishin, and Shcherbitsky, seemed mostly if not all to be Brezhnev proteges. Although holding only a party position, he was publicized much as a head of state receiving foreign delegations. Although he previously concentrated on party affairs, in 1971 he assumed leadership in diplomatic affairs. It became the norm for the astronaut or economist to make a bow to him in almost any public statement. *Pravda* published occasional glowing tributes, as of "boundless trust and unlimited love to you, dear Leonid Ilich."[15] Age was against him, however, and he lacked the obvious dynamism appropriate for a dictator. The chief impression he has given has been of outstanding dullness, and he seems to be much less popular than Kosygin, whom he has pushed politically into the shadows. It seems unlikely that he can attain absolutism like that of Stalin or perhaps even of Khrushchev in his heyday; thus far, he has lacked the ability or will to expel anyone from the inner circle. But the pendulum apparently swings back toward the single leadership which is unavoidable in a nonconstitutional regime.

For this broad turn, various reasons may be adduced. International tensions, particularly the intensification of war in Vietnam, beginning early in 1965, undoubtedly played a part, encouraging the conservatives and raising the ideological temperature. The epidemic of protests and disorders in the United States and Western Europe doubtless helped persuade Soviet leaders of the rightness of their cause. At the same time pressure against Soviet authority in Eastern Europe not only caused fears of loss of dominion over a vital area but also raised apprehensions lest a loosening of the Communist system there have serious effects on party authority inside the Soviet Union. The invasion of Czechoslovakia required ideological justification and seemed, by its success in restoring party control, to vindicate the use of force. Contrariwise, the relaxation of the world atmosphere in 1970 and 1971 seems to have been reflected in the Soviet outlook.

[15] June 12, 1971, p. 1.

Perhaps more fundamentally, the party seems to have resolved to check developments which, if they had continued as in the years 1956–1964, must have eventually been fatal to the Soviet system as Stalin built it. The leadership wishes to modernize, as Khrushchev did, but not at the cost of party rule, and extra efforts of control and indoctrination and apparently reconcentration of authority are necessary to prevent modernization from loosening the Soviet order. The Khrushchev years were, in a sense, an experiment; the leaders of the party seem to have found it dangerous.

READINGS

Robert Conquest, *Power and Policy in the USSR* (Macmillan), London, 1961.

Edward Crankshaw, *Khrushchev, a Career* (Viking Press), New York, 1966.

Alexander Dallin and Thomas B. Larson, *Soviet Politics since Khrushchev* (Prentice-Hall, Inc.), Englewood Cliffs, N. J., 1968.

Denis Dirscherl, ed., *The New Russia* (Pflaum Press), Dayton, Ohio, 1968.

Peter H. Juviler and Henry W. Morton, eds., *Soviet Policy-Making* (Praeger), New York, 1967.

Carl A. Linden, *Khrushchev and the Soviet Leadership*, Johns Hopkins Press, Baltimore, Md., 1966.

Observer, *Message from Moscow* (Johathan Cape), London, 1969.

Myron Rush, *Political Succession in the USSR* (Columbia University Press), New York, 1965.

Anatole Shub, *The New Russian Tragedy* (W. W. Norton & Co., Inc.), New York, 1969.

John W. Strong, ed., *The Soviet Union under Brezhnev and Kosygin* (Van Nostrand Reinhold), New York, 1971.

Howard R. Swearer, *The Politics of Succession in the USSR* (Little, Brown & Co.), Boston, 1964.

The Ruling Nucleus: Politburo and Secretariat

Secretariat	Politburo	
L. I. Brezhnev (General Secretary)	L. I. Brezhnev (1906)	
	N. V. Podgorny (1903)	Chairman, Presidium of Supreme Soviet
	A. N. Kosygin (1904)	Chairman, Council of Ministers
M. A. Suslov	M. A. Suslov (1902)	
A. P. Kirilenko	A. P. Kirilenko (1906)	
	A. Ya. Pelshe (1899)	Chairman, Party Control Commission
	K. T. Mazurov (1914)	First Deputy Chairman, Council of Ministers
	D. S. Poliansky (1917)	First Deputy Chairman, Council of Ministers
	P. Ye. Shelest (1908)	First Secretary, Ukraine
	G. I. Voronov (1910)	Chairman, People's Control Commission
	A. N. Shelepin (1918)	Chairman, Trade Unions
	V. V. Grishin (1914)	First Secretary, Moscow City Party
	D. A. Kunaev (1912)	First Secretary, Kazakhstan
	V. V. Shcherbitsky	Chairman, Council of Ministers of Ukraine
F. D. Kulakov (Agriculture)	F. D. Kulakov (1918)	

Candidate Members

Secretariat	Politburo	
	Yu. V. Andropov (1914)	Chairman, KGB
D. F. Ustinov (Defense Industry)	D. F. Ustinov (1908)	
P. N. Demichev	P. N. Demichev (1918)	
	Sh. R. Rashidov (1917)	First Secretary, Uzbekistan
	P. M. Masherov (1918)	First Secretary, Belorussia
	V. P. Mzhavanadze (1902)	First Secretary, Georgia
I. V. Kapitonov (1915) B. N. Ponomarev (1905) K. F. Katushev (1927) (Foreign Parties)		
	M. S. Solomentsev (1913)	Chairman, Council of Ministers, Russian Republic

Order as given by Gen. Sec. Brezhnev in announcing nominations, April 9, 1971. Positions held as of January, 1972. Birthdate in parentheses.

5. Rationale of Power

IDEOLOGY and the soviet state

Since the turbulent days of 1917, when the Bolsheviks presented their party line to the people in simple promises and exhortations, suitable for the banners of a workers' march, the Soviets have made much of slogans. It is an invariable custom to issue a set of some sixty slogans for the two great holidays, May 1 and November 7. In 1970, the first of these ran as follows:

"1. Hail the First of May, the day of international solidarity of the toilers in the fight against imperialism, for peace, democracy, and socialism!

"2. Proletarians of all lands, unite!

"3. Long live Marxism-Leninism, the everlasting international doctrine, the banner of the struggle of the toilers of all lands against imperialism, for the victory of socialism and communism!

"4. May the name and cause of Vladimir Ilich Lenin live forever! . . ."

Innumerable such statements identify the Soviet Union with a universal cause and lend it ideal purposes. It might be contended that all this is of no real importance. Ideological statements have become ritualistic, such as the official motto on coins, newspapers, and public documents, "Proletarians of All Lands, Unite!" Marxism-Leninism is seemingly irrelevant for the modern industrial society in domestic affairs, and it is not evident that Soviet foreign or domestic policies are directed to any important degree by strictly ideological considerations. Much or most of what is called "Marxist-Leninist" corresponds to understandable Soviet political interests. Ideology is whatever the party says it is; no scripture runs against the party interpretation. Hence one may incline to dismiss it as a mere verbal exercise.

However, the Soviet leadership attributes enormous importance to ideology. Hundreds of thousands of persons are full-time purveyors of ideology, and it is a part-time activity of millions. A large part of the attention of party

123

bodies at all levels is given to indoctrination and to the improvement of ideological qualifications. The attention given to ideological matters seems fully comparable to that directly applied to the guidance of industry and agriculture. In comparison with states such as France or the United States, the Soviet Union is another world, not only in the exclusion of all competitive creeds, but in the pervasiveness of what may be called political moralizing.

All states and political movements indulge in ideology to some degree, if by ideology one understands a set of ideas sustained for political utility. In this sense, ideology consists of the generalities which political leaders want people to believe, a set of propositions beyond challenge which can be used as a basis for reasoning. It is at once a statement of purposes, cause for self-righteousness, and political rhetoric. The higher reason of the state, it refers primarily to the principles of organization of society. To say that something is ideologically barred is nearly equivalent to saying that it is politically unacceptable. This does not imply that ideology is necessarily or even probably untrue in any objective sense, and it must be sufficiently plausible that many intelligent men can sincerely persuade themselves of its truth. But it removes political discussion from concrete experience and is certainly not readily demonstrable as a fact.

If all states take on something of an ideological garb, capitalist, liberal, and constitutional states—the categories are not far from equivalent—live with a great variety of morality and political ethos. There has to be agreement on the constitutional fundamentals and acceptance of certain modes of political action and basic values, but there may be agreement on little else. A loose, pluralistic state can hardly be very ideological. But political absolutism engenders intellectual absolutism. This may be almost mechanical, as the elite is in a position to exclude what it deems harmful and to propagate what it deems suitable; aside from the propensity to employ power for their own benefit, all-powerful leaders consider it their duty to educate their people to correct views. Moreover, pure force is a poor and crude means of control; obedience is not complete unless it is voluntary, preferably enthusiastic. The more of society the state seeks to manage, the greater the need is felt for ideal justification. Compulsion requires ideology. There is also an imperative demand for an integrative belief system in states lacking in natural unity, as the multinational Soviet Union, and in states suffering social strains from rapid and uneven modernization; ideology helps govern the otherwise ungovernable. The more artificial and imposed the political structure, the more essential that it find a theoretical basis in universal principles.

Ideology offers the masses some consolation for their status, as they are assured that the political ordering of society is for their benefit and is inevitable by the laws of heaven or history. Presumably for this reason, ideologies such as nazism, Soviet Marxism-Leninism, and Maoism seem to have been genuinely accepted by ordinary folk; even for the disillusioned, communism usually remains a beautiful ideal. Indoctrination, with ethical standards and guides to conduct, helps check abuse of power in a large bureaucratic system without freedom of political criticism. For the rulers themselves, ideology retards the degradation of character ordinarily induced by absolute power and gives them the sense of destiny and purpose which makes their rule both more supportable and more efficient.

Ideology is thus essential to authoritarianism or, as it has been called in extreme modern form, totalitarianism, and takes on dimensions disproportionate to the civic training of less directed states. In the Soviet Union, ideology serves to legitimize political control, excluding undesirable ideas, giving a moral cement for the divisions of Soviet society, and furnishing an ideal basis for party rule.

Soviet ideologists, in decrying "bourgeois objectivism," make clear that the interests of the state, or socialism, override factuality. Ideological changes have regularly come after changes of policy in order to justify them, rather than leading policy; Socialism in One Country and Peaceful Coexistence, for example, became doctrines well after they were policies. Party members should believe deeply but be prepared to accept new interpretations without question.

Yet ideology is a means which affects ends. It is an integral part of the political organism, and like other parts it not only serves the overall purpose of the strength and survival of the entire body, but also contributes to its character. The leaders necessarily believe something, perhaps a great deal, of what they propagate for the masses. Stalin, in the midst of his purges, may well have taken seriously his claims to be building socialism for the fullest human freedom. Ideology encourages certain ways and attitudes and discourages others, and so, in ways defying analysis, itself helps to shape the state. Nazi Germany was what it was not only because of the power and personalities of Hitler and his associates but by virtue of a set of antirationalist ideas gathered into a loose racist-nationalist ideology. Confucianist ideas, built up and refined over a long period and made the basis of the examination system, helped integrate Imperial China. Without Islamic law the Turkish empire would have been less effective and less viable. The state Church of Rome after Constantine was a vital component of the empire. The Soviet state, however it has moulded the official creed to its purposes, could not be what it presently is if the Russian empire had not come into possession of a Marxist ideological basis. Without ideology, the Soviet Union would be simply another dictatorship.

MARXISM

That the Russian empire acquired a Marxist foundation was in part a historical accident, as the war opened the way to revolutionary change while

Marxism was still a viable political faith. Essentially formulated in the middle of the nineteenth century, by the end of the century Marxism was suffering badly from the failure of its central predictions. The workers of the leading industrial countries had not become poorer but had improved their condition; they were not more alienated from the social order but had acquired, in powerful trade unions and political parties, a growing stake in it. Decades passed, and the proletarian revolution which Marx expected in 1848 seemed no nearer. Private enterprise, showing no signs of breaking down, was raising production of useful goods more rapidly than ever. The state, far from being merely an instrument of the "bourgeoisie," was responding more to the needs of the lower classes who had gained the right to vote in Britain and elsewhere. If Marxism was to retain intellectual validity, it needed updating or revision, and this was (to Lenin's disgust) being carried on in the Western countries. The result was that Marxism there had fairly well ceased to be revolutionary by the time of the Russian Revolution, and its relevance was steadily declining. In Russia also, Marxism in its original form was losing acceptability for the intellectuals at the beginning of this century. Even there, the conditions of the life of peasants and workers were visibly, although slowly, improving; and the exclusive Marxist emphasis on economic causation was incompatible with the maturing Russian intellectual atmosphere.

In the first decade of this century, however, the original Marxist creed had some intellectual force. Marx was a learned and intelligent man who formed insights in a neglected area and tried to work them into a coherent and all-encompassing theory of the universe, history and politics, promising a cure for the foolishness and wrongs of civilization. Most of his scholarly attention was directed to economics, which served as a springboard for his plunge into metaphysics, history, and politics. Examining industrializing England, he drew up a powerful critique of capitalism. The workers, he rightly claimed, did not receive adequate remuneration. If they were largely deprived, this was because the political system was organized for the benefit of the owners; the basic reality of politics was class division, class exploitation, and oppression. Marx thus grasped an idea which was fairly original and which corresponded to the spirit of an age with growing confidence in the material explanations of science. If the "class" approach was not accepted by respectable academic circles, this was obviously, as Marx saw it, because of the selfish interests of the ruling class, an interpretation which defied rebuttal. He extended the implications of the primacy of the means of production as a social-political determinant to provide a political program to abolish the social structure which he saw as oppressive to the masses.

One derivative of emphasis on economics was philosophical materialism. Just as the political structure of society and the dominant forms of culture grew out of economic arrangements, ideas and spirit in Marx's view were secondary to matter, the basic reality. However, Marx was determined to look to change and revolution, which his philosophy required to be inherent in nature. Hence philosophical materialism was diluted with somewhat mystical Hegelian principles of dialectic: change was somehow intrinsic in matter, and this change proceeded in a jagged unilinearity, with a condition or "thesis" (e.g., capitalism) giving rise to its antithesis (the workers' movement in capitalist society) and conflict (revolution) from which there emerges a new synthesis (socialism or communism). This dialectic is supposed to be part description of reality, part method of analysis, although the Soviets have great difficulty in trying to apply it to natural science.

The economic interpretation was projected backward into history and forward into utopian change. Although Marx was more realistic in recognizing noneconomic realities than many Marxists, the conflicts of the past were seen as primarily or in theory entirely as the outgrowth of the only "real" division of society, class antagonisms. The original form of society must have been communistic, with free sharing of the few goods available; there was hence no coercive power or state. The growth of specialized production and increased importance of wealth led to more complicated and exploitative institutions, the subordination of the many to the few, and a slaveholding society, as in the Roman empire. Slavery became unsuitable (for unclear reasons); and it was replaced by feudalism, appropriate for an agricultural economy. Further advancement of means of production and trade nourished within the feudal order a class hostile to it; as the bourgeoisie gained more and more wealth, it rebelled against the feudal order and burst its bonds, notably in the French Revolution. But bourgeois-capitalist society in turn nourished a contrary force within itself, the working class, which had no stake in the established order and was paid only the cost of subsistence and reproduction. But the workers must become more and more numerous, stronger and stronger. Finally, capitalism should collapse in crises and contradictions of overproduction and lack of markets, or overconcentration and inability to adapt to an age when production was de facto socialized. The historical sequence sketched here was applied only to Western Europe. Although it should be true universally if valid at all, Marx recognized that elsewhere a different "form of production" might prevail, to wit, the Asiatic, wherein political power subsumed the economic and productive property belonged to the despot and the bureaucratic apparatus.[1] But the sequence, especially the postulated replacement of capitalism by socialism, formed the basis of a political program. The workers, disciplined and class-conscious because of their conditions of labor, could bring a selfless socialist order because they had no property interests. When its historical hour had struck, the proletariat should shake off its chains and usher in the new era of

---

[1] This facet of Marxism is excluded from Soviet Marxism.

history—which should happily be the last, the end of history as previously experienced, because there would be no more antagonistic classes.

Proletarian revolution became effectively the core of Marxism, to which the rest was subordinated. It is fair to agree with Lenin that when Social Democrats ceased to be preoccupied with revolution they ceased to be true Marxists. Although Marx conceded that socialism might come by peaceful process in countries of broadly representative government, as England and the United States, this in effect contradicted his basic approach. Lenin, more consistent in this regard than the master, denied the validity of "bourgeois" freedoms and parliamentary democracy as practiced in the West. Marx shared the assumption of his age that government could and should follow the wishes of the majority. He hardly explained how the socialist society was to be ordered but took it for granted that the political problems would solve themselves once the fetters of private ownership were broken.

Marx was much more concerned with the goal, the liberation and happiness of humanity, than with strict logical consistency; and scientific utility to explain facts has never been important for the appeal of Marxism. But it struck a responsive chord as an attack on the intolerable conditions of factory labor in early industrialization, when humanitarian consciousness was rising against capitalist laissez faire and calling for governmental intervention to protect the deprived. In an age of burgeoning science, his was the political approach which most strongly claimed to be scientific. In an age of progress and optimism, Marx saw history moving inexorably to an age of perfect order, when work would be a joy, strife would be no more, and all persons should share freely in an abundance of goods. When liberals decried the power of government, Marx promised the entire abolition of government. He theorized the eminently desirable into the naturally inevitable. Prophesying automatic redemption, he insisted on the individual's role in realizing it and so exalted the intellectual. Emphasis on the importance of political action separated Marx from his socialist predecessors and made his arid philosophic and historical theories and economic interpretations interesting and relevant.

Withal, Marx created no great stir in Western intellectual life; even in socialist circles he was somewhat overshadowed by such men as Proudhon and Lasalle. His impact on the rapidly growing British labor movement was insignificant. His chosen instrument, the First International, was dissolved in wrangles with the anarchists. But Marxism spoke with accents of special truth and inevitable victory to those on the outs with Western society. For those who saw no prospects of advancement by democratic and gradual process, it offered revolution and title to the future. It excused economic failure and turned it into a virtue. It furnished an alternative for those who, for whatever reason, saw the whole system as sick and oppressive. Intelligent men are often idealistic and at odds with their Philistine neighbors; Marx cheered them with his doctrine of alienation and promised that one day all would be reversed. The completion of the circle from primitive communism to the communism of the future appealed to nostalgia among victims of industrial society for a simpler life. This feeling made Russian (and other industrializing countries) more receptive to Marxism as an answer to troubles of social disorganization. The peasant dream of a land of milk and honey was updated as "scientific socialism." This element of backward-looking futurism stands out in Marx's rejection of occupational specialization as virtual slavery, and the glorification of the proletarian as a sort of noble savage, unspoiled by the vices of civilization.

Consequently, the greatest attraction of Marxism was not and is not for the lands for which it was logically intended but for the less favored countries, for whom capitalism was alien and disliked. It especially appealed to their semi-westernized intellectuals, who found themselves at odds both with the backwardness of their native societies and with the intrusion into them of the "capitalist" West. They saw a capitalism growing up like the cruder early industrial capitalism which Marx criticized, and Marx gave them a powerful means of attacking it and Western values while adhering to a modern and seemingly scientific creed. The thesis that riches are the result of exploitation is truest of unproductive backward societies, and for these the message that the future belongs to the poor is gratifying. Hence the Russian intelligentsia around the turn of the century was far more Marxist in its thinking than that of England or France, or even Germany, where a relatively backward political system gave more scope for Marxism than in countries farther west. And Lenin made adjustments in Marxist ideas to qualify his party for Russia.

MARXISM-LENINISM

At the beginning of this century, when Western Marxists were revising theory to bring it better into accord with facts, Lenin was modifying it in an opposite direction for revolutionary utility, as discussed above. It was expedient to attack foreign capitalists and the somewhat uninspiring development of Russia which they were largely financing, mixing the envy-hatred of the lower strata for the wealthy with diffuse antiforeignism and antiwesternism. It remains the standard Soviet interpretation that socialist revolution was possible in Russia because of the factors stressed by Lenin: external added to internal exploitation, backwardness in the world capitalist framework, contradictions of modern capitalist with feudal elements, and the weakness of the ruling classes[2]—a set of reasons more political than Marxist-economic.

---

[2] Cf. *Voprosy ekonomiki*, no. 1, January, 1969, p. 3.

Lenin was impatient with the inevitable course of history and anxious to push it forward by political action. He wanted to exploit all discontents, particularly those of the land-hungry peasantry and the restive minorities, for which he appropriately reshaped doctrine. In this he could claim to be a better follower of Marx than most Marxists, as the prophet himself had been willing to compromise logic for political advantage by opining that Russia might, as the Populists urged, by-pass capitalism and leap to socialism via the peasant commune. Marx would probably also have approved Lenin's contention that the proletariat could cooperate in the bourgeois revolution and then proceed to make its own socialist revolution.

It is not impossible that Marx would have blessed the role which Lenin gave to the party, although he would hardly have countenanced the dictatorship which resulted. For Lenin, the proletariat had to be not only educated but also led by the party, which was always to be a vanguard, never to merge with the class for which it was supposed to stand. Although it was contradictory to the bases of Marxist thinking, it was realistic to recognize that the workers of themselves were not disposed to make big revolutions but to reap small benefits. The proletariat became, then, not the mover of revolution but an instrument, along with others, for its engineering by the nonproletarian party leadership.

Lenin went on to stress the dictatorship of the proletariat, a term which Marx coined but hardly used. For Marxism, government was ipso facto close to dictatorship, the instrument of whatever class ruled. Russians had little feeling for liberal democracy; there was little need to apologize for "dictatorship" as long as it was guaranteed ethically by coupling with "proletariat." The effect was to free state power from legal restrictions of any kind while giving it democratic appearances. Moreover, the Marxist relation between the economic base and the state form could be reversed. Now the people, or the party, would make the economic and social order by political will.[3]

The most remarkable fact about this Leninist adaptation of Marxism to making revolution in Russia is how little was changed when the movement turned from radical attack on the state to the defense and use of state power. Lenin was elastic in practice and made compromises with economic necessity beyond the understanding of some Bolsheviks. But, having accepted the task of building a state, he endeavored generally to sustain the original picture of the Russian Revolution serving as the opening skirmish of the world proletarian revolution, in which the Russian workers were acting as part of a universal movement. He coined the new slogan, "Communism is Soviet power plus the electrification of the whole land," while proclaiming the victory of the proletariat. Stalin, renouncing obligations to the world movement, retained it as

---

[3] N. S. Davydova, *Na puti k kommunizmu*, Moscow, 1968, p. 59, states this voluntarism as characteristic of socialism in general.

legitimation and certified that what was being constructed in Russia was indeed socialism and a service to the cause of universal revolution.

Stalin proceeded to give ideological justifications for his major policies. Collectivization of agriculture was a substitution of socialized or semisocialized for private property, and the more prosperous peasants were equated with capitalist exploiters. By eliminating the independent peasantry, Stalin gave the Soviet Union a class structure more appropriate for a state denominating itself "socialist." Stalinist industrialization had a similar good effect in providing the "dictatorship of the proletariat" with a reasonably large proletariat.

As he solidified the state, Stalin also settled the Soviet ideological picture by eliminating all independent Marxist thought and stating himself what the ideology was to be. With some skill, he set forth an unsophisticated version of what he saw as useful; this was contained in his *Leninism* (or *Questions of Leninism*), a collection of speeches and articles, and in the *Short History of the Communist Party* prepared under his direction. These were the fundamentals of party education for two decades. Stalin developed doctrines as desirable. Thus, the priority of heavy industry under planning, and by implication the preference for strength over welfare, became dogma, a "law of socialist economy." Greater vigilance and strengthening of the repressive powers of the state, which many Bolsheviks had assumed was to wither away not long after the Revolution, and hence the purges themselves, were justified by a new theory of the sharpening of the class struggle with the advent of socialism.[4] The equalitarianism sacred to the revolutionary ethos became "petty-bourgeois." Anything Stalin decreed became ipso facto doctrinally required; ideology thus came to cover far more ground than it did under Lenin. The correct literary approach, the right style of painting, and the proper interpretation of pre-Soviet history were decreed by fiat. A linguist's theory that all languages were derived from four basic syllables was official dogma until Stalin turned his back on it in 1950. The genetics of Lysenko, the most rational part of which was the supposed inheritance of acquired characteristics, was true by the sanction of the Communist Party.

Khrushchev wanted to revive idealism and make ideology more useful by making it more modern and realistic, as in the modifications in connection with his Peaceful Coexistence. But to make Marxism-Leninism realistic is to denature it politically. In Khrushchev's interpretation, "practical" Marxism-Leninism became little more than action to increase production,

---

[4] An example of Stalin's "dialectics": "We stand for the withering away of the state. At the same time we stand for the strengthening of the dictatorship of the proletariat. . . . The highest development of state power with the object of preparing the conditions for the withering away of state power—that is the Marxist formula. It is contradictory? Yes, it is 'contradictory.' But this contradiction is bound up with life, and it fully accords with Marx's dialectics." (J. Stalin, Report to the 16th Party Congress, *Works*, 1955, vol. XII, p. 38.)

coupled with a vision of Soviet greatness in the world. He would have economic growth serve as the basic inspiration, filling the role of Lenin's Revolution and Stalin's social transformation. The road to communism laid out by the 1961 Program was defined largely in terms of increased production, with little idea of structural change beyond some transfer of additional responsibility from state organs to "public" party-dominated organizations. There was evidently to be no relaxation of controls; little remained of the old promise of ultimate freedom in communism.

The collective leadership confronted the problem of ideology in a somewhat different spirit. The revolutionary generation had largely departed; the storming of the Winter Palace and the travails of civil war were only history to an increasingly sophisticated younger generation. "Class struggle" had become an almost meaningless abstraction to many or most of the people; the proletariat or "progressive" forces were practically whoever suited Soviet purposes. The Soviet "working class" was found to include not only recognizable proletarians but bureaucrats, "not only factory workers, engaged in physical labor, but those who contribute intellectual labor or carry on various auxiliary functions."[5] The increasingly conservative regime turned still more away from goals of further change. The envisioned future glowed only with promised technical and material advancement; if there was any thought of change in the order of society, it seemed to be chiefly for the perfection and strengthening of party leadership. "The broader the sweep of Communist construction, the more significance in organizedness, unity, the single direction of the activities of the toilers; without this there can be no raising of the efficiency of socialist production, no successful solution of social-political and cultural tasks."[6]

To counter inevitable weariness, the leadership has stressed symbolism of all kinds, the father-figure of Lenin, military discipline, past heroics, history, and patriotism. It has also intensified ideological work and efforts toward indoctrination, reverting toward Leninist and Stalinist fundamentalism. There is to be no thought of possible compromise; East-West bridge-building was branded "imperialist subversion," and the theory of convergence of capitalism and communism was exposed as a weapon of anti-Sovietism, while class warfare was seen as rising to new heights in capitalist countries. Any idea of national communism, or of any communism not firmly tied to the Soviet Union, was vehemently rejected in 1968 and afterwards; there could be no "liberalization" or "democratization" within the Soviet way.

The leaders claim that Marxism-Leninism cannot become obsolete because it is always being further developed. As Brezhnev said, "A creative approach to theory gives strength and confidence to the builders of socialism

---

[5] *Pravda*, December 24, 1968.
[6] *Nauchnye osnovy gosudarstvennogo upravleniia v SSSR* (Akad. Nauk), Moscow, 1968. p. 418.

and communism."[7] There has never been an attempt to codify ideology, and the chief canon is Lenin's voluminous works. In practice, it is elastic enough: bourgeois powers can be seen as conspiring for class interest or fighting one another from self-interest; capitalists repress the workers to cow them or give concessions to buy them off, or are forced to yield to their pressure; one may fight to help history or let history take its inevitable course, as convenient. It seems, however, that an enormous work of urbanization, industrialization, and education has left basic doctrine virtually untouched.

USES OF IDEOLOGY: LEGITIMATION

The central thesis of Marxism is that government and the rulership of society are instruments of the dominant economic class; this is held to be an inescapable reality. There are no absolute moral or legal standards, only expressions of class interest. The ruling class defines truth and justice, and any other pretense is a fraud. There is room in the Marxist scheme for no pluralism or separation of powers in society, as there is no doubt of social truth, and government is essentially arbitrary.

The proletariat, however, has a superior right to rule—a moral judgment creeps back into Marxist philosophy—because it is the class destined by history to succeed to the leadership of society and because it supposedly represents the large majority against the handful of exploiters. Moreover, it is morally superior by virtue of its freedom from the corruption of capital. "Mankind has never known," as *Pravda* put it,[8] "a class equal to the proletariat in its valor and willingness to sacrifice, in consciousness of social duty, in absolute dedication to serving the welfare of the toiling people . . . the social and spiritual liberation of the popular masses. . . ."

This emphasis on the rights and virtues of the workers has been useful in setting up the Soviet state as in the making of the Revolution. It helped in the recruitment of personnel of lower class origins and the exclusion from influence of those affiliated with the old regime. Workers would better execute revolutionary policies than more squeamish members of middle or professional classes. The workers were also the group most manageable by political bosses. Stalin cut down the influence of more educated Bolsheviks, as Trotsky and his student following, by flooding the party with workers. Proletarianism is a sanction for anti-intellectualism in various forms. The alleged proletarian approach to esthetics and politics could always be called upon to put down quibblers about abstract rights or artistic freedom.

[7] *Pravda*, July 1, 1969.
[8] February 14, 1969.

The rights of the proletariat in the Soviet system are important mostly, however, because they are exercisable by the party in the name of the workers. Politically speaking, proletariat means Communist Party; and the party by virtue of its mastery of Marxism-Leninism should know the true will of the workers better than they do themselves. Some thought that trade unions might, being composed of actual workers, have a right comparable to that of the party to express the will of the supposedly governing class. This viewpoint was decisively rejected from the beginning of bolshevism by Lenin's determination to have an elite party, and after the Revolution the party continued to refuse to permit the unions any real political role. This decision was confirmed by the defeat of syndicalist tendencies and the disciplining of the Workers' Opposition in 1921.

party rule

The heart of Marxism-Leninism thus became the party's monopoly of power, its right and duty to rule. Any opposition could be stigmatized as weakening the sacred cause of the workers. The party should be arbiter of right and wrong, and maker of values; its violence can only be justice. No interest contrary to that of the working class, or its party, is legitimate. The people are to be enlightened, indoctrinated, satisfied, and uplifted, but the party is the essential actor, the mother-and-father. Although the self-identification of the party with the working class is somewhat mystical, the mystique has been effective. Even the more critical Bolsheviks have found it difficult to resist what could be presented as the will of the party, which must be right because it expresses the will of the historically right class. Thus the oppositionists in 1921 subscribed to the rule banning factions, and Trotsky and many like him were paralyzed by the equation of the party apparatus with the workers.

anti-factionalism

The party's claim to know the will of the workers is "based on science, knowledge, and application of the laws of social development,"[9] the mastery of "scientific socialism." In Marxism-Leninism, political truth like facts of chemistry is knowable and unequivocal for the experts, who are the rulers. The whole structure, embracing laws of historical development, socialist revolution, dictatorship of the proletariat, and the laws of construction of socialist society, is held up as a rigorous science, no part of which may be rejected. Marxism-Leninism is supposed to give the Soviet leadership special insight; it is frequently written that party decisions are taken "on the basis of deep scientific analysis."

This authoritarian approach to truth is rooted in the thought of the master himself. His original point of departure was Hegel's Prussian philosophy, wherein truth became subordinate to power; and Marx, like Lenin, was intolerant of differences from his own views. By placing intellectual activity in the realm of the superstructure, Marx opened the way for the party to proclaim its dogma as superior to any outside and probably class-hostile teachings. Truth

[9] *Pravda*, August 11, 1970, p. 2.

in Marxism became relative to social or class needs, of which the party could make itself exponent. The workers, moreover, had a stronger claim to political correctness than the intellectuals. The latter were not and are not entitled to criticize the party, and there was no appeal against the dictates of dialectical materialism. The sophistication of the dialectic also has been helpful in drawing desired conclusions. The idea of quantitative changes adding up to qualitative change sanctioned revolution or practically any sudden change of policy. Progress by contradiction justified class struggle—and any struggle can be seen as class-based—and correspondingly strong measures; and allegations of new truth can be drawn out of the fusion of opposites.[10]

Truth is then definable practically as whatever the party, or its leadership, finds suitable. Deviations can be branded as "revisionism," "sectarianism," or "dogmatism," and wrong thinking reflects an improper "class" position. The scientificness of Marxism-Leninism then becomes the sophistication with which it is tailored for political purposes.

Acceptance of the party's leadership and its perceptions is mandatory because the world scene is one of perpetual struggle between the forces of light and dark. In theory, there is an everlasting semimilitary emergency, in which the achievements of socialism increase the hostility of its enemies and make relaxation the more dangerous. Almost any non-Soviet group or purpose can be called "capitalist" and treated as an agent of the monopolists, enemies of the oppressed people. Stalin made most use of this imagery of battle, speaking of the rightness of violence against capitalists, their hirelings, and by extension all whom he distrusted. Law being in the Marxist view a class instrument, it was fittingly turned against exploiters. Under Khrushchev there was a tendency to dilute the Marxist-Manichaean picture of the world into an incentive to outbuild the capitalists. The post-Khrushchev leaders have, however, kept up the call for unity under the party in the face of the perennial capitalist-imperialist threat.

The happiest aspect of the war of capitalism against socialism is the inevitable victory of the latter. The contentions of mankind must find their end in the overthrow of the last exploiting class. There can be nothing higher than this ideal, the prophesied paradise. It is worth any sacrifice and, by inference, justifies whatever the party may demand to reach it.

Full communism is something distant, specifically dependent on worldwide victory of the Soviet system. Khrushchev did not promise a great deal for the next two decades (although the party pledged its word in 1961 that "The present generation of Soviet people shall live under communism"), and his successors have neglected the subject. But in theory it remains essential to the Bolshevik canon. As sketched occasionally, it is to be a world of joyous intimacy, equality, mutual help, eager work, abundance of goods without the

[10] Stalin furnished a disquisition on dialectics in *Leninism* (International Publishers), New York, 1942, pp. 406–432.

corruption of money, and rather dreamlike happiness. Humans are to become paragons of broad culture and masters of Marxism-Leninism, models of saintly virtue and even of physical perfection.[11]

It is unlikely that the elite expect to see material abundance sufficient to satiate human desires, total harmony reigning, and all toiling joyously for the good of society. But the vision is appropriate. It is the ideal which any ruler might desire for his realm: complete tranquillity of the classless society with no groups capable of political action, no private wealth, no divisions among the placid subjects, all laboring dutifully and serving voluntarily. It bespeaks an immobile order, with none of the interesting and creative but bothersome turbulence of less perfect societies. Utopianism implies that the regime is entitled to control people to make them good. It also implies optimism, which has run through Soviet thinking from the fantastic expectations of the Revolution and the First Five-Year Plan down to the triumphant heroes of Socialist Realism and the rejection of Malthusian fears of overpopulation. Even though the practical measures contemplated may go little beyond rural electrification ("erasing the difference between city and country") and the expansion of education, a paradise in the future ratifies the party's role. The fundamentals of the Soviet way are inherent in utopianism: an elite to lead the way, a monopoly of truth to guide it, the perfection of man through the perfection of the political order, and an evil (capitalism) to be overcome in saving mankind.

The greatest step toward utopia is the socialization, or state ownership, of the economy. Property in consumer goods is scattered and without political significance; ownership of means of production, as Marxists emphasize, gives leverage over people. Hence, as all important property belongs to the state, in effect to the party, this enjoys an otherwise unattainable degree of control. Opposition lacks an economic base to give political effect to what may be strong but diffuse popular feelings. The party is not satisfied with major industrial enterprises, but leaves as little as possible outside of its control. When there is no employment except by party-dominated organizations, psychological independence is hard to maintain. Anyone seeking to subsist irregularly, outside

---

[11] "In the Program of our party is set forth the task of the all-round harmonic development of the personality, joining in himself 'spiritual richness, moral cleanness, and physical perfection.' Only such a personality can enter the communist society. . . .

"Physical perfection of a person includes health, high vitality, strength, resistance, and external beauty. The personality of the future will be not only highly educated, spiritually interesting, not only highly moral and agreeable to his fellows, but also strong and externally handsome. Physical development must be harmonically linked with intellectual development and moral education. It is so written in the Program of our party." (A. L. Nedavnii, in *XXIII S'ezd* [Vysshaia partinaia shkola TsK, KPSS], Moscow, 1968, pp. 219–220.)

the official framework, is subject to the charge of parasitism, or failure to contribute to the community in a recognized fashion. Hence the "ideological" antipathy for private money-making and individual commerce, despite its obvious potential contribution to the standard of living. Hence also the urge for centralization, bigger enterprises being easier to control. If only money could be eliminated, political authority would be the greater. All goods would be distributed by some sort of political authorization or order; and economic differences would disappear, leaving only differences of status.

In sanctifying the cause as "socialism," the Soviet state and party appeal to yearnings for equality and social justice. To speak of workers toiling for themselves in socialist enterprise implies that they have deep obligations to "their" enterprises. If they labor for low wages, this cannot be exploitation but service to the community. The terminology of "people's" factories is suggestive; Russians consider it less demeaning to work for the incorporated community than for a private owner whose interest is frankly gain.[12] A drawback seems to be that workers feel entitled to take for themselves what belongs to the people; and "public" ownership seems ineffective, contrary to Marxist expectations, in inspiring exceptional diligence in Soviet factories. However, the economic progress which has marked the Soviet era serves further to legitimate the party which has presided over it.

The broadly collectivist spirit of Marxism and indeed of Russian tradition also serves the party interest:

"Collectivism is characteristic of social relations in socialism and communism. If the bourgeois way of life cultivates individuality, the separation of people from one another and from society, the socialist manner of life facilitates their coming closer together and joining as equal members of society, united by common interests and aims.

"The whole process of spiritual formation of Soviet man—education, work, and way of living—is indissolubly linked with the collective. . . . 'The collective is a second family, in which the weak man is strong and without which the strong man is weak,' as metalworker S. Antonov of the Moscow 'Vladimir Ilich [Lenin]' factory correctly wrote. . . . One for all, all for one! . . . The education of all toilers in the spirit of collectivism, comradely union and mutual help is an inseparable part of the general task of communist education. . . ."[13] "Everything is done so that the individual, from the first to the last day of his life, should feel the care of the collective around him, not only in regard to his material but also his spiritual needs."[14] "Individualism and egoism, rapacious thirst for gain . . . these are the traits which the bourgeois world inculcates with its private property. . . . Our society raises a really new man, the collectivist,

[12] Cf. Günther Specovius, *Die Russen sind anders* (Econ-Verlag), Düsseldorf, 1963, p. 244.
[13] *Pravda*, July 21, 1969.
[14] *Selskaia zhizn*, October 22, 1969.

fighter, builder, patriot and internationalist."[15]   Only by seeing oneself wholly as a member of a collective can one truly develop his own personality.[16]

Even scientists should esteem collective above individual thinking. This appeal to instincts of solidarity and release from loneliness merges into a call for limitless unity: collective, party, the whole Soviet people, the world Communist movement, and ultimately all virtuous people of all races, all toilers.

Collectivism not only derogates individualism and independent thought and action; it should foster the conviction that work for the collective is honor and glory. "Man is beautified by labor."[17]   Soviet citizens, having given their all at their jobs, are expected to volunteer frequently and in large numbers for all manner of community endeavors, from cleaning up around buildings to acting as part time guardians of public order. It often appears that Soviet people are expected to display a superhuman degree of self-sacrifice and dedication in a spirit of political perfectionism; the materialistic religion of Marxism-Leninism calls for devotion beyond material interests. The citizen should spare no strength to bring in the harvest, give his free time to helping laggards in production, and risk his life to save collective property.[18] "The man dedicated to his work, giving himself fully, his strength and abilities, to socially useful labor, is doubly rich and happy, with satisfaction in his achievement and with the esteem of the collective."[19]   Probably, however, no tremendous enthusiasm is required; the party calls for the maximum to secure as much as possible.

Socialism protects the party and state from suspicion of selfishness. By definition, only private ownership can be exploitative; tyranny can only be of a possessing class. The Soviet state is consequently pure; it can represent only virtue because it stands for the virtuous working class, and there is no need to check its power. Politics, moreover, is excluded in principle, because political conflict can be only a reflection of class conflict. Any independent political action must represent, in some disguise, a class enemy attack.

USES OF IDEOLOGY: ISOLATION

Ideology serves as the spiritual or psychological foundation of the wall between Soviet and foreign societies, barring insidious influences of the West. It achieves this in part by exalting the Socialist Fatherland and its works. This is not new to Russia. In 1904 an American senator wrote of ". . . Russia

[15] *Editorial in Pravda*, March 15, 1970.
[16] *Pravda*, December 13, 1970, p. 3.
[17] *Pravda*, August 22, 1971, p. 1.
[18] *Pravda*, August 14, 1971, editorial.
[19] *Pravda*, August 22, 1971, editorial.

that looks upon other peoples as disorganized communities and dying races, and considers herself the heir of all ages . . ."[20] The Revolution made the message far more insistent and gave it a new and much more convincing basis; everything in Soviet life should be practically by definition different and better. Russia is the center of history; as the formal chief of state, Podgorny, has it, "We live in an epoch when all the most important historical changes in the world are connected with the Great October Socialist revolution. . . ."[21]

The "capitalist" world, or at least its leading and more powerful sectors, are correspondingly viewed as black; and every opportunity is taken to play up their real or alleged failures and injustices. The hallmarks of "bourgeois" society are egoism, individualism, anarchism, lewdness, hedonism, unemployment, hypocrisy, injustice, violence, and imperialism; capitalism is synonymous with venality and inhumanity. Moral degeneration under capitalism is no accident but is purposely fostered by the bourgeoisie to demoralize the workers. Even as individuals, "socialists" have a near-monopoly of virtue; no one of the "bourgeoisie" could be generous or heroic, although it is recognized that friends of the Soviet Union are "progressive." Writing on almost any social theme is likely to begin with a glowing description of Soviet conditions (as in the protection of motherhood) and comparison with the lamentable or despicable state of affairs on the other side. The Marxist thesis of qualitative difference arising from quantitative change helps to underline the complete distinctiveness of "socialist" and "capitalist" societies. "Proletarian" and "bourgeois" democracy, nationalism, law, etc., are not similar but opposites, and the latter are beyond redemption; in the black-and-white world view characteristic of the authoritarian mentality there is little shading of evil. Corporations are always referred to as "monopolies." Discussion is more normative than descriptive. The apparatus of representative government in the West is treated as mere cover for the dictatorship of capital. No credit is given for reforms. At best, concessions are exacted by the indignation of the people; and if the state seems to become more socialistic by increasing public ownership and control of the economy, this is a deception.

Marxism-Leninism furnishes in "bourgeois" a convenient label for anything disapproved. It would be possible to vilify less friendly powers or Western ways in general on a Russian-nationalistic basis, but this would be less effective than a theory which explains their vices as inherent in their form of society. Marxist socialists can congratulate themselves on being humanitarian and unselfish, while their antagonists are grasping and malicious, misled by their backward political and social structure. All evils in the world can be laid to capitalism and its offshoot, imperialism. Any deviation such as a call for freer debate within the party can be condemned as "bourgeois." Critical writers, as

---

[20] T. von Laue, in Stavrou, ed., p. 121.
[21] *Pravda*, November 7, 1969.

Daniel and Siniavsky, can be held up as agents of "imperialism"; and "bourgeois mentality" is a generic term for incorrect thinking. The vulgarity that has crept into Soviet music is deprecated as a result of bourgeois influence.[22]

It is similarly an attractive idea that wars are made not by the people but by rapacious owners; Soviet foreign policy can only be generous. The picture is convincing; ordinary Soviet citizens seem fully prepared to believe that free education, pensions, etc., are impossible under capitalism; that democracy, meaning the ability of workers to rise, is likewise out of the question; that capitalism means racial discrimination, unemployment, disorder, and war, while only socialism is pacific.[23]

Capitalism is not only bad but is inherently hostile. "In a world divided into two implacable class camps, the ideological struggle is growing constantly sharper,"[24] is a recurrent theme, especially since August, 1968. As Brezhnev put it, "there has been a further exacerbation in the struggle between the forces of socialism and imperialism, between the forces of progress and reaction. The progressive forces continue to take the offensive in this struggle."[25] Much is made of class warfare within the capitalist states; *Pravda* and other papers fairly regularly have a section entitled "On the Barricades of Class Struggle" or some equivalent. The idea of "convergence" is dangerous as it detracts from this antithesis. The hostility of the "bourgeois" is practically welcome; ten anti-Communists outside are not so bad as one heretic within the party.[26] The enmity is ascribed to the virtues of socialism; the greater its success, the more apprehensive the capitalists become lest their workers follow the example of the Russian comrades; they slander and try to subvert, and, but for fear of the might of the Soviet Union, would probably attack militarily. The worth of revolutionary actions is shown by the hatred of the reactionaries.[27]

The theme of world struggle has been useful in a hundred ways, from Stalin's terrorism to the rejection of Solzhenitsyn. The latter responded bitterly in a letter to the Writers' Union: " 'The enemy is listening.' That's your answer. These eternal enemies are the basis of your existence. What would you do without your enemies? You would not be able to live without your enemies. Hate, hate no less evil than racism, has become your sterile atmosphere. But in this way the feeling of a whole and single mankind is being lost and its perdition is being accelerated."[28] Although the quarrel with China complicated and

---

[22] *Slovo o partii* (Izdatelstvo politicheskoi literatury), Moscow, 1967, p. 134.

[23] Tibor Szamuely, "Five Years after Khrushchev," *Survey*, Summer, 1969, no. 72, p. 67.

[24] *Pravda*, May 28, 1969.

[25] *Kommunist*, no. 11, July 1969, p. 4. *Current Digest of the Soviet Press*, vol. 21, no. 31, p. 3.

[26] *Izvestia*, April 17, 1969.

[27] *Kommunist*, no. 4, March, 1969, p. 9.

[28] *New York Times*, November 15, 1969.

confused the simple two-world picture, Soviet citizens should be inspired by their role as defenders of the just socialist cause, leaders and protectors of the exploited majority of mankind. "Awareness of the fact that this great task [the building of a communist society] corresponds to the interests of the international working class and the toilers of the whole world multiplies the strength and energy of Soviet people in the struggle for new victories of communism."[29] It even spurs to new victories in agriculture. A pair of lecturers make the rounds of the collective farms, the one to talk of the international situation, the other of the techniques of planting or livestock care.[30]

Marxism-Leninism also helps to protect from undesirable, mostly foreign thinking. So far as the masses learn to think in class terms, they are protected from notions of nationalism, "bourgeois" freedom, civil rights, and the like. It is even more essential to protect the intellectuals from the Western ideas to which they are inevitably exposed. If their years of education in Marxist-Leninist categories make Western political arguments and values incomprehensible to them, the party has solved a fundamental problem of Russian government, a means of keeping out subversive, individualistic, or libertarian influences while borrowing the useful and necessary.

It is unnecessary to go into the more sophisticated parts of Soviet ideology or philosophy, which include a good deal of scholasticism regarding the laws of the dialectic, the nature of truth and knowledge, and other questions superficially remote from politics. Antireligious but not strictly materialistic, anti-idealistic yet infused with its own brand of idealism, Soviet philosophy is much more value- and politically-oriented than Western; major topics in Soviet philosophy books include tactics of political action and propaganda. In principle, it gives the last word to the proletariat; in practice, it is a means of keeping intellectuals subservient to the politicians. Its judge is not the community of scholars but the leadership of the party.

Marxism-Leninism forms a unified world view and a fairly coherent body of doctrine, parts of which are difficult to challenge without rejecting the whole structure. Though students may be bored by dialectical materialism ("diamat"), they have to absorb it; and they have no other framework for thinking about social and political questions. It becomes instinctive to judge things according to whether they occur in a "capitalist" or a "socialist" society. Even those who may come to question the right of the party to rule are checked by their acceptance of the special rights of the working class. It is not easy for Soviet citizens to understand "bourgeois" concepts of rights, and hardly any are theoretical advocates of economic liberalism. Outstanding intellectuals may find it quite difficult, after breaking with the Communist system, to assimilate

---

[29] *Pravada,* December 26, 1968.
[30] *Partinaia Zhizn*, no. 2, January, 1969, p. 52.

Western modes of thought. The Yugoslav writer Djilas, although he denounced the bureaucratism of communism in *The New Class* in 1956, for years thereafter thought in Marxist terms and categories; only in his *The Unperfect Society* (1968) did he seem to have cast them off.

USES OF IDEOLOGY: UNITY

Of the multiform ways in which Marxism-Leninism serves the Soviet system, one of the most vital is the raising up of an elastic concept, the working class, to bridge the cleavages of Soviet society. This is implied, in part, by the polarization of the world and the contraposition of Soviet socialism to imperialism and the class enemy without. More specifically, however, Marxism-Leninism decrees that differences as of religion or nationality are false and bourgeois-manufactured, whereas all Soviet citizens are really united in belonging to the broadly defined working people, builders of communism.

Class bonds should operate in all ways to overcome divisions. There should be no conflict of generations. "The party sees the key to the solution [of the problem of youth] in our conditions in the class education of the oncoming generation of builders of communism . . . the world view of our young men and girls is being formed in conditions of decisively sharpening class struggle between capitalism and socialism. Seeking to undermine socialism from within, the enemies lay their chief bet on the spiritual disarmament of the young people, seeking to weaken their revolutionary enthusiasm, to dull their class consciousness, and to oppose them to the older generation."[31]

Soviet ideology should also overarch differences of religion. When the tsarist regime wanted to make everyone Orthodox, it succeeded in little beyond antagonizing the numerous Catholics, Moslems, and other non-Orthodox peoples. But Marxism-Leninism is a faith which, although emotionally not very attractive, can be taught as a basis of morality to Turks, Balts, Mongols, and all the other peoples of the realm on the same basis, as a neutral, supposedly scientific creed, unencumbered by particular association with Russians and russification. If the mass of the people may have been resistant to the antireligious faith, it was acceptable to many of the educated and offered a long-term promise of erasing fundamental fissures. This probably has been most important with the Asiatic peoples who, less influenced by Western-style nationalism, saw their difference from the dominant peoples of the Soviet Union mostly in religious terms.

[31] *Pravda*, March 17, 1969.

The primacy of class is also applicable against racial divisions. Little is said of these, although racial frictions exist; the experience of African students in Moscow has amply demonstrated that Russians, although fairly tolerant, are by no means color blind; and the difference between the average Russian and the swarthy Central Asian is conspicuous. Religious and racial differences largely coincide, however, with differences of nationality; and it is in this regard that ideology is called upon frequently and emphatically to cement otherwise disparate peoples.

This is a problem of the first magnitude, as it has been for Russian rulers for a century or more. It is easy to think of the Soviet Union as a Russian state, but Russians proper are only about half the total population—those of authentic Russian background probably a good deal less. Of the remainder, some, as the White Russians and Ukrainians, once called "Little Russians," are fairly close to the "Great Russians"; but many others are quite alien in culture, language, and religion. The Turkic peoples of Central Asia particularly form a fairly homogeneous and indigestible group of some thirty million. The Soviet Union is the last great multinational domain in a world of strong and growing national awareness of minority and dominated peoples.

The Marxist-Leninist answer is practically to deny the reality or at least the legitimacy of the problem. Marx and Engels saw trade growing by leaps and bounds; as the world economy was growing together, it was to be taken for granted, in the priority of economic over political causation, that the nuisance of nationalism would die out in due course. The reality, in any case, was division between classes within a nation and solidarity of classes across national lines; in the oft-repeated aphorism, the workers had no country. Social change was worldwide; the socialist revolution would be international, and it would sweep away the unlamented remnants of bourgeois nationalism.

Lenin supplemented this reasoning with additions for the Russian scene. Seeing minority nationalism as an important revolutionary force, he proposed to offer full independence to the minorities. However, he also insisted on the unity of the proletariat under the united party, so he felt able in one breath to concede full sovereignty to the Ukraine and to demand that it become Bolshevik. He conceded cultural and linguistic autonomy, as he saw tsarist russification as the biggest cause of friction. However, for him, as for Marx, nationalism was a bourgeois phenomenon eventually to be overcome by assimilation and centralization.

Soviet policy hews close to this Leninist line. While in theory the fifteen Soviet republics are fully sovereign, nationalism is denounced as bourgeois poison; all the peoples must be firmly united because the proletariat must be united, and any suggestion of separatism is treason to the class cause. There can be no licit opposition to the Union, which represents the brotherhood of peoples building socialism against the opposition of the class enemy. "The working class . . . is the cement that holds together our monolithic multinational state."[32] This approach has been extended into the prerevolutionary past. As seen by Soviet historians since the late 1940's, antagonisms within the Russian empire were always the fault of the exploiting classes, the common enemy of the popular masses of Russian and minority peoples, who always aspired to harmony if not union. Nationalism has always been something ugly and regrettable, whereas class bespeaks a beautiful ideal. The Marxist ideal of socialism also serves to override nationalism. "Public ownership of the means of production and the socialist system of the economy, being completely dominant, serve as a basis for the ideological, moral, and political amity of the whole Soviet people and for friendship between peoples."[33] Ownership is vested in the central regime, and Moscow is the center of planning and much administration. To permit private enterprise would be to invite the creation of local power centers supporting divisive tendencies.

The priority of class over nation unites the Communist movement in the world and particularly in the Soviet sphere, binding the friends of the Soviet Union and dividing its enemies. Proletarian internationalism gave the Soviet Union and allied states the right, indeed the duty, to intervene in Czechoslovakia in 1968. According to a *Pravda* commentator, "Nationalism under contemporary conditions is expressed above all in overlooking the basic contradiction of our era, the contradiction between socialism and capitalism, in the rejection of class positions. . . ."[34] According to the Czech premier installed by the Russians, "Such concepts as freedom, democracy, have their class content, class forms. Where this is lost, and the class approach to problems is dulled, there rises a nationalistic wave."[35] It is the firmest of Soviet positions that the highest loyalty is due to the working class, and there can be no proletarianism, no true socialism, except in harmony with the Soviet Union.

The elevation of class over nation is more a political aspiration than description of social reality. While economic bonds have drawn nations together, education and modern means of communication have tended to solidify national feeling within many nations. The workers have usually seemed at least as aware of belonging to a nation as to a class, perhaps even when strongly organized by Communist parties, as demonstrated by frictions in Eastern Europe between Rumanians and Hungarians, Czechs and Russians, etc. The nation is a much better defined group than the class; it is easier to draw lines between Frenchmen and Germans than to divide either into "workers" and "bourgeois"; and it is much easier for a French miner to communicate with a French shopkeeper than

---

[32] *Krasnaia zvezda*, May 21, 1971, p. 2; *Current Digest*, vol. 23, no. 20, p. 38.

[33] *Social Sciences in the USSR* (Mouton et Cie.), Paris, 1965, p. 2.

[34] January 15, 1969.

[35] *Pravda*, August 22, 1969.

with a German miner. The French capitalist and worker share an economic interest in productivity and prosperity, while workers in different countries are to some extent economic competitors, having little common interest except, as the Marxists saw it, in the promotion of the socialist revolution.

It is equally likely that an Uzbek worker may feel more in common with Uzbek intellectuals who slip into bourgeois deviations than with Russian immigrants into his country, whether blue or white collar workers. Ideology has by no means solved the Soviet nationality problem, and there is considerable evidence of continuing, perhaps increasing self-awareness of peoples and discontent with centralization and alien domination. But the party's answer has been at least partially successful, and it has no other. Without some such excuse for party rule, one would expect that the realm must break into its natural fragments or at least that the character of relations among its peoples and of the regime governing them must change profoundly.

Unity is the central meaning of Marxism-Leninism, with loyalty nominally to the cause, actually to the party, to override all else. This is the bedrock of ideology, the deepest apparent commitment of the party leadership, the first principle of party organization, and perhaps the supreme value of the political system. Of all threats to Soviet unity, the gravest is that of national separation. It may be, consequently, that this is the largest single factor dictating the remarkable persistence of a revolutionary, proletarian-class doctrine as the official creed of a state which has long ceased to be either revolutionary or proletarian in spirit. If there were no Russian minorities problem, the world would have heard much less of Karl Marx during the past half century.

BURDENS OF MARXISM

The post-Khrushchev leadership, fearful of solvent trends among the intellectuals and Soviet minority peoples, and most acutely in the Soviet sphere of Eastern Europe, has done much to intensify indoctrination. Ideology is the vital cement, moral foundation, and lubricant of the huge apparatus, without which it could hardly function and perhaps could not exist. Lacking it, the Soviet Union would descend from being the maker of a new supranational world to be merely a shaky empire. Ideology seems to be even more essential in the absence of a charismatic personality at the helm of the state.

Yet Marxism-Leninism is uncongenial for the conservative, hierarchic Soviet state. Marxism bespeaks proletarianism and revolution, but a social chasm lies between the elite and the manual worker. The top men live in another world from the masses; at the same time, they must repeat that the ordinary grimy workers are the elect of history. Marxism outside the Communist sphere continues to be an inspiration for the overthrow of the established order, but the Soviet has become an established order, and the idea of revolution is horrifying to the satisfied administrators and beneficiaries of a settled society. Marxism is not a suitable foundation for a status quo. Even people who are convinced of the ideal virtues of communism observe chasms between promise and performance. Politburo members lack the common touch of Lenin and are not conspicuously self-sacrificing. "Workers" and "capitalists" are like poor and rich in the unsophisticated view, and the latter division is obvious in Soviet society. It is not difficult to apply Marxist ideas of class exploitation to the Soviet Union; not only in "capitalist" countries is there a ruling stratum.

Unless thus adversely applied, Marxism lacks emotional relevance for Soviet citizens. All antagonistic classes were supposedly eliminated decades ago. The Soviet "classes" of workers and peasants (defined in non-Marxist fashion by occupation rather than relation to means of production), along with the "intelligentsia," are not supposed to have conflicting interests. The "world revolutionary movement" is too distant and abstract, and it has dragged on too long without important results. But without struggle, Marxism is unengaging and irrelevant scholasticism, a dry theory offering no solace in hardship or inspiration in despair. Materialistic in essence,[36] as its utopia recedes it holds little for the idealism of youth; it has none of the lofty mystery of religion and no answers to the deeper questions of human existence.

The Marxist utopia not only remains distant but is uncongenial to Soviet society. Propagandists have difficulties with Lenin's predictions of an early advent of the Communist society. Marx's intentions were liberal and equalitarian, and he saw no good in the state. His ideal was individual freedom and self-fulfillment, but the Soviet state aims at maximum control. The state is not to wither but to grow ever stronger in the period of building communism.[37] The inauguration of the brotherly equalitarian Marxist dream, with all sharing in the direction of society, would require a new revolution. But much of the party's claim to rule is tied up with its historical role leading to this utopia. It is not surprising that the present leaders do not discuss the long-range future.

The Marxist utopia, however appealing to discontented intellectuals, is basically prescientific; Marx's notion that people would work by turns as farmer, artisan, teacher, etc., becomes a childish daydream in the technological age. In the Soviet Union as nowhere else, workers are specialized and materially tied to their positions. The Marxist contention that workers would spontaneously become vastly more productive and would work joyously without pay when relieved of exploitation is grossly discordant with Soviet experience, wherein productivity remains low despite innumerable spurs and incentives to

---

[36] Marx's ideas of alienation are neglected in Marxism-Leninism.

[37] M. P. Shendrik, *Obshchenarodnoe gosudarstvo—novyi etap o razvitii sotsialisticheskoi gosudarstvennosti,* Lvov, 1970, p. 8.

production. That goods can be distributed freely is belied by a half century of shortages. Marx would bring back a supposed carefree golden age of brotherly equality of pretechnological society as the highest incarnation of technological civilization.

Marx was a scholarly, at times a brilliant writer, but it was too much to expect that he might make a revolutionary contribution to economics, history, philosophy, and sociology. Overestimating the role of wealth-seeking, he largely ignored the many noneconomical drives, especially the urge to power. Not only did Marx claim to see clearly in present and past, where others were baffled by confusion, but he wanted to lay out a schematic road to the distant future. In contradiction to his own interpretation of history, he saw the "bourgeois" civilization of his day, which had barely emerged from an order he called feudal within a human lifetime, as the end, whereas it was only the infancy of industrial capitalism. He called attention to very real sufferings of exploitation and alienation, but he had only a vague notion that these should be cured by an overthrow of property relations, assuming that without capitalism there could arise no new bosses and that specialization would somehow become unnecessary. The basis of Marx's thinking was badly eroded by the social changes of the last decades of the nineteenth century. He was a child of that century, trying to answer questions which are still unanswered a century later.

It is not surprising that the expectations which served as intellectual foundation for Lenin's revolution have proved generally false, not only such assumptions as the decline of nationalism but also such key doctrines as the inevitable impoverishment of the proletariat. Marxism also gave the Soviet Union an inadequate basis for economic theory. If one contends with Marx that articles have value only according to labor inputs, "value" can mean neither price nor utility; natural resources, scarcity, ideas, luck, novelty, management, and other factors cannot influence value, and there is no way of estimating how much is due to the worker who mans the machine, to the person who provides the machine which makes labor productive, or to the designer whose ideas made the machine possible. Class struggle gives only a very partial understanding of politics, and the Soviet Union has realistically applied realpolitik in diplomacy. To look only to means of production and property relations as determinants of social order and culture, to attribute philosophies solely to class position, is a misperception refuted by Lenin's Bolsheviks if not by Marx himself, all claiming proletarian attitudes despite bourgeois origins. A soap manufacturer paid the bills for the Bolshevik party congress of 1907, and many another capitalist helped along the way, just as Engels used part of the profits of exploitation of his textile workers to finance Marx's assault on capitalism. Lenin's state has amply demonstrated the priority of the political over the economic.

Elevating the division between nonworking owners and working nonowners to the overwhelming fact of society, Marx neglected nonworking nonowners (political figures, sundry bosses, and parasites), working owners (peasants and small entrepreneurs) and many professionals between. Marxism sees society not as complex and pyramidal but as simple and two-layered. The industrial workers whom Marx saw as most exploited are often relatively well off; the truly poor are apt to be agricultural laborers and those of by-passed communities, racial or cultural minorities, who lack a role in the economy. To support the claim that Western society is becoming more proletarianized, in accordance with prediction, Soviet writers are constrained to see all manner of technicians and prosperous middle-class persons, administrators and scientists, as "working class."[38] On the other hand, persons on the bottom of the scale are often dismissed as "Lumpenproletariat." "Bourgeoisie" is also an impossibly loose concept in Soviet parlance, including almost anyone disliked. "Class" in ordinary understanding is more a social than an economic order in any strict sense; it is a political idea useful for political purposes. "Capitalism," too, has become fuzzy in times of widespread planning and governmental control, and the Russians insist that economic intervention by an unapproved government has nothing to do with "socialism."

Marxism neglects the numerous and important class of bureaucrats, officials, and political leaders. At times Marx and Engels recognized that the state was a force in its own right, but they could not reconcile this with the basic view that it was merely an instrument of the possessors. Government is not only a means of maintaining an oppressive order; it is also coordinator of society, the more necessary (as the Soviets in effect concede) as society becomes more complex. Government has also shown itself capable of giving business the kind of protection a farmer gives his sheep, sheltering in order to extract money for the benefit of the political apparatus. But the Soviet ideology contends that only economic and not political power is exploitative, and that oppression arises only from property-holding, not from possession of means of force.

This idea was necessary for the happy vision of a new society after factories, mines, and other means of production were taken away from private owners; no more owners, therefore no more classes, exploitation, and oppression. Marx did not take into account that men representing the working classes might be power-hungry and selfish, and that control of production is likely to be concentrated in relatively few hands no matter what the legal ownership. "Workers" by becoming governors gain power and privilege over their fellows and cease by ordinary understanding to be workers. The Soviet proletarian who becomes plant manager is as far from his class of origin in functions (and possibly outlook) as the American who rises from clerk to corporate executive.

The thesis that evil in society comes only from private ownership of means of production excludes basic criticism of the Soviet system. But it stands in the way of realism about present-day shortcomings as it inhibits deeper

[38] *Kommunist*, no. 2, January, 1969, p. 29.

inquiry into the disasters of the Stalin era and the reasons why so many top Soviet leaders have turned out to be, in the judgment of their successors, more or less rascals. There can be no real inquiry into the role and purposes of the party, nor any proposals for basic reform.

Political Marxism is mostly vision and therefore beyond truth or falsity. But requirements of ideology circumscribe Soviet thinking in all areas with political implications. There can be no confrontation of the Leninist contradiction of economic determinism, whereby the party, a part of the superstructure, makes the economic basis rather than vice versa. Although Soviet economists have fairly well given up the pretense of managing the economy according to Marxist prescriptions, they remain straitjacketed. They, and Soviet historians, do competent work in certain areas, but originality and deep analysis are foreclosed. The historians can hardly admit political causation but must look for class struggle everywhere; sometimes they are driven to assert that it existed in "passive" form.[39] Sociology is limited to investigations of practical utility, and political science is excluded. Truth being a political commodity, unbiased inquiry is frankly proscribed. As a learned Soviet journal put it, "We need a party approach which is devoid of any kind of objectivism."[40] The epithet of "bourgeois objectivity" is often hurled to destroy inconvenient arguments.

In the face of the modern need for critical inquiry, the Soviet Union seems handicapped by an obsolete ideology. The contradiction becomes more acute as people become better educated and more sophisticated. That many find it difficult to square ideology with reality may be indicated by repeated exhortations to improve ideological work and by the exaggerated amount of attention paid to instilling some rather simple dogmas which educated Soviet citizens have heard thousands of times. But just as tsardom had to uphold the theory of personal autocracy long after it had become outdated, the Soviet party cannot dispense with Marxism-Leninism. A sense of the growing contradiction between ideological pretense and political reality may be a prime reason for the wall of secrecy which hides all controversy within the government from public view.

LENINISM AND PRUSSIANISM

The Soviet leadership does not rely merely on somewhat uncomfortable and increasingly unsuitable doctrines of Marxism-Leninism but interweaves and supports them with symbolism, collectivist emotions, and social discipline, themes which authoritarian regimes have ever inculcated for their stability.

---

[39] Lowell Tillett, *The Great Friendship, Soviet Historians on the Non-Russian Nationalities* (University of North Carolina Press), Chapel Hill, 1969, p. 9.

[40] *Voprosy filosofii*, no. 3, 1969, p. 4.

Marxist theses often seem overshadowed by the glorious history of the party and of the Socialist Fatherland and the Russian homeland before it, by the call for collectivist and patriotic devotion, and by Leninolatry.

V. I. Lenin has become chief of the Soviet pantheon. Everyone is urged to read his works; Lenin is the greatest of world thinkers, an ultimate authority on anything. Marx is rather for the specialist; there are a hundred quotations from Lenin to one from Marx. In this non-Marxist cult of the individual, the Leninist scriptures are a canon (somewhat like "Mao Tse-tung thought") to which little authoritative has been added despite the recognized need for developing Marxism-Leninism for the very changed Soviet reality of today. A quote from Lenin may be used to support any policy, including some of which he disapproved, as tight controls of literature.

As the 1969 World Communist Conference exhorted, "Study the works of Lenin! In them you will find an inexhaustible source of inspiration for the struggle against reaction and oppression, for socialism and peace. Familiarity with them helps the younger generation to see more clearly. . . ."[41] But Lenin is even more of an inspiring personality than a doctrinal authority. His biography and the countless tales of his deeds or of meeting him are hagiography. "Lenin—every photograph, preserving his inimitable features for the ages, is priceless"[42] and much used. Especially inspiring is how Lenin would come down from Olympus to help the humble in their toil. He cannot be really dead. As school children chanted for the Twenty-Fourth Party Congress,

> "Lenin lives, Lenin lives
> In thoughts and deeds and hearts of the people!
> He teaches to live and conquer
> Never to retreat
> To go to the glowing horizons
> And we can proudly say
> Lenin today
> Is in this hall!"[43]

Men work "with Lenin in the heart," and children are taught to live cleanly and work dutifully as Lenin desired. "Lenin smiles on me and gives me courage." "Lenin's cause lives and conquers." To speak disrespectfully of him is "blasphemy." Lenin is celebrated as friend of the Indian or French or German worker as well as the Russian. He is almost as omnipresent in satellite states of Eastern Europe as in Russia; from the Elbe to Mongolia, tens of thousands of factories, schools, etc., are named after Lenin.

[41] *Pravda*, November 11, 1969.
[42] *Pravda* February 8, 1970.
[43] *Pravda*, April 2, 1971, p. 1.

Lenin, like Stalin, has been made into the symbol of unity, justice, and the authority of the party. "When we say 'Lenin,' we understand 'the party,' when we say 'the party' we understand 'Lenin.' "[44] He is frequently designated as "the leader" ("vozhd"), a term of authoritarian overtones applied formerly to Stalin. His usually stern countenance, sometimes in gigantic busts or portraits, looks down on almost every worker and every public event. To save a statue of Lenin from desecration is a feat worth risking one's life.[45] His portrait inspired soldiers in the hardships of battle.[46] The two-year preparations for Lenin's hundredth birthday in 1970, "an immense event in the history of humanity," as the Russians put it, were by far the biggest anniversary commemorations of history.[47] Almost everyone in the Soviet Union was supposed to contribute in some way, overfulfilling plans in his honor or studying his life and works. For months, Lenin filled books and periodicals. There were issued hundreds of editions of his works, and more than a dozen full-length movies illumined his life for Soviet viewers. The cult was surpassed only by that of Mao in the Great Proletarian Cultural Revolution.

The apotheosis of Lenin merges into the glorification of his party both before the Revolution and after, when it becomes practically the history of the Soviet Union. Through its struggles for the correct revolutionary line, for ideological purity, for the making of the Revolution, then winning the civil war, building socialism and defending the country in the Second World War, the party has incarnated the virtues of the proletariat. The heroic chapters are rehearsed and reviewed: the Revolution, civil war, the First Five-Year Plan, collectivization, the Fatherland War, and postwar reconstruction and the building of socialism. A large fraction of the ideological training of party cadres is devoted to this history. Basically united despite the need from time to time to expel bad elements, and above all far-seeing, the party remains infallible. As the regime rests its legitimacy more upon tradition and less upon mission of change, it stresses its roots in a sacred past.

Glorification of the party is inseparable from exaltation of the state which it has made and rules and of the people who compose it. The Soviet Union is an ideal, both as the maker of Lenin's Revolution and socialism and as a thing of unspeakable greatness in its own right. "The Soviet people opened an era of justice for all mankind," and it is taken for granted that adherence to the Soviet cause is the qualification of Communists and progressives everywhere. Ageless pride mingles with modern messianism, as *Pravda* eulogizes Moscow: "Banner-bearer, hope and bulwark of peace on earth, Moscow will live eternally,

---

[44] *Pravda*, April 26, 1970.
[45] *Pravda*, October 29, 1969.
[46] *Krasnaia zvezda*, January 27, 1970, p. 2.
[47] The actual day, April 27, was celebrated by working harder.

and human gratitude to her will never be exhausted. Because she sees an equal in every working person, a brother in every nation, she made an end forever to the law of the jungle in the mutual relations of people, nations, and governments. Now for more than half a century she has been gathering together humanity under the attractive force of Leninist ideas. And the circle of liberated peoples broadens and grows greater, new bastions of socialism and communism on earth."[48] The Russian heritage is raised to a new level by its universal mission of renewal of humanity.

Still more remote from strict dogma is the exaltation of Russian history. Stalin returned the Russian past to respectability, and old tsarist warriors were more celebrated during the Second World War than anti-tsarist revolutionaries. Khrushchev, in his effort to restore some of the spirit of the Revolution, backed away a little from the refurbishing of the image of historic Russia. But his heirs have laid new emphasis on historical continuity and reverence for the past. Towns have their historical societies. The All-Russian Society for the Preservation of Monuments of History and Culture, founded in 1965, by 1970 had four million members in the Russian republics, and other republics had similar organizations. There have been drives to renovate picturesque old towns, just as Poland and Soviet Germany have devoted large amounts of scarce resources to the rebuilding of historic Warsaw and East Berlin. Among conservative intellectuals there has been a revival of nineteenth-century Slavophilism, downgrading the West in moral terms much like those used a century ago.

The heroism of the Great Patriotic War of 1941–1945 is one of the most used historical themes, wherein the Russian, Soviet, and Communist are melted together. With the flood of stories and memoirs has swelled the glorification of military ways and virtues, discipline, and self-sacrifice, in a spirit much closer to Prussianism than Marxism.[49] Although nationalism is very bad, patriotism is chief of virtues. Newspapers are commonly graced with one or more pieces about the brave and handsome defenders of the Fatherland. Space heroes, almost all military men, are given all the personal publicity which the political leadership has denied itself. In the fall of 1969, October 12–21, *Pravda* and *Izvestia* each wrote about 82,000 words and published scores of pictures in celebration of the flight of three earth-orbiting vehicles, whose trained, disciplined, devoted, and courageous pilots are the preferred model for Soviet youth.

A militaristic streak has run through Soviet thinking at least since the civil war, when the party took on an unforeseen mission of military leadership. Maxim Gorky's tale of Danko's Heart has long been thought suitable

---

[48] November 3, 1969.
[49] See Chapter 11.

inspiration for young Soviets: a lone hero saves his people, whom he calls a flock of sheep and who act the part, by tearing out his own heart. " 'Men of duty' is the Soviet term for worthy compatriots, heroes of our time."[50] There is, indeed, a certain grimness in the Soviet outlook, with emphasis on the conquest of socialism quite drowning out, in the official view, the idea of its enjoyment. The Soviet citizen should not primarily look forward to the Marxist heaven but should think mostly of giving his all and his life if necessary for its attainment. Fear for one's self and family, a Soviet medical scientist finds, is very bad for the heart, but fear of death or suffering for a just cause strengthens the organism.[51] Loyalty, wholehearted devotion to the collective, the socialist fatherland, and the party seem to be the residue of ideology as more particular dogmas lose significance.

READINGS

Frederick C. Barghoorn, *Soviet Russian Nationalism* (Oxford University Press), New York, 1956.

N. S. Davydova, *Na puti k kommunizmu* (Izd. polit. lit), Moscow, 1968.

Richard T. De George, *Soviet Ethics and Morality* (University of Michigan Press), Ann Arbor, Mich., 1969.

Dialektika stroitel'stva kommunizma (Izd. Mysl), Moscow, 1968.

Matthew P. Gallagher, *The Soviet History of World War II* (Praeger), New York, 1963.

Robert N. Carew Hunt, *The Theory and Practice of Communism* (Macmillan Co.), New York, 1957.

E. A. Khomenko and M. I. Iasiukov, *Kurs Marksistko-leninskoi filosofii* (Voennoe izd.), Moscow, 1968.

George Lichtheim, *Marxism, an Historical and Critical Study* (Praeger), New York, 1961.

Robert C. Tucker, *Philosophy and Myth in Karl Marx* (Cambridge University Press), Cambridge, 1961.

Gustav A. Wetter, *Soviet Ideology Today* (Praeger), New York, 1962.

---

[50] *Pravda*, October 12, 1970, p. 1.
[51] *Sovetskaia Rossiia*, October 25, 1970, p. 4.

6. The Party

ORGANIZATION

Without party direction, there would be no coherent Marxism-Leninism. The party states what ideology is, interprets and applies it. At the same time the party claims legitimacy by the ideology, which sets forth basic purposes and the relation of the party to Soviet society. Party and ideology are inseparable, practically two aspects of a single political reality. The one claims monopoly of truth, the other monopoly of organization, both for the same purpose of unity and control.

Just as the essence of Soviet ideology is loyalty to the party as the incorporation of right and justice, the central principle of the Communist Party of the Soviet Union (and of the many Leninist parties patterned after it) is the maximum mobilization of wills in the name of ideology. This means a structure whereby smaller numbers dominate larger groups in a series of circles outward and downward. Thus the twenty-five men of the Politburo and the Secretariat dominate the Central Committee of nearly four hundred and the central apparatus, and at each level the secretariat or the "buro" manages the party committee; the party center guides outlying organizations, and these in turn guide organizations of smaller territorial units, and so down to the primary party organizations in factories and farms. At each level, relatively few party men watch over and to some extent direct much larger numbers of leaders in governmental, cultural, and other nonparty organizations. A minority leads the majority again at the grass roots, as party fractions within organizations assure conformity to party policy; over all, the minority of party members (under 6%) guide the entirety of Soviet society.

155

But conformity should be so far as feasible voluntary, if not eager, in order to make the apparatus effective and truly responsive to the central will. Subordinates at all levels should feel they are not merely carrying out orders but participating in the great task. Hence party structure is an intertwining of a system of command, mostly informal and exercised by customary practice but also formally sanctioned, and a system of democratic consent, mostly formal and unreal but not unimportant. The result is a complex but purposefully elaborated system. A confusing ambivalence of realities of power and appearances of democracy is inherent in the nature of the party. It is the counterpart of the ideology, designed to reinforce authority with democratic and popular ideals. It runs through all Soviet organizational practice and governmental structure.

Membership

The first organizational question is the recruitment of membership. From Lenin's little sect of revolutionaries, the party has tended to grow throughout Soviet history except for the purges after 1921 and 1933. Expansion has been most rapid when there was felt most need for support, as in the months prior to the Revolution, in the civil war, and in the Second World War; the worst year of the latter, 1942, saw the gates opened the widest. The Second World War, unlike the civil war, was followed by no large-scale cleansing, and the party has expanded fairly steadily since then. Growth accelerated under Khrushchev, but since 1966 it has slowed somewhat and expulsions have increased. At the Twenty-Fourth Congress there was decreed an exchange of party cards to weed out the less desirable, a procedure which had not been used since Stalin. Figures are as follows:

Members, Including Candidate Members, CPSU
(as of January 1 of each year)

1918	390,000	1940	3,399,975
1921	732,521	1945	5,760,369
1924	472,000	1948	6,390,521
1927	1,305,854	1953	6,897,224
1930	1,677,910	1960	8,708,667
1933	3,555,338	1967	12,684,133
1937	1,981,697	1971	14,400,000

The party has thus become a mass army, taking in at present about one-tenth of the adult population. The proportion of women leveled off to about one-fifth after 1950. Hence the party is approaching a fifth of the adult male population. This may be nearly a limit, if party membership represents real political activism.

Since party membership represents political privilege, a career or an adjunct to advancement in almost any branch of endeavor, many more probably knock at the door than are admitted in normal times. Up to 1918, all classes were welcome, and in the civil war willingness to fight on the Bolshevik side, risking death in case of defeat, was sufficient qualification. In the NEP period, as the party felt insecure at the base, it sought to recruit mainly industrial workers. But in 1925, only 8% of seven million industrial workers were members, and only about one peasant in three hundred.

In the first five years of five-year plan industrialization, factory workers were still more strongly favored. From 1933 to 1938, only enough were brought in to fill the gaps left by the purges, and emphasis turned from proletarians to Stalin's new privileged class of technicians, managers, and administrative employees. In World War II men who showed their loyalty by military competence were welcome with little regard for ideology or background. After the war, persons of all classes were admitted, with some emphasis on the underrepresented peasantry. Under Khrushchev there was some effort to proletarianize the party. White collar workers currently predominate. In 1971, the official breakdown was as follows: Workers, 40.1%; collective farmers, 15.1%; employees and others, 44.8%.[1] But it is desirable to record as many proletarians as possible, and anyone with any claim to such classification is apparently counted as such. A large part of the "workers" and "peasants" entering the party under Khrushchev had a higher education.[2]

The better one's status in Soviet society, the easier it is to become a party member, just as party membership is a means to high status. The "best people," the top layers in organizations and professions, are expected to be in the party. Likewise workers of special skills and in prestigious branches of production are more likely to be invited to join than low-grade workers. By one survey, 30% of specialists and brigade leaders of kolkhozes were members, and only 1% of ordinary hands.[3] The party represents the Soviet elite, and it is becoming a party of the educated; half of the members have a secondary or higher education, and such qualifications are considered desirable.

The party began as a nationally mixed organization, and the discontented minorities, Jews, Poles, Balts, Caucasians, etc., were much overrepresented in the leadership. At present, Russians have a slightly larger percentage of party membership than corresponds to their numbers in the general population. Georgians and Armenians, however, are a bit better represented than the Russians; Balts are somewhat underrepresented and Central Asians are seriously so. However, the underrepresentation of some minorities, particularly Central Asians, may be ascribed to their more rural character. The big cities, which are strongly Russian everywhere, are the party strongholds.

[1] Report of L. I. Brezhnev, *Pravda*, March 31, 1971, p. 9.
[2] Michael P. Gehlen, *The Communist Party of the Soviet Union*, Indiana University Press, Bloomington, Ind., p. 37.
[3] Karl-Eugen Wädekind, "Soviet Rural Society," *Soviet Studies*, vol. XXII, no. 4, April, 1971, p. 521.

The would-be party member applies at his workplace. He must be recommended by three party members of at least five years' standing, who should have known him at work for at least a year. They are theoretically responsible for his delinquencies, but this is probably serious only in case he should prove politically deficient. Youths up to the age of twenty-three (eighteen being the minimum) may join only through the Komsomol, the recommendation of a county or city Komsomol committee being taken as one sponsorship. In recent years, about half of party entrants seem to have come from the junior youth organization.

A person becomes a full member only after a probationary period of one year as "candidate." Candidates were 654,000 in 1971, slightly under one-twentieth of party enrollment. During this time, his willingness and ability are supposedly tested, as he sits with party groups and carries out assignments. He attains full membership by two-thirds vote of his local organization and the endorsement of the next higher party committee, which is guided by a special commission for the examination of new members.[4]

To join the party is a leap like marriage or taking the vows of a religious order, with no provision for resigning membership. It is a commitment to an active political life, an acceptance of special responsibilities, and an open road to advancement according to ambition, devotion, and capacities. "Above all, every entrant into the CPSU should deeply understand that from this moment he is representative of a ruling party, the guiding force in the state, which lays enormous responsibility on him. This means that he must live by Leninist principles, that means, the interests of the party first, everything else is secondary."[5]

Those who join Lenin's party belong as to a giant family by which they are possessed. They subscribe to a "Moral Code of a Communist" that is practically religious in its commandments of loyalty, love of the cause, and moral perfection—there are at least eighty-five obligations under the rules. The member must pay dues rising to 3% of his income, be a model citizen and worker, spread the party ideals, accept humbly any criticism, follow injunctions, accept any assignments, and volunteer for more. His happiness should be toil and struggle; after hours and after professional retirement, party work goes on.

Primary Organization

The basic party organizations, formerly called cells in the revolution-ary tradition, unite the workers of a factory or a division thereof, students in a school, farmers on a kolkhoz, etc. As a concession to convenience, some communists, especially retired persons, are grouped on a residential basis; in

---

[4] *Partiinaia zhizn*, no. 11, June, 1971, p. 39.

[5] *Pravda*, December 19, 1969, p. 2.

apartments the party organization may be parallel with the building management. But Communists are supposed to be active workers, and their biggest job is pushing production, so the organization is almost entirely production centered.

There are some 350,000 so-called primary party organizations, with membership from three to three hundred or more. Their characteristic is competence to handle personnel matters. But patterns are complicated; "primary" organizations are not necessarily the lowest level but may be subdivided, if large, by shop, section, or department, with as many as three lower layers of divisions or groups. These have been much developed of recent years; thus, shop organizations (with secretaries) and party groups (with "organizers") increased from 195,000 in 1957 to 670,000 in 1967,[6] and emphasis on them has increased in the following years. This means that the membership has less to do with the primary organization, which becomes more bureaucratic and which, if very large, may not have plenary meetings at all but conferences of delegates from suborganizations.

If the primary organization has less than 150 members, it should have no full-time paid staff, but there is always a secretary, and a buro is elected if there are 15 members or more, for two- to three-year terms. In a typical factory organization of 150 members there will be one elected secretary with two understudies, one for organization, the other for agitation and propaganda, supported by a buro of a dozen, backed up by an "aktiv," an eager minority. Buro members specialize in various areas, as production, volunteer work, youth organization, propaganda, etc.[7] Very large primary organizations have a committee, which implies more authority. Most secretaries at the base and nearly all above have a higher education (perhaps obtained in party schools).

Pyramid

The party narrows upward by stages corresponding to administrative divisions, from the primary organization to borough, city, or county, then to the provincial level and to the republic (except for the Russian republic, which has no party organization of its own) and to the All-Union level. Party members elect or rubber-stamp the choice of delegates to a city or county ("raion") conference. The conference forms a committee, which has its inner circle or bureau and its secretariat.[8] The conferences also elect delegates to a provincial ("oblast") conference, which likewise forms, or sanctions, a committee with bureau and secretariat. There is at all but the top level an "aktiv" of leading

[6] *Partiinaia zhizn*, no. 19, October, 1967, p. 18.
[7] *Partiinaia zhizn*, no. 1, January, 1969, p. 33.
[8] Sometimes, as among railroad workers, secondary party organizations are formed on production instead of territorial basis.

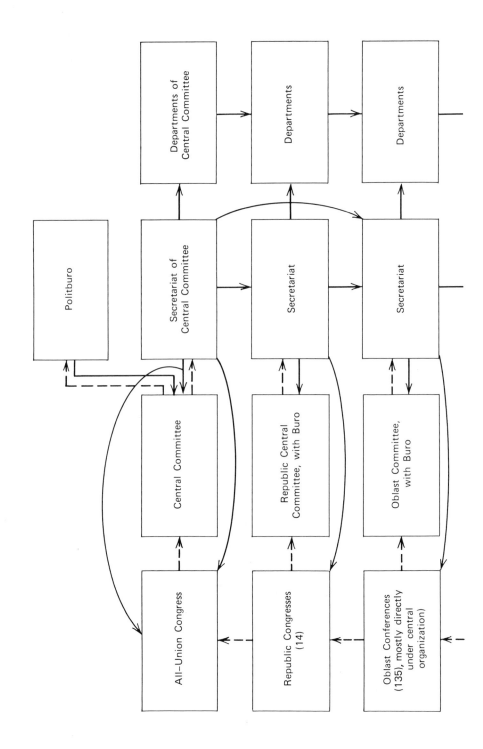

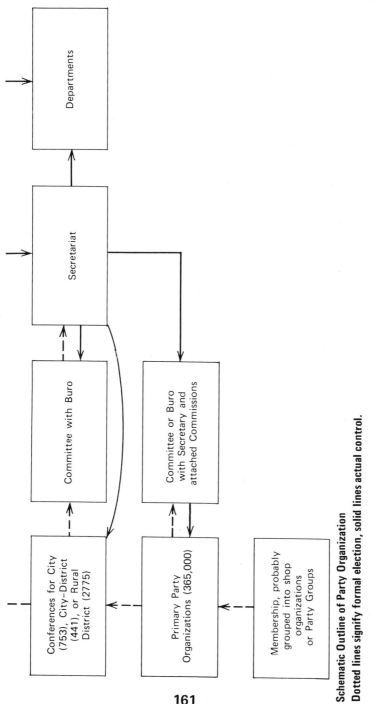

Schematic Outline of Party Organization

Dotted lines signify formal election, solid lines actual control.

party people picked to function along with the party committee and its organs. Delegates from conferences form a congress in the non-Russian republics (the smaller republics have no provincial, or oblast divisions, so the local conferences are directly represented at the republic level). Republic and, in the Russian republic, provincial conferences send delegates to the All-Union Congress in Moscow. Probably nowhere are there more indirect elections, as the ordinary member is separated from the Politburo by as many as seven electoral stages.

Participation of membership in the workings of leading bodies declines as one rises in the pyramid. The primary organization is to meet at least monthly, but it may meet only once in two or three months if it is large and has subdivisions, or delegates may replace the general membership. The local conference meets once in two to three years, the republic and All-Union Congress once in five years. The primary committee is a working body, as is that of the city and county to a somewhat lesser degree. But at the provincial and republic level, the party committee is more of a forum, meeting about three times yearly. Business is carried on in a buro of nine to twelve persons, including probably five secretaries, the chairman of the corresponding Soviet body, perhaps a chief of the control apparatus, a few other local officials, a trade union or industrial leader, etc. City and county committees have about seventy members and candidates; the size increases according to dignity up to the Central Committee of 396.

In the higher reaches the party becomes more purely apparatus and less a semirepresentative body, although a few workers and farmers are placed on committees all the way to the top. Attached to the committees at each level are specialized departments under the secretaries to carry out party work and manage the party itself. There are such departments as party organs, propaganda and the press, industry, transportation, construction, culture and schools, trade, Soviet administration, finance and planning, education, and others, the number and size increasing upward. Their officials, called "instructors," are charged with overseeing the primary cells, for approximately five of which there is an instructor. The size of the professional party apparatus is secret, but 250,000 is a reasonable guess. A few years ago there were reported 4,500 full-time party workers in Leningrad.[9] Very little is published about party finances, which are entwined with those of the state; but dues are said to provide the bulk of income, supplemented by the party press.

The key men are the secretaries. The title of "Secretary," so far as it implies someone employed to handle correspondence, is misleading; they are the line officers of the party, assisted by their troops and staff. They select party and other personnel, post and promote. They form the heart of the new nobility of service, educated and hard working, rewarded for loyal toil with great power.

---

[9] David T. Cattell, *Leningrad, a Case Study of Soviet Urban Government,* Praeger, New York, 1968, p. 33.

Although women are somewhat over a fifth of party membership, the secretaries are men only. The party secretary is like an army officer, a professional who expects to rise to another secretaryship.

Central Organs: Representative

Republic and provincial congresses and conferences are assemblages of local leaders; the Party Congress is theoretically the supreme body of the entire party, historical successor of Lenin's congresses, at which the most important pronouncements are made and whose unanimous vote, in representation of the working classes, legitimates the authority of the party. Soviet institutions are sometimes named after congresses, as the "Twenty-Third Congress Collective Farm." They are numbered from the First in 1898 and the Second in 1903 to the Twenty-Fourth in 1971. Congresses met yearly from the Revolution until 1925, then at increasing intervals (despite the rule for regular convocation) until thirteen years intervened between those of 1939 and 1952. Khrushchev held congresses in 1956, 1959, and 1961, but since then once in five years has been deemed often enough, and this has been written into party rules. They are supposed to mark eras of party history. From the time of announcement (July, 1970) of the convening of the Twenty-Fourth Congress (March-April, 1971) there was a gigantic movement to prepare for it by feats of production. "All life in our country proceeds under the sign of preparation for the Twenty-Fourth Congress of the CPSU."[10] Congresses are now timed to solemnize the initiation of five-year plans. The reports and resolutions of a congress become material for much organized study and are cited as ideological guidance.[11]

Stalin reduced the party congresses to the merest acclamatory gatherings. Khrushchev made them a bit livelier, and his congresses heard some interesting speeches, although nothing which could be called debate. This tendency was reversed after him; the 1966 Congress was very disciplined. The many speeches of the Twenty-Fourth Congress brought hardly an esoteric hint of differences, except in the reservations of a very few foreign parties. The lack of power of the congresses is underlined both by the publicity which surrounds them and their large size, which has increased from the few score of prerevolutionary days to over 1300 in 1952, and about five thousand in 1961, 1966, and 1971. However, the party apparatusmen seem to like them; like political conventions everywhere they are an opportunity to get acquainted and

[10] *Pravda*, December 26, 1970, editorial.
[11] According to the chief of the youth organization, "The Central Committee's Report has found its way to the heart of every person—it is a wonderful alloy of wisdom, extremely rich experience, comprehensive knowledge of life, and scientific foresight; and it has astonishing grandeur and sweep. . . ." (*Pravda*, April 4, 1971, p. 4; *Current Digest*, vol. 23, no. 16, p. 28.)

meet the bosses. Formerly there were also "conferences," smaller and less solemn gatherings. These became infrequent under Stalin and were formally abolished in 1952. In 1966, the rules were amended to revive the institution, ostensibly as a concession to party democracy, but none has been held.

The Central Committee, which the congress unanimously elects as a list on the suggestion of the leadership, is legally the supreme authority of the party when a congress is not in session, or almost all the time. Its membership is often pointed to as the quintessence of the Soviet elite, partly because they are obviously elect of the elect, partly because we know who they are. Currently, it has 396 members, 241 full and 155 candidates, having gradually swelled from the 23 members of 1918. The reason for having candidate members is not clear, as there is no fixed relation between candidacy and full membership.

Of the full members in 1971, there were 105 party officials, 75 government officials, 20 military, 13 diplomats, and 28 sundry police officials, enterprise directors, kolkhoz chairmen, scientists, writers, and a few leading workers and peasants. Women are 3% of membership. Almost all have a higher education, a majority have technical-professional training. Approximately one-fourth belong more or less *ex officio*, as first secretaries of republics and provinces (oblasts), central government ministers, chairmen of republic ministries, and leaders of principal mass organizations. Important persons who are concerned with the implementation of party policy in all fields are drawn together, whether to secure their understanding, concurrence and cooperation, or to learn their views. The Central Committee should meet by statute twice yearly, and remains in session several days; but it is not always convened promptly. It actually held sixteen plenums from 1966 to 1971. It cannot be a regular policy-making body, but it can act as a court of last resort, as when it saved Khrushchev in 1957 and sanctioned his removal in 1961.

Central Organs: Executive

Attached to the Central Committee is a set of departments, akin to those of lower party committees but larger, more numerous, and more authoritative. Most influential is that for Party Organs, which keeps dossiers on all higher positions. That for Propaganda trains propagandists and supervises the control of media. About a dozen departments deal with branches of the economy, overseeing respective ministries. Other departments handle science, education, the military, satellite countries, foreign parties, foreign affairs, and party housekeeping. Departments are unpublicized; this secrecy is testimony to their importance, in accord with the Soviet rule that publicity is for effect and secrecy for decision-making.

The departments are under the Secretariat. Stalin, as General Secretary, was seconded by four ordinary secretaries in his last years. He doubled this number in 1952, but it was cut back again to five after his death. Khrushchev expanded it in consolidating his power in 1961; and since 1966 it has had nine or ten members, near to the preferred number of about a dozen for decision-making bodies. For a time in 1953 no secretary was formally superior to his colleagues, but Khrushchev became First Secretary after a few months and held that title until his dismissal. The title of General Secretary was restored for Leonid Brezhnev in 1966. The party rules (no. 38) say of the Secretariat that it is "to direct current work, chiefly the selection of personnel and the verification of the fulfillment of party decisions." Four secretaries are currently full members of the Politburo; two are candidate members. Secretaries do not seem to be strongly specialized, although Suslov, for example, is known for his attachment to ideology, Ustinov for heavy and defense industry, etc. The General Secretary is legally elected by the Central Committee. Obviously, he is head of the party, but his powers remain veiled. It is a sign of authority that the General Secretary has his own secretariat to oversee the various departments.

The policy bureau, or Politburo of the Central Committee, set up to guide the Revolution, was formalized in 1919; it immediately tended to become the center of decision-making at the expense of the then still manageably small Central Committee. Stalin enlarged it to twenty-five members and eleven alternates in 1952 and called it the Presidium. However, on Stalin's death it was disclosed that there had been an inner bureau of the Presidium; and these men, taking charge, reduced it to handier size. It has since then varied only slightly; at the Twenty-Fourth Congress the number of full members was increased from eleven to fifteen, supplemented by six candidate members. In 1966 it got back its old name of Politburo.

Full members now include the General Secretary (Brezhnev), the Chairman of the Council of Ministers (Kosygin), the Chairman of the Presidium of the Supreme Soviet (Podgorny), secretaries of the Central Committee (Suslov, Kirilenko, and Kulakov), First Vice-Chairmen of the Council of Ministers (Polianskii and Mazurov), head of the trade unions (Shelepin), First Secretary of the Ukraine (Shelest), First Secretary of Kazakhstan (Kunaev), Moscow party chief (Grishin), head of the Party Control Commission (Pelshe), Chairman of the Council of Ministers of the Russian Republic (Voronov), and Chairman of the Ukrainian Council of Ministers (Shcherbitskii). The Politburo thus includes representatives of principal Soviet organs, except the armed forces. Among candidate members are representatives of important minority nationalities. This body thus serves some representative function, and it is a sort of collective head of state, acting as honorary presidium of many gatherings. Members are listed alphabetically, which handily places Brezhnev at the head. Where and when it meets is not known, but weekly gatherings have been indicated. Apparently, it sets up commissions of Central Committee members and others for various questions, but nothing is divulged about them.

There are other central bodies of secondary importance. The Central Auditing Commission, according to the rules (no. 36), "supervises the proper handling of business by the central organs of the party" and audits accounts. Its work and importance are obscure, but it sometimes sits with the Central Committee and seems to be a reserve for its membership. There is also a Party Control Committee, which handles disciplinary questions.

MANAGEMENT OF THE PARTY

Unity

As a member of a privileged closed group, a party member shares a profound interest with the elite. He can only lose by setting himself against party principles or the established leadership. The more he gives to the party, the more he has to lose by falling from its good graces. If persons disinclined to bow to dictation are unlikely to subject themselves to party discipline, they are even less likely to be invited to enter. Every effort is made to select men totally devoted to the system of party rule, in accordance with Lenin's original idea; the party should be composed of unconditionals, with whom there should be no real problem of control.

Among the obligations of a party member is submission to the rules of "Democratic Centralism," the basic doctrine of party management adopted in 1906 as a concession to Menshevik criticisms of Bolshevik discipline. Democratic in appearances and centralist in effect, this permits criticism but stringently limits it. Criticism and discussion of policy are permissible only so far as the party has not taken a position on a question. This does not mean that critical and incisive discussion is not desired. The leadership frequently scolds local organs for inattention to criticisms from ordinary members and calls for plain speaking without respect for personalities and frank acknowledgement of errors. It seems to be a duty of members to speak out with reasonable frequency; records are kept of all who take the floor. The ideal party meeting might open with hard-hitting rundowns of deficiencies in the implementation of the latest resolution of the Central Committee, analyze recent failures and measures taken to overcome them, and adopt a firm resolution to do better in the future. Some criticism and controversy are necessary to avoid stagnation, to enable the upper leadership to assess opinion, and most of all to keep local bosses on their toes.

The bounds are narrow, however. There is no criticism of those near the top (criticism of high party figures even by their equals is almost invariably indirect and perceptible only to the initiated), no discussion of fundamentals of the Soviet system, no questioning of policies accepted by the party. It is inadmissible to disagree with any party decision; it is not even licit to put a question on the agenda without agreement of the authorities. Criticism should be coupled with self-criticism; it should not be spontaneous and wide ranging but organized and specific, as Soviet writers point out.[12] Party members can express opinions only before the decision has been taken, be it a major decision of the higher leadership or a minor resolution of the local organization. Afterwards, all members must take the official decision as their own. Persons who have opposed a particular policy may be assigned to present the arguments for it publicly. As stated by a party organ, "Real freedom of criticism consists not in ignoring the regulations and norms of party life but in carrying them out conscientiously and unswervingly."[13]

The formation of factions to present different views has been prohibited for fifty years, the rule having been adopted against the kind of opposition which came to the fore at the party congress of 1921. Any attempt to form any unauthorized grouping is seen as a threat to party unity, leading potentially to independent centers and splits. No faction can be contemplated within the party except that of the insiders, the secretaries and those around them. It is ironic that the party rules (no. 30) provide that a third of the membership can call for the summoning of a congress; if half a dozen got together to make such a demand, they would become a punishable faction.

The rule against factions is strict. Party members are not to address a joint petition to higher-ups; they are limited to speaking individually in official meetings on matters open for discussion and should not even concert a position. There is no way a party member can properly ascertain, except by speaking up in the face of the leadership and watching faces, whether there is widespread sympathy for his views. A lower party body is not to address itself as a group to a higher one, nor is it to have any horizontal contacts with other party organizations except through the superior body. Party members who heard a complaint without reporting it were in one case expelled from the party for "Antiparty actions and participation in a conspiracy,"[14] although this was considered incorrect by the central authorities, as it was judged that the conspiracy charge was only a cover-up for failures. In another case, a party member was subject to disciplinary action because he advised two workers to make a complaint to the local party committee.[15]

It is hard for ordinary party members to criticize because they have no information as to how important decisions are reached, what considerations were involved, or who is responsible for them. Secrecy within the party was another Stalinist innovation, excused on grounds of necessity for the First Five-Year Plan. Different layers of the party are given access to material of

[12] *Partiinoe stroitelstvo,* Moscow, 1968, p. 107.
[13] *Partiinaia zhizn,* February 3, 1969; *Current Digest of the Soviet Press,* vol. 21, no. 7, p. 5.
[14] *Pravda,* January 19, 1962.
[15] *Pravda,* January 11, 1971, p. 2.

differing degrees of confidentiality, just as some material is divulged to party members but kept from the general public.

Core

At each level, power is concentrated in those closest to the chain of command, the buro and especially the secretaries, who manage the *nomenklatura*, naming personnel to positions within their purview. At every level, conferences or congresses ratify what has been decided in advance by the apparatus. Thus, the oblast conference is something of a show, to inform delegates, inspire them, and indicate their expected roles.[16] Debate is managed by the secretaries; if there is criticism, it is a sign that the victim has already been disgraced. Even the oblast committee, which is mostly composed of lower secretaries, is not to decide policy but to consider its better implementation, and its sessions likewise are fully organized in advance.

The big party congresses are acclamatory, not decision-making bodies. Although for morale and communication it would seem clearly desirable to convoke party bigwigs oftener to a pseudorepresentative and authoritative assembly, there must be apprehension lest many important men get together and exchange undesirable views. Meetings lasting ten days or so once in five years seem sufficient for legitimation and propaganda uses. There has been no evidence that the congress in any way checks the apparatus even informally or in closed meetings.

Meetings of the Central Committee also are too short and infrequent for it to interfere much in the running of affairs. The party can function without it; only three meetings were held in Stalin's last twelve years. From his death through 1971, plenary sessions averaged three yearly, lasting from a few hours to several days; and members have other jobs, mostly away from Moscow and the fountain of power. Its principal function is probably legitimation; party decisions are decreed in its name, the secretaries and various committees are attached to it, and it is the officially sovereign head of the party except when a congress meets. Through most of Soviet history it, like many other Soviet bodies, has gained membership and lost effectiveness. The 1971 increase of its full members from 175 to 241 implies a further diminution of its ability to influence policy. However, it has functions of coordination and information, as it brings together several hundred of the highest-placed Soviet leaders of various branches of government, party, and all important organizations with whom the top leaders find it advantageous, if not indispensable to consult. Khrushchev permitted some fairly lively debate; if there has been any since, it has not been publicized. The Central Committee can exercise some real power if the inner

---

[16] Stewart, *Political Power in the USSR* (Bobbs-Merrill), Indianapolis, 1968, p. 27. This study treats the work of the Stalingrad oblast party.

circle is divided, as in 1957 and 1964. It may have checked Brezhnev in July, 1970, when two plenary meetings were held in ten days.

A really powerful body will not usually expand because the members do not welcome dilution of their position, and the Politburo has stayed close to its present size, apparently considered optimal for policy discussion, except when Stalin wished to weaken it in 1952. Perhaps at this level the leadership is small and united enough that most decision-making can proceed by consultation, the Politburo being called upon to decide more controversial or graver questions. The Politburo then would act collectively as top of the party pyramid and final arbiter. Recently it has also served as formal spokesman in place of the Central Committee, making pronouncements in its own name. It assumed responsibility for approving the Ninth Five-Year Plan.[17]

Power also comes to a focus at the Secretariat of the Central Committee, which lacks candidate members and which has usually been smaller than the Politburo. The Secretariat also meets weekly, according to Brezhnev. But the Politburo is to some extent a representative body, and its members mostly hold high positions outside the central party apparatus; that is, they oversee execution of party policy. Several of them have posts away from Moscow. The Secretaries, on the other hand, have no nonparty positions. Hence it is probable that the Politburo is judge of policy but the Secretariat is master of personnel and general party overseer as suggested by the party rules. In the later Stalin years, the Secretariat was the only functioning high party body. In the Soviet republics, the secretariat is superior to the buro of the republic central committee. The ouster of Khrushchev was incubated within the Secretariat, decided by the Politburo, and ratified by the Central Committee; this probably indicates the usual roles of the three bodies. The Secretariat, with its general control over party positions, perhaps decides who enters the Politburo.

Democratic Centralism

The strongest provision of "Democratic Centralism" is the requirement of obedience of all lower party bodies to higher ones. Stalin aptly compared the top ranks of the party to generals, the next layer to officers, and the apparatchiks to noncoms; and the situation in this regard has not changed. As Lenin is cited, discipline must be absolute: "Refusal to submit to the leadership of the centers is equivalent to a refusal to be in the party, equivalent to destruction of the party."[18]

Various practices contribute to making subordination effective. Local party bodies do not use their own funds but are financed from the center.

[17] *Pravda*, October 17, 1971, p. 1.

[18] *Partiinaia zhizn*, no. 3, February, 1969, p. 10; *Current Digest of the Soviet Press,* vol. 21, no. 7, p. 3.

At all levels "instructors" attached to party committees advise party bodies below them and sit in on their meetings; it is a bold organization that opposes their will. Party departments at each level are subject not only, indeed not primarily, to the committee to which they are attached but to the corresponding department of the next higher party committee. No party center below the apex has command even of its own apparatus. Finally, by the party rules, each party secretary must be confirmed in office by the next higher party committee.

Against these faculties the democratic aspects of Democratic Centralism are featherweight, intended to serve appearances. One of them is accountability of higher to lower, which means little more than the holding of meetings at which leaders appear, review achievements, and make policy statements. There seems to be sharp questioning of superiors by hierarchic inferiors only at the lowest level.

The other democratic element of Democratic Centralism is the election of higher bodies by lower ones, from the bottom through several stages to the top. Party members have the right, of which they are commonly unaware,[19] to propose and discuss candidates. But there can be no electioneering or even, theoretically, talk of a candidacy in the corridor. A member can speak up only in the regular electoral meeting, conducted under the eagle eye of a superior instructor or secretary, who sits on the presidium to "raise the ideological level," interpret the rules, and comment. He is supposed to persuade rather than to command, but his guidance is considered essential to avoid "haphazard" results. He proposes candidates and may even bring in an outsider to "strengthen" the organization.[20] The participation of higher-ups in electoral meetings is "a clear expression of the democracy of party life," according to Politburo member Shelest.[21] The key men, the secretaries, are not even formally elected by the membership but by the respective committee or buro.

If a member opposes a candidacy, he should present his objections quietly behind the scenes. If a candidate is challenged, an open vote is taken on his inclusion in the list; this is then voted by secret ballot.[22] Supposedly names can be written in, but apparently the number of candidates is regularly equal to the number of positions to be filled, and scratching a name is more or less conspicuous. There were once complaints in party journals that some party secretaries stubbornly insisted on permitting more candidates than vacancies, with the result that good men failed of election.[23] The local body may rebel

[19] *Pravda*, January 11, 1970, p. 2.
[20] *Partiinaia zhizn*, no. 16, August, 1970, p. 40.
[21] Ibid., no. 22, November, 1970, p. 54.
[22] Ibid., no. 16, August, 1970, pp. 38–40.
[23] Boris Meissner, *The Communist Party of the Soviet Union* (Praeger), New York, 1956, p. 41.

against the suggested nominee to force the naming of another, but this seems to be rare. In primary party elections in 1969, less than one in one thousand party committees were disapproved.[24] In any case, the instructor can simply inform them that an upstart candidate will not be approved, and any candidate whom the higher-ups dislike can be ordered to withdraw. The party electors, in other words, are supposed to act from conviction but to make the approved choice.[25] Rebellion is feasible only if a local body can look to higher support against abusive officials.

Nonetheless, it is felt necessary to hold elections. The occasional skipping of the formality is sternly castigated, and it is a firm obligation of members to participate. It is desired that there be an opportunity for criticism of local bosses; the discussion of merits and shortcomings is intended to be educational for both candidates and electors. To be periodically subject to scrutiny and possible blackballing is salutary for apparatchiks. When Stalin introduced the secret ballot in 1939 it was not for democracy but as a means of checking local abuses of power in a terrorized party.

This check applies, however, to the lower levels and less rigorously to the secretaries. While committees, conferences, etc., are subjected to secret ballot, the secretaries and inner guiding bureaus are elected by open voting, in which no sane person would oppose a party decision. Very little is published about elections above the local level. The Central Committee apparently gives instructions as to the size and general composition of all "elected" party bodies.

The practice of managing the party from the center was inherent in Lenin's conception of it. From the first, nominally elective positions were in fact appointive. It has not always been possible for the center to impose strict control throughout, but as the party became able it has done so. It would be generally fair to state that from the top down, secretaries name secretaries. A secretary tells his inferior, "I was getting ready to promote you."[26] The apparatus recruits itself.

There are also ample means of control of the individual Communist. He may not change employment without the party's consent and must accept any assignment at any location. He must obey any decision of his or a superior party organization. He is expected to exude virtue, and in theory (although practice seems often to be the reverse) he should expect to be punished more severely than ordinary citizens for any infraction. Anything which can be interpreted as "antiparty action" may be cause of disciplinary sanctions. His private life is not private; the party may inquire into his affairs and require penitence for errors; contrariwise, the party may give comradely assistance if he

---

[24] *Partiinaia zhizn,* no. 5, March, 1969, p. 9.
[25] As is frankly stated (*Partiinaia zhizn,* no. 12, June, 1971, p. 43.).
[26] *Pravda,* January 16, 1971, p. 2.

is in trouble of any kind. Members are ideally responsible not only for themselves but for their comrades. "It is necessary to maintain constant party control over every Communist, regardless of the position which he occupies. It should not be bothersome, injurious to personal dignity and harmful to initiative, but comradely and principled. . . ."[27]

If one should stray, sanctions are first to be applied by the local committee, which may conduct a sort of trial before the assembled membership, to re-educate as well as to test the errant member and to enlighten others. If the case is grave, the Party Control Committee may reach down from the center to decide. The maximum penalty is expulsion from the party. Expulsion fairly well ends a man's career prospects, and the status of an ex-member is much worse than that of a nonmember. In recent years some 50–70,000 yearly have been expelled, the large majority apparently for nonpolitical misdoings, as drunkenness, bribetaking, misuse of state property, and the like. There are also reprimands of various degrees of severity which may go into the party book and become a permanent handicap to advancement. Moreover, any misstep, although it leads to no formal sanction, may cause an entry in the secret dossier which is kept on each member, like a military personnel record.

The best way to forestall trouble is the infusion of "party spirit, which long ago came to stand for all that is best in a person."[28] It is the duty of Communists not only to teach others but to learn, forever to raise their "ideological level." There must be no complacency, but the member should ever strive for ideological improvement, pondering by day and dreaming by night how better to fulfill the wishes of the party. Members should periodically give an accounting of their work to their party organization, expose themselves to comradely scrutiny, and deeply criticize themselves.

Few Communists can approach the ideal. But it is probable that many are convinced that unity is the key to political success if not survival and come to speak and think in terms not of "I" but "we," to abdicate autonomy of thought and to accept the guidance of the leadership. Relieved of moral and intellectual responsibility by the infallible party, they have only to believe in its mystique to find purpose and security. Their own power—and even the rank-and-file member is psychologically and materially privileged—rests on the whole system of party control. Adherence to its way and truth is the way of the ambitious, and the man who can adapt himself to the system of principled subordination can hope to enjoy the fruits of power as a manager of men. Although the apparatchik is humble toward superiors, he is powerful over his inferiors, a boss in his area. It is in his interest to support the system whereby, as the party is above the people, the apparatus manages the party, and each layer of the pyramid rules that on which it rests.

[27] *Pravda*, August 12, 1969.
[28] *Slovo o partii* (Izd. polit. lit.), Moscow, 1967, p. 7.

YOUTH AUXILIARY

The organization of youth is essential for the mobilization of young hands, for ideological training of the oncoming generation, and for the preparation and selection of new recruits for the party. It is a common feature of one-party states, and the Soviet youth program has some resemblance to those of Maoist China, Hitlerite Germany, and Fascist Italy.

It was not easy, however, to form a youth movement in the first months of the Soviet regime. For several years, membership grew slowly, approaching half a million in 1920. Only in the 1930's did the Komsomol (officially, "All-Union Leninist Communist League of Youth") become a truly "mass organization." Since then, it has grown to comprise about half of the eligible age bracket, fourteen to twenty-eight, or over twenty-seven million youths. Nearly everyone of suitable age can join if he desires. It represents a limited political commitment, from which one may drop out honorably or graduate to the party, if found worthy.

The Komsomol serves as apprenticeship for the party, whose organization it closely parallels, from local cells at work places or schools, with their committees and secretaries, through the regional conferences, committees, and buros, up to the big national congress, Central Committee, buro and Secretariat. The upper layers are professionals, who thereby become candidates for careers in the party apparatus. Elections through the Komsomol organization are handled in much the same way as in the party, with the significant difference that balloting in primary cell elections is by open show of hands only.[29] Girls comprise over two-fifths of the membership; but, as in the party, very few have higher positions.

The party rules (no. 63) state that, "The Komsomol works under the guidance of the Communist Party of the Soviet Union. The work of the local Komsomol organizations is directed and controlled by the corresponding republican, oblast, district, city, and county party organizations." The slight independence the Komsomol enjoyed in its first years has been eliminated. At the base, party organizations recommend Komsomol leaders; and the percentage of secretaries of primary Komsomol organizations who are party members grew from 14.7% in 1966 to 32.5% in 1970. The Komsomol apparatus is composed of party members paid by the party; more than 70% of delegates to the Komsomol Congress of 1970 were party members. Komsomol officials are exempt from the upper age limit. First Secretary Sergei Pavlov was forty-one when he was replaced in 1970 by Yevgenii Tiazhelnikov, aged forty-three. Individual party members are supposed to give the young people the continual benefit of their

---

[29] Allen Kassof, *The Soviet Youth Program* (Harvard University Press), Cambridge, Mass., 1965, p. 56.

political maturity; party men attend Komsomol meetings, and the two organizations often meet jointly. In 1956–1957 there were some stirrings of resistance, as many locals reportedly refused to accept candidates handed down from above and it was sometimes necessary to hold repeated elections. Discipline was reimposed, however, and the organization seemingly returned to full conformity; it did not even share visibly the limited liberalization of 1958–1965. Its advantage is monopoly; its great difficulty, to judge from complaints in the Soviet press, is boredom and apathy as members fail to attend and pay dues.

The Komsomol has served as a valuable reserve of volunteer labor. In the First Five-Year Plan, many thousands of dedicated youths tackled projects under the most difficult conditions. The last undertaking which seems to have aroused much enthusiasm was Khrushchev's Virgin Lands program in 1956–1957. Recently, however, the Komsomol was reported to be patronizing one hundred major industrial or construction projects, to which it contributed 300,000 volunteers.[30] Everywhere, Komsomol members are supposed to be an example in voluntary work and even more in their steady devotion to their jobs in field or factory.

The more important task of the Komsomol seems to be educational-political. It carries on many lectures, seminars, inspirational entertainments, and so forth, not only for its own members, who are generally supposed to participate, but for nonaffiliated youth and others. It works with military authorities in military training, paramilitary activities, and indoctrination. Komsomol groups in industry and agriculture cooperate with party and trade union organizations to raise production. The Komsomols provide most recruits for the volunteer police helpers; and they, or the activists among them, regard themselves as guardians of Soviet orthodoxy and morality.[31] If girls dress immodestly (limits of modesty being rather narrow) or if boys drink too much, the Komsomol may take them in hand, whether they are members or not. The Komsomol seems to regard itself as custodian of the interests of all young workers. When a group of Lithuanian workers got together a few hundred rubles and planned to give themselves a trip to the Baltic shore, the Komsomol local demanded indignantly to share in deciding how the money should be used.[32]

The role of the Komsomol is more critical in higher education than in production because the more educated are politically more important and more exposed to subversive ideas. Membership in the Komsomol and its recommendation are practically requisite for admission to a higher institution. The student is subject to Komsomol jurisdiction; if he falls foul of it, he may suffer in career prospects or even see his education truncated.

[30] *Partiinaia zhizn*, no. 19, October, 1970, p. 17.
[31] There may be some relation between the Komsomol and the secret police. Shelepin, Semichastny, and Andropov, the last three police bosses, all graduated from Komsomol to security leadership.
[32] *Izvestia*, August 28, 1969; *Current Digest of the Soviet Press*, vol. 21, no. 35, p. 23.

The Komsomol provides guidance for the school children, "Young Pioneers," even as the party leads the youth. Komsomol members are leaders of Pioneer brigades, which normally include nearly all children in school classes of ages ten to fifteen. The chief effort is directed toward moulding the psychology of the future Soviet citizen. Kept busy with wholesome social activities, from games to volunteer jobs, to camps and military games and training, the Pioneers should learn to regard themselves primarily as members of a collective and ultimately of the world Communist movement. In preparation for Soviet citizenship, they learn to draw up plans for group activity, allot responsibility for fulfillment, and verify results.[33]

WORK OF THE PARTY

The Communist Party is a supergovernment in a polity not of executive, legislative, and judicial powers, but of party and its instruments. The government formally based on the soviets is merely one of the means, along with the economic administration, the trade unions, and other organizations, whereby the party carries out its mission of rule. Responsible for social and political cohesion, the party has made itself into a governing elite beyond Western conceptions. The rationalization of the party's status is that it represents the rightfully ruling proletariat, or sometimes that it embodies the true interests of all Soviet society, in which no legitimate conflicting interests can be acknowledged. It might be contended, in semi-Marxist logic, that there is no room for competing parties because one group controls the entire economy.

Opposition to the party has always been held to amount to opposition to the people, or treason; and the rule of the party has been uncontested since it was consolidated shortly after the Revolution. After Stalin mastered the party, he seems to have felt distrustful of it and sought to balance it with the administrative apparatus, the police, and the army, which he managed and coordinated through the party secretariat and his personal staff. But he always upheld the theoretical supremacy of the party and governed in its name.

For a year and a half after Stalin, Malenkov seemed, as Chairman of the Council of Ministers, to be the leading maker of policy, an indication of the importance of the governmental apparatus in its own right. But if the quarrel between Malenkov and Khrushchev was in part a contest between governmental and party bureaucracies, the latter won. Khrushchev, relying entirely on the party, restored whatever it had lost of its primacy. Since Khrushchev and especially after 1967 there has been a further elevation of the party, seen more than ever as omnicompetent guide of government, economy, and culture. "It

[33] Kassof, *Soviet Youth*, furnishes the most detailed information on the Pioneers as on the Komsomol.

[the Communist Party] directs the activity of all governmental and social organizations for the building of communism, defines their place and role in this task, organizes the Soviet people and carries out the education of the masses."[34]
As embodiment of Soviet patriotism, personified in solemn rituals, it is held the instrument of historical inevitability, indispensable to the existence of the Soviet state. It is the unconditional trustee of Soviet society. Its guiding role is not to wither, but to expand as the Soviet Union comes nearer the perfect state of communism; the strengthening of the party is decisive for the building of the communist utopia.[35]

Article 126 of the Soviet constitution states that "the most active and politically conscious citizens in the ranks of the working class, working peasants, and working intelligentsia voluntarily unite in the Communist Party of the Soviet Union, which is the vanguard of the toilers in their struggle to build Communist society and is the guiding nucleus of all organizations of the toilers, both social and state." Similarly, the party rules state in the preamble that the party is "the leading and guiding force of Soviet society." The party should bind all peoples and sectors of Soviet society for a single, albeit vague purpose fixed by itself. To fulfill this duty, the party sets policies and supervises their administration; it leads practically all permitted organizations (the chief exception being some religious groups); it selects responsible personnel in all fields; it propagates ideology and makes, or tries to make, morality; it stands at the head of the world Communist movement. It concerns itself with everything from the Near East to literature, milk production, and bus service.

The party does not merely direct the government and other organizations at the top; it supervises in the republic, province, county, city, village, and enterprise. Paralleling the formal state, the party organization exerts pressure at all levels. This sophisticated and well-engineered scheme reduces to the minimum the de facto independence of large bureaucratic organizations. Political leaders elsewhere have to rely on the compliance of a probably sluggish governmental apparatus to carry out their decrees, and they may watch helplessly as their purposes are watered down by indifference and inertia. Soviet leaders have their own apparatus, unburdened by direct administrative duties, to see to it that their will is done at every stage; if in fact inertia and bureaucratic resistance creep into the Soviet system, this shows that the best political engineering is imperfect.

The Soviet rulership thus has a control agency composed of men dedicated to party rule, whose careers depend upon success in executing its will, and whose powers are indefinite. They should be exempt from the vices of the administrators as they are from responsibilities. Their prime qualification is dedication to the ideological world view which gives the party the special

[34] *Partiinaia zhizn*, no. 13, July 1970, p. 14.
[35] *Partiinoe stroitelstvo* (Izd. Mysl), Moscow, 1968, p. 4.

mission of management and control. This may be the greatest reason why the Soviet Union has managed thus far to keep within bounds the official corruption which cursed the tsarist regime.

In all branches and at all levels, men should heed the voice of the party more than that of their administrative superiors. The first secretary is the boss of his district and is sometimes referred to as such in Soviet writing; a Soviet paper refers to "The party worker, the manager of the collective."[36] The provincial party organization concerns itself with everything in its area except the armed forces, for which there is a separate and especially elaborate system of control. "The raion committee answers for everything in its raion."[37] It is taken for granted that the party, the only place in which political talent should find expression, has the last word on anything political, and almost anything is political in the Soviet system.

Party Action

The means by which the party controls Soviet society are much like those by which the center controls the party. It preferentially persuades rather than coerces, takes advantage of the monopoly of organization and political leadership, and preserves appearances of consent while assuring conformity. The party organization, while it firmly upholds its authority, should avoid simple dictation and take wishes into account so far as compatible with party policy. Party leaders receive lengthy instructions for handling people; they should be accessible, politely modest, and responsive to complaints and reasonable requests. Sternness should be balanced with comradeliness, and inexorable demands should be explained by superior knowledge and judiciously stated to appeal to ideals. Local bodies and organizations should be taught to look to the party for guidance of their own volition.

The party has a monopoly of purposeful organization. It is illicit even for a handful of people to meet regularly without a very good excuse, and no organization is permitted except as specifically authorized by competent authority. Even chess clubs and pensioners' recreational societies are subject to strict party control. In any organization there should be some party members, and these (being three or more) form a party fraction. The party fraction (the only allowable subgrouping of the membership) is responsible for the guidance of the organization. Unless very small, the party fraction probably has a secretary, never the formal head of the organization, who answers to a party body.

To monopoly of organization is added control of personnel. A large part of the business of the party at all levels is the education, selection and

---

[36] *Selskaia zhizn*, December 10, 1968.
[37] *Pravda*, August 23, 1969.

posting of cadres. Each party body has a list of positions in government and the economy for which it is responsible, to which it may name personnel or for which its assent is required. This list, called the *nomenklatura*, is short for local bodies but includes many thousands of positions for higher ones; it is a vast field of patronage but it carries responsibility if nominees turn out badly. Party organizations are to keep their eye on other appointments of importance, even though not on the *nomenklatura*, and call attention to deficiencies. Thus all important careers, except some specialties, are tied practically into a single service by the *nomenklatura*; even assignments of gang leaders on farms are party business. The party has almost complete control of the channels through which a Soviet citizen can advance himself materially or achieve anything of recognized significance.

Directions come down in various ways. Party men are guided by the broader teachings of ideology and the pronouncements of high figures. There are also instructions of the Central Committee, both public and confidential. This body sometimes addresses itself to problems in general terms, underlining a preoccupation of the moment, for example directing attention to the raising of the ideological level, innovation in production methods, or efficiency of retail trade. Ordinary business goes through the departments attached to committees at all levels, which act as reporters, checkers, and agencies of liaison, allocating cadres, keeping dossiers, and inspecting compliance. They work with official and unofficial bodies at their own and inferior levels, with lower party bodies, and the specialized departments of the latter. They take on trained specialists to facilitate control of the professionals with whom they have to deal. At the lower levels, city and county (raion) or below, they are assisted by large numbers of volunteer and spare time inspectors. To check malfeasance, the Party Control Committee reaches down from the Central Committee, with powers to look into anything and to discipline not only party but governmental personnel.

As Lenin stated in *What is to Be Done*, in 1902, "The movement must be led by the smallest possible number of the most similar groups of tried and experienced professional revolutionaries. There must be engaged in the movement the largest possible number of the most varied groups of the proletariat (and other classes of the people). . . ." One need only substitute "state" or "entire society" for "movement," and "politicians" for "revolutionaries," and one has the present essence: the broadest possible control of as many as possible by a nucleus as small, and hence reliable, as possible. Stalin looked mechanically to

the "transmission belts," the "levers," and the "directing force" which in their totality constitute "the system of the dictatorship of the proletariat" (Lenin) and with the help of which the dictatorship of the proletariat is accomplished. . . . To sum up: the *trade unions*, as the mass organization of the proletariat, linking the Party with the class primarily in the sphere of production; the *Soviets*, as the mass organization of the working people, linking the Party with the latter primarily in the sphere of state administration; the *cooperatives*, as the mass organization mainly of the peasantry, linking the Party with the peasant masses primarily in the economic sphere, in the sphere of drawing the peasantry into the work of socialist construction; the *Youth League*, as the mass organization of young workers and peasants. . . ."[38]

Khrushchev carried the idea further by proposing more use of "mass organizations" centered on and directed by the party. Khrushchev also stressed implementation of the party will by "activist" volunteer groups, politically forward citizens working with party cells and commissions. Adding to party capacities without sharing power, the activists lack any larger organization and so have not even the small potential of trade unions or national sport organizations to develop a will of their own. They were said to number in 1969 over twenty-five million.

Managing the Economy

Not only does the party fix goals and set the main outlines of national policy, including economic plans; it oversees administration at all levels. Party leaders check and coordinate institutions in their area. Control of media of information is of special importance; party committees at various levels have direct charge of leading newspapers and journals and give instructions to others. "[The party] guides all the creative work of the Soviet people, gives it an organized, planned, scientific character."[39] The party watches over the selection of entrants to higher education, their instruction, and the administration of the schools; a party group may veto a university administrative decision. When boarding schools in Kirghizia are poorly organized, first the party and only secondarily the ministry are called upon to attend them. Play needs party guidance: "Practice confirms the utility of party control over the plans for development of sports and their quality."[40] No field is too technical: "The party and the government pay great attention to the prevention of cancer. . . ."[41]

But much the greatest preoccupation of the party, to judge from the huge volume of instructions, criticisms, and comments, is the overseeing of industry and agriculture. "The chief concern of the party is the further advancement of the national economy,"[42] and "Material production is the chief

---

[38] J. V. Stalin, *Works*, vol. 8, Foreign Language Publishing House, Moscow, 1954, p. 37.
[39] *Partiinoe stroitelstvo*, p. 6.
[40] *Pravda*, November 16, 1969.
[41] *Pravda*, September 3, 1969.
[42] *Pravda*, April 26, 1970.

area of application of the forces of party organizations."[43] Khrushchev's splitting of the party up to oblast level into agricultural and industrial sections shows the primacy of this preoccupation. The party rules (no. 60) specifically confer appropriate authority: "Primary party organizations of industrial plants and trading establishments, state farms, collective farms, design and drafting agencies, and research institutes directly concerned with production have the right to control the work of the administration."

The party secretary, although often inconspicuous, is probably the real boss in the factory. Not burdened with detail, he is in a better position to observe and criticize results. The party has most to say about personnel, as jobs of different importance are in the purview of higher or lower party authorities, although the administration has formal responsibility. In one case, a chief of a geological party in Siberia had trouble with an alcoholic subordinate. The matter was taken up not with the superior economic administrator but with the party, which made the decision; in this and other ways, it seemed clear that the supervisor was responsible primarily to the local secretary.[44] If a manager comes into conflict with the party body at his level, he appeals ordinarily, it would seem, not to his ministry but to the next higher party body.

For better control, the office of manager is not only kept separate from that of party secretary, but they must not be in any way related nor be close friends. The secretary is not permitted to receive any emolument from the enterprise. Even his salary as a worker goes through the party; the enterprise pays the party, which pays the secretary.[45]

The party is to control but not supplant administration; and there has been a great deal of difficulty in determining where the line is to be drawn. At times, especially in Stalin's later years, there was a tendency to give more latitude to the administrators and to restrict the party to general supervision and indoctrination; recently, on the other hand, the party has been encouraged to go more into specifics, which requires an increasing number of party leaders to have technical qualifications.

The main emphasis is on general guidance. The party is to concern itself particularly with morale, nonmaterial incentives, and organization of work. As an article in *Pravda* has it, "We Communists have to work with people, with means of acting on human character, on people's moods and their capacity for initiative. You can't get along here with standardized norms and ready-made recipes. This 'technology' is decidedly complex."[46] The party is also to be the

[43] *Partiinaia zhizn*, no. 12, June, 1971, p. 30.

[44] *Pravda*, September 28, 1969.

[45] A. Avtorkhanov, *The Communist Party Apparatus* (Henry Regnery Co.), Chicago, 1966, p. 132.·

[46] August 23, 1969.

generator of ideas. When the "liberal" journal *Novyi mir* ventured to credit mathematical economists with the ideas leading to the economic reform of 1965, the economics journal *Voprosy ekonomiki* (no. 4, 1969) sternly corrected it: the party was real creator and inspirer.

The rule of the party is at least as complete and direct in agriculture. Nearly all collective farm chairmen are party members and, although nominally elected, are chosen by the party and removed by it if deficient.[47] In kolkhozes, the party office is responsible even for appointments to brigade leader. The party secretary or the raion instructor may have more to say about humdrum work assignments than the farm chairman; they have complete say-so as to the employment of party members.[48] The party looks to the quality of production and the technical training of farm workers. "If the state farm could get over the difficulties, it was only because the raion party committee closely followed the implementation of the economic experiment and gave timely assistance. Committee workers came often to the farm, and not only on visits but to go deeply into one or another question, to decide measures to be taken. . . ."[49] If milk production goes up, "Such is the effect of party guidance of production!"[50]

Governing the Government

As in the management of the economy, the party acts as a sort of supergovernment, pronouncing basic policy and taking leadership so far as it sees fit. In foreign affairs, for example, Brezhnev has emerged as principal spokesman and negotiator without benefit of governmental position, and in his state visits abroad he had been accompanied mostly by party rather than foreign ministry officials. But the party also controls the administrative apparatus at all levels. By the party rules as amended in 1971, party organizations in governmental agencies have approximately the same rights of control as over productive enterprises. They should supervise, strengthen discipline, combat bureaucratism, observe and report on shortcomings, coordinate, select personnel, educate and indoctrinate, advise, and cut red tape. A city party committee typically prods bureaucrats to put in utilities, helps a parent get his child in a nursery, hears complaints of discrimination, etc.[51] The party enjoys the advantage over the government as over productive enterprises of dealing with longer-range and general affairs while remaining free of detailed administrative burdens. The party

---

[47] *Pravda*, July 18, 1971, p. 3.
[48] *Partiinaia zhizn*, no. 11, June, 1969, p. 49.
[49] *Pravda*, September 4, 1969.
[50] *Pravda*, July 7, 1971, p. 1.
[51] *Partiinaia zhizn*, no. 4, February, 1970, p. 43.

is frankly exempt from state law,[52] but it makes law, "obliging" party and government workers to prescribed actions, sometimes mentioning its decrees as having full legal force. While ministries are often and sometimes bitterly criticized, party organs are seldom subject to attack, and party policy never. All higher government officials are party members and so under party discipline, as are nearly all judges, army officers, and probably all or nearly all police.[53]

Demarcation between party and government is indistinct. The Central Committee approves the Five-Year Plan and "authorizes" the Council of Ministers to proceed with it, and the Central Committee approves the budget before the Supreme Soviet goes through the motions. Control Commissions carry out party as well as formally state policy; there are joint party-state decrees at all levels; some enterprises formally pertain to both state and party, as newspapers that are organs at once of the republican or regional central committee and the council of ministers. But the party is the only unified organization, and it seems clear that each ministry is more under the aegis of the corresponding department of the Central Committee than under the Council of Ministers. Ministries, like army, press, courts, etc., in theory have no will or policy of their own. Local party bodies are apt to control local government so closely as practically to take its place. In 1939, the Central Committee secretary in charge of naval affairs was clearly superior to the nominal head of the branch, with whom he discussed policies in considerable detail.[54] The nominal legislative bodies or soviets at various levels are entirely chosen and managed by the party.

THE PARTY AND GROUP INTERESTS

The directing role of the party does not preclude asking about other and differently based influences acting on or through the party to shape decision-making. The American Congress passes laws, but the analyst wishes to know who has lobbied for or against, and what civic, social, or perhaps especially economic interests are served thereby. The party is to a certain extent a representative body. People in all professions and categories belong to it; and they do not cease to be industrial managers, army officers, writers, etc., when

[52] "The situation of the party as political organization and nucleus of all organizations of the toilers excludes the possibility of legal regulation by the government of concrete functions of the party organs and organizations, of forms and methods of party leadership." (G. B. Barabash in *Sovetskoe gosudarstvennoe pravo* [Izd. jurid. lit.], Moscow, 1967, pp. 148–149.)

[53] See T. H. Rigby, *Communist Party Membership in the USSR 1917–1967* (Princeton University Press), Princeton, N. J., 1968, p. 449, for information on party membership in various professions and categories.

[54] S. Bialer, ed., *Stalin and His Generals*, p. 96.

they acquire a party book. It is hence desirable, perhaps indispensable, for the understanding of Soviet policy formation to learn as much as possible of basic influences which doubtless go into the thinking of the party, probably suggesting some policies and advocating, altering, or impeding others.

For this reason, the study of group tendencies in the Soviet Union, their divergences, indications of autonomy, and possible influence has attracted much attention.[55] The study, however, is difficult and often baffling. Differing positions on major policies are usually expressed covertly and mildly, only in terms of different priorities and emphases, perhaps by indirection, as a trend may be berated in vague terms. Since important figures may not be overtly criticized, they are attacked with a subtlety which makes the message difficult to decipher. Who are the "certain circles" or "some people" who may be needled for ideological shortcomings? Content analyses of press organs show different slants, but it is seldom clear how much this may be due to differing outlooks and how much to the fact that the various organs speak to different audiences. For example, the army paper, *Krasnaia zvezda*, shows no enthusiasm for disarmament talks. If military men are not ardent for them, one must also remember that there is no reason to trouble soldiers with such an uninspiring topic. On the other hand, army leaders may have much more divergent views than they are permitted to express.

No group can present itself frankly as a corporate entity seeking support or concessions for itself; all must claim to express the public interest, of which the party is recognized guardian. It is a matter of judgment whether or to what extent one thinks of institutional groups (as the police), occupational categories (as industrial managers or scientists), or agglomerations that may be formed over broad issues (as "liberals" or "hardliners" in the Kremlin[56]). Usually, in fact, merely personal followings may be more evident than these,[57] as adherents of Brezhnev or Podgorny. Alignments are somewhat uncertain; for years, Brezhnev seemed to stand more for heavy industry and Kosygin for consumer goods; but their positions at the Twenty-Fourth Congress were slightly reversed.

In some ways, the party apparatus may stand—or stood, in the first years after Stalin—in opposition to the state bureaucracy; perhaps in more ways, divisions within the two sectors outweigh the division between them. At best, there are shadings of opinion and fluid groupings. There have been hints of

---

[55] A selection of the literature is given by H. G. Skilling and F. Griffith, eds., *Interest Groups in Soviet Politics* (Princeton University Press), Princeton, 1969.

[56] Philip D. Stewart, "Soviet Interest Groups," *World Politics*, vol. XXII, no. 1, October, 1969.

[57] T. H. Rigby in Fleron, ed., *Communist Studies and the Social Sciences* (Rand McNally and Co.), Chicago, 1968, p. 24.

opposition within the party apparatus between the secretaries who are purely party men and those charged with relations outside the party. If most writers on economics take the expectable position of favoring latitude of managerial decision-making, there are others to insist on the primacy of planning and party direction. The army is perhaps better prepared organizationally to form a coherent group, but the ground forces diverge from the rocket forces, the technicians from the line officers, and the political from the operational officers.[58] The secret services have played an important part in the past and may, for all the outside world knows, have a large role in policy formation behind the scenes today. There is apparently rivalry between the civilian security forces (KGB) and military intelligence. In 1970, the Ukrainian party organization tried to cover up a bribery scandal which the Ministry of the Interior was trying to expose.[59]

Experts and specialists play an increasing role in the modernizing Soviet economy, and they have in recent years been able to speak out on issues concerning which the party has not fixed a position. There have been something like debates on educational reform, economic planning, agricultural organization, and legal reform. Institutions or groups obviously can forward their own interests. Industrial interests have at least partly frustrated the official policy of restricting the growth of the biggest cities. It appears that the profitability of tobacco and alcoholic beverages has a good deal to do with their large-scale use in the Soviet Union as in the United States. From 1960 to 1970 tobacco consumption per capita nearly doubled, according to a Soviet paper.[60] Although the party conducts antiliquor campaigns to check absenteeism and crime, retail stores push the sale of vodka, and consumption steadily grows.[61] When youth cafes were set up in 1961 to get young people off the streets, the Ministry of Trade turned them into liquor outlets. *Pravda* praises good wine like potable sunshine, "the sun in a glass."[62] A different example was the outcry raised in 1969 by scientists and lovers of nature over a paper mill which would have seriously polluted Lake Baikal and destroyed much of its unique biota. Authorities responded with stringent conservationist measures. There has been disagreement between those interested in electric power and those concerned with the flooding of useful land by hydroelectric projects; the ministers of power and agriculture stressed opposite sides of the question in speeches at the Twenty-Fourth Congress.

It is to be assumed that party bodies make policies, at least when no broad ("ideological") issues intervene, with consideration of who is for and who is against; but it will have no other body in a position to exert competitive

[58] Roman Kolkowicz, *The Soviet Military and the Communist Party* (Princeton University Press), Princeton, 1967.

[59] *Radio Liberty Dispatch*, February 2, 1971.

[60] *Literaturnaia gazeta*, August 18, 1971, p. 13.

[61] Cf. David E. Powell, "Alcoholism in the USSR," *Survey*, vol. 16, no. 1, Winter, 1971.

[62] November 20, 1970, p. 6.

political pressure. It seeks to impose a fusion of all interests by its penetration and direction of all organizations and particularly by its control of staffing through the *nomenklatura*. It alone can represent unity of policy and philosophy, and those who are not prepared to accept this are ineligible for positions of influence. Communication between persons who might join in support of a certain position is irregular and unorganized; anything like a faction is as prohibited outside the party as it is within. The influence of any group is the more restricted because the party oligarchy cannot tolerate any of its members looking outside the party for support and so making himself the spokesman of an interest.

If outsiders have authority, it is mostly because they are skilled and valuable. Their relation to the party is of consultation, not bargaining. In return for their services, they are given material advantages but not freedom or influence, much as Lenin paid bourgeois specialists more than party men even while surrounding them with suspicion, and Stalin overrewarded his experts while terrorizing them. The relation is like that of a home-builder to his architect. The builder picks the professional, sets the specifications, and heeds or disregards his recommendations as he will. But because he wants a proper house, much decision-making necessarily rests with the expert. Moreover, the builder knows that his architect will work better if he is treated with consideration and heard with attention even though his recommendations may not be fully accepted.

The party controls allocations, decides which experts are to speak, requires that their criticism be in terms of helpfulness to the general or party cause, and takes their advice so far as it pleases. Any special claims to authority are to be made only through the party, on which everything centers. The most influential must be those whose work is close to that of the party itself, the military, heads of government departments, trade unions, Komsomol and such semipolitical organizations, and managers of major industries; purely technical or professional specialists, as engineers, scientists, teachers, or artists, come far behind.[63] The party strives also to keep decision-making to itself by bringing into its higher ranks experts highly dedicated to party purposes. Of nine secretaries of the Central Committee, seven have a technical background.

Organizations grow up and develop some institutional momentum from the difficulties of planning and controlling everything from a single center. The party and state must increasingly secure the cooperation of well educated and intelligent men trained for special work; this means both emphasis on indoctrination and permitting and heeding discussion. In Stalin's day, the party made foolish errors trying to direct science; it no longer does so, although it stresses the political education of scientists. Party interference may recede in other areas if the technological level continues to rise and political dynamism

---

[63] Stewart, op. cit., p. viii.

declines. Much depends upon the unity of the central elite. In a succession crisis or in case of disagreement within top party circles, outside groups can hope to assert themselves. Each real public debate permitted has reflected a division within the upper circle. For example, Khrushchev looked to outside support for his educational reforms, against the resistance within the party elite to his democratizing changes.

If the evolution of the Soviet state proceeds like that of other authoritarian systems, it is likely that the ability of the center to reach and enforce decisions will decline gradually, even apart from presumptive effects of technology. The apparatus grows older, stiffer, and less responsive; vested interests develop and learn covertly to defend themselves. If the party has less will of its own, it becomes more of a mediator and aggregator of different interests, speaking less for itself and more for others who speak through it. But the divergencies emerging in Soviet society may at best be comparable to the self-will of various departments within the government of the United States; few sectors of the Soviet system seem to have nearly as much autonomy of the Politburo as the State Department has of the American president, who is legally its master.

No political structure, however despotic, is really monolithic. There are always conflicting wills behind the scenes. The despot rarely sees his orders carried out in quite the way he would like; and he is always dependent upon his apparatus, often at its mercy. Even within armies, there are organizational and personal frictions. Under the tyranny usually recalled as the model of totalitarianism, Hitler's Third Reich (not to speak of such loose-jointed regimes as those of Mussolini or Franco), there was much more evidence of group autonomy than in the Soviet Union today. Elite groups contested bitterly, while Hitler acted as supreme arbiter, dependent on the bureaucratic structure, seldom trying to overrule the majority of his inferiors.[64]

Like any political system, the Soviet must reconcile and adjudicate a multitude of interests. The most remarkable political fact about the Soviet system is the degree to which Lenin's party has been able, by purposeful organization and ideological commitment, to minimize the ability of any group to press for its own policies. "It would be a profound mistake to suppose that such exceptional harmony in the coordination of different complex aspects of social existence, which any bourgeois government might envy, comes of itself. It is the result of the titanic organizational work of the Communist Party, based on the great ideas of Marxism-Leninism."[65] Much depends upon how effectively it can maintain the present degree of harmony.

---

[64] Edward N. Peterson, *The Limits of Hitler's Power* (Princeton University Press), Princeton, 1969.

[65] A. Aimbetov et al., *Problemy sovershenstvovaniia organizatsii i deiatelnosti mestnykh sovetov* (Izd. Nauka), Alma Ata, 1967, p. 87.

READINGS

A. Avtorkhanov, *The Communist Party Apparatus* (Henry Regnery Co.), Chicago, 1966.

A. Denisov and M. Kirichenko, *Soviet State Law* (Foreign Languages Publishing House), Moscow, 1960.

Ralph T. Fisher, *Pattern for Soviet Youth: a Study of the Congresses of the Komsomol, 1918–1954* (Columbia University Press), New York, 1959.

Michael P. Gehlen, *The Communist Party of the Soviet Union* (Indiana University Press), Bloomington, Ind., 1969.

Allen Kassof, *The Soviet Youth Program* (Harvard University Press), Cambridge, Mass., 1965.

Partiinoe stroitel'stvo (Izd. "Mysl"), Moscow, 1968.

John S. Reshetar, *A Concise History of the Communist Party of the Soviet Union* (Praeger), New York, 1964.

Leonard Schapiro, *The Communist Party of the Soviet Union*, 2nd ed. (Random House), New York, 1970.

Slovo o partii (Izd. polit. lit.), Moscow, 1967.

Spravochnik partiinogo rabotnika (Handbook of the Party Worker), 7th ed., Moscow, 1968.

7. Governmental Structure

The Soviet government is not clearly bounded. It includes the apparatus of civilian order, the power which conducts foreign relations and defense, makes rules and punishes for their infraction, and carries on through ministries and departments of state the functions ordinarily filled by governments. However, the greatest activity of the Soviet government, administration of the economy, is managed differently and separately from regular civil functions. Moreover, the armed forces, security police, courts, and economic ministries are tied together only by common responsibility to the party. The system of pseudolegislative bodies, the soviets, also forms a separate branch which intermeshes with the administration to some extent, especially on the local level, but which has no real relation to rule-making and which is also an instrument of the party. On the other hand, the deciding of significant policy is kept in the hands of the formally nongovernmental party. To further complicate the picture, party and government-administrative spheres and personnel overlap. Various other organizations, as the trade unions and Komsomol, perform official duties. The former, notably, administer the social security system. It is likewise unclear where a line can be drawn between party policy and regular law.

Some of this fuzziness results from the fact that the party's control leaves no clear sphere for the state. In part, however, it derives from the fact that the revolutionaries of 1917 assumed that they came not to reform the state but to abolish it. Lenin spoke of "dictatorship of the proletariat" but (except in the naively anarchistic views of *State and Revolution*) he did not spell out what this meant in terms of institutions. When the Bolsheviks undertook to set up an

189

administrative apparatus, they claimed that their government was essentially different from that of earlier states because of its "class content." Its theoretical basis was the system of more or less proletarian councils, in Russian, "soviets," which sprang up in the vacuum caused by the collapse of tsardom. Lenin envisioned working people gathering briefly to vote on the right course of action, and going back to their jobs. This would imply leaving the real business of government to men who were in a position to devote full time to it; and there was never much prospect of the assembled proletarians deciding very much.

From the very first, an executive committee took over most of the business of the Petrograd Soviet and an inner circle took over the direction of the executive committee. The Congress of Soviets to which Lenin handed power was sent home after endorsement of the new regime and its initial proclamations. Subsequently, as the Soviet government gained strength, it reduced the powers of soviets, local and regional as well as central, to triviality or fiction. It also looked very much as if the old bureaucratic apparatus had revived, with ministries (named "commissariats" until after the Second World War), secret police, and centralized administration. The soviets remained, however, the formal basis for equating the will of the party with the will of the masses, the legitimating foundation for an amorphous administrative structure.

CONSTITUTION

It soon appeared desirable to formalize basic structures, so a constitution was provided for the Russian territories in 1918 and for the Soviet Union in 1923. In 1936, Stalin, consolidating his absolutism, had drawn up a new document supposedly reflecting the advances toward socialism. This "Stalinist" Constitution, as it was called during his lifetime, followed closely upon the line of its predecessors, except for certain democratic improvements, as direct elections to higher soviets. Khrushchev set up a ninety-seven-member commission in 1962 to draft a new constitution, but nothing was heard of it until after his ouster, when it was reconstituted with Brezhnev at the head. The subject seems to have been dropped since then.

In Marxist thinking, a constitution does not limit the power of the ruling classes but at best describes its exercise. In this light, the Soviet constitution reflects the principles of "dictatorship of the proletariat," proclaiming ostensible rights for the people without restraining the governing power. A considerable effort was made to give the constitution a democratic aura. It was made the subject of organized public discussion, in which over thirty-six million persons were said to have participated, although all of their deliberations led to only one amendment of substance. The constitution provides a complete framework for democratic government, with parliamentary bodies elected by universal secret ballot from bottom to top, governments responsible to these, and an impressive set of rights. The latter include freedom of speech and the press, inviolability of persons and of the home, and the like. Not merely "bourgeois" liberties are guaranteed; Soviet citizens have a constitutional right to work, to leisure, to maintenance in case of need, and to education. The right to freedom of the press goes much beyond Western constitutions: it is to be made effective for the masses by "placing at the disposal of the working people and their organizations printing presses, stocks of paper, public buildings, the streets, communication facilities, and other material requisites for the exercise of these rights." (Article 125)

This constitution was used to cast Stalin in the role of a great democrat, and many persons not only in Russia but abroad saw it as a statement of excellent intentions if not an actual realization of liberty and equality. Bukharin was associated with its drafting; shortly before he was blood purged, he seems to have believed that it would protect the people from dictatorship.[1] It was widely assumed that the right of public organizations to nominate candidates was seriously intended and thus that there would be freely contested elections, unknown in Soviet practice since 1917.

Careful reading of the document should have discouraged optimism. The right to work (Article 118) is balanced by the duty to work (Article 12), and such a general obligation as "to respect the rules of socialist behavior" (Article 130) can mean nearly anything. The definition of treason is broad. Political rights are for "organizations of the working people," and these are such organizations as are approved, permitted, and party controlled. The role of the Communist Party is specifically underlined (Article 126) as "the leading nucleus of all organizations of the working people, both public and state," and the party is given the privilege of making nominations for soviets.

The constitution is not taken very seriously. Its guarantees may be simply ignored; for example, kolkhoz land is frequently taken away despite the promise of perpetual possession (Article 8), and union republics have been deprived of territory without authorities bothering to register their consent. It is not judicially cited, although some literary defendants are reported to have brought it up (without helping their cases). It is easily amended by the Supreme Soviet, which has never cast a vote in opposition to any official proposal, and minor amendments (as of the lists of ministries) are made frequently. Despite this, the government has several times ignored the constitution in its measures, only later making the requisite amendments. Some provisions are propagandistic, as the unequivocal statement of the right of Soviet republics to secede (Article 17), any attempt to exercise which would be treason. There is a

---

[1] B. Nicolaevsky, *Power and the Soviet Elite* (Praeger), New York, 1965, p. 25.

fundamental contradiction between the ostensible status of the elected soviets as the legitimate source of power and the party's real use of the soviets as "transmission belts" for mobilizing and guiding the masses. The real constitution of the USSR is the well-understood supremacy of the party.

ELECTIONS

Soviet elections are exemplarily democratic in all ways except in failure to permit voters to elect, that is, to choose. Much is made over the equality of the franchise for races, sexes, and nationalities and of its universality; no Western nation can boast of participation approaching 100% as can the Soviet Union. They are also direct at all levels. But the fact that prior to 1936 elections were by show of hands and indirect,[2] and that certain classes were discriminated against, indicates at least a fear at that time that elections might have some practical effect; if Stalin made them direct and equal, and also formally secret, it meant that he feared no complications from them.

Elections are held every four years for supreme soviets (of the Soviet Union and constituent republics), every two years for local soviets. There is no legal reason that these should not be real contests, and the instructions on the ballot imply a plurality of candidates: "Leave on the ballot paper the name of ONE candidate for whom you vote, cross out the remainder." Soviet authors state, "As for the bourgeois propagandists' allegation that the Soviet electoral system permits only one candidate in each constituency, it is the result of either ignorance or deliberate slander."[3] However, as a more candid source puts it, "The party directs social organizations and toilers' collectives in the nomination for deputy of worthy workers, collective farmers, and members of the intelligentsia, in the careful consideration of candidacies."[4] The party authorities at each level sieve candidates and decide on the nominee in the single-member districts. He is then presented to a nomination meeting of some organization, as a trade union, perhaps open to the public. The nomination and all motions related to it are normally approved unanimously. It is possible sometimes, especially in villages, that the suggested candidate proves so unpopular that he is withdrawn, but information is lacking. It was formerly customary to nominate several candidates, all but one of whom would withdraw according to the suggestion of the party. Recently it seems that there has been

[2] Lenin, with some flexibility in the use of words, said indirect elections made the Soviet apparatus "more accessible" to workers and peasants. (*Works*, vol. 7, Moscow, 1946, p. 130.)

[3] A. Denisov and M. Kirichenko, *Soviet State Law*, Moscow, 1960, p. 362.

[4] *Gosudarstvennoe pravo SSSR* (Izd. iurid. lit.), Moscow, 1967, p. 156.

only one nomination per district, except that high leaders receive honorary nominations, all but one of which they decline. The electoral commissions, composed of representatives of organizations, are authorized to exclude candidates, but they have not had to exercise the power.

Probably the party tries to choose, as it says, "the best people," in the sense of getting men devoted to the cause, respected by their fellows, and qualified to carry out their duties of assisting mobilization, leadership, and relations with the public. Nomination is also an honor and reward for good work. Along with a few exemplary workers and farmers, persons of influence and importance are nominated, including party workers, managers, and commanders of the local garrison and of the police. While lower party bodies seem to pick candidates, higher authorities apparently give instructions as to the composition of soviets, the percentages of women (about one-fourth in the Supreme Soviet, two-fifths in local soviets), party members (three-quarters in the Supreme Soviet, about half in local soviets), Komsomol, government officials, manual workers (about a third by doubtless liberal definition), and peasants. That proportions of such categories are practically constant indicates that quotas are fixed, which is known to have been the case under Stalin.[5] About half of the two million deputies nominated each time are new.

As the party controls nominations, it might well permit two or more trusted individuals to contest the election. This would make it vastly more interesting, would be a challenge to the candidates, and would greatly improve the image of the Soviet Union without detracting from the power of the party. A Soviet explanation is that the presentation of candidates by the bloc of Communist and nonparty people is "a sort of constitutional custom, born of the moral-political unity of the Soviet people, based on the unlimited authority of the Communist Party in Soviet society but not stated in legal fashion."[6] As a trade union spokesman told an American student, "It would indicate a lack of confidence in the candidate if you were to nominate two men for the same post."[7] A more cogent reason is fear of the entering wedge of division. If two candidates vied for support, it would be difficult to prevent their touching upon real issues and exposing fissures in Soviet society. It would also encourage feelings of independence, because victorious candidates would owe their position not entirely to the party but in part to the voters.

The campaign consists of about two months of meetings, speeches, and exhortations. It is a time of speeches praising the Soviet system and the virtues of "socialist democracy" as against "bourgeois" elections, which are

---

[5] See M. Fainsod, *Smolensk under Soviet Rule*, p. 94.

[6] A. Aimbetov, M. Baimakonov, and M. Imashev, *Problemy sovershenstvovaniia organizatsii i deiatel'nosti mestnykh sovetov* (Izd. Nauka), Alma Ata, 1967, p. 81.

[7] Max E. Mote, *Soviet Local and Republic Elections* (Hoover Institution), Stanford, Calif., 1965, p. 29.

allegedly controlled by capitalists and marked by bribery, intimidation, and discrimination. Agitators try to talk individually with every voter, meetings are graced with entertainments, and scarce goods appear in the shops. The candidate meets the voters, listens to their requests, and promises to do his best. But the publicity is not for his benefit. The issue is not the merits of individuals but confidence in the party.

It is considered a privilege to vote; as a poet was inspired to sing,

> Today I vote
> For our wise government,
> For its great right
> affirmed in battle.
> I vote for our bright
> Life of labor,
> For the friendship of machines and plowlands. . . ."[8]

It is also an unofficial obligation to cast a ballot, and according to the record less than .05% fail to do so. Electoral helpers rouse people from their apartments and carry ballot boxes to the hospitals. Travellers passing through vote also, although they have no past or future contact with the candidate. Failure to appear at the polling place can be checked by the register. Contumacious refusal to participate may be cause for banishment.

There are no write-ins, and the voter has only to drop the ballot in a box. To cast a negative vote is rather conspicuous, an act of defiance without utility, but from one to four voters per thousand vote against the "Communist and nonparty" candidates according to Soviet figures.[9] The votes are to be counted by electoral commissions, but little is said and no show is made of the tallying of the ballots. The veracity of the results announced is questionable. The nationalities which Stalin deported for disloyalty, and the Baltic states immediately after sovietization in 1940, showed the same near-unanimous results as the rest of the country.

Voters in small villages and settlements may, however, sometimes make themselves felt. To be counted elected, a candidate must receive a majority of favorable ballots. Roughly one out of twenty thousand local candidates may be announced defeated. The number of defeated candidates rose from 102 in 1948 to 289 in 1961, but was down to 129 in 1967 and 101 (out of 2,165,168) in 1971.

The party may make a mistake, and a deputy can be recalled at any time—an outwardly democratic procedure which fosters conformity. The recall procedure is less democratic in form than the election. It is initiated by the

---

[8] *Literaturnaia gazeta*, June 17, 1970, p. 1.

[9] Cf. Everett M. Jacobs, "Soviet Local Elections," *Soviet Studies*, vol. 22, no. 1, July, 1970, pp. 61–76.

nominating organization, that is, by the party; and the decision is taken by open voting at irregularly organized meetings. About one deputy in four thousand suffers this indignity in a given year.[10]

Elections furnish "a powerful demonstration of the monolithic unity of the Communist Party and the people."[11] It is also desirable that all citizens engage in a symbolic act of support for the Soviet government, even though this is only dropping a piece of paper in a box. The elections also serve propagandistic purposes abroad, like the rights enshrined in the constitution and the pseudoparliamentary institutions. They conform to model democratic patterns in many ways, and they influence not only the naive but many intelligent persons looking for potential democracy in the Soviet system.

The elections may also be fairly convincing for many or most Soviet citizens. In capitalist countries, they are told, ordinary people have no means of putting forward their candidates, but in the Soviet Union the union nominates a good worker to the high legislative body. The people know very little of democracy; government is high and far, and to be consulted is a concession. Long indoctrinated with the necessity of unity, they are apt to regard the idea of competing parties with repugnance.

Some know enough of democratic practices, however, to see the Soviet nonelections as a humiliating comedy. It can only be confusing that the Soviet press reports the successes of Communist parties under capitalist tyranny, thereby making the Soviet variety seem more farcical. However, elections are part of the apparatus of the modern state, of which the Russians have borrowed appearances, and they cannot easily be renounced.

SUPREME SOVIET

The Great Hall of the Kremlin, where all major Soviet conclaves meet, is host to a colorful assembly of about 1500 Kirghiz herders, Ukrainian tractor drivers, Baltic factory workers, and their counterparts from all over Russia, along with staid managers and important party secretaries. In a bow to the federal pattern of Soviet administration, the Supreme Soviet is divided into two chambers. In the Soviet of the Union, seats are allocated on the basis of population; the other, the Soviet of Nationalities, is composed of thirty-two deputies from each of fifteen union republics, eleven from each "autonomous republic" within the Russian, Ukrainian and Georgian republics, five for each "autonomous region," and one per "national area." The two chambers often meet jointly. Constitutional provisions for resolving differences between them

[10] *Sovety deputatov trudiashchikhsia*, no. 5, May, 1969, p. 96.
[11] *Partiinaia zhizn*, no. 3, February, 1969, p. 7.

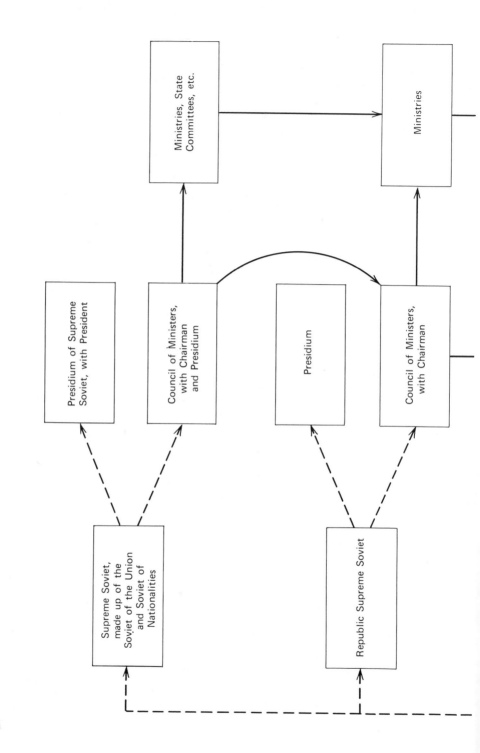

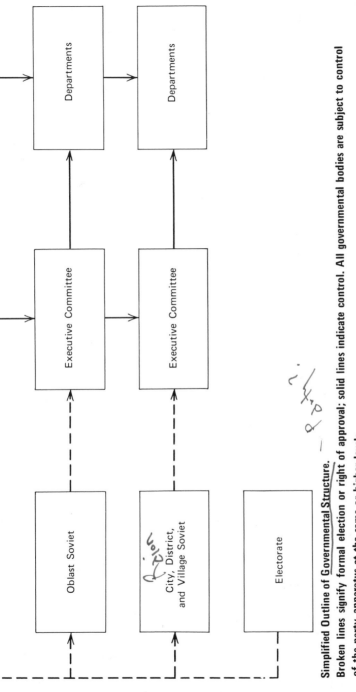

Simplified Outline of Governmental Structure.
Broken lines signify formal election or right of approval; solid lines indicate control. All governmental bodies are subject to control of the party apparatus at the same or higher levels.

Departments

Departments

Executive Committee

Executive Committee

Oblast Soviet

City, District, and Village Soviet

Electorate

197

are elaborate, but there has never been a hint of disagreement with official policy in either.

Of the 1970 Supreme Soviet 45% are classified as workers and peasants, 40% party and government officials, 10% "intelligentsia," and 5% military. A majority of deputies are new at each election, as the reward is passed out to the deserving. The deputies continue their regular employment in order to "live in the midst of the popular masses, know their cares and needs, express their interests."[12] In theory, the deputy is to be legislator and controller of the government (he has no office and no staff) and to carry the laws to the people while holding a full-time job. But there are no residence requirements and many deputies are probably nonresidents of their districts.

It is the formal function of the Supreme Soviet to approve the ministry, to ratify laws and decrees issued in its absence, to pass a few laws, and to approve the state budget. It is particularly the duty of the Supreme Soviet to sanction the economic plan and promote its fulfillment. Most time in session (about four hours daily in two yearly sessions totalling three to five days on the average) is given to hearing official reports. Deputies also report on the progress of their constituencies, praise the government and its proposals, and sometimes suggest minor changes or mildly criticize execution of programs. Questions may be used as a peg for government policy statements, especially in foreign affairs. Speeches of deputies last usually only two to five minutes, to permit twenty or thirty deputies to speak during the day. They are practically indistinguishable in style and substance. Criticisms seem as conformist as praise, speakers in the two houses making the same proposals at the same time, even in practically identical wording.[13] Votes, which are by raising hands, are always unanimous, no abstentions having been recorded. In 1955, the resignation of Malenkov was sprung as a surprise, but the deputies unanimously approved it without discussion.

Each chamber of the Supreme Soviet has some ten "standing commissions" for the budget and such fields as industry, agriculture, construction, culture, etc. These are selected from the membership, and are probably chaired by the party secretary charged with the corresponding subject. As inner circles meeting secretly, they are entrusted with more authority than the larger body. They meet more often and seem to have some role in the consideration of laws.

The apparently increased activity of the commissions in the Khrushchev era could be interpreted as a germ of parliamentary institutions. More attention was also paid to the Supreme Soviet after Stalin; it had been much in the shadows during his last years, meeting even more briefly and seldom. For a few years after Stalin, it met ten days yearly on the average. There

---

[12] *Selskaia zhizn,* December 5, 1969.
[13] See for example *Pravda*, December 18, 1969.

was a little questioning from the floor of the assembly, and some Soviet writers felt able to suggest that the people's representatives should have a slightly more active role. However, since 1954 the Supreme Soviet has been kept around only about half as long.

Even if the Supreme Soviet should be activated, unless electoral procedure were changed it would signify little more than another mode for the party to check the official bureaucracy. The Supreme Soviet is nonetheless a valuable means of liaison. It enables desk-bound Moscow leaders to meet and talk with persons from many walks of life and all parts of the country. It brings together worthy people to learn about and be inspired by official policy. Having been honored and informed, they are to carry the word back to the grass roots. The deputies' authority is raised by giving them sundry favors to take home, from a bridge to a new school or a statue of Lenin—although the deputy must think not of special privileges but of the needs of the whole country. It is also useful to solemnize certain laws, especially those touching very many people, like that on military training, by passage by the Supreme Soviet. This body thus serves like the tsarist Council of State to register decrees.

The other obvious purpose of the Supreme Soviet is to serve as democratic facade. It is felt necessary to have an institution to correspond to the claim that the state is servant of the people. Much publicized, even by foreign correspondents, the Supreme Soviet is referred to as the "Soviet Parliament" (despite Lenin's vehement rejection of parliamentary government). Soviet "parliamentarians" exchange visits with French Deputies and British M. P.'s. It is extremely useful to have something like the Supreme Soviet to support claims to represent the people. "Our parliament is much more democratic than the American Congress," Soviet citizens repeat, "because in the Congress there are no farmers or workers."

Giving the Supreme Soviet a little more leeway in consideration of policy would make it both more interesting and more effective as a simulacrum of democracy. Probably the party does not make this use of it, just as it does not enliven the elections, because of obsessive fears. No large consultative body is kept together long enough for members to establish personal relations and gain coherence as a group.

PRESIDIUM

The Presidium of the Supreme Soviet is theoretically an elected executive committee of that assembly but in practice is a separate organ. It serves to some extent as a linkage to the state apparatus of the union republics, as the chairman of each republic supreme soviet is on the Presidium, by custom although not by law. Most of the other twenty-one members are drawn from party posts and the leadership of sundry other organizations. It is also a dignified shelf for superannuated dignitaries, as civil war hero Budenny and ex-president Mikoyan. The Presidium by the constitution possesses most of the powers of the Supreme Soviet during the 98% of the time that the latter is not in session; that is, it passes laws, approves ministers, and the like. It names the electoral commission for elections to the Supreme Soviet after nominations by party and other bodies. It is the institutional peg for the standing commissions of the Supreme Soviet, which seem to have some functions in the absence of their parent body. The greater part of the published acts of the Presidium consists of the granting of honors and the making of diplomatic appointments. When, where, or whether it really meets remains a mystery.[14]

The President of the Presidium is the formal head of the Soviet state. Formerly the post was purely decorative, its duties being mostly handing out medals and receiving foreign ambassadors. It was filled for many years under Stalin by the only genuine peasant among Bolshevik leaders, Mikhail Kalinin, then by a trade union official, Nikolai Shvernik. For the last decade it has been occupied by solid political figures, Brezhnev, Mikoyan, and Podgorny. It has recently seemed to become more significant than ever, as Podgorny has apparently acquired second place in the Soviet hierarchy; but how it exercises political power is obscure.[15]

COUNCIL OF MINISTERS

The top of the state bureaucracy is the Council of Ministers, which includes heads of about fifty ministries, mostly economic (the number has fluctuated greatly), heads of a dozen State Committees, a few other government agencies or councils, and the fifteen chairmen of the councils of ministers of the republics. Perhaps this group of eighty or ninety men (and one woman, the Minister of Culture) never meets as a whole; but it has a presidium consisting of a chairman, two first vice chairmen, and nine or so ordinary vice chairmen. The Council of Ministers, or more probably its presidium, serves as something of an administrative coordinator. It is also the principal Soviet issuer of laws, or decrees with the force of law, somewhat contrary to the letter of the constitution, which grants it only a power of administrative regulation in implementation of laws.

[14] On its role, see: D. Richard Little, "Legislative Authority in the Soviet System," *Slavic Review*, vol. 30, no. 1, March, 1971, pp. 57–74.

[15] It may have been given more prestige to offset the authority of the Chairman of the Council of Ministers, whose administrative responsibilities might furnish a solider power base.

The presidency of the Council of Ministers is one of the most important posts in the Soviet system. Lenin occupied it rather than any specific party position, and Stalin assumed it as clouds gathered in 1941. It seemed briefly a sufficient base for Malenkov's leadership, and Khrushchev occupied it in addition to the First Secretaryship as soon as he was able to do so, in 1958. It is no solid power base, however. The present holder, Aleksei Kosygin, has tended to lose stature since assuming it.

Ministries are of two kinds. About half are "All-Union," operating throughout the USSR in their own name. The other half are "Union-Republic," operating through the corresponding ministries of the republics. For the most part, matters best handled at the All-Union level are under All-Union ministries, as Merchant Marine and Defense Industry. But the formal division is not entirely logical. Foreign Affairs and Defense are nominally Union-Republic as a concession to the theoretical sovereignty of the republics, although in reality totally centralized. There are dual lines of control: from central ministry to republic ministries and from the USSR Council of Ministers to the republic councils of ministers, while innumerable committees and councils contribute to making the world's most complicated administrative setup.

The apparatus under the ministers, whatever the bureaucratic vices denounced in the Soviet press, is hardly a bureaucracy in the classic sense. Administrative superiors lack control of appointments, promotions, and posting, which are the concern of the party group or department. There are no regularized career ladders with rules for advancement; and there is no formal security of tenure, although bureaucrats in practice hold their places for long periods and seem strongly to protect one another. Lines of authority are multiple and often confused, to judge from complaints of evasion of responsibility. One may surmise that coordination within the governmental maze is to a large extent informal and that decisions are reached (as often happens in other governments) by irregular consultation and personal contact.

FEDERAL STRUCTURE

Efficiency demands some devolution of administration, and ethnic divisions of the USSR are primary units for this purpose. The fourteen non-Russian "union republics" were formed as a result of the resubjection of breakaway peoples after the Revolution, while pretending that they retained independence. There are also twenty "autonomous republics" which do not enjoy trappings of sovereignty. Sixteen of them are within the huge Russian republic, and a principal reason for their less dignified status is that their non-Russian peoples are situated in the interior of the Russian domain and were never able to move for independence. Their autonomy consists chiefly in legal use of the minority language.

Much is made of the sovereignty of the "republics," and they have some utility in foreign affairs; Stalin obtained United Nations membership for the Ukraine and Belorussia, and Asian republics are sometimes used for dealings with neighboring powers. In practice, however, the republics are only administrative subdivisions. Their governmental structures are largely laid down in the Union constitution, and their constitutions are essentially identical with that of the Union, even in phrasing. The chief differences are that some provide for different subdivisions or ministries, according to local needs, as a ministry of cotton production in Uzbekistan. Republic councils of ministers are subordinate to the Union council of ministers and subject to its decisions (Article 81). It is a seemingly needless backstop that the central government has the right (Article 69) to annul acts of republic governments. Important ministries are of the Union type, which operates without reference to the republics; six of thirty-nine economic ministries are Union-Republican, which means that the republic ministry operates under the direction of the central ministry. Only social security, local industry, road building, and the like, are administered through the republics. Any rights under the constitution can be removed by constitutional amendment without consent of the republics. Democratic Centralism, obedience tempered by consultation, applies in the governmental as well as the party structure.

Nonetheless, a good deal of administration seems to go forward at the republic level. Practical and local details are written into the framework of All-Union laws, and policies may be implemented at a different tempo in the various republics. The latter, although they have practically no revenues of their own, fill in the specifics of budgets handed to them from the center. They also have legal responsibility for the local governments beneath them. Of the total governmental apparatus, it was reported, 15.4% worked at the republic against only 6.2% in the All-Union level (18.7% being in provincial government and autonomous republics and 59.7% in local units).[16]

LOCAL SOVIETS

Each administrative layer has its popular-representative legitimating soviet. The supreme soviets of the republics are much like that of the Union, large bodies which seldom meet; they only lack the publicity surrounding the Moscow body. Down the scale, soviets decrease in size, meet oftener, and have

[16] *Nauchnye osnovy gosudarstvennogo upravleniia v. SSSR* (Akademiia Nauk), Moscow, 1968, p. 301.

somewhat more work to do, in parallel with the party congresses and conferences. Regional soviets should meet at least four times yearly, those at the bottom level six times. Apparently they often fail to comply with these requirements, and the sessions are likely to be one day or less, although central authorities repeatedly press for regular and frequent meetings and for greater activity on the part of the soviets.

The indifference of the men on the spot reflects their lack of autonomy. Subject to a multitude of orders from above, they do practically nothing on their own. In a reversal of the traditional role of parliamentary bodies, the soviets are not to decide policy but to assist in its execution. Party leadership is absolute. "Expressing trust and gratitude for the Communist Party, the electors send many of its members to local soviets, and the deputies elect leading workers of party bodies (most often first secretaries of obkoms, gorkoms, raikoms) to the corresponding executive committees."[17] Party instructors attend sessions of lower soviets and sit with their executive committees. Officers of the soviets generally seem to be named from outside, and they are frequently nonmembers of the soviet despite the ease of electing whoever may be desired. The soviet has little say-so over personnel formally subordinate to it. For soviet members there are courses, indoctrination sessions, and party schools.

In principle, there is ample business for the local soviet. It should interest itself in transport, roads, schools, trade and service facilities, and public order. It is to guide and plan for industry of purely local significance and to watch over but not interfere with other enterprises on its territory. It should look into agriculture (if rural), direct the use of fertilizer, storage of hog food, and care of machines; it helps get foodstuffs delivered to the state. It assigns children to orphanages and authorizes exchanges of housing. It has a sort of residual jurisdiction over matters that no superior body cares to preempt. With theoretical powers of examination and interrogation, it is to act as watchdog of local administration, combatting bureaucratism and (as the party directs) localism, protecting state interests in general.

In practice, the work of the local soviet is unexciting. Its control function may be activated if the party decides to exert pressure in a certain area, but criticism is hazardous when deputies face the ire of local officials. Complaints should in any case go first to the agencies or authorities affected, and deputies should take them up only if not properly handled; the chief recourse, if the bureaucrats do not give satisfaction, is publicity in the press or appeal to higher powers. Deputies are in any event adjured to consider suggestions and petitions in the light of broad significance, that is, party policy. The soviets have no funds of their own but only small allotments from above.

[17] *Sovety deputatov trudiashchikhsia*, no. 8, August, 1969, p. 49.

The meetings, which are closed to the public, tend to be dull and formal, the Soviet press complains. The approximately 24,000 local deputies of the Kirghiz republic used their right of inquiry only six times in 1969 and eight in the first half of 1970.[18]

The main occupation of deputies is to carry on relations with the people. Deputies hold office hours at least once weekly, mostly for persons seeking a way through red tape. This relieves the burdens of the local party organization. At least once in six months deputies should hold meetings to give an accounting to the citizens and to hear their views. They should look for troubles which paternalistic intervention may solve. If a worker is falling down on the job, the model deputy investigates, talks with all concerned, and resolves the marital discord at the root of the trouble. The two million deputies, like party members, should be all-around propagandists, helping to make the new Soviet man. The soviets might well be considered under the rubric of opinion control.

The local soviets also serve as the principal focus for the organization of volunteer activities. All manner of groups for civic purposes, mostly of control, are organized formally under the auspices of the soviet, perhaps with the participation of a deputy or a group of deputies, those representing a section of the community or those interested in some activity. There are apartment committees, street committees, borough or ward committees, parents' groups, hospital councils, and the like. Probably most important are the "standing commissions" of the soviets, in which 1,700,000 deputies are joined by 2,500,000 outside activists;[19] this is also a means of associating qualified persons with the work of the soviets. The commissions, of which there are more than three hundred thousand, deal mostly with such matters of local concern as education, the militia (ordinary police), health, transportation, housing, juvenile affairs, parks, and retail trade, working with and supplementing the regular local administrative apparatus. A total of twenty-five million activists are said to cooperate with local soviets in various ways.[20]

LOCAL ADMINISTRATION

In the Petrograd Soviet of 1917 decision-making fell to an inner group called the executive committee, and the center of local administration at all levels below the republic is so designated. Theoretically an emanation of the elected soviet, the executive committee is actually a different body, as the

---

[18] *Sovety deputatov trudiashchikhsia*, no. 2, February, 1971, p. 9.

[19] *Izvestia*, February 6, 1971, p. 2; *Current Digest*, vol. 23, no. 6, p. 18.

[20] L. I. Brezhnev, in *Pravda*, October 30, 1971, p. 1.

Presidium of the Supreme Soviet, a part not of the soviet but of the administrative apparatus reaching down from the center. Its members may but do not have to belong to the corresponding soviet. It is a cabinet of paid state officials, probably about a dozen in small cities, twice as many in larger, whose chairman is ceremonial head with no important power, and it has departments like ministries. Around and below the executive committees there is a proliferation of agencies, party and government bodies often being inseparably intermingled in personnel and functions.[21] Neighborhood councils bring together representatives of party, Komsomol, Soviet executive committee, Dosaaf (the voluntary military organization), the volunteer militia, and local administrative agencies to carry on political work with the masses.[22] In the villages, peasants gather (in an assembly called by the name "skhod," used in tsarist times for the village get-together) to listen to local executive committee members; in the cities, there are bureaus for small groups of apartment buildings and offices in individual buildings to register and deal with the tenants.

The field of local government includes everything higher authorities prefer not to handle directly, such as local transportation, services, retail trade, schools, and perhaps housing, although this is more likely to be associated with industrial enterprises. The local administration coordinates collective farms, local industry, and cultural institutions even though these are under other agencies. The principle of dual subordination means mostly responsibility to central agencies, by-passing not only the local soviet but also the executive committee. Heads of city departments are not merely checked by the respective ministry but named and dismissed by it.[23] Local administration is also under watchful eyes of the party, the Control Commission, inspectors from ministries, the Ministry of Finance, the State Bank, and others.

Despite the multiplicity of controls it is difficult for the central authorities to make sure that subordinate agencies follow the spirit of directives. Even the letter may often get lost, particularly in the economic sphere, because of shirked responsibility, confusion of directions, and overloaded communications. Here as everywhere the Soviet leadership wishes to secure initiative on the part of those who are called upon to execute policy and to get them to apply rules intelligently. But it is difficult to cause local institutions to be both energetic and wholly obedient; the problem is as old as empires.

One answer is to enlarge slightly the areas of autonomy and invite more policy-making and hence responsibility by men on the spot. In parallel with the limited economic decentralization of Khrushchev, 1957 and after, there

[21] Cf. B. M. Frolic, "Municipal Administrations, Departments, Commissions and Organizations," *Soviet Studies,* no. 3, January, 1971, pp. 376 ff.

[22] *Partiinaia zhizn,* no. 20, October, 1970, p. 50.

[23] David T. Cattell, *Leningrad, a Study of Soviet Urban Government* (Praeger), New York, 1968, p. 31. This is a valuable analysis of Soviet local institutions.

was some tendency to increase local rights, mostly for the benefit of the republics, but only timorous steps were taken. Movement more recently has been rather in the contrary direction; "decentralization" is no longer ostensibly on the agenda.

Central reins are combined with local spurs. Citizens are organized in the standing commissions of the soviets and innumerable controller groups to scrutinize deficiencies of the authorities; amateurs, perhaps inspired by general dislike for the entrenched bureaucracy, are to keep the professionals in line. Like deputies, local officials are supposed to give an accounting of their actions from time to time and face questioning by popular gatherings. Their office doors are always to be open; and citizens are encouraged to present complaints about all manner of abuses and failures in local administration and services, from unsafe streets to poor meals in restaurants. There are strict rules about the processing of demands, and superior authorities are to be informed concerning eventual disposition.

The Soviet press gives to understand that this works better in theory than practice. The people can exert only a feeble moral pressure unless they can arouse the interest of a superior body. There can be no independent organization to push for improvement; the party is the mover of the volunteer and controlling groups, and the party organization very likely sympathizes with the bureaucrats, who may be prominent in it. Ordinary folk are apt to be much at the mercy of local power-holders, while they usually have little personally to gain, except moral satisfaction, from making trouble. They are sufficiently tame that when a city soviet illegally imposed a fine of five rubles on those who failed to show up for volunteer work, the only complaint came from a man who had actually done his stint.[24]

DEMOCRACY WITHIN DICTATORSHIP

A remarkable Russian invention is the amount and variety of democratic forms that can be used to reinforce an authoritarian state. Democratic institutions everywhere serve to raise the authority of law and government; the Soviet success is to have them serve this end while giving more instead of less security to the established rulership. The compatibility of pleasant facade and unpleasant reality is shown by the introduction in the worst year of the terror of the "most democratic constitution in the world." Democratic appearances help more effectively to suppress criticism as "antipopular," and the official preemption of the vocabulary and phraseology of rights and freedom

---

[24] *Izvestia*, June 4, 1969; *Current Digest*, vol. 21, no. 23, p. 31.

psychologically disarms the opposition. As long as the party monopoly of information and organization remains absolute, small steps overtly in the democratic direction may be designed further to affirm party rule. It is a major advantage of the formal separation of party and state that democratic and constitutional appearances can be introduced into what is called the "government" without troubling the monopoly of power in the governing party.

The Soviet rulership is nonetheless apprehensive of a potential loosening of the state. Thus they decline to make the use of elections and soviets that would seem at first sight quite feasible in order to preserve the front of unanimity. To legitimate any political contest would require drawing up effective rules for the allocation of power; this might prove dangerous for the monopoly of the center.

Discussion of issues is also nearly excluded. "Debates," as of the draft constitution in 1936, the Party Program in 1961, and the revised collective farm charter in 1969, were kept within very narrow limits and had no obvious relation to decisions taken. Under Khrushchev there was some controlled discussion of real issues, as family law, educational reform, and changes in the planning system. It seemed, especially in 1956–1960, that the Soviet Union might be moving toward legislation by consultation, and Soviet writers claimed this as a virtue of their system. But the idea of an open forum has receded since Khrushchev. No use has ever been made of referendums or plebiscites, though they were provided by the constitution (Article 49 e) and promised by Khrushchev as the basic means of legislating. This democratic form was useful to such rulers as Napoleon and Hitler, but the Soviets apparently find it undesirable to call upon the people to sanction major decisions.

To keep issues within the inner circle and to veil the gap between facade and reality, the workings of the system are shrouded in secrecy. There is no public weighing of the merits of anyone in an important position; it is not even felt necessary to give explanations of promotions and demotions, unless the individual is to be used as an example. Lines of real command and practically everything to do with policy-making are concealed; if a meeting is publicized it is not important. When in Khrushchev's time differences within the elite came to the surface, they raised questions as to the infallibility of the leadership and suggested the possibility of differing views. To divulge divisions of any kind would also encourage many persons of the upper tiers of government, if not the common people, to believe that they might have a claim to influence the decision.

Secrecy hence becomes a principle; not only is it impossible for Soviet writers to analyze issues or personalities in politics; they cannot even write critically of the mechanics of government. But the effects of secrecy are negative, undoing much of the benefits of the theater designed to demonstrate the popular-democratic nature of Soviet government. The separation of rulers from ruled makes for apathy and cynicism; the uninformed are indifferent. Probably a series of lesser screens between different layers of authority reduce trust and understanding and contribute to the unresponsiveness of the bureaucracy.

The Soviet commitment to democratic forms is equivocal. The Soviet Encyclopedic Dictionary (1963) defines democracy as "The form of government in which the will of the majority is legally recognized as the basis of authority, and freedom and equality of citizens are proclaimed." Democracy is thus treated as a matter for formal recognition and proclamation. In other connections, democracy is defined primarily in terms of social rights, people's ownership of the economy, and above all, citizens' participation in the execution of policy.

The number of persons who work in and with local soviets is the best proof of Soviet democracy. According to Brezhnev, "The strength of the socialist government lies in its firm links with the people, in the involvement of the broadest masses in the administration of the country and in social affairs. Socialist democracy is called upon to assure precisely this. Its improvement and broadening comprise the principal direction of the development of Soviet society on the road to communism."[25] The more persons mobilized, the more popular the government. So far as people can be involved in the web of Soviet organization, in supervised and guided political participation, they are giving consent and support to the regime; activism and idealism are directed not merely into harmless but into positively useful channels.

In *What is to Be Done* Lenin wrote that "broad democracy" in Russian conditions was only a *"useless and harmful toy"* (emphasis by Lenin), [26] a remarkable statement in view of the usual readiness of those out of power to subscribe to democratic rights. On the eve of the Revolution he wrote, in opposing the proposition that the Congress of Soviets should assume power peacefully, "The people have a right and are obliged to decide such questions not by voting but by force."[27] Brezhnev quoted Lenin at the June, 1969, congress of Communist parties: " 'Pure democracy' is a deceitful liberal phrase to make fools of the workers."[28] It is enough to say that free elections destroy the "unity of the working class," and there can be no freedom for "antisocialist elements."[29]

Soviet writers do not hesitate to decry "arithmetic" or "mechanical" majorities when votes go contrary to their purposes, and to speak of the necessary "dictatorship of the proletariat" even while claiming the most

[25] *Pravda*, July 7, 1969.
[26] *Collected Works*, vol. 5, Moscow, 1961, p. 479.
[27] *Sochineniia*, 3rd. ed., vol. 21, p. 263.
[28] *Pravda*, June 8, 1969, p. 4.
[29] *Pravda*, June 1, 1969.

democratic of governments. They are frank in admitting that "socialist democracy" is not to be measured by the standards of "bourgeois democracy." The great sin of the Czechs before August, 1968, was to move toward democratization of socialism, which was an anti-Soviet ploy.[30] This was subversive of the dictatorship of the proletariat; and, "Any attempt, regardless of the subjective views and desires of individuals, to blunt the class approach in the name of a falsely understood humanism contradicts the true interests of the working people. . . ."[31] Democracy hence proves to be inadmissible unless redefined in the Soviet manner, just as "socialism" means the Soviet system and little more.

The essence of the Soviet way is "consciousness" over "sponta- neity," to use the terms of Lenin seventy years ago. There is little room for separate individual or group urges apart from the ideal of the system or the purposes of those who stand at its head. "Discipline is one of the unvarying conditions of democracy. The requirements of discipline are deeply democratic, because they assure unity of will for the attainment of the common goal, the successful functioning of the state."[32] The leitmotif and theme is always unity. "To permit the free play of all political forces in socialist countries in the present situation would mean the suicide of socialism."[33]

READINGS

Harold J. Berman and John B. Quigley, Jr., eds., *Basic Laws on the Structure of the Soviet State* (Harvard University Press), Cambridge, Mass., 1969.

David T. Cattell, *Leningrad: a Case Study of Soviet Urban Government* (Praeger), New York, 1968.

Max E. Mote, *Soviet Local and Republic Elections* (Hoover Institution), Stanford, Calif., 1965.

Philip D. Stewart, *Political Power in the Soviet Union* (Bobbs-Merrill), In- dianapolis, 1968.

[30] As in *Izvestia*, July 24, 1969; *Current Digest*, vol. 21, no. 30, p. 13.
[31] Ibid.
[32] *Nauchnye osnovy gosudarstvennogo upravleniia v SSSR*, p. 418.
[33] S. Kovalev in *Znania*, March 1971, pp. 187–199; *ABSEES*, July 1971, p. 24.

8. Economic Front

INDUSTRY

The basic Soviet claim of superiority is that the means of production belong to the people. With no private ownership of wealth-producing property, there should be no exploitation; the vices of the selfish bourgeois-capitalist order should be cast away; production should soar as capitalist anarchy is replaced by rational socialist order; peace and happiness should reign as conflict ceases.

A small fraction of production is still private. Household garden plots and livestock make a remarkably large contribution to the Soviet diet. Individual artisans can legally make some articles without employing labor. Until 1960, producers' cooperatives accounted for a few percent of industrial production, but they were nationalized and their members became state employees. The greater part of agricultural production comes from nominal cooperatives, but they are in reality as controlled as the state farms. For the rest, transportation agencies, stores and distribution agencies, service establishments, banks, manufacturing plants, and mines are alike state property, directed by state agencies. In the United States and other "capitalist" countries, production is in principle by private entrepreneurs; the state intervenes to control or sometimes operate when necessary. In the Soviet system, the state owns and operates as a matter of principle.[1]

[1] Of all areas of Soviet life, economic management is best illuminated by a large volume of publication. Much is missing, and indices are often unreliable, but economists usually have some confidence in specific figures so far as it is clear what they refer to. Data became more accurate under Khrushchev, but the improvement has not continued in recent years.

211

Planning

In the civil war, nearly all industrial production was by command, goods being transferred by order without payment. To remedy the economic disaster that resulted from the conflict and overcontrol of the economy, Lenin made a major retreat in his New Economic Policy of 1921. Small-scale private enterprise was permitted, and state-owned manufacturing trusts were placed on their own so far as possible, told to keep accounts and to make a profit.

But the Bolsheviks never dropped the idea of central direction of the economy. Even in the abysmal times of 1920, as the Bolsheviks were still struggling to end the civil war, Lenin was dreaming of the electrification of Russia, which he equated with communism. An agency to plan development of electrical power began attempting some prospective planning for major industries. From 1924, as recovery proceeded, there was strong emphasis on heavy industry; and from 1925 to 1926 and after, the state planning agency, Gosplan, began issuing target figures for basic production.

By 1928, Stalin, having vanquished his chief rivals, felt able to embark on a much more ambitious program. The goal of his First Five-Year Plan was mostly the rapid building of heavy industry, especially the production of steel and machinery. Targets were continually raised in a spirit of "Bolsheviks can do anything"; and despite inexperience and lack of managers, fair success was registered in basic industry, although at the cost of consumer goods production. The hallmark of Stalinist industrialization, along with concentration of resources and attention on heavy industry, was centralization. Industry was administered by central ministries and planned in detail from Moscow. Stalin also emphasized the monumental and grandiose, giant plants and towering furnaces, palatial subways and cities carved from the wilderness—a romanticizing of industrialization which contributed not only to economic growth but to awe of the ruler.

By the time of Stalin's death, the Soviet economy had outgrown his stifling controls, and it was widely felt that relaxation was necessary for continued expansion. Many small steps were soon taken to give managers a little more discretion in the use of resources; some materials were released from allocation, plants were permitted to sell unneeded equipment, republics were given more administrative authority over a number of branches, etc. But more was needed, and in 1957 Khrushchev, in opposition to the Stalinist old guard, put through an extensive decentralization. Although central planning was retained, nearly all the economic ministries in Moscow, except those related to defense, were dissolved. The enterprises under them were transferred to a hundred-odd Economic Councils responsible to the soviet executive committee and the party boss of their territory, usually an oblast or a small republic.

This decentralization was no innovation but mostly a return to an administrative structure like that of the 1920's. It was designed to bring the bureaucrats closer to the industries they supervised and to reduce transportation costs. The central ministries had been much inclined to autarky, which meant shipping goods far and wide without taking due account of needs and resources near at hand. However, decentralization led to some localism, raising the specter of national or other divisiveness. Within a few years larger regional units were being created over the Economic Councils and many of these were amalgamated. By 1962, only forty-seven remained, with much reduced powers. At the same time, industrial growth failed to improve and declined fairly consistently through Khrushchev's tenure and markedly toward its end.

Economic reform was hence high on the agenda of the new government. Kosygin in 1965 outlined extensive changes toward both decentralization and recentralization: managers of industrial enterprises were to be given more latitude and encouraged to strive for a profit instead of merely fulfilling output figures; but the central economic ministries were to be restored. Of these two sides of the reform, the first was the more publicized, but recentralization proved more operative as the liberalizing reforms were watered down in practice. Although the Brezhnev-Kosygin setup has partly reverted to Stalinist patterns, it has been more rational. There was no more grand campaigning, as when Stalin gave steel all-out priority and Khrushchev turned to the chemical industry as a cure-all. Light industry received a slightly higher share of investment, in the vicinity of 12%, whereas under Khrushchev it had been down to 8%. Targets were scaled down, and the plans became more realistic.

The main ideas of planning have changed little since the First Five-Year Plan. The conventional period has been five years, although Khrushchev scrapped a five-year plan when it was floundering half through and replaced it with a seven-year plan. Longer projections, for ten or twenty years, are made; but these seem to have little meaning. The five-year plan itself is mostly a political goal, although it is described as legally compulsory. It may be a year or two late in getting formal sanction. Year-to-year plans meshed with the national budget are more operative. These are projections based mostly on experience and the performance of the previous year.

The principal planning agency, Gosplan, assisted by a number of commissions, translates party directive into figures primarily of goods to be produced but also covering many other performance indices, as labor productivity, cost reduction, return on investment, material consumption, and innovation. Quotas are allotted to the republics and oblasts, which divide obligations among smaller divisions. The plan is made more detailed stepwise down to individual factories, shops within factories, brigades, and even individual workers, with study and consultations at each stage. The process is lengthy and seldom completed by the beginning of the period which the plan is to cover. There is always a contest between superiors, who want those beneath them to promise to produce as much as possible with the least input of resources, and inferiors, who wish to get maximum labor, capital, and materials for minimum assignments.

Assignments are crucial because the main levers to secure fulfillment of the plan are rewards for reaching or exceeding quotas and penalties for shortfalls. Managers and to some extent workers get bonuses or higher pay rates for everything over the quota laid down in the plan, whereas underfulfillment brings loss of income, probably reprimand, and perhaps more severe penalties. Ever since Stalin decreed ambitious output goals with little regard for cost, plan fulfillment has been the prime criterion of success for the producer (to a large extent also for transportation agencies, distributors, et al.). Within the limitation of planned goals, multiple controls, and the restrictions that materials should be bought from prescribed suppliers and sales made to prescribed users, the manager buys and sells and employs the resources at his disposition as he decides best. He cannot make major investment decisions, as capital is allocated by the state, formerly without charge and still usually with little or no interest. He cannot fix prices, which are set by the State Committee on Prices or ministries, and which partly reflect costs and partly priorities, as producers' goods have been kept cheap to favor expansion. He cannot ordinarily fix wages nor set the total wage fund. But he operates on a budget and tries to make a profit, part of which he, like an American corporate executive, can retain for various uses, and part of which, as in the United States, goes into the state treasury.[2]

Planners' Troubles

If the planning system were able rationally to order the economy to maximize output, the Soviet Union would have long since outstripped the best of the disorderly capitalist countries. In practice, the planned Soviet economy has been able to direct a large share of the national income into investment, and it has achieved a good rate of growth over a long time by concentration on essentials, but its success is qualified.

A basic difficulty of planning lies in the measurement of output; whatever criterion is adopted leads to distortions. It is impossible to have quotas for each product except in the simplest industries, so planners have usually chosen a gross aggregate measure, as weight, numbers, etc. But if, for example, cloth output is measured by weight, it is made as heavy as possible; if by area, thin; if by length, narrow; if by price, costly. Machines added up by weight become steel monsters. To fulfill plans, railroads send freight a roundabout route. Geologists are rewarded according to the amount they drill, which is

---

[2] The state's share of industrial profits furnishes over one-third of revenues. The second largest item is the turnover tax, which amounts to a sales tax at rates which are not publicized but which vary from about 20% to 300% or more on luxury goods. A state lottery contributes to revenue. Inheritance tax was abolished in 1943. Income tax is low, with a maximum rate of 12%, except for private professionals and artisans, charged about half of their incomes. [Cf. Robert J. Osborn, *Soviet Social Policies* (Dorsey Press), Homewood, Ill., 1970, p. 35.]

easily measured, not the discoveries made, which are irregular and hard to evaluate. Sometimes for simplicity the plan has been in terms of materials consumed, an invitation to maximize waste. Builders can satisfy their plans more easily by using more expensive materials.[3] Since producers make not what the market needs but what the plan calls for, unsalable goods began piling up in warehouses as soon as the economy rose out of extreme shortages in the latter 1950's. On the other hand, many needed articles are not produced because there is no incentive. The shortage of screws is such that manufactures are shipped without. A light bulb factory must make its own fine wire, because wire producers have plans by the ton.[4] Similarly, there are places in nursery-kindergartens for older but not younger children because the former are easier to care for.[5]

In calculating prices, in Marxist theory and Soviet practice, there is no good way to take into account capital employed, land or natural resources used, scarcity, innovation, anything but labor and material inputs. This means careless use of resources and prices bearing little relation to the desirability of goods. Many prices remain unchanged for a decade or more, while difficulty in getting reasonable prices fixed by distant authorities deters bringing out new products. It is difficult to take quality into account. A fertilizer plant began to lose money when it improved its product but it could not raise the price; the solution was to lower the quality.[6] Setting prices on the basis of cost of production gives incentives to fictitious or real inflation of costs.

Because there has been no penalty on tying up capital and because supplies are irregular and costs often relatively unimportant, plants strive for self-sufficiency, hoarding materials and making countless small items and parts at great expense by hand or with primitive facilities. The way for a plant to be sure of having adequate materials is to ask for too much; the way to be sure of getting supplies in time is to store them; the sure way to get spare parts is to make them. Excess materials or machinery are also useful to barter for needed supplies. Labor is widely hoarded and then paid overtime in "storming" to meet deadlines. Six chemical factories were reported to employ eight times more workers than similar plants in the West.[7]

Carelessness with capital, difficulty of getting equipment and materials, confusions of planning, and fondness for new projects, mean that construction may be dragged out interminably. It may be hard to complete buildings, because they are prematurely declared officially finished and so written off the construction plan. A Soviet economist proposed that projects

[3] *Pravda*, October 19, 1970, p. 2.
[4] *Pravda*, September 14, 1971, p. 2; September 11, 1970, p. 2.
[5] *Pravda*, July 17, 1971, p. 3; *Current Digest*, vol. 23, no. 29, p. 8.
[6] *Izvestia*, July 15, 1969; *Current Digest*, vol. 21, no. 28, p. 28.
[7] *Voprosy ekonomiki*, no. 10. October, 1969, p. 29; *Current Digest*, vol. 22, no. 1, p. 15.

underway be reduced by half to permit expeditious termination of the remainder. Half a year later, exactly the same proposal was semiofficially repeated.[8]

A chief preoccupation of the party is to promote the modernization of technology. But there is no way to measure innovation, and conservatism is built into the planning system. Changes in processes or products not only require extra effort but are likely at least temporarily to endanger the plan. Unless there is a stern drive from above for improvement, as in military wares, it is more advantageous to go on making obsolete goods or using obsolete machinery. Since the use of diamonds in metalworking was regarded as very modern, the planners rewarded firms for using as many as possible; the result was waste.

The authorities far from the local scene are unable to keep up with a million details. They fix prices on more than 8,000,000 articles, including, for example, 700 varieties of cherry preserves. Plans are detailed in the extreme; thus, each garage, collective farm, etc., has a quota for the number of used tires it should turn in for reconditioning.[9] Since orders go through headquarters, a plant may get from thousands of miles away supplies obtainable next door. "Irrational transportation is brought about to a large extent by the planning system, under which the increase of transportation costs goes into the planned cost of production, and does not prejudice the interests of the enterprise or productive branch, although the economy as a whole suffers grave losses thereby."[10] A factory with an oversupply of bags could get no orders to dispose of them and was forbidden to sell; as a result they rotted.[11] For a long time only dark tasseled lampshades were sold because there was no price for any others; when attention was called to this folly, the manufacture of the old style was forbidden by decree of the Central Committee and Council of Ministers. *Pravda* stated[12] that it was good for small-scale industries to be started on collective farms because it took too long to get ministerial approval of conventionally organized industrial plants.

Because of overcentralization, decisions are made without adequate information; but producers are buried in reports and questionnaires. The fishing trust is described as sailing on a paper sea. The Amur Gold Trust arbitrarily demanded about fifty types of reports with 16,000 indices to be furnished daily or weekly.[13] Before a new dress could go into production, it had to be approved by over a hundred authorities. There is great duplication in administration. In Krasnodar, seven organizations with 1436 bureaucrats administered 2600

[8] *Pravda*, July 24, 1969; *Izvestia*, January 18, 1970.

[9] *Pravda*, September 26, 1970, p. 2.

[10] *Pravda*, October 29, 1971, p. 3.

[11] *Partiinaia zhizn*, no. 2, January, 1969, p. 64.

[12] November 15, 1969.

[13] *Pravda*, March 20, 1969.

fishermen.[14] Ninety-eight retreading plants are under twenty-one different authorities.[15] Controls are self-defeating in their multiplicity. Ten or more organs, including the Gosplan, the state bank, the ministry of finance, the relevant industrial ministry, the local government, the local party organ, and control commissions, frequently give contradictory instructions to a plant. A few years ago a Soviet mathematician projected from the growth of the apparatus that by 1980 planning would require the work of the entire population.

Despite or because of all the efforts to control, there is fudging, cheating, and some positive corruption. Since quotas and allotments are so important in terms of bonuses, there is every incentive to fool those higher up both as to needs and capacities. Inflation in production figures is inevitable, scrap is counted as output, and managers pad costs and labor needs. The ministry may not desire to uncover the fakery, because this would detract from its own results. When a subordinate denounced the director for inflating production figures, a storm descended not on the director but on the denouncer; even when the party put the matter straight, the guilty man received only a reprimand.[16] In view of low fixed pay, workers sometimes refuse to work unless time sheets are falsified;[17] and factory bureaucrats fill fictitious jobs.[18] It appears to be rather easy for directors of firms with a construction department to make equipment and materials available to themselves. Goods are written off as scrap. A fishing crew takes the ship out at night and sells the catch.[19]

It is probably impossible for a manager to fill his plans, in view of deficiencies of supply, without engaging in illegal operations. Fixers and expeditors play a major role in the Soviet economy, as they seek ways around red tape; half of all travel in the Soviet Union is said to be connected with deficiencies of the supply system.[20] Although the Soviet press in 1971 was lamenting the increasing numbers of fixers, the planners are usually glad for the factory to get materials as best it can. Black or gray market private enterprise looms large and has probably been growing in recent years. Illegal buying and selling in controlled markets means easy enrichment; for example, dealers who found a supply of beans could make a profit of 1,000%.[21] It seems to be quite normal for collective farms to buy lumber from unofficial dealers, and no one minds unless the dealer turns out to be a cheat. Local industries are set up to

---

[14] *Pravda*, July 31, 1970, p. 3.
[15] *Pravda*, September 26, 1970, p. 2.
[16] *Partiinaia zhizn*, no. 15, August, 1970, p. 36.
[17] *Pravda*, September 11, 1969.
[18] *Izvestia*, May 21, 1969.
[19] *Izvestia*, August 11, 1970, p. 4.
[20] *Izvestia*, January 21, 1971, p. 3.
[21] *Bakinskii rabochii*, October 31, 1970.

manufacture such things as curlers and pens from materials of unknown, that is, illegal provenance.[22] Small construction jobs are apparently quite often done by private operators.

Soviet economic planning suffers not merely from inefficiency, however, but from the elevation of political values over economic. Control is desired not only for the sake of production but for the sake of control. The Soviet monopolies have many of the rigidities and vices associated with monopoly in the West. The manager is probably an engineer, skilled in the technology of production; but he needs, above all, political skill in a bureaucratic maze. Political considerations, especially cooperativeness with party leaders, weigh heavily in his career. "There was a time when almost the only criterion in the selection of a candidate for a responsible position was his honorableness, his devotion to our cause. Beyond a doubt, these qualities are necessary most of all today. . . ."[23] His success comes less from producing useful goods than from fulfilling bureaucratically defined norms and, perhaps even more, from his success in getting a good appraisal from superiors. The plan itself is politically shaded, as bargaining among authorities takes the place of economic calculation, and allocation of capital is determined by considerations of influence and prestige.

The result is not that the system cannot produce but that production is costly and poorly adapted to needs of the market. The system functions well in those areas which receive closest attention from central authorities and enjoy high prestige. Soviet armaments are apparently equal to the best; and related branches, as aircraft production and watches, have also done well. Planning is relatively successful in industries which have simple, large-scale and unchanging products, as coal and steel. But progress means more fabrication, more specialized expertise and an ever increasing number of products, with interrelations in the economy growing approximately as the square of the number of products. In the post-Stalin years it was no longer possible to concentrate on a few big objectives. It became ever harder to decide what should be produced and to get the right product mix. Waste grew and useless goods piled up. Rates of growth not only of industrial production but of productivity of labor declined, and the return on capital investments decreased. By 1964, the need for change was obvious.

Remedies

One potential remedy was coercion. Stalin was able to get the managers to perform fairly well by rewarding generously and punishing cruelly, but his methods ceased to be applicable to the maturing industrial economy. In

[22] *Pravda*, January 24, 1969.
[23] *Ibid.*

1970 and 1971 there were campaigns for discipline and threats to apply criminal sanctions to lazy workers and careless managers, but this could be no real remedy.

Khrushchev tried devolution to regional authorities, but this led to unacceptable localism. Tinkering with the planning mechanism and proliferation of state committees and councils in the latter Khrushchev years probably hurt more than it helped. There have been hopes that computers would come to the rescue of the central planners, with sophisticated new approaches, as cybernetics, input-output analysis, and linear programming. But the complexity of the economy outran the capacity of computers to keep up. Far from rushing into the computer age, the Soviet Union remained relatively backward in that respect, with less than one-tenth of the American stock; and the emphasis in introduction of computers has been on production, not planning.

More promising has been the effort to give managers more independence, shifting emphasis from gross planned output to cost reduction and profitability. From shortly after the demise of Stalin there was some relaxation of controls, and suggestions were made for obvious reforms, such as crediting the manager not with total production but with goods sold and giving incentives for economy of capital and labor. Khrushchev, a few months before his ouster, permitted two clothing factories (performance having been particularly unsatisfactory in this area) to operate experimentally under a system whereby the enterprise took orders from stores, negotiated prices with them, purchased materials as desired, gave workers bonuses not for plan fulfillment but for quality, and used its profits to expand production. It was a great success in terms of consumer satisfaction as well as profits. After Khrushchev was forced out, his successors extended the new system to hundreds of other plants, mostly in light industry.

In September of 1965, Chairman Kosygin, talking like a businessman, announced sweeping reforms looking to a partial liberation of management. The economic ministries were restored, but they were to be general overseers instead of detailed controllers. The number of planned targets was to be much reduced. The manager was to be given assignments in total sales, kind of production, wage fund, investments, basic tasks of innovation, and material supplies. He would then seek maximum profitability in use of resources and retain a larger part of profits. To induce economy in use of capital, interest would be charged on loans. A "Factory Charter" spelled out extensive rights of management. In 1967, a price reform made many industrial prices more realistic. A reform of the construction industry in the same spirit was designed to stimulate completion of projects. The Soviet Union seemed to be heading toward a market socialism, with obvious potential political consequences.

The reforms were, however, so delayed, qualified, and diluted in application as to be negated. Applied to a few showcase factories, the new rules worked well; when they were extended widely, the bosses kept on bossing much as they always had. Provisions for use of profits and the like became extremely complicated, and new indices were added until managers had little more freedom than before.[24] It was feared that the reforms would cause unemployment, or that they would lead to emphasis on consumer goods, where most profit was to be made. It was complained that plants allowed to use funds at their own discretion spent the money frivolously. The authorities preferred to allocate capital at their volition, so capital charges (at rates varying according to purpose) were not widely introduced. If many in the West saw the stress on profit as a turn toward capitalism, many in the Soviet Union did likewise and did their best to restrain it. After the reform movement of the spring and summer of 1968 in Czechoslovakia heightened fears of any liberalization, "market socialism" and "market relations" became forbidden terms. Even discussion of economic reform was dampened. Neo-Stalinists rejected the whole idea of "money-based commodity relations" as harmful to socialism and called frankly for increased centralized controls both in industry and agriculture. The economist Yevsei Liberman, whose name was attached to the reform movement, discovered that free markets were "anti-Leninist."

Contrary tendencies continued to pull the Soviet economy in opposite directions. In 1968, a chemical plant was given freedom to use its wage fund as it saw fit, letting unneeded workers go and raising the pay of others, a great innovation which was only a small part of the reforms promised three years before. It was reported a tremendous success, like the earlier experiments, and in October 1969 the Central Committee called upon all ministries to emulate it. But talk of autonomy gave way to a campaign for combination. Under the slogan "unification is progress," industrial plants were amalgamated into larger combines covering regions or the entire Soviet Union. The call was for a crackdown on shirkers:

> While generously rewarding outstanding workers for their honest, conscientious work, it is necessary more decisively to catch up the wrongdoers. Forgiveness and failure to punish do great harm and morally pervert other people, especially the youth. . . . One can hear it said that, in the course of building communism [disorganizers of production] will gradually be re-educated under the influence of the healthful mass of toilers and then at some stage will disappear.

> No! One cannot agree with this point of view. Persuading these hardened loafers, drunkards, slovens, pampering them—unhappily it still goes on—brings no good. Besides, why should society be humane with them if they do not behave humanely with society?[25]

[24] See Keith Bush, "The Implementation of the Soviet Economic Reform," *Osteuropa Wirtschaft*, vol. 15, no. 5, October, 1970.

[25] *Pravda*, February 8, 1970, p. 2.

Basic reform is difficult. The fact that all productive goods are owned by the state makes political management seem natural; transfers of materials are not truly sales, as ownership does not change. Prices are more or less arbitrary and so not an adequate basis for economic decisions. Planners, wielding political power, think in terms of solving problems by command or administrative action. They prefer having a commission control quality or product assortment to leaving it to consumer preference. The idea of individual or group gain is uncongenial to the collectivist society. It is ill regarded if men earn consequential amounts of money by useful work. Workers who got a few hundred rubles for collecting scrap metal were expected to turn it over to "social" organizations.[26] If managers show a substantial profit, political controllers are likely to take it away.[27] Perhaps managers are satisfied to have the simpler task of filling a gross output quota without too much attention to costs, while potential profits go to salaries, bonuses, and perquisites.

Politically more acceptable than profits earned by economic calculation are moral incentives organized by the party. Nonmaterial incentives fit very well the Marxist critique of "bourgeois" society as grossly monetary and the idea that people should work for joy in the society of the future. Moreover, they suit the controlled society as they are dispensed at the discretion of authorities. Honors for good workers were introduced soon after the Revolution; Stalin made much use of them, as did Khrushchev in his effort to restore Communist zeal. His successors proclaim them as a major stimulant for production. Emphasis on moral stimuli seems to be a major peculiarity of Soviet wage policy.

The distinctions to which the diligent may aspire include many orders, some of which, as Hero of Socialist Labor, carry material benefits such as a pension, preference in housing, and free transportation. Worthy workers are elected to honorary positions, given medals, written down in books of honor, posted on boards of fame, and praised in the press. "On houses along the village street there are heavy plaques informing passers-by that here lives an honored collective farmer or a famous milkmaid."[28] Leaders in production are allowed to sign reports to the party congress. There are also prizes, and it is deemed better to give a desirable article, as a radio or a motorcycle, than cash. On the other hand, slackers and drunks appear on the board of shame, are caricatured in the wall newspaper, are reprimanded in front of their fellows, or have to eat in a disgrace corner of the lunchroom.

Many awards are distributed by "socialist competition": individuals, brigades, factories, even cities and provinces compete to fulfill plans, reduce waste, etc. Apparently a large majority of Soviet workers engage in such emulations for glory, wherein the losers are supposed to emulate the leaders, and

[26] *Izvestia*, August 28, 1969.
[27] *Izvestia*, August 7, 1969; *Current Digest*, vol. 21, no. 23, p. 21.
[28] *Pravda*, December 10, 1969.

these are supposed generously to help the rest to raise themselves. Good workers may form a "Brigade of Communist Labor," a title the Komsomol was authorized to grant in 1958. Toilers so honored should be not only model workers but morally perfect citizens. Their motto is, "All for one and one for all"; sharing joys and troubles, they should help one another raise productivity. There has been some tendency for the brigades to pool incomes, but this is frowned upon as narrow.

Great efforts are made to apply indoctrination to industry; the success of a party group's ideological work is measured by production. There is endless exhortation to produce more, better, and cheaper, to save raw materials, to use machines carefully, or to innovate. Patriotic themes are used to inspire, and feats of labor are coupled with battlefield heroism. The universal cause inspires: "The toilers of our country by their labor make a weighty contribution to the cause of strengthening peace and friendship of peoples, of bringing nearer the universal brotherhood of all nationalities of the earth."[29] The workers are told that they have the joy of working for themselves while workers under capitalism are humiliated in toiling for grasping private owners. As proud Soviet citizens responsible for their share of the Five-Year Plan, it is their joy to fill quotas early. Towns, factories, brigades, and individual workers pledge over-plan production, even when results are out of their control, as in the case of the locomotive driver who promises to haul so many thousand tons of freight. Consumption-mindedness is degrading, while "Man is glorified by Labor." The motto is, "Love your factory, esteem its honor, be proud of the worker's labor."[30] "You should be happy in the feeling of joyous exaltation which you experience when you go to work in your collective. . . ."[31]

The effectiveness of moral incentives seems to be uneven, however; perhaps the best thing about the Brigades of Communist Labor was that they qualified for substantial bonuses, recently several hundred million rubles yearly. Russians take medals seriously, even wearing them on the beach; but awards are more appropriate and doubtless more effective in a priority industry filling a great national need. Medals for productivity must carry more weight in a tank factory than a sausage plant. The purpose, however, is more than to reward the outstanding workers. It is to call attention to the performance of the best workers and their techniques, and to put pressure on others to do likewise.

Moral incentives are the affair of the party, and this has been called upon to take a stronger direct hand in overcoming the difficulties of the economy. Whatever relaxation of administrative control there may have been under the economic reforms seems to have been fully compensated by party controls. "The reform evoked deep moral-ethical advances, it placed the accents

[29] *Bakinskii rabochii*, February 11, 1971, p. 3.
[30] *Pravda*, February 22, 1970.
[31] *Izvestia*, December 16, 1970, p. 3.

in a new way on the mutual relations of persons in the process of production. . . ."[32] While still maintaining that its role is not administration but political mobilization and organizational educational work, the party seems to have gone far toward taking charge of the nuts and bolts of production. For example, "The paper industry should be under the firm control of party, soviet, and economic organizations";[33] and there is not much apparent difference between the kind of control exercised by each. The party group gets credit for the successful laying of a pipeline.[34] Party guidance takes place behind closed doors and is less discussed than administrative direction. But economic decisions not only at the top but at all levels are likely to be examined first in party committees.

The party makes special efforts to look to matters with which planners have most difficulty, particularly honesty, quality of production, and innovation. Party discipline and spirit should compensate for the deficiencies of planning, as the party strives "to combine trust for the cadres and the development of their self-reliance and initiative with high exactingness and precisely imposed control."[35] Men should do what is right for the country and the party and find their rewards in their conscience and the esteem of the party. The party should dissuade the manager from seeking lower assignments and inspire him with a passion for modernization in the name of Lenin. If it were not that party leaders share many of the purposes of the managers and so collude with them, the party-ideological approach to production might be quite effective.

Trade Unions

The trade unions are important auxiliaries of the party in the stimulation of production and promotion of labor discipline. They are organized by industry—there were recently twenty-two—in parallel with the party, with regional councils and a central organization. Like the party, the trade unions have big congresses every few years, although Stalin held none from 1932 to 1949. Nearly all workers, except the temporarily employed, are members; and unions include not only bench workers but managers, who may be quite influential within the workers' organization. There are also "production councils" alongside the union organization at the lowest level, composed of a delegate for six to ten workers. Introduced with much fanfare and promise in 1958 as a step toward industrial democracy, they were given outwardly large consultative powers; but they have largely disappeared from view.

---

[32] *Izvestia*, January 15, 1970, p. 3.
[33] *Pravda*, November 17, 1969.
[34] *Pravda*, October 5, 1969.
[35] *Pravda* editorial, January 18, 1971.

The trade unions are controlled from top down, in much the same way as the party; and union officials, like party secretaries, are subject to confirmation. They are also controlled by the party at each level. Elections are in the party manner, indirect for the upper bodies and open for officers, by secret ballot for primary committees, with slates proposed by the party fraction. As Soviet authors put it, if the unions themselves proposed candidates, this would be harmful to the dictatorship of the proletariat.[36] The party seems to pay some heed to the feelings of workers in the trade unions and directs fairly suavely, with ostensible respect for democratic forms.[37] But rulership has been complete since 1930, and the duty of the trade unions to follow the party was written into the statutes in 1938. Trade union committees may meet jointly with party committees, and the All-Union Central Council of Trade Unions may join the Central Committee and the Council of Ministers in the issuance of decrees on labor matters. Work in and through the unions is a large part of the activity of party groups in factories; "party committees and primary organizations [should] improve their leadership of trade unions, raise higher and higher [the unions'] role as schools of administration, schools of economic management, schools of communism."[38] The agenda of the trade union meeting is likely to be identical to that of the party group. When the Central Council of Trade Unions met in July, 1969, the only item on the agenda was, "Results of the International Meeting of Communist and Workers' Parties."

Although after the Revolution unions were promised control of the economy, there has been no question of a political role since their share of industrial management was ended in 1929. A suggestion in that direction would be "anarcho-syndicalism." Any independence of unions would immediately bring out latent conflicts of interest between workers and the state which runs the factories, and such conflict is inadmissible.

As agents of the state, trade unions handle social security benefits (except pensions), health services, and sanatoria; they sponsor and largely finance vacations for deserving workers. They patronize organized sports,[39] recreational facilities, and production training; they have some voice in housing assignment, the payment of overtime, job classification, and the expenditure of collective bonuses. Unions also should protect the worker in various ways,

[36] A. Aimbetov, M. Baimakonov, M. Imashev, *Problemy sovershenstvovaniia organizatsii i deiatel'nosti mestnykh sovetov* (Izd. Nauka), Alma Ata, 1967, p. 84.

[37] Emily C. Brown, *Soviet Trade Unions and Labor Relations* (Harvard University Press), Cambridge, Mass., 1966, p. 147.

[38] *Pravda*, October 30, 1969.

[39] Organized sports are as politicized in the Soviet Union as they are commercialized in the West. Administered under party direction by the trade unions or for paramilitary purposes by military groups, they are to fill leisure with approved activities, offer emotional outlets and involvement for the masses, provide heroes for the young, and improve both labor productivity and defense capabilities.

looking to the enforcement of the rules against managerial caprice and to safety standards. They must be consulted regarding disciplinary actions, especially dismissal, a serious blot on the record of a Soviet worker. It is important for a worker to stand well with his union.

Unions sign collective contracts with management, but wages are fixed by the government. The collective contracts deal mostly with the joint efforts of workers and management to fulfill the plan. This is the most important function of the unions, which help secure the cooperation of the workers not only by propaganda and moral pressure but by their ability to reward the zealous and impose sanctions ranging from public reprobation and formal condemnation to deprival of benefits and bonuses, even of union membership, social security benefits, etc.

It is also a function of the unions to prevent strikes and work stoppages. Although wages are not at issue, there have been occasional reports of strikes from sundry exasperations.[40] A strike means that union leaders (as well as party and management) have failed, and they can expect to be appropriately punished. Labor discipline, however, is laxer in practice than theory; many observers have reported that workers seem to spend more time relaxing on the job than producing.

Labor

A large majority of Soviet workers are paid by piece-rates, a system denounced as exploitative in capitalist countries. The fixing of wages is very complex, with bonuses, over-norm premiums, differential categories, extras for various regions and working conditions, and sundry deductions. Despite central control over wages, the manager has some leeway in classifying jobs and applying norms. Consequently, because cost is still less important than output and workers are legally free to shop around, there has been some upward pressure on wages. The draconian disciplinary law of 1940 (issued allegedly on recommendation of the trade unions) is no more; workers can leave their jobs on two weeks' notice. Only students, obliged to take assigned positions for two years after graduation, are legally bound.

There is still restriction on movement, however. Housing is ordinarily tied to employment, as are some of the benefits trade unions can dispense. The ability of employers to make negative entries in the work book, which must be presented to get a job, is a deterrent to change. To get work in another town, one must have a residence permit and a place to live, which is difficult to procure in the desirable cities. However, the ability of the government to direct

---

[40] In 1963, Soviet authorities, to demonstrate the workers' freedom, reported a strike: longshoremen refused to load coal for France in solidarity with a French miners' strike. (Brown, op. cit., p. 235.)

its people is limited. Doctors and teachers shun the village for the metropolis. The efforts to populate Siberia, where the great treasures of raw materials lie, have been unavailing. Despite blandishments, career opportunities, exhortation, and bonuses, about one million more persons emigrated from Siberia in the decade of the 1960's than were induced to go there.

Much of Soviet industrial growth has come about from the expansion of the work force, which is somewhat larger than that of the United States. But it is no longer possible to draw many more from the countryside, already drained of youth, and the labor force is growing only very slowly. On the other hand, there is a great deal of underemployment because managers refrain from firing workers who may be needed at some future time. There is an undisclosed amount of unemployment, also, from technological change, lack of skills, lack of coordination between employers and technical training institutes, and planners' failure to take labor supplies into account in locating factories. Officially, unemployment was abolished in 1930, and by Soviet doctrine it cannot occur under socialism. There is no unemployment relief, although there is some provision for retraining; to be jobless may be equated with parasitism.

In the Soviet view, everyone should work, unless he can qualify for a disability pension. The sexes are emphatically equal; and since only families in the upper brackets can make ends meet on one salary, women make up about half the labor force—more than half in unskilled labor. Although recently a majority of medical students have been men, medicine (a relatively low-paid occupation) has been a women's specialty, over 70% of physicians being female. But as in the political domain, fewer women reach the higher ranks; chief doctors are usually men. The farm brigade leader is probably a man, the chairman surely; the pig-tender is probably a woman. Women shovel snow, men run snow-clearing machines. While the Soviet birth rate declines, raising fears for the future labor supply, large families are discouraged by the extensive use of female labor. According to the party program, this dilemma should be solved by communal eating facilities and nurseries. Little progress is made in this direction, however, and for the present, women hold jobs and do the housework as well.

AGRICULTURE

The Soviet system functions better in industry than in agriculture. The productivity of Soviet labor in industry is about one-half of the American, in agriculture only one-fourth. Mechanization has not strikingly improved the situation on the ordinary Soviet farm; a prize was once given for an arrangement whereby seventy peasants worked together on a single grain thresher.[41] About

[41] Alec Nove, *The Soviet Economy* (Praeger), New York, 1969, p. 164.

30% of the labor force is still engaged in agriculture, against 6% in the U.S. For a long time, agricultural output was less than before the Bolsheviks took charge. A major grain exporter in tsarist times, Russia in 1963, 1965, and 1966 had to import large quantities to avoid bread rationing. Fresh fruits and vegetables in Moscow are of poor quality and costly. Stalin's successors have tried to move agriculture from its doldrums, cutting down compulsory deliveries, raising prices, and investing larger (although still relatively small) amounts in mechanization of agriculture, production of mineral fertilizers, and even electrification of the countryside. While the standard of living of city workers rose gradually, that of the peasants doubled and tripled in the post-Stalin years. Nonetheless, the peasant remains low man in Soviet society; a milkmaid may go to work at 3-4 a.m. and return home at 8 p.m.[42] The 70% output increase promised by the Seven-Year Plan (1959–1965) came to only 10%, no more than population growth. The following Five-Year Plan projected an average increase of 4% per year; the 1971–1975 projection is the same, half the rate of expected industrial growth. In 1970, the Central Committee and the Council of Ministers demanded better attention to the procurement of wild fruits and berries and wild honey.[43] In July, 1971, there was a campaign for city volunteers to help bring in the hay.

Natural conditions are unfavorable. Arable land, despite the immensity of the country, is only two-thirds of that of the United States, and many areas suffer early frosts or frequent drought. The productivity of the private peasant plots, however, shows that the failure is essentially political. Agriculture has always had low priority, the farmers have been made to bear costs of industrialization, and political controls have proved less workable in the countryside than in the cities.

Marxism was not for peasants; they did not fit its theory, and it had little to offer them. So far as the peasants supported the Leninists in the civil war, it was as the lesser evil, and grain requisitions destroyed most of whatever sympathies they had for the Soviet regime. There were very few party members in the villages, except as bosses or administrators, until after Stalin. The proportion of party members among collective farmers remains much the lowest of all occupational categories.

There remains some of the old superiority of urban, modernizing Russia for the "dark people." The peasant lived and lives still to a large extent in a world much less promising to the future-oriented revolutionary; ignorant and intractable, he represents little more than an obstacle. "Collective farmer" in Soviet speech is equivalent to "hayseed." Industrialization promised social transformation, a desired industrial proletariat, and an economy controllable by the party. Industry is prestigious, and it promised much more rapid increase of wealth than any foreseeable modernization of agriculture. Industry meant

---

[42] *Pravda*, September 16, 1970, p. 2.
[43] *Pravda*, April 7, 1970.

military power. Agriculture bespoke consumption goods, always of secondary interest, and has shared the neglect of light industry. For similar reasons, agriculture has commonly been neglected in underdeveloped countries; it does not appeal to leaders as the way out of backwardness to power and glory.

Collectivization subjected the peasants politically and harnessed them economically, facilitating the expropriation of the greater part of the harvest. The Stalinists in the 1930's would have preferred to put the peasants into purely state-owned farms, sovkhozes, but they lacked administrators to manage the "grain factories," and those which were established mostly proved expensive failures. Moreover, hiring the peasants as laborers for the state implied paying them wages; it was more attractive to let them take care of their own subsistence while exacting as much as feasible in compulsory deliveries. Hence the basic organizational form of Soviet agriculture became the collective farm, or kolkhoz, theoretically a producers' cooperative modelled after traditional communal organizations.

The administration of the kolkhoz is untraditional, however. The assembly of members "elects" the chairman, board, and inspection committee for three-year terms. General assemblies usually have been held only once or twice yearly, although the 1969 statute suggests four times. General assemblies are also replaced by meetings of delegates from brigades or other units. Membership was theoretically voluntary at first, but it soon became fixed; and a peasant can withdraw from the kolkhoz (or even make a trip to the city) only by permission. His grown children become kolkhoz members automatically, unless they decline to return after military service or manage to place themselves in higher educational institutions.

The inclination of the peasants at first was to divide equally whatever was left after the state had taken its part and the needs of the collective were satisfied. But this did not suit the Stalinist way, and they were given a complicated system of piecework pay, including exaggerated bonuses for exceeding norms. One would earn a "labor-day" for plowing a hectare or tending so many pigs or milking so many liters; all the labor days were added, and after the harvest each received a share of the net product according to his accredited labor-days.

In Stalin's time the peasants could subsist only thanks to compromise with individual enterprise. To make collectivization bearable, each household was left a garden plot of as much as one-half a hectare, on which the family could raise potatoes or vegetables and keep a cow with calf, or perhaps some pigs, chickens, or other small stock, according to the region. The peasants were also entitled to pasture the cow on kolkhoz land, to receive some feed, etc. It was permitted to sell produce of the garden plots (along with pay received in kind from the collective) at free markets. The peasant was required, at least in theory, to make the trip himself to sell his eggs or melons and could not even give a neighbor a commission to do it. Although Stalin taxed the private plots and demanded compulsory deliveries from them also, they were so much more productive than the collectivized fields that they became the major source of income. In a sense, putting in the required number of labor days for the collective was the price for being allowed a household plot, somewhat as serfs were permitted use of parcels of land in return for working on the landlord's estate.

Since mass collectivization, the kolkhozes have been completely controlled by party and state. However, they are legally an anomaly in the Soviet system, a sector of theoretically nonstate ownership of means of production; and administratively they stand slightly outside the regular system of economic controls. For ideological-political reasons, the Soviet ideal has always been the fully integrated sovkhoz, as much a part of the apparatus as a steel mill, directly and unequivocally under ministerial orders. Consequently, the thrust of Soviet policy since the Second World War has been toward the fuller incorporation of the kolkhozes into the Soviet system, ultimately toward doing away with the distinction between the two kinds of farms.

No sooner had the government finished restoring order in the kolkhozes after the Second World War than Khrushchev set about amalgamating them. They were reduced from 254,000 in 1950 to 54,000 in 1959 and were down to 36,000 at the beginning of 1970, the average kolkhoz now having some 10,000 hectares of land, 1,000 head of cattle, 40 tractors, 427 households, and 1400 people.[44] The stated purpose was efficiency, but in fact they are inefficiently large. Their amalgamation, however, made possible more effective use of the limited number of reliable party members in the countryside. In 1969, all the kolkhozes were drawn into a single network, with councils established at district, province, republic and All-Union levels, with indirect elections in the usual manner.

The enlarged kolkhozes in 1958 were given control of agricultural machinery, which Stalin had kept under separate management, thereby becoming more like state agencies in handling their own equipment. For the machine operators and other skilled personnel there is a trade union, which functions much like its counterpart in the factory, striving for labor discipline and political education; it organizes sports, social services, and vacation facilities, and it makes a collective agreement with management as though the kolkhoz were a state farm.

There has also been an effort to pay collective farmers regularly to make them more like wage-earners with more or less guaranteed wages, thereby to increase willingness to work on the collective fields and to reduce dependence on private plots. Payments in kind were discontinued, but remuneration was still

---

[44] *Narodnoe khoziastvo SSSR v 1969 g.*, Moscow, 1970, pp. 285, 304.

very complicated; a machinist might receive thirteen kinds of wage supplements.[45] From 1965, there were also moves to provide pensions for collective farm workers, to be paid from a fund based on contributions of the members. Superannuated kolkhozniki were receiving twenty rubles per month in 1971, but it was hoped to raise this to the sovkhoz level of forty rubles.

Further to approximate kolkhoz to sovkhoz, there has been intermittent pressure on the peasant plot. Khrushchev once proposed agricultural towns wherein workers would live in cities and tend no land for themselves except window boxes. But liberalizing measures after Stalin's death tended in the opposite direction, removing burdens on household production. From 1958, however, many measures were taken by local authorities to induce or compel peasants to give up individually-owned livestock and by kolkhozes to squeeze the private sector. These unpopular actions were halted by Khrushchev's successors very soon after his removal, and taxes on peasant livestock were ended. However, the general purpose remains. By persuasion and the increased profitability of the collective economy, the peasants should be gradually weaned from private enterprise.

Another step toward making kolkhozes into properly socialist enterprises has been to permit and encourage them along with state farms to establish small industrial plants, primarily but not necessarily using agricultural raw materials. This is an old dream of Russian revolutionaries and is sensible, as farm workers have had little to do much of the year. It was not allowed by Stalin, who wanted industry where he could control it. There was some opposition to this move, and local authorities seem to have been tempted to crack down if enterprises became profitable. There is no notion of letting farmers produce what they wish; a man and woman were sentenced to ten and twelve years of imprisonment for making paint brushes, rope, etc., on a kolkhoz without authorization.[46] But it shows increased confidence that the party is prepared to license kolkhoz industries.

As the kolkhoz became very like a sovkhoz, it can have made little difference to the member that he was summoned occasionally to use his symbolic right to approve a chairman instead of receiving a director frankly appointed by higher powers. Even so, the share of kolkhozes in Soviet agriculture has shrunk. New farms set up, as in connection with Khrushchev's Virgin Lands program and expansion of the cultivated area by irrigation, have been sovkhozes; and after 1957 many kolkhozes were converted into sovkhozes by the will, theoretically, of the membership. The state farms have approximately tripled their percentage of agricultural output since 1950 until they have half of the cropland and more than half as many workers as kolkhozes.

The state farms average about three times as large as the nominal cooperatives, and they are better mechanized and much more productive. But

---

[45] *Pravda*, February 13, 1970.
[46] *Radianska Ukraina*, December 2, 1970, p. 4; *ABSEES*, April, 1971, p. 37.

this remaining difference is decreasing as the kolkhozes modernize. The difference of the forms has also been lessened by a reform of the state farms. Formerly selling to the state at low prices and in return receiving subsidies, they have been going over to a system of accountability like that of the kolkhozes. The sovkhoz is even to distribute part of profits like the kolkhozes' sharing out.

The giant state farm, spread over tens of thousands of hectares and comprising dozens or scores of villages, should approach the Communist planners' dream. It has its several specialized departments, of agronomy, animal husbandry, communal services, construction, planning, etc., each headed by supposed experts and staffed by specialized workers more like proper proletarians than individualistic, tradition-bound peasants. It should, in the Marxist way, be growing toward an urban style of life, with large apartment buildings, cafeterias, nurseries, cinema, and the like. However, it is something of a white elephant, expensive and cumbersome. Both sovkhoz and kolkhoz, as Soviet economists are well aware, are badly in need of decentralization, much as industry needs more latitude for economic profit-and-loss management.

The debate has gone on in agriculture even longer than industry, as efforts have been made to enlarge or restrict the "link" as a unit of production and accounting. Under Stalin there were moves to let "links" of some six to twelve peasants take charge of a fixed parcel of land with livestock and as much equipment as feasible and cultivate it as well as they could for their own material benefit. By the "lease," the farmers would pay a "rent" in the form of sales of fixed quantities of produce at fixed prices; whatever else they raised they could merchandise freely. The idea was rejected by Stalin on "ideological" grounds, because it would lead to too much independence; the preferred work unit remained the brigade of about one hundred peasants attached to no particular piece of land. Under Khrushchev's successors, as industrial reform was in the air, it was again mooted that the link be made the basic unit. The experiment was reportedly tried on both kolkhozes and sovkhozes on a limited scale, and yields, returns, and profits were as much as doubled. But it was again feared that such a change might lead to the break-up of the collectives and retreat from economic planning, to weakening of the party's position in the countryside and dissolution of much of the administrative apparatus; resistance prevented generalization of the idea.[47]

Controls and Difficulties

As Pravda headlines, "The first commandment of agriculture is grain for the state."[48] The party has long been concerned with controlling peasants and agriculture even more closely than factory workers and industry. Lines of

---

[47] See Dimitry Pospielovsky, "The Link System in Soviet Agriculture," *Soviet Studies*, vol. XXI, no. 4, April, 1970, pp. 411–435.

[48] September 2, 1971, p. 1.

authority go through the Union and the republic ministries of agriculture, the soviets, and the party. So close is the attention given the kolkhozes that it might seem that the state farms, likely to be under any of various ministries and departments or even food-consuming industrial groups, as a coal combine, railroad administration, or a trade enterprise,[49] may be able to operate a little more freely. Primary responsibility for management of agriculture lies with the county (raion) administration, which looks to deliveries and gives relevant orders. Village soviets are to work with the farm administrations to help carry out directions, which are extremely numerous and detailed, fixing virtually all collective farm programs.

At any level the real boss is probably the party secretary, and the party manages not only through the administrative apparatus but in its own name, both through agricultural departments and primary party organizations. As in industry, the party is concerned not only with morale, indoctrination, and organization, but with production. Communists are supposed to study techniques, to spread the advances of the best farms and best workers, and particularly to foster innovation, for which economic incentives are inadequate, and push the work generally. "The raion party organization at the moment has no more important task than bringing in the harvest promptly and without losses."[50] The needs of the world struggle against imperialism are impressed on collective farmers. Moral incentives are used as in industry. The leading combine sports a flag of victory in socialist competition as it cuts a swath across the field, and good workers become "Master of Agricultural Production" or "Honored Machine Operator." Children of collective farmers should be made to want to stay on the farm by inculcation of better attitudes and by giving more dignity to the calling. On entering the ranks of full-fledged kolkhoznik, a youth should go through an initiation ceremony with a solemn oath and should be handed a labor book for a formal record of his achievements.[51]

The party picks the kolkhoz officials, the oblast committee naming the chairman, the raion committee naming the brigade leaders. The peasants can vote for but hardly against them, as the balloting is open; at best they might appeal to a higher party body. The chairmen seem to be regularly brought in from the outside to check tendencies to self-seeking on the part of the kolkhoz. Socially and politically superior to ordinary members, they are professionals probably trained in special schools,[52] whose advancement depends on satisfying not the farmers but the party hierarchy. As bosses, they are more powerful than industrial managers, because the collective farmers are more scattered than factory workers and have less recourse to agencies which might protect their

[49] *Sovety deputatov trudiashchiksia*, no. 1, January, 1969, p. 9.
[50] *Selskaia zhizn*, August 31, 1969.
[51] *Selskaia zhizn*, January 8, 1969.
[52] *Partiinaia zhizn*, no. 20, October, 1970, p. 72.

rights. The prerogatives of the chairman approach those of a feudal lord. He can dispose fairly freely of kolkhoz funds and property as long as he fulfills his obligations. He assigns jobs and issues orders binding on all under him, who are not free to leave the estate. He assesses fines at his discretion. He may even require his subjects to give blood.[53]

It is more difficult to plan and manage agriculture from a distance than industry, as farms have their particular problems in endlessly varied local conditions, and the variable seasons are forever presenting unplanned necessities. Despite this, the men in Moscow have long given overriding directions for the conduct of Soviet agriculture, prescribing what was to be raised and how. Khrushchev gave only a little relief from Stalinist strictures, and he went on to impose numerous panaceas. His program for plowing marginal "virgin lands" was carried out capriciously and in disregard of scientific counsel. The corn planting campaign was comical in its exaggeration; to please the leader, corn was allotted the best land, most fertilizer, and most careful cultivation, thereby compounding the delusions. A later campaign to plow fallow and grassland promised a quick return but increased erosion and reduced fertility.

Capricious and arbitrary command has been at least as prevalent on the local level. Each layer is under pressure from above to extract as much as possible from those below; and party and state agencies interfere constantly, with or without strict legal authority, to overcome what they see as selfishness on the part of producers. If a farm produces a large amount of milk or grain, its quota is likely to be raised. If farmers make money by producing high quality pickles, they are scolded and warned that wealth will not bring them happiness.[54] Even though a farm shows a loss, it may have to pay income tax.[55] A good harvest may actually be harmful, as it encourages the secretaries and directors to interfere and squeeze the household plots, while a bad harvest inspires respect for realities.

Planning encounters many troubles similar to those in industry. The demand for paperwork is insatiable. The stream of instructions and queries is said to be such as to occupy most of the time of specialists; a section of the Ministry of Agriculture dealing with irrigation and drainage wanted 1,166 items of information from a kolkhoz.[56] A sovkhoz, with 15,000–16,000 indicators in its long-range plan, may be expected to supply 50,000–60,000 indices through the year.[57] The measurement of performance is difficult. When the chicken-tenders were paid by the weight of chickens raised, they produced hens that were

[53] *Izvestia,* January 7, 1970, p. 2; *ABSEES*, July, 1970, p. 84.

[54] *Sovetskaia Rossia,* October 30, 1970, p. 2.

[55] *Izvestia,* September 4, 1969; *Current Digest,* vol. 21, no. 36, p. 24.

[56] *Pravda,* May 30, 1970, p. 2; July 28, 1970.

[57] Morris Bornstein, "The Soviet Debate on Agricultural Price and Procurement Reforms," *Soviet Studies,* vol. 21, no. 1, July, 1969, p. 16.

too fat for laying; it proved necessary to go to such criteria as the amount of vitamin A in their livers and the size of the oviduct.[58] Judicial sanctions are used to supplement economic incentives; loss of cotton in harvesting is punishable by one year's imprisonment, two years if the fiber is taken for home use.[59]

The price system is even more irrational in agriculture than industry. Under Stalin, some prices were insufficient to pay even the cost of transportation to market. Such anomalies have ended; but a farm, with quotas to fill for fifteen to twenty items, will show a loss on some which it is expected to make up on others; sometimes the farm is driven to purchasing in the market. There are different prices for different producers, quantities, and regions. Prices of perishables are constant through the year, discouraging storage and off-season production. Prices are still generally too low for adequate incentive. When it is announced that farms can sell freely or at higher prices their produce over fixed quotas, this is negated by calls for voluntary overfulfillment, for joyous contributions to socialist competition, or for generous assistance to less fortunate kolkhozes.

Under these conditions, Soviet agriculture has suffered lethargy and inefficiency. A large part of agricultural machinery is frequently reported idle and in need of spare parts or repairs. Every fall, much grain is lost because of lack of storage and transportation facilities. A major reason for losses seems to be determination of authorities to remove harvests rapidly from the farms lest the peasants help themselves. Misuse of collective assets seems to be rife. A measure of the inefficiency of the politically ordered farms is the productivity of the household plots, which with 1% of the cultivated land produce one-third of agricultural output. In 1970, they accounted for 60% of potatoes, 45% of vegetables, 40% of meat and milk, and 60% of eggs, figures which had declined only slightly over the previous decade. Privately owned Soviet pigs performed about as well as the American average; socialized pigs put on less than one-half as much weight.[60] The productivity of labor seems to be as high on the diminutive plots as on the immense collective fields with all their machines and large-scale facilities.[61]

Despite this poor record, however, the Russian village is gradually growing into the twentieth century. The Stalinist neglect is no more; agriculture is no longer called upon to finance industrialization but receives growing investment funds. Allotments for 1971–1975 are set at 77.6 billion rubles, 70% over the previous five-year period. Electric lines are creeping across the countryside, and television sets are no longer a rarity.

[58] *Sovetskaia Rossia*, October 30, 1970, p. 2.

[59] *Pravda Vostoka*, November 5, 1970, p. 2.

[60] W. Klatt, in Roy D. Laird, ed., *Soviet Agriculture: the Permanent Crisis* (Praeger), New York, 1965, p. 140.

[61] Eric Strauss, *Soviet Agriculture in Perspective* (Praeger), New York, 1969, p. 289.

RESULTS AND PROSPECTS

Not only because of shortages, stresses, and priorities, but in its campaigning, relative neglect of the consumer, and use of noneconomic methods and moral incentives, the Soviet is somewhat like a war economy. By comparison with those of "bourgeois" Western societies, it is sharply skewed. For some purposes, it is effective, perhaps uniquely so. It is able to shift resources, to make major decisions, and concentrate on objectives which the planners or the party deem crucial. It should be well equipped to plan urban development, at least in broad outlines. It produces magnificent displays, from May Day celebrations to spectacular theatricals. Some basic services, as medicine and education, are well organized and more freely available than in most countries. Public transportation is mostly efficient and inexpensive; Soviet trains and subways are good to excellent. Military wares are outstanding both in quality and quantity.

The level of Soviet technology and productivity varies somewhat according to relation to military and national political purposes. The space program, run by the military, was ahead of the American as long as it could ride on military rocketry and fell behind only when the United States developed rockets larger than militarily useful. Various items, as helicopters and cameras, benefit from the military priority. The Soviet fishing fleet is modern and efficient, although crews are about double those on comparable Japanese or Norwegian trawlers. It seems easier to mechanize fishing than egg production; the fishing fleet has much naval and political utility. The Russians have much to their credit likewise in areas essential to military production. Steel technology has been up to international standards, and production indicators for Soviet furnaces are quite high. A good deal of Soviet machine-building has been of outstanding quality; the Russians are the world's leaders in gigantic machinery.

If the record in agriculture and consumer goods industry has by contrast been deficient, these branches have been starved and called upon to pay for requirements of heavy industry. Their backwardness also results from lower morale and the greater difficulty of central planning in these areas. Trade and distribution have suffered at least as much. Commerce seems to need freedom even more than industry; but distribution is a state monopoly (except for the kolkhoz markets) run on plans for turnover and fixed margins, with few incentives for initiative and many controls. Scorned as nonproductive, retail trade is one of the least desirable of professions.

By virtue of concentration on heavy industry and mobilization of resources, the Soviet Union has shown historically rapid growth. Industrial production increased yearly 12–14% in the decade after 1928 and at similar rate in the decade after the Second World War. Soviet industrial production was about 13% of that of the United States in 1913, but has been about two-thirds of that of the United States since 1963. In the late 1920's, Soviet steel production was less than one-fifth of the American, but it currently has been about nine-tenths. It is not true, however, that "Such growth is impossible in the world of capitalism."[62] According to the national statistics reproduced by the United Nations, China (Taiwan), El Salvador, Greece, Iran, Israel, Japan, Republic of Korea, Mexico, Pakistan, and Spain all showed more rapid industrial expansion, 1963–1969, than the Soviet Union, some by a wide margin. In some respects the Soviet economy is decidedly backward. For a larger population, the volume of mail and the number of telephones are less than one-tenth of the American figures,[63] and the rise of the Soviet standard of living has not been comparable to industrial growth. Consumption per head is ordinarily estimated about one-half of that of leading Western European countries[64] and one-fourth of that of the United States, although comparisons are subjective and uncertain.

The average wage was supposed to reach 122 rubles monthly in 1971, with prices mostly irregularly higher than in the United States.[65] But quality, assortment, and availability are as important as wages and prices. Rents are low, in the range of $5–10 per month for small apartments; but housing is very short, with most urban families doubled up; housing per capita in the cities is still much under the prerevolutionary level. Construction has not gotten back to the 1959 figure of 2,710,000 units (mostly two-room apartments). Tenants may have to make repairs or replace defective fixtures shortly after moving in. Many prerevolutionary buildings in Moscow and Leningrad are in excellent condition, while Soviet buildings frequently become shabby in a few years. To this day, tourists in the principal cities are likely to be lodged in tsarist-built hotels. A large proportion of apartments lack running water; it still seems exceptional for water to be piped into village homes.[66]

Production of passenger cars is about one-twentieth of the American, two-thirds of them destined to official use. The Togliatti auto plant, built with foreign help, should triple this by 1975, producing vehicles basically of 1960 design; but the country is totally unprepared for the automotive age in roads, repair facilities, and service stations, of which Moscow recently had one per million population.

Many mundane goods are likely to be scarce or nonexistent, as fresh fruits and vegetables out of season. Food processing is backward; the gap is very incompletely filled by imports, mostly from Eastern Europe. From time to time

---

[62] As claimed by Soviet professors, *Sovetskaia Rossia*, February 5, 1971, p. 1.

[63] *Statistical Abstract of the United States*, 1970 ed., pp. 831, 832.

[64] Cf. Hanson, *The Soviet Consumer*, p. 41.

[65] See Keith Bush, "A Comparison of Retail Prices in the USA, USSR, and Western Europe in April, 1969," *Bulletin*, Institute for the Study of the USSR, vol. XVII, no. 3, March, 1970, pp. 13–32.

[66] *Partiinaia zhizn*, no. 11, June, 1971, p. 63.

meat or eggs may be nearly or entirely unavailable. Little items, as nylon stockings, needles, irons, or hairpins, may be first unobtainable and then a glut, as planners overreact. During much of 1969, matches were a black market commodity. There is incomprehensible slowness in the introduction of new products. Transistor radios came to the Soviet Union with a lag of a decade, and the planners simply did not interest themselves in numerous trivia, as cellophane tape, pencil sharpeners, can openers, and ball point pens. Principal Soviet cities in the latter 1960's opened shops wherein all manner of otherwise unobtainable and good quality merchandise could be purchased only with foreign currency. One commodity almost always to be bought for rubles at moderate prices and in fair quality is vodka and other alcoholic beverages. The reason seems to be that sale of alcohol is an easy way to meet turnover norms and show profits, and it brings large revenues to the state.[67]

Most services are poorly run; shoe repairs or dry cleaning are real problems for the ordinary Russian, and campaigns and decrees bring little improvement. The average Russian spends several hundred hours yearly waiting in front of shops or in line. For many goods, there is rationing by queue, as a shipment of stylish sweaters or pretty dishes is likely to be sold out in hours. Productivity of labor is reduced by workers' taking time off to get things repaired, do their shopping, or deal with official red tape. Time is lost by the system of queuing thrice for one purchase, first to select, then to pay, then to pick up the goods. One learns of what is to be had only by word of mouth or by making the rounds of stores; commercial advertising is far behind political and is almost limited to such injunctions as "Drink coffee" or "Scallops are good eating." It has become possible to buy appliances on installments deducted from wages, but the Soviet citizen has no such convenience as a charge account or a checkbook. One result of shortages and unrealistic official prices is much speculation despite harsh legal sanctions.

Compared to the average person in most of the world, the Soviet consumer is decidedly well off. Many appliances, for example, television sets, refrigerators, and washing machines, are gradually becoming available to the mass of the population. It is in terms of results compared with ostensible efforts that the Soviet economy falls short; exhortation, prodding, indoctrination and organization, and the long-term dedication to building up the economy with the sacrifice of today to a promised tomorrow have not brought results commensurate with the effort and resources invested. Soviet achievements in education have been remarkable, but the claim that the Soviet Union has three times as many engineers as the United States raises serious questions about the utilization of resources. The great political effort to raise productivity seems to be offset by a corresponding amount of politically induced waste.

[67] Cf. Gertrude E. Schroeder, "Consumption in the USSR," *Studies on the Soviet Union*, vol. X, no. 4, 1970, pp. 1–40.

For some years, roughly 1950 to 1960, the outlook was excellent. During those years, output of steel, electricity, and other basic materials increased steeply. Capital investment tripled from 1950 to 1959, when Soviet industry acquired new equipment in the amount of $18 billion while new American industrial equipment came only to $9 billion. Soviet machine tool production was more than double the American in 1960. Aware of the harm which isolation had brought to Soviet technology, the Khrushchev leadership expanded foreign trade and exchanges of all kinds; foreign exhibitions became commonplace in Moscow and Leningrad. Foreigners were no longer stared at. Consumer goods became much more abundant and varied. Cosmetics and fashion shows appeared, and a few Russians acquired such luxuries as pet dogs. There developed something of a modest night life and cafe society in the major centers. Life was becoming materially more comfortable and graceful, and it seemed likely that the Soviet Union might soon offer its people at least more or less the same range of goods as Western Europe. The Soviet government promised categorically in 1961 that "in the current decade the Soviet Union . . . will surpass the strongest and richest capitalist country, the United States of America, in production per capita."

That promise, like Khrushchev's earlier boast that the countries of the Soviet sphere would have over half of world industrial production by 1965, has remained empty. The gap between the Soviet Union and the United States has been little narrowed in the time which the Soviet leaders gave themselves to end it, despite the fact that for a decade Soviet investments in the economy have probably exceeded American. Japan, with less than one-half the Soviet population, threatens to surpass Soviet industrial production and is already far ahead in such modern branches as electronics and optical production. The share of the Soviet bloc in world trade has remained virtually unchanged. *Izvestia* boasted (October 30, 1970) that the "Socialist Commonwealth" had 32% of world industrial production; as much was claimed in 1957. It is widely agreed that the Soviet technological lag has increased in the past decade; in computers the Soviet Union ranked sixth in the world behind France at the end of 1970. Having come within shouting distance of the leading industrial powers, the Soviet Union has been unable to sustain its relative progress; and Soviet growth rates have ceased to be a real argument for the superiority of the Soviet way. Price inflation seems to have distorted upward official indices, and the overall expansion of industrial output is about as rapid as that of Russia in the last decade of the nineteenth century.

Many reasons have been suggested for this slowdown. It is no longer easy to raise production by bringing in large numbers from the countryside; it has rather become urgent to find ways to keep capable youths on the farm. Some supplies of easily accessible raw materials have come toward exhaustion, elevating costs. The abundant natural resources lie in Siberia where workers do not like to go, and larger investments are required for their development. As the Soviet economy becomes fairly modern, gains from borrowing technology abroad are no longer so easy and spectacular. But such explanations are inadequate. With higher technology, returns on capital should improve rather than fall off. There is no real pressure on the labor supply, and the educational system is turning out large numbers of highly trained young people. No other nation is so well supplied with raw materials. There remains a great deal of technology to be borrowed, and the Russians purchase Western equipment and installations on a large scale.

The real problem seems to be the overuse or abuse of power.[68] In the Soviet system, a man can acquire goods and status much more readily by skill in dealing with people than by contributing to the production of material things. Most jobs, and all the really important ones, are political; and managers and technicians are subordinate to political bosses. The criterion for the allocation of resources is primarily utility for the party and its leadership. The attitude toward money, profit, and gain is negative; yet the striving for gain is practically inseparable from the striving to produce goods.

The economy is tied up in regulations and buried in paperwork. Fifteen minutes were required for filling out forms for the repair of a child's boot, which took only five minutes.[69] Innovation is necessarily inhibited in the bureaucratic setup because it implies risk. There is fear of producing profits lest they be removed, and managers and workers know that if they exceed norms this is an invitation to their being raised. Simple measures of decentralization are unacceptable because they would represent some loss of control or an opportunity for local people to become wealthy. Competition between nationalized enterprises would promise radical improvement for the market; this also is politically excluded. With no expenditure, the Soviet leadership could rapidly ease shortages by permitting small-scale private enterprise in services, trade and manufacturing, as is done in several East European countries. But it is inadmissible because it would infringe the principle whereby all things must hang on the will of the party, and it would permit large numbers of persons to earn their livelihood outside the official economy and so to enjoy economic and potentially political independence. From the Soviet point of view, a person who earns money by individual endeavor is a parasite, antisocial, that is, antistate. Authorities seem more anxious to prevent private gain than to improve production; when a man rigged up a gadget radically cutting the time and cost of unloading cement, this was rejected lest he profit thereby.[70] Overregulation nullifies initiative; people sit and wait for orders. It also means that a great part

[68] Gertrude E. Schroeder, "Soviet Technology: System vs. Progress," *Problems of Communism*, vol. XIX, no. 5, September-October, 1970.
[69] *Pravda*, September 13, 1970, p. 3.
[70] *Pravda*, August 4, 1971, p. 3.

of the energies of the population is spent unproductively on control. The more regulations there are, the larger the army of checkers, listeners, keepers of records, and digesters of information.

The maturing economy, however, presses against its bonds; the thesis that modernization entails liberalization of the political order is not without merit. The complexity of the economy defies the controllers, who cannot know nearly as much of what goes on as the producers. It raises a large class of technicians who are more rationally and less ideologically inclined than the party bosses. A more educated society grows impatient with political myth-making. Rapid technological change makes it harder to sustain a fixed view of the world. It becomes more difficult to keep Soviet society essentially isolated from the heretical outside world. Scientific industrial development needs freedom to experiment and innovate, to generate and apply ideas. It threatens to breed the same kind of pluralism which enfeebled tsarist autocracy in its last decades.

The conflict of interest cannot be gainsaid, as Soviet leaders see consumerism loosening their state; they want economic growth but fear it may entail political change. It can hardly be assumed that the economy of great abundance is a priority Soviet aim. Industrialization has served party rulership by furnishing a power base and motif of mobilization, as much as party rulership has been designed to forward industrialization. The orientation toward heavy industry has been maintained during all of Soviet history. For the first time, the 1971–1975 plan promised a larger increase in consumer goods, 44–48%, than producers' goods, 41–45%; but fulfillment has always been poorer in the first than the second category. Equally significant may be proposed increases of 70% in machine building and steel investment; they bespeak a fundamental power orientation of the economy.

The Soviet leadership, we may assume, wishes to see the people decently fed and housed and sufficiently well supplied with goods that there is ample impulse to work for money and satisfaction and pride in the Soviet system. But material well-being per se is less important, to judge from the Soviet press, than productivity. Workers should have nice apartments and pleasant surroundings so that they will work more efficiently,[71] vacations so they will remain productively healthy.[72]

Socialized consumption is strongly preferred to individualistic. When income takes in part the form of schooling, medical services, entertainment, pensions, cheap vacations, tours, etc., control remains with the authorities and the dependence of the people is correspondingly increased. People are expected to be grateful for benefits they receive without direct charge, taxes being indirect and hidden. It is politically desirable to furnish living space at a nominal cost, although economically it is troublesome; it means that shelter is not bought

[71] *Selskaia zhizn*, March 19, 1969.
[72] *Sovetskaia Rossia*, November 15, 1970.

or rented by the individual as an equal but is dispensed by the authorities. One has an apartment not because he has paid for it but by fiat of higher powers. Somewhat curiously in view of the ordinary deficiencies of restaurant services, much effort is made to socialize eating. It is sufficiently desirable to have communal child care that facilities have been established exceeding demand in Moscow and Leningrad. Despite urgings that mothers should avail themselves of the nurseries, they have been seriously underoccupied.[73] When the society of the future is mentioned, emphasis is not on abundance but on "communism," in which economic independence would become zero. Not only is personal property to be eliminated, but in the apartment of the future, meals, laundry, recreation, and child care are to be communal.[74] Yet the apartment collective must in no wise be a group apart.

It is questionable how much the elite might be willing to sacrifice to give the average Russian the kind of prosperity which would give the masses the mobility and independence of a private automobile and the urge to travel abroad. Ordinarily, authoritarian states have not been directed toward welfare and a maximum of goods for all. In any case, the elites have abundance, and their privileges are greater as they are exclusive. It is probably impossible to organize such a tight system as the Soviet on the basis of dedication to popular well-being. If economic development leads to difficulties for the controllers, if there is a conflict between political stability and raising productivity of industry and agriculture, the leadership will face a very difficult choice.

The Soviet Union can relieve some of the pressures for liberalization by importing technology and to some extent capital. Thus the Russians have invited Japanese investment and skills to play a major role in the development of minerals and timber in Siberia. In the 1960's the Soviets returned to the practice of the early 1930's of importing industrial plants and technicians, not only to install them but in some cases to operate them. The auto works at Togliatti on the Volga are perhaps the most modern in the world; their equipment is entirely foreign. It may not even be necessary for the Soviet leaders themselves to perceive their needs. In 1969, an Italian group, taking note of the backwardness of Soviet merchandising, took all the initiative of planning and persuading to get orders for several million dollars' worth of fully equipped supermarkets. This is a confession of failure for the state which was to lead the way into the future, but the Soviet Union can thereby improve its technology with minimal modification of its political system.

The basic pattern of foreign trade of the Soviet Union remains that of a less developed country, exporting mostly bulk raw materials and importing the fruits of the inventiveness of less organized societies: gas is sold to Germany in return for the pipe which is to carry it, and chrome ore is shipped to Western

---

[73] *Literaturnaia gazeta* June 4, 1969.
[74] *Literaturnaia gazeta*, November 6, 1969; *Current Digest*, vol. 22, no. 3, p. 16.

Europe in exchange for computers. The Soviets likewise export raw materials to countries of Eastern Europe and predominantly receive from them machinery and manufactured consumer goods. This corresponds to comparative advantage; the Soviet Union has large natural resources and in its planned economy is best prepared to produce simple, relatively homogeneous and unchanging goods.

The Soviet Union is a model of economic development only for relatively backward states. It represents less a new departure than a modernization of timeworn ways of authoritarianism. The Chinese have called it state capitalism of a new bourgeoisie, and it has shown many of the features of monopolistic capitalism. The owners of the economy are not troubled by wage demands, the unions cooperate tamely in helping production, and everyone buys in the company stores at prices fixed by the company. Far more than in any Western country, the entire economy is controlled by a very small group, who can well mock the influence of Western financiers and captains of industry. According to Marxism, the owning class is the ruling class, but nowhere is this identity so complete as in Leninist countries; it is the peculiarity of "bourgeois" society that economic and political power are somewhat separated. The full joining of the two makes possible a relatively unified, orderly and purposefully directed but stiff and inefficient society.[75]

READINGS

Fyodor Abramov, *One Day in the "New Life"* (Praeger), New York, 1963.

Mikhail Bor, *Aims and Methods of Soviet Planning* (International Publishers), New York, 1967.

Robert Campbell, *Soviet Economic Power* (Houghton Mifflin), Boston, 1966.

George R. Feiwel, *The Soviet Quest for Economic Efficiency* (Praeger), New York, 1967.

Jerry F. Hough, *The Soviet Prefects: the Local Party Organs in Industrial Decision-Making* (Harvard University Press), Cambridge, Mass., 1969.

James R. Millar, *The Soviet Rural Community* (University of Illinois Press), Urbana, Ill., 1971.

Alec Nove, "Soviet Agriculture under Brezhnev," *Slavic Review*, vol. 29, no. 3, September, 1970, pp. 379–411.

[75] This is not to imply that the United States or any other country has a satisfactory answer to the major problems of this age. The roles of private vs. public interests, entrepreneurial freedom vs. state control, labor vs. capital, raise all kinds of questions and dilemmas. There is enormous waste and irrationality in the American economy. But it seems clear that the challenge and strengths of the Soviet system are not economic but primarily political.

G. V. Osipov, ed., *Industry and Labour in the USSR* (Tavistock Publications), London, 1966.

Barry M. Richman, *Soviet Management* (Prentice-Hall, Inc.), Englewood Cliffs, N. J., 1965.

Nicholas Spulber, *The Soviet Economy, Structure, Principles, Problems* (W. W. Norton & Co., Inc.), New York, 1969.

Vladimir G. Treml, ed., *The Development of the Soviet Economy* (Praeger), New York, 1968.

On special topics:

Emily C. Brown, *Soviet Trade Unions and Labor Relations* (Harvard University Press), Cambridge, Mass., 1966.

Robert Conquest, ed., *Industrial Workers in the USSR* (Praeger), New York, 1967.

Philip Hanson, *The Consumer in the Soviet Economy* (Northwestern University Press), Evanston, Ill., 1968.

Roy D. Laird, ed., *Soviet Agriculture: the Permanent Crisis* (Praeger), New York, 1965.

Alec Nove, *The Soviet Economy*, 2nd. ed. (Praeger), New York, 1969.

Robert J. Osborne, *Soviet Social Policies, Welfare, Equality, and Community* (Dorsey Press), Homewood, Ill., 1970.

Erich Strauss, *Soviet Agriculture in Perspective* (Praeger), New York, 1969.

9. Psychocultural Front

PERSUASION

For Lenin, the party paper was almost as important as the party organization. His party carries on political advertising by all conceivable means and media—the Russians call a pipeline "Friendship," and a sausage may show the hammer and sickle in cross-section—using censorship to exclude deviant expression. It is not enough that a factory produce according to plan; it must also constantly raise the political level of its workers.

Political culture is conceived in the West as produced by the press, schools, broadcasting, cinema, etc., more or less independently of the government, along with popular traditions and inherited attitudes. In the Soviet Union all organized opinion-making (with a slight exception of churches) is closely directed by the party. Marxism claims that the ruling classes make a cultural superstructure to reinforce their position; nowhere do they do this so thoroughly and purposefully as in the Soviet Union. The monopoly of organization means a monopoly of mass communication.

Propaganda is less wasteful and less dangerous than sheer coercion, which embitters and may lead to a reaction. Police and especially armies always represent some political menace, since they are potentially capable of removing the men in the highest seats. But propagandists have no arms other than their message and are not only harmless but the most loyal.

The lesser aspect of opinion control is (officially unacknowledged) censorship under the Ministry of Culture. Closure of hostile newspapers was one of the first acts of the fledgling Soviet government in 1917, and it has always been insisted that the press should be entirely in the service of the party; only the intensity of control has fluctuated slightly from the looseness of the mid-1920's to the Stalinist absolutism, the post-Stalin thaw, and recently again toward strictness. Phonograph records, radio and television, plays, movies, circuses, placards, etc., are all subject to official scrutiny and approval. Only party and a few government publications are considered sufficiently reliable, and some scientific publications sufficiently technical, that specific authorization is dispensed. Actual censorship comes only when material is put into print, and editors should be the primary watchdogs through their knowledge of what is expected.

To be a Soviet journalist is to be a specially reliable Communist. "Ideological work" being peculiarly the province of the party, the Central Committee department has divisions for each medium or type, central press, regional press, books, movies, etc. Most of the press is directly under party management, while radio and television are run by state committees. Leading papers are organs of the Central Committee; *Izvestia* speaks in the name of the government. With minor exceptions, all periodicals are published by party-controlled organizations, ranging from ministries to the Union of Writers. Although they may be directed to special audiences, as the military or the industrial workers, papers carry a very similar message and publish the same speeches and proclamations. Most authoritative is *Pravda*, claimed to have been founded by Lenin in 1912 and decorated with two orders of Lenin, which it sports on the masthead. On rare occasions papers have mildly criticized one another; *Pravda* may criticize others, but no one criticizes *Pravda*.

"The press of the USSR is a most important means by which the party speaks with the people concerning vital questions of the building of communism, the development of the economy and culture, and the education of the new man."[1] The press is a lever for the organization of the people, a coordinator of campaigns, and a means by which they learn the party line and concerns of the day. It is also a control organ. On the basis of letters received (major papers claim to receive one thousand or more letters per day) and information from reporters with rights of access to lower-level offices, to question and examine almost anyone or anything, it is an adjunct of more regular enforcement agencies. Millions of nonpaid correspondents help the press to encourage good work and denounce lapses. When even a local paper barks, party organizations jump, not to speak of nonparty ones. When *Pravda* growls, it is grave.

It is a duty of the party to promote the press, and it is considered desirable that people buy more papers (or spend more time with TV) just as it is that they produce more kilowatts. The quality of Soviet papers is low in relation

[1] *Pravda*, August 13, 1969.

to the importance attributed to them. Paper, printing, and pictures are mediocre to poor. They ordinarily have only four pages, *Izvestia* having six about twice weekly, and *Pravda* six except Monday and more for important speeches. Ten of twelve pages on March 31, 1971, were given to Brezhnev's report to the Party Congress. Despite this, leading newspapers fill space with tales of no great interest or ideological value. The same *Pravda* which carries an unsophisticated analysis of world affairs may also carry articles on physics much more technical than any American daily would venture. Many verbose statements seem intended for ideologists or party men only, and sometimes newspapers read like an official gazette. *Pravda*, on March 25 and 26, 1970, gave about three-quarters of its space to listing electoral districts, with about half a page of what would ordinarily be considered news. Such protocol events as the visit of a delegation from a "fraternal socialist" country or the publication of theses of the Central Committee are likewise prominent. Reporting of the 1971 Party Congress consisted of innumerable speeches, without commentary or summaries. There is no space for such things as crime (unless to point a moral), merely personal news, and transportation or industrial accidents. Natural calamities ordinarily trouble only the non-Soviet world. Sensational foreign events are often unreported, at least until the Soviet line is decided; the simultaneous hijacking of four planes by Arab guerillas in September, 1970, was not mentioned for several days and then only briefly noted. Even Communist affairs may be neglected; there were only the scantiest accounts of the August, 1970, meeting of party and government leaders of the Warsaw Treaty Organization. Soviet citizens often complain that "The paper is uninteresting, dull, tedious."[2] Khrushchev's son-in-law once attempted to enliven *Izvestia*, and Soviet readers took to it eagerly, but this belongs to the past. Training in journalism is undeveloped, and very little has been published about propaganda techniques and theory. The most attractive Soviet publications are those for the foreign market, such as *Soviet Life* and *Sputnik*.

Every means of conveying information, from banners to speakers on the railroads, should likewise advance the "struggle for communism." Billboards give the slogans or caricature leading capitalist powers, and hardly a square is without its statue of Lenin. Radio Moscow gives the word; it takes precedence over local stations, which mostly relay its programs, in the same way that central papers stand above local organs. About half of radio outlets are wired speakers. Soviet radio has some competition, however. Jamming of foreign broadcasts was begun in 1948 as the Cold War chilled, ended in 1963 as the relaxation came to its height, and resumed in August, 1968. However, shortwave radios are common, and many Russians are said to listen to Western broadcasts.

Over six million television sets were made in 1970; and fairly soon nearly all Soviet citizens should have access to television. Moscow has four

[2] *Kommunist*, no. 7, July, 1970, p. 71.

programs, although broadcasting hours are much shorter than in the United States. The Russians also make much use of motion pictures, not only long films but documentaries, newsreels, and educational movies, somewhat as the American armed forces employ training films. The average Muscovite is said to attend sixty times yearly.[3]

But in the age of television, the party stresses face to face contact, which ranges from lectures and guided discussions to talks to the workers as they eat lunch; agitators are supposed to go around parks and kolkhoz markets engaging people in enlightening conversation. Workers or farmers should gather frequently for "agitation" sessions; the occasion may be lightened by music or other amusement. The propagandists, said to number over 2,000,000,[4] perhaps a half million of them professionals, have to be informative and interesting yet stress correct ideology. They must "exclude any trace of a lofty approach to people and their needs and build on deep respect for human dignity, an attentive approach and consideration of their moods. . . ."[5] Great efforts should be made to involve the people in their own edification, to speak not so much to them as with them, to carry them along in the development of ideas. The newspaper can be rejected,[6] but it is much harder to ignore the arguments of a man speaking personally. Volunteer labor, combining agitation and involvement with production, should help to fill leisure time. 119,200,000 persons are reported to have toiled on a Communist Saturday.[7] "Millions and millions of Soviet people begin this nonworking day with dedicated labor in a joyful, festive atmosphere of general inspiration."[8]

A more singularly Soviet means of molding opinion is through party schools under the Propaganda department of the Central Committee. At all levels of sophistication and importance, and in many forms, these schools train both party and nonparty people, from high-ranking ideologists to part-time agitators to citizens brushing up on their Marxism-Leninism. Everyone in a political position, from the leader of a party group up, is supposed regularly to participate in some form of political education. At the pinnacle is the Academy of Social Sciences with a three-year course of instruction. Slightly less sophisticated instruction is given in Higher Party Schools in Moscow and republic capitals, with fulltime and correspondence courses; their students include chairmen of republic councils of ministers, leaders of oblast party

[3] *Sovetskoe kino*, January 17, 1970, p. 2; *ABSEES*, July, 1970, p. 3.

[4] A. C. Unger, in *Problems of Communism*, vol. XIX, no. 5, September-October, 1970, p. 31.

[5] *Pravda*, May 28, 1969.

[6] According to a refugee writer, a whispering campaign was used to justify the invasion of Czechoslovakia because people believe much more of what they hear from their neighbors than what they read in the press. (*New York Times*, August 21, 1969.)

[7] *Pravda*, May 1, 1970.

[8] *Pravda*, April 11, 1970.

committees, etc.[9] Below them are scores of party higher educational institutions and local political schools in considerable variety for the elite and the nonparty, including universities of Marxism-Leninism, Basic Marxism-Leninism schools, elementary party schools, party aktiv schools, study circles, theoretical seminars, People's Universities, and Houses of Political Enlightenment. The Komsomol has a smaller network of political schools. There are also many "Schools of Communist Labor" and the like where vocational training is mixed with political.

Under Stalin, political education was for party members only, but Khrushchev greatly expanded it until in 1964 it supposedly involved thirty-six million people. Khrushchev's successors again restricted as they moved away from his concept of "party of the whole people"; still, in 1969 there were reported to be fifteen million students. More than one million Muscovites (about one-fourth of the adult population) were recently reported studying Marxism-Leninism under 90,000 instructors and lecturers, 200,000 agitators, and 52,000 "political informers."[10] More than a million party members are reported active in the schools.[11] The figures of massive activity may, however, be a bit misleading; sometimes party "schools" meet only twice a year.[12]

Party schooling takes up Marxist fundamentals, material production as the basis of social development, the class struggle and its role in history, and the proletarian revolution as the way from capitalism to socialism. It goes on to the biography of Lenin and party history; at the more advanced level it deals mostly with party structure and work, which merges into the study of management techniques and organization for the promotion of production. Special skills are taught; there are courses for producers of wall newspapers and posters, as well as for party workers in different branches. It is very virtuous to participate; and students are supposed to combine study with practice. In theory it might, like the old Chinese bureaucrats' study of Confucianism, continue all one's political life. It is a prime means of assuring maximum uniformity of views in the party.[13]

The purpose of propaganda is less to explain or justify than to shape attitudes and character, less to convey information than to implant broad attitudes. *Pravda* laments that "in some places to this day propaganda is dominated by educational, not to speak of scholastic methods."[14] It should lead Russians to believe that their lives are happiest in the hands of the party, and

---

[9] *Pravda*, June 10, 1971, p. 3; *Current Digest,* vol. XXIII, no. 23, p. 19.

[10] *Pravda*, November 13, 1970, p. 2.

[11] *Pravda*, October 17, 1970.

[12] *Partiinaia zhizn*, no. 11, June, 1971, p. 36.

[13] Cf. Ellen P. Mickiewicz, *Soviet Political Schools* (Yale University Press), New Haven, Conn., 1967.

[14] July 19, 1971, p. 1.

make them loyal, cheerful, selfless, and nonindividualistic, Spartan builders of the political order.[15] It should convince the people that they live in blissful freedom, while the victims of bourgeois exploitation suffer misery, slavery, and anarchy.

There is little effort to make the people feel participants, or even spectators, of the process of government. No debates and no differences are reported; there is no interpretation, and only the barest announcement is made of the replacement of high officials. Even indirect criticism is eschewed; in discussion of the fall of the birth rate there is no mention of housing shortage and the need for women to work. Bad news is hardly ever published except as a call for improvements. No suicides are news. Tourists are not supposed to photograph the shabbier aspects of Soviet life, and a documentary of Siberia shows only spring and summer. The people are not told about drought until it is stated as a reason for agricultural shortcomings. Labor is joyous; "My Love, the Factory," is the title of a newspaper eulogy.[16] The usual format of reports, as of party meetings, is: we celebrate successes, but there are shortcomings to overcome. No one must doubt ultimate victory, but we must not relax. There is a great deal of symbolism, emphasis on honor and ceremony, Soviet patriotism, and, of course, Lenin. Anniversaries are frequent news, from the celebration of ten years of a Soviet-Mongolian friendship treaty to the birthday of Aeroflot.

Propaganda compensates in quantity, emphasis, exclusiveness, and consistency what it may lack in liveliness and interest.[17] By hammering its points unremittingly and backing them with evidence which the people are not in a position to refute, it can at least make contrary opinions difficult to sustain. It mostly calls for generally acceptable things, fighting hooliganism, the improvement of production, proper attention to the harvest, and good character, practically making morality equivalent to support of the political system. Berating slackers and troublemakers shows that errant individuals are to be blamed for troubles. Our policy is peace, the opposition is therefore for war and crime. Communism, the Soviet way, is associated in every way with peace, prosperity, and the better life; capitalism means imperialism, suffering, and decadence. To doubt the Soviet way is to oppose rational order and progress.

The Soviet press and radio endeavor to avoid outright misstatements of fact. They deal somewhat freely, however, with the observable world. Thus, it is flatly denied that anti-Semitism exists in the Soviet Union, while the United States is condemned as anti-Semitic; a conference of Communist parties which broke up in failure is reported as a grand success; etc. It is insisted that Soviet

---

[15] These are essentially the same qualities which ideologists of tsardom sought to instill. (Cf. R. Byrnes in Stavrou, ed., *Russia under the Last Tsar*, p. 65.)

[16] *Pravda Vostoka*, November 7, 1970.

[17] "If sometimes, to tell the truth, in the heat of the attack my knees were gripped by a cold horror, I always remembered [my party book]." (Poem by Vladimir Gribanov, *Sovetskaia kultura*, February 21, 1970.)

citizens are free to travel—no law forbids it. Printed speeches do not necessarily correspond exactly to the words of the speaker. Concrete data are sometimes suspect; for example, *Pravda* reported[18] that 68% of the young workers using the library of Gorky automobile factory regularly read the works of Lenin, and that nine-tenths of the young people visiting the central library of Magnitogorsk ask for the same author.[19]

EDUCATION

Soviet dedication to propaganda is inseparable from dedication to education. The one should make politically schooled people; the other should train productive, morally and politically tempered citizens. Education is also an area of major success of the Soviet system, which takes pride equally in having raised the country from relative backwardness to the world's second industrial power and in having turned a largely illiterate nation into one of the most advanced in technical training, with by far the world's largest pool of scientists and engineers. Secondary education is to be made general by 1975. In the Soviet Union, education is the road to advancement as perhaps nowhere else. A large part of the working people improve their qualifications by correspondence or evening classes, and as perhaps nowhere else it is expected that one prepare formally for his work. Not only mechanics and miners should have their diploma; there are institutes for textile workers, retail clerks, and whatever profession is deemed essential. "There is a whole network of service training institutions in the country, one in almost every city. There, along with tailors, appliance repairmen, and barbers, we could prepare future piano tuners."[20]

Upgrading of labor skills through education is a chief source of industrial growth, more important now that the labor force has ceased to grow rapidly. Education is also a chief credit of the regime and a claim to the gratitude of the young, while the beneficiaries of Soviet education, especially those who have climbed to the top, seem in the large majority to accept the fundamentals of the Soviet order.

The educational system is under centralized and multiple control and guidance; and centralization has been carried further in recent years. Since 1966, the Moscow Ministry of Education and the Ministry of Higher Education have had full control of curriculum and staffing, the granting of higher degrees, and appointments to professorships. With slight deviations, all Soviet children of

[18] November 11, 1969.

[19] In 1970, a new Soviet atlas showed cities all over the country misplaced by as much as twenty-five miles, possibly to confuse American nuclear targeters. (*The Economist*, January 24, 1970, p. 32.) In Stalin's day, maps were not to be had; in Khrushchev's they were accurate.

[20] *Sovetskaia kultura*, August 14, 1971, p. 2.

a given age should be studying the same lessons on the same day. Trade union organizations, in concert with the party, have a voice in the placement of teachers and share in the administration of higher educational institutions. The party group can decide to fire the rector of a university.[21] Instructors in higher institutions are mostly party members, especially in social sciences. All university teachers are supposed to carry on ideological work, and it was proposed in *Pravda*[22] that all candidates for higher degrees be required to show competence in Marxism-Leninism. Local party committees and party organizations in schools supervise the teaching of history and social studies in the schools, assess the qualities of courses, consider staff nominations, and forward the political education of teachers.[23] As a teacher relates, "The Communists in the school study the materials of the XXIV Congress with great enthusiasm and deep interest. . . . Every day in the teachers' room the talk is about the plans of the party and how to fulfill them."[24]

The Soviet school has come full circle from the revolutionary years, when entrance requirements, examinations, and grades were abolished, and "learning by doing" was the motto. Discipline is strict, and students are expected to acquire a large amount of information in both humanities and sciences. Originality is not stressed; art lessons are exercises in copying. Scientific and technological courses comprise over half the curriculum of primary and secondary schools. The labor training which Khrushchev stressed has been reduced to insignificance. There is not much consideration of special individual needs or abilities. By Soviet theory, all normal children should be able to master the work, so there is no need for testing of intelligence or other capacities; all are expected to pass. For a very few, among whom children of the elite may figure prominently, there are rather remarkable secondary schools specializing in some art, science, or foreign language. Higher education is extremely specialized, designed not for enlightenment but skills, to prepare persons for particular slots in the national economy; having chosen his field, the student has practically no electives.[25] There is no tuition and students receive stipends, depending on their standing, up to 60 rubles monthly. Facilities are uneven, from the first-class universities to neglected rural schools; and schools suffer some of the same kind of troubles as the economy, from shortages of textbooks to difficulty of innovation. But Soviet education seems to produce a great deal of technical competence.

[21] *Pravda*, May 17, 1970, p. 2.
[22] March 18, 1970.
[23] *Pravda*, February 17, 1970, p. 2; *Partiinaia zhizn*, no. 10, May, 1971, p. 40.
[24] *Partiinaia zhizn*, no. 11, June, 1971, p. 54.
[25] Of 600,000-plus graduates of higher schools, nearly half were engineers or agronomists, a fourth were teachers. (*Pravda*, March 20, 1970.)

However, "the Soviet school does not merely prepare educated people. From its halls there should come forth politically trained, ideally convinced builders of communism, patriots and internationalists."[26] "We want to educate our children to be toilers, persons for whom labor is the alpha and omega of life, its meaning and highest joy."[27] In kindergarten, children sing about Lenin and his love for them. They learn to sit immobile and respect the teacher, to admire heroes of war and labor, to love their "Socialist Fatherland," to respect their elders, and to behave honorably as Lenin would wish. Stress is laid upon collectivism and duty, belonging to the class group and to the country. The class is organized somewhat as a party group, with its own committee and the teacher as secretary; the discipline and standing of the group are the responsibility of each. Competition is avoided; better students should help the weaker as all progress together. The chief chastisement (corporal punishment being disapproved) is censure by the collective, class, or Pioneer group, perhaps ostracism. All share in the disciplining of deviants and thereby benefit from the lesson. There are multiform honors, the board or book of honor, badges, etc. There is socialist competition as in industry. Most of all, the child is to become accustomed to functioning as part of an organized group engaged in planned activities. As a result, young Russians are said to be decidedly more mannerly and better disciplined than their American counterparts.[28]

In elementary school the child learns about the inevitable victory of communism, the leading role of the party, the evil of bourgeois ideology, and the misery of the masses under capitalism. History shows class struggle, and classical Russian literature carries lessons of oppression and dedication to the revolutionary cause. Foreign language textbooks give some space to foreign workers, more to Soviet achievements translated from Russian. Specific study of Marxism-Leninism, which is supposed to be helpful for the mastery of Russian and mathematics, begins in secondary school, and a new school law of 1970 required its intensification. The youth should emerge with an overwhelming sense of duty. As *Pravda* comments, "It occurs in some families that they drag out, as a reason for studying, the undesirable contention, 'Study is for you, not me, you study for your own benefit.' This formula is deeply wrong. It is necessary to convince children otherwise: 'Study because this is necessary for the country, the people. The educated person increases our strength. Study because, when you are grown, you must return a hundredfold what you receive in childhood. . . .' "[29]

---

[26] *Pravda*, August 22, 1969.

[27] *Izvestia*, December 18, 1970, p. 4.

[28] Cf. Urie Bronfenbrenner, *Two Worlds of Childhood* (Russell Sage Foundation), New York, 1970.

[29] *Pravda*, September 22, 1969.

Ideology becomes more critical in higher education because temptations are greater at the higher level while higher education is increasingly the qualification for entry into the upper strata. This makes problems, as parents resort to pull and bribery to open doors for their offspring.[30] It also compels to conformity. Entry depends not only on academic considerations but on political acceptability, attested by the Komsomol, or trade union or party if the candidate has been at work. There are party commissions for the supervision of admissions.[31] Entrance examinations, which are mostly oral, lend themselves to political discrimination.

Having leaped the hurdle into the university, the student does not seem to have to study very hard, but he has every reason to be careful. The security police have representatives at higher institutions. The Komsomol is primarily responsible for discipline, which may include withdrawal of stipend and in extreme cases expulsion—and the student knows there are a hundred outside waiting to take his place. To get his degree, he has to pass his courses in dialectical materialism. "The central pedagogical task of the higher school is the ideological education of the students."[32] Ideological problems are severest in social sciences; better students prefer the physical sciences. However, it is not easy to escape politics; in the party's view even mathematics instructors should carry on ideological work.

The Soviet leadership wishes to have rational and creative scientists and engineers who will not bring into question the party's supreme right. Much of the future depends on how far this is possible.

LITERATURE AND THE ARTS

In the creative arts as elsewhere, the party faces the fundamental contradiction between the initiative requisite to productivity and ideological-political discipline. Creativity in all areas, from industrial design to theater, is essential for the modern state and for the party's mission of shaping thought and character. Yet writers and artists cannot be simply left free to express their genius. Political feelings are like a river which, dammed here, overflows elsewhere. If the newspapers are entirely conformist, people look for frank speaking in journals or books; if none is to be found in print, they read criticisms in painting or even music. Policy regarding the arts has consequently fluctuated like economic policy and in step with it; the state of Soviet literature is a good barometer of political pressures.

[30] *Izvestia*, September 12, 1968.
[31] *Izvestia*, August 5, 1970, p. 3.
[32] *Pravda* editorial, February 6, 1971.

The Revolution was greeted as liberation for the arts, and censorship was for a long time not unlike what it had been under the tsars; nothing was to be published attacking the Soviet system. In the enthusiasm for change and experimentation, modernism and futurism flourished; if Lenin did not approve, he did not try to repress them. In the 1920's, art was practically given over to private enterprise, and the party took the position that various tendencies could contribute to socialism. Artistically, this was the most productive period the Soviet Union has known.

After 1928, Stalin harnessed the arts. All private art groups, organizations, and schools were dissolved by official fiat. Publishers were ordered to emphasize socially useful literature, and the authorities began stating more explicitly what authors should say. Stalin called writers "engineers of souls" in the five-year plan and invited them, in effect, to become part of the privileged apparatus, with corresponding material and moral rewards. In 1932–1934, the Union of Soviet Artists and the Union of Soviet Writers were set up as sole organizations within which artists and writers could function. The obligatory style became "Socialist Realism."

It is not easy to define Socialist Realism beyond stating that it is the broad style which Stalin and Soviet leaders since have found most suitable and flattering for their state and themselves. Officially, it is "realist in style, socialist in content." Its style is clear and pseudofactual, with photographic detail, somewhat in the way of Russian classics, which were restored to grace in the 1930's. Socialist-Realistic writing should be sober, without flourishes, rather suitable for elementary school textbooks. It permits no art for art's sake. Its socialist content is support of the party and its purposes; under Stalin this degenerated to rather simple-minded propaganda, in the style of boy and girl love tractor. It is anti-individualistic and antisubjective, strong for positive thinking; it glorifies work, discipline, and self-sacrifice for the state and the party. Its heroes are heroic and its villains despicable, in the black-and-white Soviet view of the world. The heroes always win; Man, uplifted by the party, can achieve anything. This has remained the ordinary mode of Soviet writing to this day, just as Stalin's state has endured basically unaltered. Soviet readers have grown to take it for granted; even oppositionist writings follow its manner.

Stalin imposed his unsophisticated personal taste, which favored the ornate but despised music which he could not whistle. The Second World War brought some relief, as Marxism-Leninism retreated and artists could apply their talents to patriotic themes. Tightening was resumed as early as 1943 after the victory of Stalingrad indicated that victory was no longer in doubt. Nonconformist writers came increasingly under attack, until by 1948–1949 Soviet literature was compressed as never before. Writers received directions to compose works on specific subjects. Many were purged, and it was not easy for those who remained to conform sufficiently to political standards to escape criticism, despite the best of intentions. As a result, hardly anything of real literary worth, except some wartime pieces, was published in the Soviet Union from 1932 to 1953.

By 1952, even Stalinists called for more originality and better characterization, and they recognized that there could be human conflicts within socialism. There was some relaxation of controls, and more realistic works were published in the first part of 1953. Upon Stalin's death, there appeared a rash of critical novels of a sort not seen for nearly a generation. A sign of confidence was the holding in 1954 of a writers' congress, the first since 1934.[33] In the latter part of 1956, because of the troubles in Poland and Hungary, the official line retreated somewhat. But from 1958, when Boris Pasternak was forced to renounce the Nobel Prize, there seemed to be gradually developing a semifree Soviet literature. Despite setbacks from time to time, the scene became increasingly varied and interesting through the remaining Khrushchev years.

At no time did the party consider surrendering its overlordship of art and literature. Khrushchev felt that he, not the writers, should decide what was to be criticized, and he at times reviled them loudly. In 1964, near the height of his liberalism, a nonpolitical young poet was sent to labor camp for "parasitism." But Khrushchev permitted young rebels to speak up and, within limits, to publish or show their works. Lack of solidarity within the party hindered full control; to attack neo-Stalinist rivals, Khrushchev permitted in 1962 the publication of a concentration camp novel, *One Day in the Life of Ivan Denisovich* by Alexander Solzhenitsyn, thereby arousing exaggerated hopes in Soviet intellectuals and stimulating many others with equally picturesque memoirs to seek publication. In 1962 and after, there were some small, unannounced and brief expositions of modern art. The Sino-Soviet dispute, Khrushchev's desire for the support of foreign Communist parties, and his anxiety to improve the Soviet image in the world all impeded a crackdown. The poet Yevtushenko, could publish more freely because he was a valuable roving cultural ambassador. The intellectual community was growing steadily, and its less conformist members could look to expanding support. The scientists patronized modern art, and the public flocked to applaud less conformist poets. The party encouraged literary "conservatives," but it could not make their works popular; conservative literary journals lost circulation to liberal ones. The liberals gained and for some years held some control of the writers' and artists' organization. Many demanded more integrity and humanity, more opening to the West, and a degree of freedom within the generally accepted framework of socialism and party direction.

The first moves after the ouster of Khrushchev further heartened the liberals. The rapid and thorough repudiation of Lysenko's genetic charlatanry

---

[33] Time between congresses was an indicator of degree of distrust: the party went 13 years without one; the trade unions, 17; the writers, 20; the peasants, 34.

was encouraging, and *Pravda*[34] advocated an "environment of search, experiment, and the free expression and confrontation of opinions, the presence of various schools and trends, various styles and genres competing among themselves and at the same time joined by the unity of . . . Socialist Realism." But there were warning notes in the summer and fall, and writers were criticized for concentrating on unlovelier aspects of Soviet reality and private feelings instead of political verities. *Pravda*, on September 8, took *Izvestia* to task for "unhealthy criticism of young writers"; but the *Pravda* editor was removed soon thereafter, and in following months most major papers and journals received new heads. In September, 1965, two writers, Daniel and Siniavsky, were arrested, and a few months later they were sentenced to forced labor for publishing abroad works deemed anti-Soviet. A small compensation was that the defendants, unlike Stalin's victims but like those of the later tsars, refused to plead guilty but defended themselves energetically in their semisecret trial.

Since then, the collective leadership has worked steadily to restore full party control. Their style has been different from that of Khrushchev and more effective. The leaders have avoided personal commitment, speaking only seldom and in general terms. They have let hack writers, jealous of the popularity of those with greater talent, and cultural bureaucrats wage the battle with quiet party backing. A pall of uniformity thickened; more and more movies and books glorified the party line, patriotism, and the military. Even plays of Chekhov were rejected because they might be interpreted as critical of Soviet society. After August, 1968, there were fiercer denunciations of Western influence, and remaining liberals were removed from journalistic positions. Solzhenitsyn, whose writings in recent years had been published only in the West, was expelled from the Writers Union. In February, 1970, Tvardovsky resigned from headship of *Novy Mir*, the last slightly deviant journal.

Contrary to the expectations of those who saw the death of Stalin as freeing the Soviet Union to pursue a natural course toward modernization and release of energies, the redomestication of the arts is suggestive of Stalinist "partyness." Writers, like other workers, prepare for the party congress with feats of production. With somewhat more sophistication than in Stalin's day, literature continues to extol production; e.g., "Fair are the forests, fields and flowers/But the world contains no more beautiful beauty/Than the beauty of molten metal."[35] "The duty of writers is to make patriots."[36] "The party expects of cultural workers . . . significant new works which . . . actively assist the formation of the spiritual image of the builder of communism, bring out in Soviet people high moral qualities, loyalty to Communist ideals, civic feelings, and dedication to Soviet patriotism and socialist internationalism. . . . It be-

---

[34] February 21, 1965.
[35] *Pravda*, January 29, 1971, p. 3.
[36] *Literaturnaia gazeta*, June 2, 1971, p. 15.

comes especially serious in a situation of sharpened ideological struggle on the world arena."[37] Further, "Our enemies strive to use any crack through which to introduce the venom of doubts, discord, slander; and we fighters of the ideological front must be dedicated to our task. Only a clear party position permits the all-around analysis of the class reality of things. . . ." Poets have been among the freest of writers, but, "The white heat of ideological battle demands that our poetic weapon be in good working order and not miss the target. For, 'song and verse, these are bomb and banner,' as Maiakovsky wrote."[38] Soviet music, too, must be "on the forefront of ideological battle. It must still more actively attack rotten bourgeois ideology, more persistently and clearly affirm Communist ideals . . . the ideas of socialist humanism, educate our people, especially the youth, in the spirit of Soviet patriotism and proletarian internationalism, of constant readiness to defend the conquests [of the Revolution]."[39]

There is no room for atonal music, and popular songs must be cheerful. There must be no individualism. A poet is chided for expressing special love for her own children. Heroes are collectivists: "It is today possible to imagine a genuine literary hero only in active participation in some area of Communist construction."[40] There are to be no doubts or hesitation; a literary encyclopedia was berated for "unwillingness or inability . . . steadfastly to resist any attempt to slur over the class nature of things . . . spirit of objectivism and academic impartiality."[41] Can the Soviet state "permit its achievements to be used for the propagandizing of hostile views, in counterrevolutionary, antipopular purposes? No, it cannot."[42]

Party policy is carried out not only by censorship (and sometimes the police) but also by the artists' unions, which have lost the limited independence they had in Khrushchev's day, and to which artists must belong if they are to be considered professionals eligible for publication. Party cells within them are responsible for directing them, in the same spirit as party groups guide enterprises toward higher productivity. Party members should carry on political education and teach Marxist-Leninist esthetics to their fellow artists, who should accept ideological guidance as a worker would receive technical instruction.

Obedience is sweetened with material rewards. On admission to the Union of Artists or Union of Writers on the basis of competitive examination or work submitted, one is assured of lifelong comfort with moderate exertions, and of a very high income by Soviet standards if he shows exceptional ability. Writers are paid by the page or line, rather than in royalties for copies sold,

[37] *Pravda*, September 11, 1969.
[38] *Pravda*, October 21, 1969.
[39] *Pravda*, December 21, 1968.
[40] *Literaturnaia gazeta*, August 11, 1971, p. 2.
[41] *Pravda*, June 30, 1969.
[42] *Sovety deputatov trudiashchiksia*, no. 10, October, 1969, p. 11.

which reduces dependence on public taste. The Union provides housing, free vacations, rest homes, financial support for projects, and ultimately pensions; very few are prepared to reject all this in the name of an ideal of truth.

However, if the writers are among the least worked and best paid in Soviet society, they need special skills to interest their readers and satisfy the party at the same time. Intellectuals are naturally critical of their society, and readers likewise ordinarily prefer critical to laudatory works. The writer should draw, interestingly and convincingly, a picture which he knows to be more or less unreal. It is particularly difficult to portray the party plausibly as it wishes to see itself; yet it is impossible to deal with much in Soviet life without taking the party into account.[43] It is not easy to secure suspense when the triumph of virtue is almost foreordained; even Swan Lake has received a happy ending. Comedy is difficult because there can be no joking at the expense of authority. Crime is usually unacceptable. Heroes should be without blemish; in reply to the notion that they should be realistically portrayed, *Literaturnaia gazeta* queries, "Can't the dramatist portray his hero at the moment when the sun stands at the zenith and the hero has no shadow?"[44] There should be no disquiet, unsolved problems, or dark premonitions. There should not even be much individual feeling; and the mainstay of Western entertainment, sex, can be used only in careful doses.

A fundamental problem is that there are supposedly no real conflicts within Soviet society, wherein the interests of all must basically harmonize. To find conflicts the Soviet writers turn to the class struggles of the prerevolutionary past or of the "capitalist" world for genuine heroes and villains. They particularly dwell on the heroic times of the Soviets, the civil war or the Great Patriotic War, or have glorious security police trap perfidious foreign spies. Or they write nature stories or children's books. Plays or novels which treat contemporary Soviet reality are likely to have trouble with the censors; in those which pass, the plot is likely to rest on accident. "The present-day scene is for some reason treated mostly in satiric, comic, vaudeville manner. The heroic note is heard only in plays dealing with the past."[45]

The problem is equally difficult for the party. Ideologists encounter skepticism and indifference; as one wrote,

I asked a famous artist about her ideological-theoretical development. She looked surprised and suddenly asked, "Do you sing?" I answered no, I did not sing, that this was not the affair of a philosophy instructor. "So why then," she went on, "should I both sing and study theory, while you

[43] A party man lamented that he couldn't find in the libraries a single book "where the hero was a true leader of Communists gripped by a high ideal." (*Pravda*, July 21, 1971, p. 3.)

[44] March 11, 1970, p. 11.

[45] *Pravda*, August 30, 1970, p. 3.

only deal with theoretical questions?" I tried to explain the importance of social science for persons of all professions, but I do not know whether I succeeded.[46]

It is inherently impossible to make the creative artistic intelligence a faithful instrument of party-political purposes. There is always pressure for the staging of popular plays instead of correct ones, for the showing of entertaining, especially foreign, films instead of inspiring ones. For the party to denounce a work is to guarantee its popularity. Conservative journals have spiced their offerings with stories by less approved writers to keep up readership. There is always the competition of less ideological classics; and there is a black market in undesirable works, either old or smuggled, with which to contend. Western literature is difficult to exclude, despite prohibitions and the closing off of sections of libraries. Russian writers find holes in the censorship and carry on the nineteenth century tradition of "Aesopian" language; people become alert to political hints, as in suggestive anti-utopias of science fiction. The highly educated are likely to be repelled by Socialist Realism. It does little good for the party to castigate writers for not dramatizing properly the deeds of the workers and collective farmers and failing to concentrate on the generation of virtue. It cannot even discuss the real problem.

DISSIDENT INTELLECTUALS

Under Khrushchev the Soviet intellectual community grew up, enjoyed a little freedom and self-respect, and came to take itself seriously. If this freedom has been largely removed, the regime has not been able to crush the intellectuals or has deemed the cost too high. The result is that for essentially the first time in Soviet history the regime faces an opposition class, tiny but gifted and mutually protective. In this as in other ways, the new Russia reverts toward tsarist patterns.[47]

The chief manifestation and achievement of the opposition is a substantial underground literature. From the latter 1950's there has been circulating an ever increasing volume of unpublishable writings, publications of "Samizdat" ("Self-Publisher"), sometimes handwritten but mostly typewritten privately or in offices. This can perhaps be done largely at government expense, so a book by Samizdat is not necessarily extremely expensive. Most of the material seems to be poems or novels, some of them translated; countless satirical songs also defy censorship. Works are not

[46] *Sovetskaia kultura*, August 19, 1971.
[47] Cf. Lewis S. Feuer, "The Intelligentsia in Opposition," *Problems of Communism*, vol. XIX, no. 6, November-December 1970, pp. 1–16.

necessarily anti-Soviet. Most of them seem to be rather apolitical, simply deviant from official canons; occasionally they are approved for publication after circulation underground.[48] There are also critical statements such as the essay by a leading nuclear physicist, Andrei Sakharov, calling for intellectual freedom and cooperation between the Soviet Union and the United States.[49] Dissidents write letters to Brezhnev or the Central Committee, which are circulated by Samizdat and come into the possession of Western broadcasters, who proceed to make far larger numbers of Russians aware of them. Since April, 1968, there has circulated every two months a "Chronicle of Current Events," devoted mainly to the defense of rights of Soviet citizens. A single issue has some thirty pages, and its coverage shows an extensive informational network.

Active oppositionists are not numerous and apparently almost confined to Moscow and Leningrad, strong only in the widespread though mostly passive support of many of the educated elite. Six demonstrated against the occupation of Czechoslovakia, August 25, 1968; a hundred gathered to show indignation at the trial of Daniel and Siniavsky; twenty met in Red Square to protest an expected rehabilitation of Stalin on his birthday in 1969. The protest against another literary trial was signed by 738,[50] who must have comprised a large proportion of the intellectual opposition. Of 6,790 members of the Writers Union, only eight protested the ouster of Solzhenitsyn. In November, 1970, Sakharov and two other physicists formed a "Committee on Human Rights," the first open unauthorized political organization for nearly half a century; but it apparently formed an army of generals without troops when it was subsequently (ineffectually) ordered dissolved.

The opposition is also ideologically weak. The protesters usually accept the premises of the regime and use its vocabulary. Even as they defend themselves with quotations from Marx or Lenin, they place themselves at a disadvantage by discussing in the party's terms. They have little understanding of free political institutions. It is hard for them to espouse democracy, because the mass of the people follows the party or may regard the complaining writers as privileged ingrates.

Hence the skeptical intellectuals have no real alternative program and no unifying philosophy. Most do not seem to wish to overthrow the regime but merely to secure the implementation of the proclaimed rights; they see their mission in terms of purifying the party and getting back to the true ideals of Marxism-Leninism, without realizing that these provide no firm basis for political freedom. A few apparently take a neo-revolutionary or Maoist position,

---

[48] Selections are given by Abraham Brumberg, ed., *In Quest of Justice* (Praeger), New York, 1970.

[49] Published as *Progress, Coexistence and Intellectual Freedom* (W. W. Norton & Co.), New York, 1968.

[50] Amalrik, op. cit., p. 53.

rejecting the Soviet system as a reversion to capitalism. Some look to Western models and wish to open up and liberalize the system to make Soviet democracy a reality, warning that reforms are essential to prevent the Soviet Union from falling behind in competition with the West. Others mingle Marxism-Leninism with Russian nationalism or nostalgic Pan-Slavism, calling for a return to popular roots, perhaps with religious overtones. There are also neo-Stalinists, who have nothing in common with the liberal intellectuals except opposition to the establishment. Divided and uncertain, the oppositionists can only suggest reform, not radical remaking of the system; their chief demand is freedom of expression.

Nonetheless the regime is concerned. Hundreds of protesters have been consigned to psychiatric wards, where they are mingled with the truly deranged and subjected to treatments hardly separable from torture. They are thus degraded without the confrontation of a formal trial. Many have been sent to forced labor or exiled to Siberia for possession or circulation of "anti-Soviet propaganda." Still more are spied upon, lectured and threatened, or dismissed from positions. Even prominent scientists have occasionally been arrested. But the fact that some dissidents can continue to live normally and publish works abroad betrays an un-Stalinist weakness. The abundance of Samizdat publications bears witness to an ineffectiveness of the police, which may have, like the tsarist Okhrana, some vested interest in the opposition movement. It may also indicate that the holders of power have lost conviction in the absolute validity of their official ideology. Feeble as it is, the intellectual opposition generates doubts and brings the basis of the Soviet regime into question.

SCIENCE

The strongest allies of disaffected writers in the struggle for freedom of opinion are scientists. Scientists, like writers, are among the privileged; and most of them are politically passive if not convinced adherents of the regime. But they are aware of science in the Western world and its achievements, usually superior to their own; they receive foreign journals and may meet Western counterparts in international conventions. They know that scientific theories are confirmed by confrontation of hypotheses and conflict of opinions, and they have ventured to suggest this in Soviet publications. Science is oriented toward change in an increasingly conservative society, and toward developing technology for the general benefit, whereas the ruling creed elevates political means and class struggle.

Consequently, a few scientists, particularly those of exceptional talent and relatively secure position, speak out for reforms or new approaches which they perceive as essential for scientific progress or human well-being. The memorandum of Sakharov has been mentioned; he also wrote a bitter denunciation of censorship in a letter to Brezhnev which was circulated by the underground press. Another physicist, Peter Kapitsa, attacked Marxist dialectics in the Soviet press (in 1965, when this was permissible) as a hindrance to scientific progress, has given a critical assessment of the state of Soviet science, and has spoken (outside the Soviet Union) for the idea of convergence of Soviet and American societies. Frequently, Soviet scientists have expressed their boredom and indifference to official ideology. They also shrug off Socialist-Realist art; they are the chief patrons of the Soviet Union's small corps of modernist painters and sculptors.

It is not easy for the party to coerce the scientists. Their skills are vital for Soviet progress and strength, and scientific and technical achievements both raise the Soviet stature in the world and confirm the rightness of party leadership. The scientists seem to have some confidence in their importance, and they are prepared to fight injustice against any of their colleagues as a threat to all of them. The party handles them gently, rewarding cooperation with the perquisites of the elite. Rather luxurious accommodations were provided at Akademgorodok, in central Siberia, to get them away from Moscow and make them feel more a part of Soviet construction and less of the international fraternity of science. Scientists are organized under the prestigious Academy of Sciences, which no longer has the limited independence it enjoyed in Khrushchev's day, when it once successfully refused to accept a candidate sponsored by Khrushchev. The institutions on which scientists depend are party-controlled; the party groups in them (as in the academy), including all employees, not merely scientists, were given stronger supervisory powers in 1971. The scientist's career is subject, like that of nearly everyone else, to party scrutiny, not only informally but formally. Under a recently established procedure, all scientists are to undergo an examination every three years by a panel including trade union and party officials along with scientists, testing not only scientific but political qualifications.

Even mathematicians are warned against individualism and urged to work with collective and party spirit for the Fatherland and the proletariat, as directed by the party.[51] That a scientist should concern himself only with science is cause for alarm. According to a resolution adopted by the Academy of Sciences in the relatively liberal period, "The international obligation of Soviet scholars is to intensify the criticism of bourgeois ideology. . . ."[52] An attack on ideological enemies is essential for any positive approach to science.[53] The party group in the scientific institute must concern itself with everything in the

[51] *Sovetskaia Rossia*, July 14, 1970, p. 2.
[52] George Fischer, *Science and Politics, the New Sociology in the Soviet Union* (Cornell University Press), Ithaca, New York, 1964, p. 4.
[53] *Kommunist*, no. 4, February, 1970, p. 8; *ABSEES*, July, 1970, p. 56.

collective and with the moods and thoughts of the researchers.[54] All scientists should participate in political training and so far as possible publish on "philosophy."[55]

The ideologists claim that their ideology is deeply scientific and essential for the guidance of science. "It is no secret that both the fruitfulness of scientific research and its implementation depend largely on the ideological maturity of the people of science themselves, on the clarity with which they perceive their place in socialist society and the depth of their feelings of responsibility to the people."[56] On the more abstract level, they should apply Marxist or Leninist dialectics, although this has no operative significance and, strictly interpreted, is inimical to ideology in that any idea generates a new antithesis. As *Pravda* assures, the success of engineers, teachers, doctors, scientists, and artists "depends on their mastering the dialectics of analysis and party principles in scientific research and ideological work."[57] Only the conscious application of materialistic dialectics really frees the student from one-sidedness and philosophic prejudices. . ,."[58]

Scientists can often satisfy the formal requirements by making an initial bow, citing Lenin, and getting on with their scientific results. But in some areas and at certain times, ideology has seriously interfered with science; and political pressures, along with the priorities of the Soviet system, have caused unevenness in Soviet achievements. Mathematics and physics have fared best, the first an old Russian specialty too abstract for the ideologists, the second closely associated with military power in the nuclear age. This is not the entire story. Low-temperature research and astronomy have prospered, and the Russians have made excellent progress toward controlling nuclear fusion. Under Stalin, the theory of relativity was theoretically banned, and some principles of quantum mechanics, as complementarity and uncertainty, were tabu; but physicists used them anyway. Because of secrecy, inferior instrumentation, and military bent, the Soviet space program has reaped far less scientific data than the American. Soviet oceanography is first-rate, perhaps because of naval implications. Chemistry is backward for reasons not immediately evident.

In biological sciences, ideology has been more damaging. The virtual murder of Soviet genetics by Lysenko is notorious, but it can hardly be exaggerated.[59] Stalin and Khrushchev were seduced by Lysenko's easy answers

[54] *Kommunist*, no. 8, August, 1970, p. 68.

[55] *Partiinaia zhizn*, November, 1970, p. 9.

[56] *Kommunist*, no. 18, December, 1968; *Current Digest*, vol. 21, no. 1, p. 3.

[57] July 8, 1969; *Current Digest*, vol. 22, no. 27, p. 31.

[58] *Pravda*, August 29, 1969.

[59] Zhores A. Medvedev, *The Rise and Fall of T. D. Lysenko* (Columbia University Press), New York, 1969, pp. 167, 175. This is a very illuminating study of the Lysenko affair. The author was discharged from his research position and in June, 1970, was arrested and confined to a mental institution; he was released after widespread protests in the scientific community.

for agricultural troubles and so they made official his crude doctrines of acquired heredity. Scientific genetics was simply outlawed by party fiat. One of Lysenko's ideas was that, in starting forest belts to improve the climate of southern Russia, some thirty acorns should be planted in each hole so that all but one would sacrifice themselves to the strongest seedling, since intraspecific competition was a capitalist invention to justify oppression. This scheme, put into practice without verification, cost hundreds of millions of rubles. Another was more fanciful: by mixing manure with an equal amount of earth, one would transmit the qualities of the manure to the earth and so double the supply. Geneticists were driven from their positions or in some cases, under Stalin, more violently purged. Something was saved of Soviet genetics only because research continued under the guise of space science or in radiation laboratories under the patronage of nuclear physicists. The political meddling is illustrated by an episode in 1962. A regional boss heard that Medvedev had been condemned by the Central Committee for opposition to Lysenko. Only a telephone call was required to secure the dismissal of a Medvedev he located in a research institute, although this man had nothing to do with the controversy.[60]

Ideas somewhat related to those of Lysenko continued, long after his disgrace, to influence Soviet evolutionary theory, as the role of genetics was rejected, the succession of forms was interpreted as "negation of the negation," and the whole picture was colored with Marxist "progressivism." There have been comparable impositions by decree in linguistics and anthropology. Soviet psychology has suffered from the mandatory assumption that there can be no real conflicts. Freudianism is excluded not only by official prudery (which negates sexual psychology in general), but also by the fact that the personality is not to be shaped by things like libido and the unconscious but by the state and the party. Orthodox Soviet psychology has been based on the work of Ivan Pavlov, a great scientist who would certainly not approve of his theories being turned into dogma. The conditioned reflex seemed to Stalinists to promise the easy training of the perfect Soviet man.

Medical research was long dominated by neo-Pavlovian insistence on the primacy of the central nervous system in health and disease.[61] Soviet medicine is extremely varied in quality. A few Soviet instruments have been borrowed by the West; but the Soviets have contributed practically nothing to the medical revolution of the past generation. Ideology becomes antimaterialistic in asserting a "qualitative" difference between the living and nonliving, hence it was felt that there was no need for doctors to study chemistry. Soviet medical researchers are also handicapped by lack of published statistics regarding diseases, causes of death, etc. The health hazards of tobacco are discussed in

[60] Medvedev, op. cit., p. 207.
[61] For example, diabetes "develops after intense emotional strain or cerebral tension." [V. Kristman, *Internal Diseases and Nursing* (Peace Publishers), Moscow, n. d. (1965?), p. 276.]

terms of Western, mostly American data.[62] In the 1960's, some Soviet doctors used leeches to bleed patients, advised mud baths for rickets, and, to judge from press accounts, subscribed to many quackish remedies. *Pravda* urges the better development of mineral baths and radioactive waters.[63] The excellence of Soviet medicine is not in its science but in its organization, which has produced the world's largest corps of doctors and through which medical care is made readily available.

It is in social sciences that the shadows of ideology and party direction have most stunted inquiry. Closely linked with Marxism-Leninism and "scientific socialism," one of its main functions is the unmasking of "bourgeois" falsehoods. There has been good scholarship in archaeology and ancient history, but this is hindered by the necessity of squeezing history into Marx's periodization. Treatment of recent or contemporary issues is severely restricted. Soviet philosophy is "a weapon in the ideological struggle of socialism against capitalism in the world arena,"[64] although in the Khrushchev era it became possible for Soviet scholars seriously to study Western philosophers and even acknowledge some good points. The study of economics exists to serve production, hardly as general theory. Political studies must be politically useful, and the Soviet Union has not followed Eastern European countries in the establishment of political science as an academic subject; the answers to all political questions are given by the party, and secrecy covers practically everything that might be called politics in the Soviet state.

There has been some effort to create a science of administration, and there is a little research which may be called sociological. Yet there has not been a single graduate in sociology from Soviet universities.[65] Soviet sociologists, counted in dozens,[66] look into such questions as labor turnover, leisure time utilization, incentives, and vocational plans. "Researchers regularly visit the departments of the factory, studying the psychological condition of the workers, their work attitudes and mutual relations."[67] Their results are sometimes of considerable interest. But their function is to assist in the management of society, as the Soviet leadership seeks to look to more refined and scientific means of social control.

Soviet science suffers the same vices as the economy. Research is overcentralized and overcontrolled; scientists are supposed to plan results in accordance with demands from above. They are even more burdened by bureaucracy and paperwork than American investigators; scholars spend a large part of the time on administrative matters. There is overspecialization, and

---

[62] *Literaturnaia gazeta*, August 18, 1971, p. 13.
[63] October 11, 1971, p. 2.
[64] *Pravda*, January 22, 1971, p. 4.
[65] *Literaturnaia gazeta*, March 18, 1970, p. 12; *ABSEES*, July, 1970, p. 57.
[66] Fischer, op. cit., p. 25.
[67] *Pravda*, October 13, 1971, p. 2.

scientists in one area fail to profit by work in another, since secrecy reduces cross-fertilization. Soviet science is decidedly hierarchic;[68] conservative senior academicians dominate institutes and may bar the way to new men and new ideas. Equipment is often obsolete, and innovation meets much resistance. Overstaffing is widespread, by foreign terms, with too many heads for the available facilities or insufficient facilities for the personnel available. As in economic fulfillment, data may be shaped to desired ends. A study of the "sound wave" of the Soviet supersonic transport plane found it completely harmless.[69]

The Soviet Union can get good results by massive expenditure, compensating less productivity per worker by large numbers of workers. Expenditures on research and development are approximately equal to those of the United States. But Soviet science has failed markedly to come up to the expectations of 1957–1960, when Western scholars predicted that it would lead the world within a decade. It still lags substantially behind the United States and in many areas behind Western Europe and Japan. The application of science to production has been still less successful, despite strong Soviet emphasis on applied as against basic research. But where the Russians wish to concentrate resources on priority objectives, there is no reason to doubt their capacities.

RELIGION

Even skeptical rulers of the past have regularly wished their subjects to be religious, because the discipline and code of religion normally make people more law-abiding and obedient to authority. But traditional religion represents a challenge to the official Soviet creed and the claimed monopoly of truth about human purpose and destiny. Marxism-Leninism must contain, or provide the basis for seeking, answers to all questions; but religion states that there are divine laws above human laws. The party, not priests, tradition, or scriptures, is to determine right and wrong. Salvation is to be sought through the party, not in relations with any higher power with or without the mediation of a church. Religion draws away from the guided mainstream of Soviet life. Churches represent ideological and potentially political rivals; if they could be eliminated there would remain no nonparty-dominated organization in the Soviet land. Religion might encourage the separatism of non-Russians, especially Catholics and Moslems. It has also seemed antimodern to the Bolsheviks. Atheism stood for science, industrialization, and the progressive society, while religion, as practiced in tsarist Russia, stood for superstitious conservatism, blessing crops instead of mechanizing.

[68] *Science*, vol. 173, no. 3999, August 27, 1971, p. 798.
[69] *Izvestia*, June 20, 1969; *Current Digest*, vol. 21, no. 25, p. 33.

A revolutionary party in Russia in 1917 was inevitably opposed to the Orthodox Church, which was practically a department of the old state and devoted to it. The Bolsheviks were anathema to the church, while Lenin was more bitterly antireligious than Marx. Consequently, the Bolsheviks on attaining power launched a frontal attack on the former official church. Its real estate was nationalized, and it was deprived of juridical personality. Church buildings might be used by groups of believers, but from 1919 religious instruction of children was forbidden. Many priests and bishops were arrested, a few were shot; and in the first years there were thousands of clashes with religious peasantry.

With the end of the civil war the Soviet regime moved toward a modus vivendi with the church, although antireligious propaganda was continued. Forcible attacks were renewed in 1928 and went into high gear in the collectivization campaign. A secondary purpose of collectivization was to separate the peasants from the church; the priests no doubt opposed it so far as they dared. Countless churches were closed and priests were driven out with the kulaks. According to a Soviet account, this was successful: religious observance among male peasants age 25–39 decreased from 71.4% in 1923 to 3.2% in 1934, while observance among those age 40–59 fell from 100% to 14.5%.[70] By 1939, only about one hundred churches were functioning in Russia.

Upon the German attack, religious leaders surprised the Bolsheviks by immediately calling on the people to resist. By 1943, an informal concordat was worked out, whereby the church was tolerated in return for its support of the war effort and Soviet foreign policy. Some 20,000 churches were reopened and relations at times approached cordiality. This arrangement outlasted the war, as Orthodoxy was useful for the extension of Soviet influence in the Balkans. Antireligious propaganda, however, was revived after victory. Khrushchev intensified the attack. Atheistic lectures, books, movies, and television programs flooded the Soviet media. Churches were closed by pressure against believers. The eight small Orthodox seminaries of 1957 were reduced to three by 1964. Taxes on churches were increased, and a majority were closed under one pretense or another. Children were forbidden to attend (except for baptism), and believers were excluded from party and Komsomol.

The campaign continues. The school teaches science as the answer to man's needs, the truth of the party, and the reactionary nature of historical churches. Among the duties of teachers and schoolchildren is atheism. Many publications and programs play on themes of the backwardness of religion, its antisocial nature, and its class significance as a means of exploitation and oppression. The ministers or priests are accused of profiteering and immorality, in many cases of being agents of foreign interests. There are special schools to train atheist propagandists, who work through a multimillion member atheist

[70] *Obschestvo i molodezh* (Izd. VLKSM), Moscow, 1968, p. 231.

society ("Znanie," or "Knowledge"). Communists are supposed to go around leading religious persons back to Soviet conformity. Church membership is a bar to higher education. Because many persons were going to church for the climactic ceremonies of life, since 1959 there have been developed competitive civic-Soviet institutions. Young Russians are married with music, flowers, champagne, and an inspirational talk by a minor dignitary in "marriage palaces." There are also Marxist-Leninist baptisms and funerals. Soviet holidays are magnified to detract from religious ones, most importantly the New Year festival overshadowing Christmas. Lenin has been made into something like a personal deity.

Theoretically, religion should be bested by argument, if not simply outgrown in the absence of class exploitation. But the legal arsenal of Soviet atheism is impressive. Practically nothing is permissible but the bare bones of services. Even this is not assured, as the lease of the church to the congregation can be terminated. Theoretically, twenty believers can apply for permission to open a church, but this right is difficult to exercise even if twenty times twenty sign a petition. It is a crime to allow one's house to be used as a church. Only a few dozen Orthodox priests are trained yearly; there is only one training center for Moslem mullahs and none for rabbis. Practically no religious publications are permitted; the chief one is the dull *Journal of the Moscow Patriarchate*. Proselytizing is illegal, and it is forbidden to attempt to persuade anyone to "abandon public activity." Monasteries are forbidden to engage in economic activities to support themselves. Income of priests may be taxed up to 83%.[71] Only parents can legally give religious instruction to children, and these are not to be forced to participate in religious exercises even in the home. No one under eighteen may join a church, and it is illegal to baptize a child unless both parents sign a formal request, thereby becoming subject to pressures.

Since it is a black mark on leaders to have a religious community in their territory, pressures have gone beyond these legal measures. Reports of children being taken from parents to prevent the inculcation of religious faith are treated approvingly in the Soviet press. "Religious fanaticism" may be, like political dissidence, regarded as insanity and grounds for confinement.[72] Komsomol squads make rounds of houses and apartments to halt religious observances and enforce Soviet morality, and the door must be opened to them. Refusal to participate in Soviet affairs is cause for imprisonment. Religious dissenters are said to be a substantial fraction of the prison population.

It is remarkable that there are any believers left aside from the aged. A Soviet study a few years ago found 5.5% of the people in the 18–25 age group holding religious belief and 13.4% among those 26–30, with the percentage

---

[71] George L. Kline, *Religious and Antireligious Thought in Russia* (University of Chicago Press), Chicago, Ill., 1968, p. 156.

[72] *Partiinaia zhizn*, no. 6, March, 1969, p. 57.

rising to 43.8 of those 51–60, and 55.7% of those 61–65. But religion was definitely for the poor. In the Voronezh oblast, the religious or uncertain were 14.6% of collective farmers; 13.4% of unqualified workers; 10.2% of first-year recruits; 3.1% of skilled workers; 2.1% of schoolchildren; 1.7% of students; and only 0.7% of intellectual workers.[73] Large areas of the Soviet countryside and many large new cities, even of half a million or more, lack churches or formal ministers of religion. There were more than 54,000 Orthodox churches in 1913; 10% may now be functioning.

The Orthodox Church has been not only much reduced but tamed. Under the official Council for the Affairs of the Orthodox Church, it is financially supported; in return it accepts the state power and supports the government which proposes its extermination. Perhaps as the party waits for the church to die out, the church waits patiently for the regime to appreciate its usefulness.

Other large organized religions have mostly been reduced to ineffectiveness. Lithuania has few Catholic priests, and there are few Lutheran pastors in Latvia and Estonia. The Uniate Church (Orthodox recognizing the Papacy) was unceremoniously returned to the Orthodox fold. Soviet Judaism is practically without rabbis; of several thousand synagogues of tsarist times, a few dozen remain. Over nine-tenths of the mosques have been shut. The Armenian Church, which is useful as a focus for the diaspora, is domesticated like Russian Orthodoxy, but retains vitality; recently it gathered more adherents than ever.[74] The Baptists are split between those who compromise with the regime and those who resist. But the weakness of conventional churches seems to spawn the growth of the unconventional. Many groups, more or less associated with larger faiths, have resorted to informal meeting places, in homes or outdoors, under amateur leaders. Radical and illegal sects, as Seventh-day Adventists, Pentecostals, or schismatic Baptists, seem to have thrived in recent years; it is against these that most Soviet ammunition is directed.

The Soviet state can perhaps squeeze religion to impotence but cannot replace it. There is ample testimony to a revival of religious feeling in recent years. Large numbers of infants are presented for baptism, said to be more than half of all births in some places. The potential sanctions seem to have lost deterrence. Russian and Slavophil stirrings among some of the intellectuals and young people have been reflected in renewed interest in the ancient faith, with its national as well as spiritual meaning. Under the Old Regime, intellectuals were antireligious not because of intellectual doubt but because religion was a crutch of the state. Now religion appeals as an alternative for those dissatisfied with the official creed. Possibly, if the regime becomes more conservative and Marxism-Leninism becomes less relevant, the leadership will rediscover religious

[73] *Obshchestvo i molodezh*, pp. 224, 232.
[74] *Zhurnal moskovskogo patriarchata*, December, 1969, p. 4; *ABSEES*, July, 1970, p. 49.

values. Speakers at the Twenty-Fourth Party Congress spoke much about minority nationalism and other problems but said not a word against religion.

PUBLIC OPINION

Even Soviet leaders may have little knowledge of the true feelings of their people or how they would react if free to please themselves. Although the police presumably informs on this score, it is not in the Soviet way to inquire into what people believe but into how they may be brought to correct beliefs. Quite possibly, many or most Russians have little real opinion about political questions. Soviet society is much divided, and communication other than that sponsored by the party is haphazard and limited to narrow circles. The Russians have well learned that it is better to give proper answers.[75] If a person has dangerous doubts, he can only guess how far they may be shared. It is difficult to speak of political belief unless there is some weighing of alternatives. But the Russians have little conception of a political order other than "socialism" or a political philosophy other than Marxism-Leninism. They are accustomed to not being consulted on political issues, to not knowing what goes on inside the Kremlin, to not reading political articles, and to not thinking about what is not supposed to concern them. Some resort to "internal emigration," the divorce of private thoughts from external behavior. A Soviet writer who defected in 1969, Anatoly Kuznetsov, made himself an accomplice of the political police, the KGB, while scheming to defect. Others who shape their words and actions to serve their careers may never know how far they believe in what they say and do.

The visitor who mingles privately with the people encounters some who complain bitterly and some who seem to have taken the slogans entirely to heart; but the dominant impression is of indifference. This is confirmed by the meager effect of an immense amount of exhortation, particularly to work better. Soviet papers frequently attack apathy; this, not positive opposition, is the propagandists' problem. Political activities tend to degenerate into formalism, despite the continual struggle to inject life into them. Komsomol units fake minutes for meetings they should have held.[76] As seen on Soviet TV, audiences doze during political speeches. There are idealists and activists as well as overt cynics, but most people seem simply to look to their own interests within the framework of the system, skipping the editorials and speeches in the newspapers

---

[75] According to *Pravda* (September 18, 1970, p. 4), when factory workers were polled as to what they most esteemed in a person, 90% answered, "Love of work."

[76] Allen Kassof, *The Soviet Youth Program*, pp. 133–134.

but probably studying evenings to get ahead, minding their tongue, with no wild thoughts of changing their universe. They give the party not enthusiasm but conformity.

It is difficult to keep political writing interesting in the absence of political contention. Propaganda may work in contrary ways; sputniks stimulated not only admiration for socialism but also questioning as to why housing was so bad. Frequent reports of the protests of opposition parties in the "capitalist" countries must lead many to wonder why there should not be freedom of speech under socialism. If life is so loathsome in the West, Soviet citizens may wonder, why should they not be free to travel there? People become inured to the repetitive message and tend to rely on information by word of mouth. They may even react negatively; according to the Komsomol paper,[77] sales of vodka regularly soar when there is a press campaign against alcoholism, so outlets stock up when they see antiliquor articles in the press.

Western influences also pose an insoluble problem. As tourists to the Soviet Union learn, there is an irrational fondness for foreign styles and clothing, which harmonizes poorly with Soviet ideology. Many youths are captivated by Western music and dances; the biggest attraction of the Voice of America is not its news but its songs. Forbidding such imports makes them more desirable. Tourism brings in foreign currency but may infect the population. The importation of needed Western science and technology cannot be quite separated from political ideas. It is particularly difficult to insulate the intelligentsia, who may participate in international gatherings and know foreign languages.

Russians with a good memory have cause for skepticism. The changes of authority of the past twenty years, the denunciation of Stalin, then of the "Anti-Party Group," finally of Khrushchev, cast doubt upon the present-day validity of the word given by Brezhnev. All previous heads and near-heads of the allegedly perfect party except Lenin have been degraded.

All our evidence indicates, however, a large measure of acceptance. People grumble about many things, from shortage of meat to poor pay, but they are grateful for social services and opportunities and pleased with Soviet power in the world. Not many seem to reject the right of the party to rule. It is much as in nineteenth-century Russia, when the bureaucrats were violently blamed for all manner of misdeeds but few questioned the legitimacy of the tsar. Many who suffered from Stalin's terrorism shrank from questioning the power that maltreated them, only wondering that it made mistakes; some met death with Stalin's name on their lips. Even those who have come to reject the Soviet regime ordinarily accept its philosophical bases, the picture of the world as dominated by the contest of capitalism v. socialism, and the idea that theirs is

---

[77] *Komsomolskaya pravda*, January 6, 1970; *Soviet Studies Information Supplement*, no. 26, April, 1970, p. 57.

somehow a "workers' " regime. Those who criticize usually do so in the name of Communist ideals. A large percentage of wartime refugees, although they considered themselves anti-Soviet, took for granted the ideas of inevitable class struggle and the basic Marxist concepts of history and were inclined to believe capitalism decadent and imperialistic.[78] Apparently not many Soviet citizens believe in freedom of information in the abstract; writers who want release from censorship for themselves may believe that the masses require indoctrination.

When one receives a message constantly and from all sides without overt rebuttal for many years, he is likely to cease to pay attention; but it is impossible fully to exclude it and difficult to maintain its falsity. As commercial advertisers know, claims dressed up with good appearances and pressed relentlessly do not have to be inherently very plausible to affect consumer behavior. For many Soviet citizens, it seems to be unthinkable to consider political questions without reference to the party's teaching. And there is much attraction in the party's doctrine. It appeals to fundamental ideas of human justice; and very few have the political sophistication to perceive the deeper relations of justice with freedom. Holding up its mission, the party speaks with outward self-confidence. The prosecutor in a literary trial asked a defendant, "Surely you don't think that today, in the fiftieth year of Soviet power, a Soviet court is capable of making a wrong decision?"[79] Much is made of the superiority of Russia, stated in terms of the party's world-historical role. Marxism-Leninism makes Russia the universal leader and the most perfect society; the Russians are persuaded that they are "active champions of everything progressive and growing, of the way of the future."[80]

To go against the system is to exclude oneself from possibilities of advancement and influence; if one is troubled by doubts, it is, from the individual's point of view, rational to suppress them. Even if one's ambition is nonconformist, to gain autonomy, to travel and get to know the world outside, this is to be attained by holding one's peace, endeavoring to satisfy the powers above, and climbing up the ladder of authority. But doing so consumes the urge to freedom. Belonging to the apparatus and sharing its material and psychological interest in the established order means acquiring at least a little of the conformist official mentality.[81] Great efforts are made to occupy energies in acceptable causes. No Soviet citizen should complain, as did Lenin's brother before his execution, "We are encouraged to develop our intellectual powers, but

---

[78] Raymond A. Bauer, Alex Inkeles, Clyde Kluckohn, *How the Soviet System Works* (Harvard University Press), Cambridge, Mass., 1956, pp. 33, 97, 124 ff.

[79] Pavel Litvinov et al., *Dear Comrade* (Pitman Publishing Corp.), New York, 1969, p. 15. This compilation of Soviet statements is revealing for both proregime and antiregime sentiments.

[80] *Pravda*, February 3, 1970.

[81] A point stressed in Amalrik's essay.

we are not allowed to use them for the benefit of our country."[82] Ordinary workers were found to participate rather little in "public assignments," but shop chiefs on the average went to four meetings weekly and took part in 4.5 service organizations.[83] It is a great psychological burden under these conditions not to identify with the state and its purposes.

From childhood, the Soviet citizen is taught always to think first of the group or collective, always to consider his own feelings secondary, and to depend socially and psychologically on the collectivity, guided by the party. There is no reward for individuality, no esteem for intellectual originality. For a long time, it was held reprehensible to save; all security was to come from the state. The result is psychological dependence. The principal hardships of refugees in the West are insecurity and the burden of having to make countless decisions which in the Soviet Union would have been made for them. As an ex-Soviet artist, Vladimir Ashkenazy, put it, "A Soviet-educated person that goes to the West finds that he is suddenly on his own. You feel like a baby thrown into the sea."[84]

The party seeks to convince people that there is no alternative to its rule. There is no idea of a really different political system as an abstract proposition; Soviet citizens, possessing limited and distorted knowledge of the political institutions of the world without, have difficulty envisioning a different state. They are led to believe that a multiparty system would mean only anarchy and disorder. The only conceivable way of change would be through the party. Even the Czechs, in their brief time of free discussion in 1968, seem to have envisaged reform only in the framework of the Communist Party. For the Russians, the party, whatever its faults, is the only visible exponent of the national purpose. They are probably right in that only the party and its ideological base hold together the Russian-dominated "Socialist Common-wealth." Moreover, the party has done a good deal to earn this acceptance. It has led the Russian people finally, albeit after much tribulation, to rising standards of welfare, far ahead of the old Russia though still behind the West. And it has brought them, as leaders of a grand unifying movement, to their acme of historical power.

In view of this, one must wonder at the need for the intense perennial drumbeat of propaganda to keep up the present level of acceptance. There is so much effort to point out the advantages of socialism that these cannot be self-evident. From time to time there are warnings against "bourgeois" radio broadcasts, even against the dangers to "unripe persons" from magazines left behind by tourists.[85] The regime feels unsure of its citizens after fifty years of control not only of means of production but of all political organization.

---

[82] Adam Ulam, *The Bolsheviks*, p. 11.
[83] *Kommunist*, no. 12, August, 1965, p. 50.
[84] *Manchester Guardian Weekly*, August 28, 1968.
[85] *Partiinaia zhizn*, no. 4, February 1969, p. 70.

READINGS

Andrei Amalrik, "Will the USSR Survive until 1984?" (Harper and Row), New York, 1970.

George Z. F. Bereday and Jaan Pennar, eds., *The Politics of Soviet Education* (Praeger), New York, 1960.

Keith Bosley, ed., *Russia's Underground Poets* (Praeger), New York, 1969.

Robert Conquest, *The Politics of Ideas in the USSR* (Praeger), New York, 1967.

Yuli Daniel, *This is Moscow Speaking* (E. P. Dutton & Co., Inc.), New York, 1969.

Roland Gaucher, *Opposition in the USSR* (Funk and Wagnalls), New York, 1969.

Constantin de Grunwald, *God and the Soviets* (Hutchinson & Co.), London, 1961.

Max Hayward and William C. Fletcher, *Religion and the Soviet State* (Praeger), New York, 1969.

Mark W. Hopkins, *Mass Media in the Soviet Union* (Pegasus), New York, 1970.

Alex Inkeles and Kurt Geiger, eds., *Soviet Society, a Book of Readings* (Houghton Mifflin Co.), Boston, 1961.

Priscilla Johnson, *Khrushchev and the Arts* (MIT Press), Cambridge, Mass., 1965.

John Kose, *Two Generations of Soviet Man* (University of North Carolina Press), Chapel Hill, N. C., 1962.

Ervin Laszlo, ed., *Philosophy in the Soviet Union* (Praeger), New York, 1967.

Deana Levin, *Soviet Education Today*, Monthly Review Press, 1963.

Metodika partiinoi propagandy (Izd. polit. lit.), Moscow, 1967.

Inge Morath and Arthur Miller, *In Russia* (Viking Press), New York, 1969.

William Taubman, *The View from the Lenin Hills* (Coward-McCann, Inc.), New York, 1967.

10. Coercion and Law

Every state is coercive, but the Soviet state is exceptional for the size and elaborateness of the apparatus of compulsion, the scope of its actions, its intermingling with the political direction, and the mixing of education with coercion. The Soviet state, despite dedication to indoctrination, requires the use of not less but more force than more open states, partly to sustain the monopoly of propaganda and power, partly because more regulations mean more infractions.

By Marxist theory and the aspirations of the Revolution, crime should disappear in socialism. Lenin expected this to happen and only belatedly undertook to provide his state with laws and courts. It is an embarrassment that after five decades crime, typical result of capitalism, remains a major problem. This is probably the main reason that there is very little reporting of crime, except as incidents to make a moral point. Only vague statements are published, always to the effect that criminality has decreased. These become implausible; thus a Soviet legal book gives year-to-year comparisons which, if gaps are ignored, would make criminal convictions in 1962 about 10% of those in 1922,[1] when the Soviet court system was still on wobbly legs.

The Soviet press, while claiming victories over crime, ever returns to the attack; and new measures are always found necessary. A frequent explanation is that crime is ascribable to the imperialists' subtle propaganda and insidious poisoning of minds. The view that crime can be considered nonclass, like disease, is specifically rejected; it is held transitory in principle, conditioned by class conflict, the product of "bourgeois" selfishness and individualism.

[1] *Kurs sovetskogo ugolovnogo prava*, T. 1 (Izd. Leningradskovo Universiteta), Leningrad, 1968, p. 191.

Where present capitalist or foreign influences cannot be blamed, crime is the result of survivals of prerevolutionary ways and mentality. It is admitted that social consciousness lags behind material conditions,[2] despite education and propaganda.

In more realistic discussions, many other causes are admitted, including mismanagement of the economy which causes speculation, poor education, bad living conditions, lack of supervision for juveniles, and improper organization of security forces. A large fraction of crimes, especially crimes of violence and "hooliganism," are attributed to alcoholism. Whatever the theory of causation, since the ascent of Stalin the individual has been held entirely responsible. His fault is greater because he breaks the rules of a near-perfect society. Moreover, ordinary civil crime, in the Soviet system, merges into political crime. Just as it is an expression of loyalty and Communist discipline to work well, it is politically bad to cheat or steal public, or state property, or in any way to contravene the purposes of the regime. Contrariwise, political oppositionists are treated as speculators and unprincipled coveters of Western material rewards.

Arbitrary Force

The Soviet state has always been inclined to deal with the most important crimes, which are political, in a political, more or less arbitrary fashion, without the restraints of a regular court procedure, much less public trials with guarantees of impartiality. Lenin organized a political police, the Cheka, and put it to work soon after the Revolution while the Soviet court system was still embryonic. Illegal executions began in February, 1918; and Lenin frequently berated his heavy-handed lieutenants for softness. Trotsky freely executed even veteran Communists in the civil war despite the tradition of revolutionary camaraderie. After the wounding of Lenin in August, 1918, thousands of persons unconnected with the deed were executed, and terrorism in the civil war did much to give the Bolsheviks a reputation of scourges of civilization.

With the end of the civil war, the Cheka was not curtailed but given the power to sentence persons to five years of labor camp when evidence was inadequate for judicial procedure. But repression through the 1920's was relatively mild, and political prisoners were usually treated fairly leniently, somewhat in line with the tsarist custom. This was reversed as the dictatorship slaughtered millions to secure its monopoly. Stalin set up special purge boards to deal with those whom it was not convenient to try in court; and the police apparatus, successively named GPU, OGPU, NKVD, or MVD, became one of the major components of his state.

[2] Op. cit., pp. 155–156.

The political importance of the police rose to its height shortly after Stalin's death, but it was cut down with the execution of Beria. Thereafter, the security police, now called KGB (Committee of State Security), was reduced to inconspicuousness through successive changes of its leadership; its representatives in the Supreme Soviet decreased from twenty-three in 1954 to twelve in 1958. Khrushchev, following the implications of de-Stalinization and realizing the counterproductive effects of terror, appeared desirous of ending arbitrary procedures altogether. He even abolished ministries of justice, transferring many of their functions to higher courts in the interest of regularization and decentralization; and there was begun an overhaul of the codes for the sake of "Socialist Legality."

Khrushchev's successors have reverted to semi-Stalinist methods. Much has been done to glorify the KGB, whose agents, often called by the romantic name of "Chekists," are extolled as the essence of proletarianism and given credit for the safety of the Fatherland. The KGB, half a million strong, has recovered some political importance, its head, Andropov, being a candidate member of the Politburo; but it is covered by secrecy. The KGB has been linked with many intrigues, and it is widely regarded as a conservative, anti-Western force. Its claim to importance is as the watchdog against Western subversion, a danger which it will certainly not minimize.

The Brezhnev government has thus far shown no inclination to revert to terrorism even on the reduced scale of Stalin's last years, probably because of fear that it would get out of control. However, it carries on quiet and inconspicuous repression. Many citizens are kept under surveillance, lectured, and threatened. Some are arrested, imprisoned, or deprived of residence permits. Others are made ineligible for promotion, threatened with loss of jobs, or fired; if discharged, they may be considered parasites and become subject to deportation. A student who refuses to participate in elections or signs a petition may be expelled from school and denied his degree; one who passes out pamphlets may be sent to labor camp. There are several political mental hospitals, as the Soviet state has made common the practice very rarely indulged by the tsarist, of regarding as insane those vocal in disagreement and subjecting them to treatment by KGB men in white blouses. Drugs and other modern means are said to be employed to alter mental processes.[3] Of fifty-four signers of a petition to the United Nations in June, 1969, calling attention to violations of human rights in the Soviet Union, nearly all were subjected to reprisals in following months.

Ordinary Russians learn of such actions only by gossip, however, and repressive measures lose much of their effectiveness because they are unpublicized. For this reason and because critical attitudes have become respectable, some Russians speak with considerable indifference to possible consequences.

[3] *New York Times*, March 20, 1971.

Formal Justice

The regular system of law enforcement comprises the ordinary police ("militia") and a conventional court system. It is a peculiarity of the militia that they have, like the armed forces, political officers. They operate under close party supervision, especially in regard to selection and training. Like factories, they carry on socialist competitions. Unlike the armed forces, they do not appear in the published budget, and their numbers are a matter of conjecture.

The police turn offenders over to a court system formally resembling that of Western European countries, particularly that of Germany. The basic court for civil and criminal cases has a judge, usually a woman, "elected" by the people, and two laymen called "assessors," drawn from a panel made up by the party and accepted by workers' meetings. In 1970, there were 3849 of these "People's Courts" with 8074 judges and 582,771 assessors.[4] Above them are regional courts, republic supreme courts, and a USSR Supreme Court, nominally elected by corresponding soviets. All presidents of republic supreme courts are members of the Union Supreme Court, in parallel with the practice of the Presidium of the Supreme Soviet. In 1967 the Supreme Court had among its members two prominent KGB men. The judges have five-year terms, and judgeship seems to be a profession. Judges can be recalled, however, and have no security. Higher courts, without lay assessors, mostly hear appeals, which can be by either defense or prosecution. In the latter case, the higher court may order a new trial and suggest the correct verdict. The courts are little used to remedy illegal acts of local authorities; the appeal is ordinarily to higher administrative powers.[5]

There is some pretense of independence of the judicial system, and judges are supposed to act on the evidence of the case. But Soviet political theory rejects separation of powers, and Soviet sources candidly proclaim the party's guidance of the courts and the prosecutors, as of other institutions. If a party body interferes improperly in the course of justice, it may be checked or reversed only by a higher party body. Judges are nearly all party members, as are nearly half of the assessors.[6] Judges comply with the directives of the hour, as a campaign against speculators. In March, 1970, the Supreme Court, pointing to instructions of the Central Committee, ordered all courts to crack down on violators of labor discipline.[7] Courts heed the voice of the people, as expressed, for example, by a group of workers. Since Stalin, however, much has been said of "socialist legality," and the state has increasingly tried to follow definite

[4] *Izvestia*, October 31, 1970, p. 1.
[5] *Literaturnaia gazeta*, October 14, 1970, p. 11.
[6] *Izvestia*, February 19, 1969.
[7] *Pravda*, March 26, 1970.

rules; a regime interested in fixity has to subscribe to some rule of law. Apparently some evidence is usually required for conviction, even of political defendants; and these have on occasion been able to make use of laws and the reluctance of the prosecution to admit a scandal.

The conduct of trials differs from Western custom both in procedure and spirit. Guilt or innocence is mostly determined in a pretrial investigation, in which interrogation is unlimited and the accused has no counsel. This is presumably as fair or as callous as the police or procuracy which conducts the inquest. During investigation a man may be legally imprisoned as long as six months, longer in practice; there is no bail. Trial in court, using evidence adduced during the investigation, is principally to fix degree of guilt and appropriate punishment. Court procedure is decidedly informal, unhampered by rules of evidence. The judge largely conducts the trial, does most questioning of witnesses, and decides the sentence, which may be harsher than that requested by the prosecutor. The two lay assessors, who take the place of the jury of tsarist times, in theory are equal to the judge, both in the trial and deciding the verdict; but they seem to play a largely ornamental role. One of their functions is to explain decisions to the people and generally to support the law; they are another means of linking official organs with the masses. A prosecutor, called "procurator," and a defense lawyer are usually present, although these may be dispensed in minor cases. It is not clearly provided that the defendant is innocent until found guilty, but it is up to the procurator to demonstrate guilt. Confession, which was held to be the best evidence in purge times, is no longer to be considered sufficient of itself. The defense plea is usually mitigating circumstances or good character.

Much of the trial is likely to revolve around the attitude of the accused and his record as a worker and Soviet citizen, a fact which should serve as a general incentive for proper conduct. The direction of the crime is significant; it is theoretically much worse to steal state than private property. The social nature of the crime is made clear to both defendant and spectators, and the trial is not only for the benefit of the accused, but also for the edification of the public (unless it should have political significance and hence probably be closed). "Public accusers," representatives of various "social organizations," may be brought in on either side. Much is made of the didactic importance of trials, which may be held at factories or elsewhere outside regular courtrooms to make them accessible to large audiences.

The procuracy is an important organ of the Soviet government, with powers like those it enjoyed in the eighteenth century. Highly centralized and independent of local powers, the procurator's office should be a general guardian of legality, always on the watch for violations of law. It decides whether to prosecute, unless this decision is taken by a party organization, which may hold a sort of pretrial and decide whether the accused is to be let off, reprimanded, or turned over to the state arm. The procurator can enter or appeal any case. He is to be at once a party to the case and an impartial agent of justice who may help the accused. He has a uniform like that of a naval officer. The central Ministry of Justice, established in 1936 and abolished in the de-Stalinization of 1956, was reestablished in September, 1970, to supervise judicial institutions and strengthen law enforcement.

The defense attorney is relatively humble, low in status, pay, and prestige. Lawyers are not numerous; in 1962 there were about 1,000 in Moscow,[8] and only as many jurists are graduated in the Soviet Union as in Hungary.[9] They are members of colleges of advocates under republic councils of ministers or soviet executive committees. The defendant can pay and choose his lawyer, but fees are fixed and do not depend on winning the case. A lawyer's salary and career depend on pleasing not litigants but the authorities. He is bound to protect not only the interests of the defendant but those of society as interpreted by the party. He may plead guilty even though the client is innocent,[10] because "It is a commonly held view that if the defense counsel's opinion does not coincide with the decision of the court, then the defense counsel is in the wrong and deserves to be rebuked."[11]

Once brought to trial, the Soviet defendant soon knows his fate. Trials last only a few hours or at most days, and appeals seem also to be speedily dealt with. Acquittals as well as convictions may be appealed, however, and there is no rule against double jeopardy. If the convict is well regarded, he may be remanded to the custody of a collective, for example his factory, for re-education. But there may be severe penalties for rather minor infractions; stealing a fur hat may bring two weeks to five years hard labor. A nonparty first offender was sentenced to a year's imprisonment and fined 850 rubles for killing one deer.[12] The maximum term is fifteen years, with parole possible after ten.

Capital punishment has had a checkered history in Russia and the Soviet Union, and the legal existence of the penalty has not had much relation to the number of persons put to death by the state. Nicholas I had men beaten to death in lieu of a nonexistent death penalty. In 1927, the Soviet state abolished capital punishment except for counterrevolutionary activity, but it became a common practice well before it was formally reinstated in the purges. In 1947, it was again abolished as executions continued apace. It was restored in 1950 for treason, etc. In 1958 and 1961, as most of the world was moving in the opposite direction and Khrushchev's Russia was entering its most liberal phase, capital punishment was considerably broadened for a number of grave crimes of

[8] Feifer, op. cit., p. 235.
[9] *Sovetskaia iustitiia*, no. 19, 1970, pp. 4–6; *ABSEES*, January, 1971, p. 30.
[10] *Literaturnaia gazeta*, February 4, 1970, p. 13; *ABSEES*, July, 1970, pp. 35–36.
[11] *Literaturnaia gazeta*, no. 2, January, 1970, p. 11; *Current Digest,* vol. 22, no. 3, p. 5.
[12] *Selskaia zhizn*, September 16, 1969.

violence and then for large-scale economic crimes, such as currency speculation, embezzlement, stealing of state property; and it was frequently applied, mostly to Jews. There were no announced death sentences for crimes against property from the early 1960's until the summer of 1970.

When sentenced to confinement, a person goes not to a prison, which is for those awaiting trial, but to a work camp. There he is to be at once made useful and spiritually redeemed by healthy labor and "political training" sessions. There are several types of camps of varying degrees of severity; under the ordinary regimen, five visits and three parcels per year are permitted. Labor camps are supposed to be self-supporting if not profitable; prisoners are paid low wages and charged for room and board. The prison population is a matter of speculation. The man who has served his time is often not free to go home, as he may be denied a residence permit or assigned to another area.

Law

Law, like lawyers, has small prestige. It is not a moral good but a provisional necessity, theoretically to be done away with in the communist future.

The nascent Soviet state thought to get rid of law immediately. Tsarist courts were abolished, and the old codes were to be applied only in terms of "revolutionary legal conscience." Soviet law was hardly more than the will of the party. With the end of the civil war and the retreat to a mixed economy in the NEP, codes were adopted, blending Bolshevik, tsarist, and Western legal ideas, to regularize relations within a stable society. Up to the end of the 1920's Soviet theorists still looked to the fairly imminent demise of state and law; but in the 1930's this idea was branded counterrevolutionary. Stalin maintained that the state had to be strengthened in its repressive functions as the class struggle sharpened in the victorious march of socialism. In the purge period, law was emphasized as the instrument of proletarian dictatorship.

After Stalin, the law of analogy, an elastic clause under which an act could be condemned as "analogous" to a prohibited act, was dropped; there were to be no more secret criminal laws; confession was no longer to be held sufficient proof of guilt; and the accused was given some guarantees. This movement toward legal order was climaxed by a new criminal code in 1958. Soon afterwards, however, there was a countertrend toward more "popular," or party-guided justice, with irregular "Comrade Courts" and mass meetings given power to exile "parasites." The post-Khrushchev leadership altered little in the legal structure. Some new codes were issued, but the most signal change was recentralization. Under Khrushchev, the republics were given a little latitude in the adoption of their own codes, and there were some significant variations. But subsequently, civil, criminal, and corrective labor codes were required to conform to the all-Union model; and the Ministry of the Interior was recentralized. Emphasis has turned from the "withering away" of the law to its "supreme flowering under socialism." The theory of law continues to be Marxist-Stalinist. By Marxist principles, law is part of the superstructure and a means of class rule, a political instrument. Soviet law is hence regarded as the tool of the ruling "working class." There seems to be growing reliance on criminal penalties to secure economic or social aims. For example, in view of increasing traffic accidents, it was decreed in October, 1970, that drivers in fatal accidents might receive up to fifteen years imprisonment; pedestrians who caused accidents were made subject to five years. It is a criminal offense to fail to control weeds in cultivated areas.

Marxism implies that the law of a socialist state should be entirely different from that of a capitalist one, and Soviet law is exalted as qualitatively distinct and much higher than any known before. For the most part, however, its provisions parallel those of other states. There are some special prohibitions. It is a crime to give religious instruction, to buy and sell for a profit, to hire help to make something for sale, or even to make something alone for sale without specific license. It is forbidden to photograph or draw not only military installations but harbors, waterworks, railroad junctions, tunnels, railroad and road bridges, industrial establishments, research institutes, construction bureaus, laboratories, power plants, radio stations, and telephone and teletype establishments. Soviet law also has peculiar fields, such as housing rights; occupancy of an apartment is almost a species of property. There are some differences of approach; for example, the planning of a crime is held equivalent to its commission.

Soviet law is also marked by its applicability to political offenses. The judge does not need to go outside the law or to have recourse to secret statute; articles in the published code cover any conceivable undesirable behavior. The prohibition of espionage can be applied to almost any information about the Soviet economy, technology, or culture, as well as defense. The effort of some Westerners to distribute leaflets in Moscow (February, 1970) was charged as "malicious hooliganism," maximum sentence five years, without reference to the content of the leaflets. The constitutional guarantees of freedom of speech, etc., must be exercised "in conformity with the interests of the workers and in order to strengthen the socialist state." Laws against anti-Soviet propaganda apply to religious and nationalistic agitation; as a Soviet encyclopedic dictionary puts it, "antisoviet agitation and propaganda [is] one of the especially dangerous crimes covered by article 7 of the law on the responsibility for political crimes . . . (oral or written, public or private) . . . distribution, preparation, or possession of antisoviet literature."[13] Penalty: up to seven years. The Crimean Tatars who petitioned for return to their homeland were convicted of this crime in August, 1968. Anti-Soviet jokes come under the

[13] *Entsiklopedicheskii slovar pravovykh znanii*, Moscow, 1965.

same rubric, while any unwanted gathering may be "disturbance of the public order." Those who demonstrated against the occupation of Czechoslovakia were punished for "interference with traffic." The judge in the Daniel-Siniavsky case was awarded the Order of Lenin for "strengthening socialist legality."

No matter what the law says, what counts is its application. This may operate in favor of the ordinary citizen, as strict rules may be diffidently applied or allowed to lapse. For example, Stalin's decrees on labor discipline were a dead letter for years before they were formally repealed. On the other hand, authorities may be capricious. Stalin's daughter was prevented from registering marriage to an Indian because the Presidium did not like him. Or systematic practice may be counter to the letter of the law. Thus, the prohibition of emigration is an essential of the Soviet system. It is very difficult for ordinary Soviet citizens to get permission to depart the homeland, and to attempt it illegally is a capital crime. To apply for an exit visa is a bold step. Yet according to the law, travel is completely free.

Justice by the People

Having renounced Stalinist terror, Khrushchev developed, or revived, several agencies of popular control, the volunteer police, "druzhiny," the informal petty "comrade" courts, new procedures for exile of undesirables from the principal centers, and a variety of volunteer controller groups. The ostensible purpose of these organizations was to prepare for the transition to the goal of pure communism, and they were supposed to represent a transfer of coercive authority from the official state to "social" organizations. When this transfer could be made complete at some date after 1980, presumably the state would finally be on the way to withering away, and there would remain only administrative agencies for the economy and popular, party-guided groups, through which people would keep order among themselves. The "popular" agencies, however, did not replace official organs, only supplemented them.

The "druzhiny" are youths, led by Komsomol activists, who give an evening now and then to patrolling the streets, with red arm bands, on the lookout for antisocial behavior. They function directly under party organizations. The druzhinniki have the authority to detain persons and bring them to the militia or other authority. For their activity they earn honors, vacations, and presumably political credits. The calls for the druzhiny and gratitude expressed in the Soviet press for their intervention indicated a real need. In 1969, there were reported to be 6,500,000 druzhiny, one-third being Komsomol members.[14] The Soviets here succeeded where a tsar failed. Alexander III early

---

[14] *Komsomolskaia pravda*, March 2, 1969. Less formally than the druzhiny, Komsomol groups often act as vigilantes, organizing "raids" on factories, farms, or, more commonly, calling deviationist young people to order, censoring clothing, music, dances, etc.

in his reign tried in vain to organize volunteer police auxiliaries, called "druzhiny," against anti-tsarist elements.[15]

The antiparasite program was also reminiscent of prerevolutionary practice. Not only was exile by administrative action a common tsarist punishment; peasant communes could also expel undesired members. Laws passed 1957–1961 provided that committees under the cognizance of the local soviet could call neighborhood meetings to exile persons without satisfactory regular employment to remote regions, where they were subject to a strict work regimen. This was directed at nonconformists, persons living from black market dealings or renting houses or automobiles, professionals not supposed to exist in Soviet society as prostitutes and beggars, or anyone living outside the approved framework, as artisans or handy men without official employment. The requirement that everyone have an approved full-time job also impedes deviant political activity.

The idea of neighborhood crowds exerting this power caused some protest, however; and the measure was not very successful, either for re-education of the "parasites" or development of Siberia. In May, 1970, a new procedure was established whereby a man is given fifteen days to get a job; if he does not, he is assigned to work; if he fails to work, he is sent to labor camp.

The comrade courts fulfill a broader function. These are something between courts of justice and indignation meetings summoned by the party to castigate minor evildoers. Comrade courts are formed under the aegis of the trade union or of the local soviet executive committee. There may be 300,000 in the Soviet Union. They have a chairman and secretary but no prosecutor, defense attorney, or fixed procedure. They deal mostly with drunkenness, disorderly conduct, or petty quarrels, but they also handle antisocial behavior with political significance. They can place a reprimand on one's record, impose small fines, and suggest stronger measures, such as demotion in employment, eviction from housing, up to fifteen days physical labor at the work place, etc. This verdict can be appealed to the local soviet executive committee, which may return the case for retrial. But their purpose is primarily educational, to make an example of the wayward before the assembled citizens. There are also other semiofficial courts of "parental honor," "workers' honor," and the like. In minor infractions, the militia may turn the culprit over to his employer for chastisement.

In such ways, nonconformity is discouraged without adding to the direct burdens of the enforcement agencies of the state. Soviet citizens are legally called upon—as provided by the law of 1959 on comrade courts—to see to it that their fellow citizens obey the law; and the party mobilizes the willingness of some to watch their neighbors, judge, and improve them. There are many

[15] Anatole Leroy-Beaulieu, *The Empire of the Tsars and the Russians* (G. P. Putnam's Sons), New York, 1902, vol. 2, p. 147.

agencies for this end. Apartment committees assist political education, prevent violation of apartment rules, protect buildings, keep young folks from going astray, save marriages from breaking up, and help the police. Street committees sponsor lectures and other political entertainment, fight petty crime, etc. Juvenile affairs commissions, composed of soviet deputies, teachers, militia, etc., have extensive duties of guiding juveniles as well as rights of punishment including authorization to take children from their parents. Village assemblies are sometimes used to shame offenders. Local soviet administrations can assess fines for moonshining, failure to control weeds, poaching, etc.

People's and Party Control

The most important agencies of social control are the "people's control commissions." From 1919, when there was established the Workers' and Peasants' Inspectorate to bring proletarians in to check the waxing bureaucratism of the party apparatus, there have been a series of usually ineffective control commissions. In 1962, Khrushchev injected new life into the idea by establishing the Party-State Control Committee and organizing a vast network of regional and local committees or commissions officered by apparatus-men and staffed by volunteers. By 1963 he claimed two and one-half million party members working full time as controllers.[16] After his retirement the hybrid body was divided into the Party Control Committee and the People's Control Committee. The first of these bodies works in the party and government, mostly at higher levels, as has been discussed above. Headed by a Politburo member, it has been superior to the People's Control Committee; it may be, however, that the appointment of a Politburo member to direct the latter means improvement of its standing.

The People's Control Committees are set up in parallel with the party and soviet organization, almost as another arm of the political system. Leaders of local control committees direct control "groups" and "posts," of which there are about a million,[17] manned by seven million volunteer inspectors and controllers.[18] The powers of the controllers are mostly of investigation, and they are to have full access to records. Having uncovered errors or wrongdoing, they may suggest changes, denounce the guilty to higher authorities (including the procurator), or publicize their findings; they may levy fines for damages and suspend officials from their positions pending further inquiry.[19]

Controllers are supposed to forward the decisions of government and party. In the retail trade, they uncover wrong prices, overcharging, hiding of

[16] *Pravda*, April 5, 1963.

[17] *Partiinaia zhizn*, no. 2, January, 1969, p. 10; *Pravda*, September 19, 1969.

[18] *Ekonomicheskaia gazeta*, no. 4, January 20, 1969; *Current Abstracts of the Soviet Press*, vol. 2, no. 2, p. 3.

[19] *Partiinaia zhizn*, no. 2, January, 1969, p. 14.

goods, and faulty scales.[20] In the factory they compensate for deficiencies of the planning system, point out ways to increase production, reduce waste, cut down administrative expenses, get workers to stop loafing, promote innovation, and check quality of output. On the farm, they see to the cleanliness of milk, the quality of grain, the drying of hay, and the adequacy of storage facilities.[21] On the construction site they look into supplies of materials and the state of the machinery. Pilferage of state property is their particular concern. They also carry on strictly political activities, studying the ideological and moral qualities of workers, helping to educate and organize the cadres, and perhaps recommending candidates for responsible positions. They should act as the conscience of the apparatus; if ministries ignore rules for reducing transportation costs, the people's controllers should step in to overcome irrationalities caused by the planning system.[22]

The direct responsibility of the party for the people's control apparatus was weakened in 1965, and it seemed that the latter might be made a governmental adjunct. But 1968 legislation put it squarely in the hands of the party; the affiliation with the soviets seems to be only formal. Leaders of control groups are party members, while presidents of party control committees are generally party secretaries or committee members. The party also undertakes the political education of people's controllers, who are likely to be candidates for political advancement. "Party leadership and party support are the basic factor determining the effectiveness of the work of the groups and posts. . . ."[23] "The Communist Party organizes the whole business of control in our county."[24] The people's control apparatus is, in short, part of the system of "Soviet Democracy," another transmission belt through which as many as possible are engaged in the work of the party. Its true importance remains to be seen, but the volunteer enforcers of law and morality could be the answer to an autocrat's prayer. They cost little, occupy many idealistic people, give a sense of participation in public affairs, and keep everyone in society under some kind of surveillance; yet they represent no political force.

Problems of Control

The apparatus of law enforcement, like that of political education, approaches the limits of the practicable, with a large part of the adult population supposedly watching over the remainder. When the welter of supervising and controlling organizations fails to work as it should, the leadership calls for

---

[20] *Pravda*, November 17, 1969.
[21] *Selskaia zhizn*, July 30, 1969.
[22] *Pravda*, October 29, 1971, p. 3.
[23] *Pravda*, September 19, 1969.
[24] *Sovety deputatov trudiashchiksia*, no. 6, June, 1969, p. 19.

expanding and strengthening it, sometimes for reorganizing, hardly ever for pruning away.

There are armed guards for bridges, railroad stations and yards, and collective farm fields at harvest time. Passes are required to enter universities, libraries, and most public buildings. It is assumed that the porter reports to the police, that hotel rooms are bugged, telephone conversations monitored, and letters subject to opening. Russians suspect that almost any neighbor might be a police spy. Citizens over age sixteen are required to have internal passports, and changes of residence must be registered with the police. Children should be made to feel that everything they say or do is subject to the scrutiny of the house committee; it is even advocated that all over age seven should be registered and induced to report any misbehavior within the family as well as out.[25] Yet crime apparently does not decrease. In 1966, Moscow introduced a 10 p.m. curfew for minors, and since then there have been several campaigns against juvenile delinquency. Narcotic use seems to have been spreading. Soviet citizens who formerly did not lock their houses now do so, and the Moscow police began offering burglar alarms, at a fee, for apartment dwellers.[26] Game poaching is a major problem; the poachers in one case were equipped with a helicopter, hardly obtainable but from the armed forces.[27]

It seems in many cases expected that people will defy the rules. The people's controllers at the big Gorky automotive plant found that only 40% of vehicles taken out for a test run were driven over the prescribed route; the remainder were used for pleasure driving. The controllers did not try to secure compliance with the rules but advocated testing the vehicles on a stand and hailed this as a great innovation.[28] A prosecutor in Siberia urged that a man be arrested because he might feel free to leave town after his daughter finished school and would thus be lost—a reflection on the passport and registration system.[29]

Laws make crimes; for example, people enter fictitious marriages to get residence in desirable cities. Countless functionaries are in a position to help or hurt people by giving or denying a permit, releasing goods, assigning lodging, etc. Bureaucratic management of the economy, with artificial prices and shortages of goods, creates countless opportunities for illicit gain. Producers are tempted to cut quality or tamper with reports, to sell goods illegally at higher prices, or to produce goods other than those demanded by the state. While directors contravene the rules to meet their quotas, workers help themselves to

[25] *Komsomolskaia pravda*, June 26, 1969; *Soviet Studies Information Supplement*, no. 26, January, 1970, p. 12.

[26] *New York Times*, October 6, 1969.

[27] *Pravda*, September 29, 1969.

[28] *Pravda*, September 19, 1969.

[29] *Pravda*, September 29, 1969.

the factory's supplies, especially since they likely cannot buy in shops the paint or lumber they need. When a warehouse guard used his position to get workers to fix his dacha, paying with vodka, he was brought before a comrade court, but he received only sympathy from the audience.[30] When one gets free building materials, others want no less. It is said, "And why not please them, if it costs nothing? Personally, of course. But the government doesn't get poor, you know. Our government is rich."[31] Authorities hardly seem to try to stop pilfering, clamping down only on those who make a business of it. But amounts involved may be very large. It was reported that 10% of the meat which went into the slaughterhouses of Georgia was irregularly removed.[32]

Shortages and theft run together. Teenagers rip out telephones to get string for guitars, which is otherwise unobtainable. Tractor drivers can make money using tractors to do errands because of the lack of cars. Selling stolen goods is easy. In the economy of shortages, there are speculators handling almost anything, and the gray market merges into the black. A man was sentenced to four years for reselling a prize-winning lottery ticket which entitled him to an automobile.[33]

Since every subsidiary authority is a little power center, inclined to take care of itself, controllers have to be careful whose toes they step on. A guilty official may get a slap on the wrist, after which he can perhaps proceed to exact vengeance from his accusers. The worker who demands fulfillment of the law may get formal satisfaction after petitions and investigations; but the director remains in charge and it seems to be taken for granted that he will take reprisals against critics.[34] A worker may be punished for questioning the inflation of production figures or for protesting the director's arbitrary appropriation of recreation facilities.[35] Not only managers but fellow workers may take it out on an unfortunate controller who brings malversations to light, pressing all manner of accusations and practically hounding him out of the factory.[36] Charges, criminal or otherwise, are pressed against a party member only with the consent of the party organization; and if he stands well with it, every effort will be made to shield him. If there is an appeal to central authorities, the easiest thing for them is to ask for a report from the person or organization against whom the appeal is raised. The malefactor very likely has local protectors who profit from his improper enterprise or share his interests, and who can arrange excuses or shift the blame in the maze of conflicting and overlapping responsibilities.

[30] *Izvestia*, November 22, 1970, p. 4.

[31] *Izvestia*, October 30, 1970.

[32] *Izvestia*, August 7, 1970, p. 4.

[33] *Pravda*, January 16, 1970; *Current Digest*, vol. 22, no. 3, p. 17.

[34] *Pravda*, December 24, 1970, p. 3.

[35] For examples, *Pravda*, September 19, 1969; January 8, 1971, p. 3; February 28, 1971, p. 6; *Sovetskaia Rossia*, January 29, 1971, p. 2.

[36] *Pravda*, October 29, 1971, p. 3.

READINGS

Andrei Amalrik, *Involuntary Journey to Siberia* (Harcourt Brace Jovanovich), New York, 1970.

Peter Archer, *Communism and the Law* (Dufour Editions), Chester Springs, Pa., 1963.

Harold J. Berman, *Justice in the USSR*, 2nd. ed. (Harvard University Press), Cambridge, Mass., 1963.

Uyacheslav Chornovil, *The Chornovil Papers* (McGraw-Hill), New York, 1969.

Robert Conquest, *The Soviet Police System* (Praeger), New York, 1968.

George Feifer, *Justice in Moscow* (Dell Publishing Co.), New York, 1964.

John N. Hazard and Isaac Shapiro, *The Soviet Legal System* (Oceana Publications), Dobbs Ferry, N. Y., 1962.

Anatoly Marchenko, *My Testimony* (E. P. Dutton & Co.), New York, 1969.

11. The Military

It was a promise of the Revolution that armies would be ended; or, if a defensive force were still needed, it would be a people's militia entirely unlike the traditional standing armies. But when the Bolsheviks failed to overcome the German army in the same way that they had dealt with the tsarist, by propaganda, they had to put together a big, clumsy, undemocratic army strong enough to win the civil war.

Because of poverty and fear of its influence, the Soviet leadership kept the army relatively small from the end of the civil war until the mid-1930's. The army then began a steady program of expansion which continued up to the attack of June, 1941. Stalin made the army more national and traditional, but he battered the forces so severely in the purges that they remained politically paralyzed as long as he lived.

Released from Stalin's grip, the Soviet army has been an important although unweighable political force. The armed forces have remained large, and they have received first priority in the economy. There is daily testimony to their prestige in the Soviet press, and they are the only visible alternative to the party as a governing organization. Not only do they have the physical force to take control whenever they might resolve to do so; they have esprit de corps, coherence, and a unified command as does no other Soviet sector except the party itself. There is no real constitutional or ideological bar to their undertaking to remove what they might consider a defective leadership or insisting on political changes for the safety of the land. It is yet possible, in the unforeseeable turns of politics, that the old Bolshevik fear of a Bonapartist turn may one day be realized, turning the Soviet Union toward the common pattern of outright military dictatorship so common in the world.

293

Party in the Military

To forestall this possibility, the party leadership has always taken great pains to permeate the military establishment and check it in every possible way. The party has sought to indoctrinate soldiers and officers in the necessity of absolute obedience to it, much as any army indoctrinates its men in absolute obedience to the command structure. The party has made itself the supreme military command with its special lines of authority into every military unit.

The party's apparatus of control in the military is elaborate as nowhere else. One arm is the security police under the KGB, with agents at the regimental staff level and above. Called the "Special Section," "OO" by the Russian initials, it has regular ranks and uniform but operates under its own command structure. Security officers are concerned with morale, manifestations of anti-Soviet feelings, desertion, sabotage, etc., as well as counterespionage. They also check on the work of military and political officers, keep dossiers, and approve promotions. As party members, they participate in the party organizations in the armed forces and should cooperate with the party secretaries.

Control is also effected through party and Komsomol organization. About four-fifths of recruits are Komsomol, and only 5% of junior officers are reported nonparty.[1] Senior officers are all or nearly all party members. Battalions or divisions have primary party organizations, while subsidiary units have party groups; regiments with over seventy-five members form party committees.[2] There are party organizations corresponding to larger commands, as the Baltic military district or the Baltic fleet or the Moscow district antiaircraft forces, but little is publicized of these.

The party organization in the army differs from that in civilian life in that its head is not the nominally elected secretary but the appointed political officer of the unit. There is a political officer, or "deputy for political affairs," "zampolit" in Russian, for units the size of a company (about 150 men) or larger. He belongs to the hierarchy of the Chief Political Administration, a department of the Central Committee. The CPA is a coequal part of the armed forces, with a chain of command parallel to that of the army from top to bottom. Its chief is first deputy to the Minister of Defense and by protocol number three in the forces.

Zampolits, some 80,000 in number, are descendants of the commissars, reliable Bolsheviks set to watch tsarist officers recruited for expertise in the civil war. The commissars held a veto power over the officers until 1925, when an adequate number of Bolshevik-trained officers had become available. They recovered it in 1937 when Stalin purged the army, but lost it in 1940, when

[1] *Krasnaia zvezda*, April 5, 1969.
[2] *Krasnaia zvezda*, November 13, 1970, p. 2.

failures of the war against Finland showed the need to give the regular officers a freer hand.

Military and political training are inseparable. Political officers are given technical military training, and regular and political military careers are mixed. Officers should be qualified in both capacities, and may be transferred from one to the other. Commanders are customarily members of party committees and are much involved in political work. But the political deputy remains primarily a morale officer, working mostly through the party groups and the party members, who, including the commander, are under him as party leader and whose promotions depend on his reports along with those of the KGB representative. He is chaplain, educator, morale-builder, censor, organizer of entertainments, and instructor, working with a staff of full-time propagandists and secretaries of party and Komsomol committees.

Daily instruction on foreign and domestic affairs and party policy is obligatory for all enlisted personnel. There are lectures, so numerous as to interfere with military duties, discussion groups, indoctrination movies, and radio and television programs. Special importance is attached to newspapers; it is the duty of party and Komsomol to get them to soldiers despite whatever obstacles. There are political schools, with two-year courses and three levels of instruction, and people's universities. Above all, the political educators must work by personal agitation, in which they help, like fathers, to resolve personal problems and build character. Even more than in the factory, nonmaterial incentives are applied. There are socialist competitions between companies, titles, medals, books and boards of honor, and the like. The party organization keeps the "room of military glory," with its treasured relics of the unit's past and its wartime feats. The soldier who performs best may have his photograph taken with the regimental banner, or be commended publicly or praised to his home town or factory collective.

"Political preparation" seems almost as important as the strictly military. "Ours is an army in which the officer as well as every soldier is called upon to be a political warrior, an active propagandist and agitator."[3] On the eve of battle, soldiers are not to rest or polish their weapons but hear a lecture on the international situation.[4] Two hours of political instruction daily should convince soldiers that the leadership of the party is virtuous and indispensable, the prime source of the army's strength, and it should make them "skilled and ardent propagandists of the ideas of the Communist Party."[5] The political section and the party must mould warriors who are totally inspired and obedient, completely immune to "bourgeois" ideology, vigilant against hostile infiltration, and ever mindful of their "patriotic and international duty."

[3] Marshal Grechko, *Krasnaia zvezda*, November 27, 1969.
[4] *Partiinaia zhizn*, no. 2, January 1969, p. 51.
[5] *Krasnaia zvezda*, June 12, 1969.

But "the political worker is concerned with everything, responsible for everything."[6] Since 1956 the political apparatus has been responsible not only for political but for general military training. The zampolit, having a broad military education, helps teach men how to handle tanks while he is inculcating their Soviet-patriotic and proletarian-internationalist duty. The party apparatus concerns itself with general policies, personnel questions, and rather technical aspects of military assignments, much as it looks into organization of labor and techniques of production in industry. If soldiers are sloppy or insufficiently respectful of the sergeants, the party intervenes.[7] Much work is carried on through the Komsomol; there are also people's controllers in army, navy and air force units, apparently working somewhat as their counterparts in the economy to check waste and maladministration.[8] The commander himself is supposed to undergo self-criticism at party meetings and may be called upon to justify his professional competence. Although his orders are not to be criticized, the party may sit in judgment over his treatment of subordinates.[9]

Military in Soviet Society

If the party permeates the armed forces, the military has tentacles throughout Soviet society. If the party indoctrinates the army, this indoctrinates the people. "In contrast to capitalist countries, where the ruling circles make every effort to separate the army from the people," in the Soviet Union every effort is made to bring the two together.[10]

Linkage is close at all levels. Over a score of top commanders are members of the Central Committee, and military men are high in party leadership in the oblasts or republics. At a lower level, party rules require that party bodies in the forces "maintain close contact with local party committees and keep them informed concerning political activities within the military units. Secretaries of military party organizations and heads of political bodies participate in the work of local party committees." (No. 67). Many officers are deputies in local soviets. Military party groups are directed to maintain close contact with factories and farms of the area where they may be stationed, telling the workers of the successes of the warriors and vice versa, and helping to cultivate love for the army and navy among the people, especially the youth.[11] Trade unions and factories respond by sponsoring military units in their vicinity, organizing entertainments, sports, and outings for the fighting men. Conversely,

[6] *Krasnaia zvezda*, July 30, 1970, p. 1.
[7] *Krasnaia zvezda*, November 25, 1969.
[8] *Partiinaia zhizn*, no. 2, January, 1969, p. 10.
[9] *Krasnaia zvezda*, July 25, 1969.
[10] *Partiinaia zhizn*, no. 3, February, 1970, p. 18.
[11] Iu. P. Petrov, *Stroitelstvo politorganov partiinykh i komsomolskikh organizatsii armii i flota* (Voenizdat), Moscow, 1968, p. 445.

soldiers sometimes help out on construction projects, even the building of apartments.[12]

The soldier is held to be a representative in the armed forces of the collective from which he came; the factory or farm sponsors its draftees, and it is up to them to show themselves worthy. Those who excel are eligible for a place on the board of honor not only of their company but of their former work place. Military service (ordinarily two years, longer in special branches, one year for persons with higher education) is not a mere interlude but an integral part of the life of the Soviet male. It is in some ways a part of entry into manhood, as it ideally transforms the raw youth into a modest but self-assured, strong, self-sacrificing, disciplined Soviet citizen. Entry into the army is celebrated as the beginning of real participation in the great Soviet brotherhood, where common soldiers and marshals serve the cause together. On the solemn day, for which they should specially prepare themselves,[13] the new recruits are welcomed by veterans, hear inspiring speeches and stirring music, and take the military oath in the presence of the assembled citizenry, surrounded by banners and mementoes of dead heroes. A factory stops work to give its draftees a proper send-off.[14] A man's eyes take on a new glow, and he departs with an inspiring charge from the workers he leaves behind: "Be upright, honorable, brave, faithfully fulfill all military rules and commands. Do not shame the collective in which you worked and studied and your near ones, guard worthily the fame for valor in work and battle won by your father or older brother! Protect the peaceful and creative labor of our people, building commu- nism.... We await your return to our collective at the end of your service."[15] When active duty is over, the youth is to be a soldier of production; he also remains a reservist for ten years, bound to training every summer.

The draftee should come well prepared, for he has had ample opportunity through boyhood to absorb military spirit and familiarize himself with the ways of the soldier. Of the two leading children's magazines, one increased its military-patriotic material, 1966 to 1970, from 6% to 19%; the other, from 30% to 42%.[16] As Pioneers, children engage in an endless round of semimilitary ceremonies with accents on struggle and brotherhood, and are trained, inspired, and hardened in play battles.[17] When they grow up a bit they exercise with real artillery and tanks under the guidance of army officers.[18]

---

[12] *Krasnaia zvezda*, November 21, 1969.
[13] *Pravda*, July 10, 1970.
[14] *Krasnaia zvezda*, November 22, 1969.
[15] Iu. I. Kolodina, *Sevodnia Komsomola Buriatii*, Ulan Ude, 1968, p. 66.
[16] *Der Spiegel*, vol. 25, no. 5, January 25, 1971, p. 104.
[17] *Pravda*, July 1, 1969.
[18] *Pravda*, August 8, 1970, p. 3.

"It was entirely like the fulfillment of a responsible assignment in war. At the appointed hour each of the "scouts" received an envelope with a wax seal and the inscription "absolutely secret." In it were crisp, military-style directions and a map. The participants, each separately, were ordered to seek out one of the local monuments related to events of the October Revolution or the Patriotic War and to gather as many details as possible.

So operation "Absolutely Secret" began. The "warriors" made their way through forest paths to fulfill the assignment. Then, using the map and password, they gathered at the appointed time [to report]... The "Scouts" were village boys and girls, members of the youth club.... [They then went in a procession, torches held aloft, to a cemetery of victims of fascism.] Youths and maidens swore to be true helpers of the party, to fight for peace and happiness on earth. Then military campaign songs resounded over the meadow."[19]

In the Urals district, it was reported in 1969, military authorities sponsored 35 orphanages and 815 schools; there were 235 divisions of "Young Friends of the Soviet Army," 438 military sport clubs, 418 military museums, and 5,186 "corners of military glory." About 1,200 soldiers were leaders of pioneer brigades and 200,000 school children were guests on trips to army posts.[20] "In the schools are set up small but unique war museums, and feats are chronicled; from the school door begin excursions to places of military and labor glory of the Soviet people. Thousands of schools cooperate in the All-Union Exhibition of military-patriotic work, proclaimed by the CC of the Komsomol, the CC of the Dosaaf, the USSR Ministry of Education, the Staff of civil defense of the country, the Academy of Pedagogical Sciences of the USSR, and the newspaper Izvestia."[21]

Civil defense lessons begin with the fifth grade. Formal, obligatory military training has begun, since 1967, after the eighth grade, whether the boy continues in secondary school or goes to work. Girls learn medical and auxiliary specialties. Directors of schools, enterprises, farms, etc., are legally responsible for seeing to it that the youths under them receive proper military instruction.[22] This is conducted by the army, which details active or reserve officers as instructors. The Soviet paramilitary defense organization, Dosaaf, and the Komsomol cooperate. Students in higher education also must pass military courses throughout their university career. Otherwise they are subject to draft as privates instead of qualifying for officer status upon graduation.

The name of Dosaaf is composed of the Russian initials for "Voluntary Society for Cooperation with the Army, Air Force, and Fleet." With

---

[19] Sovety deputatov trudiashchiksia, no. 5, May, 1969, pp. 40–41.

[20] Partiinaia zhizn, no. 3, February, 1969, p. 61.

[21] Izvestia, January 28, 1971, p. 3.

[22] Krasnaia zvezda, June 27, 1969.

a membership burgeoning since Stalin to forty million (in 1964), it is one of the great organizations of Soviet society and an important link with the masses.[23] Its structure parallels that of the party; and party, trade union, economic, and especially Komsomol organizations are obliged to cooperate with it. With branches in factories, farms, and higher schools, Dosaaf carries on civil defense instruction and trains in military skills and sports. It carries out war games and contests for young and old, teaching especially such sports as motorcycle riding, fencing, marksmanship, grenade throwing, and obstacle racing. It holds mass parachute jumps and long marches in winter and summer, frequently led or supervised by army officers. Other sports are also encouraged for their utility in hardening bodies and training minds to coordination and teamwork. Dosaaf invites boys to learn to operate radio equipment, to pilot planes, and to scuba-dive. It trains a million or so technical specialists yearly. Factories have military instruction sections, probably under a reserve officer, for firing practice and other exercises as well as general morale and the fostering of the "military and revolutionary traditions" of the Soviet people.[24]

"Now, as never before, there is an immeasurable expansion of the role of military-patriotic education of the toilers, especially of youth."[25] Millions of boys and girls are taken on pilgrimages to the innumerable war monuments and shrines which hallow battles of the civil war and the Great Patriotic War, where they stand before the symbols of death and victory, meditate on the sacrifice of those who fell there, and dedicate themselves equally to serve the Soviet Fatherland. Outstanding military heroes are kept busy addressing groups, especially of school children, and participating in ceremonies; they hand out to sixteen-year-olds the passports which attest their citizenship. The county (raion) should have its patriotic museum of "military and labor glory" and hold regular sessions at which veterans speak of the "heroic traditions of party and people."[26] There are observances of Navy Day, Army Day, Militia Day, Rocket Forces Day, Border Guards' Day, Tank Day, Victory Day, and Recruit Day.

The Soviet soldier is both the bearer of proletarian internationalism and heir of the glories of Russian armies of ages past. Russian nationalism is tied to Soviet Marxist supranationalism, as medieval battles are interpreted both as Russians against Germans or Mongols and as the people against would-be enslavers. Past invasions of Russia are used to show the necessity of strength; the Second World War especially is the supreme vindication of the Soviet system.

[23] For a description, see Ellsworth Raymond, *The Soviet State* (Macmillan), New York, 1968, pp. 287–290.

[24] *Partiinaia zhizn*, no. 4, February, 1970, pp. 59–60. Cf. *Krasnaia zvezda*, January 12, 1971, p. 2; *Current Digest*, vol. 23, no. 2, p. 12.

[25] Lt. Gen. N. Denim, First Vice-Chairman of Dosaaf, *Krasnaia zvezda*, September 24, 1969.

[26] *Partiinaia zhizn*, no. 21, November, 1970, p. 42.

This fearful and heroic conflict has never been allowed to fade from the daily awareness of Soviet citizens; in the last several years it has been made subject of a flood of writing and movies. Military themes are perennial in all media, particularly newspapers, books, and television, in tales and reminiscences of past wars, accounts of training exercises and the day-to-day duties of soldiers, especially the ever-alert border guards, and dramas of successes in battling the enemy.[27] The army paper, *Krasnaia zvezda* (*Red Star*), produced not only for military personnel but for the public, has a circulation in the multimillion range of *Pravda* and *Izvestia*. Papers dedicated to literature, art, and the economy also give ample space to military themes. The Military Publishing House puts out a great variety of literature, including suitable novels, 2,819 of them in 1961–1968, in 134 million copies.[28]

Nothing may detract from the heroic aura. Presumably for this reason, maimed veterans have been kept out of sight, despite the large numbers left by the Second World War. No statistics of war losses have been published. When feeble tendencies toward realistic portrayal of war appeared in the years of maximum relaxation of the early 1960's, they were firmly put down as sordid and unpatriotic. As *Pravda* put it, "Consistent fidelity of military-patriotic literature to the heroic outlook is the decisive condition of its success. It is important to underline this proposition as a matter of principle, for in days past (and even today) there appeared 'fears' concerning the allegedly limited possibilities of the heroic aspect in the portrayal of the Soviet citizen in war . . ."[29]

Military Economy

Announced Soviet military appropriations, recently somewhat over seventeen billion rubles, are very modest for such a large country. But a realistic guess would be three times larger. Military training is charged to education; research and development and advanced weapons can be covered by appropriations for science and heavy industry; Aeroflot provides services for the air force; etc. The monetary yardstick is elastic in application to the armed forces. Manpower is paid at subsistence cost, as soldiers receive only trivial pocket money (partly to spare them the temptation of vodka);[30] procurement prices

[27] "What a word 'soldier'! In its very rhythm one hears the precise cadence of the parade march, and the iron roar of winds at the front, and the victorious, ancient, yet new Russian 'Hurrah!' But not only that. We say, 'Soldier of the Fatherland' and we see before us a man of high goals and lofty duty, a man of generous spirit and warm, challenging heart. With the word 'soldier' are indissolubly bound concepts of valor, faithfulness, discipline, and friendship, pure as a mountain spring, hard as adamant. . . ." (*Kazakhstanskaia pravda*, February 18, 1971, p. 3.)

[28] *Krasnaia zvezda*, October 24, 1969.

[29] July 20, 1969.

[30] *Krasnaia zvezda*, June 18, 1970, p. 4.

are very low, shifting much or most of the cost to the producer. A ruble spent by the armed forces may have ten or twenty times the purchasing power of a ruble in the hands of a consumer.

Soviet military expenditures can thus be estimated by the results. The Soviet Union maintains armed forces of about the same size as those of the United States and equips them with weapons universally rated as first quality, in many cases the world's best. It has a great variety of advanced planes and develops new ones. Soviet military transport showed great efficiency in the 1968 air-borne invasion of Czechoslovakia. The Soviet navy, which Khrushchev downgraded, has been rapidly expanded to a world-girdling force with indefinite perspectives, comparable to the American navy in size and much newer. The Soviet submarine fleet is by far the world's largest. From 1965 to 1971, while the number of American intercontinental missiles rose only slightly, the Soviet force increased five fold, to about 1,500, against 1,054 on the American side. The explosive power of the Soviet weapons, moreover, is several times larger than the American, so total Soviet megatonnage at the end of 1971 is reportedly more than five times that of the United States.

Since the Soviet economy is approximately half the size of the American, it may be roughly estimated that its military component is proportionately about double that of the American. The Soviet economy has been oriented to heavy industry since the First Five-Year Plan; and heavy industry has served primarily to create the foundations not of consumer goods production, which has steadily lagged, but of military production. Military and industrial management are closely associated. The armed forces have special schools to qualify officers in the technology of various branches of production, as aircraft, chemical, artillery, etc.; and officers are attached to heavy industrial enterprises to expedite military production and coordinate mobilization planning.[31] Soviet lead times in weapons development have been consistently shorter than American, and the quality and imaginativeness of Soviet military goods has contrasted with that of civilian goods.

The result has been rising confidence. From the latter 1950's the Soviet military posture has been visibly shifting from simply shielding the homeland to protecting communism or Soviet influence abroad. Soviet strategic writings, moreover, have turned away from the theory that nuclear war would mean only mutual annihilation to contend that the better prepared country will win. There is no need to be terrified of a nuclear attack, because civil defense is perfectly feasible;[32] and according to Marshal Grechko, the Soviet Union is capable of destroying missiles far from their targets regardless of their height and speed.[33]

[31] For a discussion of Soviet military-industrial coordination, see Raymond, *The Soviet State*, pp. 334–343.

[32] *Nauka i zhizn*, no. 1, January, 1969; *Current Abstracts*, vol. 2, no. 2, p. 3.

[33] *Pravda*, February 23, 1970.

Military and the Party

In contrast to its evident potential, the army has played through Soviet history a remarkably modest political role. In the civil war, it was strongly infused with Marxist-revolutionary feeling, as its officers were militarily experienced but politically distrusted, while the commissars were militarily unqualified but politically reliable. After the civil war, the army was cut down to about half a million men, and it remained practically out of the political picture. The reaction to Stalin's forced collectivization spread into the army, composed largely of peasants; but it posed no serious resistance. In the purge of 1937, the military leadership bowed humbly as Stalin's police agents murdered most of them. Perhaps because they were cowed by the purges, the generals accepted unquestioningly Stalin's right to command during the Second World War, when conditions were most propitious for their self-assertion in the name of national safety.

After the war, Stalin showed his apprehensions lest the military leaders claim a share of power as reward of victory by scattering the most outstanding of them. However, the relative decline of the party as an instrument of rule in Stalin's last years gave increased importance to the military, as shown by the fact that all the alleged victims of the Doctors' Plot, except the long-dead Zhdanov, were military. After the decease of the dictator, the party needed the support of the army against Beria's police. The execution of the latter and the reduction of the power of the security forces benefited the military element as well as the party. De-Stalinization came to dilute the generals' respect for the party's infallibility. In 1957, the army, supporting Khrushchev because of the resistance of Molotov and company to the rehabilitation of Stalin's victims, played a decisive part in Khrushchev's victory.

By his intervention, Marshal Zhukov earned promotion from candidate (which he had been since February, 1956) to full member of the Presidium (Politburo) of the party, first real military figure to enjoy this station. If he had remained, the army might have staked out a place at the political summit. But Khrushchev expelled him from the Presidium and the post of Minister of Defense, in October–November, 1957, with no visible resistance from the army. Zhukov's most obvious sin was being too powerful, but he was accused of seeking personal glory, inferentially of having sought to seize power. Specifically, he was charged with opposing party controls in the armed forces and partially dismantling the political organization. Since 1956 he and other high officers, unhappy with the expansion of the party's field from political indoctrination to military training and policy, had been wanting to reduce the demands of political education upon officers' time and to check criticism of commanders by subordinates in party meetings.

As a result of the crisis, the party moved to strengthen the role of the political officers and broaden their responsibilities. But the place of the military in the Soviet political picture expanded as the authority of Khrushchev became less firm after 1960 and particularly after the humiliation of the Cuban crisis in 1962. They were conspicuously more successful than any other Soviet group in securing posthumous rehabilitation for purged comrades. Having sided with Khrushchev on de-Stalinization, the generals became apprehensive of his consumerism and protested his efforts to reduce the size of the forces.

The military leadership had little share, so far as has become known, in the intrigues which led to the downfall of Khrushchev; but the plotters must have been encouraged to move by the awareness that the forces would be happy to see him gone. The ouster of the innovative chairman represented a victory for the conservative-military point of view, the influence of which became more evident after Khrushchev. In September, 1965, General Dumenko, executed not under Stalin but under Lenin, was rehabilitated with much publicity. In 1967 it was reported that the marshals had rejected a nonmilitary candidate favored by a majority of the Politburo for the position of Minister of Defense and secured the nomination of one of their own, Marshal Grechko.[34] The latter became prominent as an executor of Soviet policy in relations with countries of the Soviet sphere. Many foreign military delegations came as guests not of the Soviet government but of the marshal. Military integration was more effective than economic in Eastern Europe, and the army could credit itself with saving the Soviet position by intervention in Czechoslovakia in 1968. Soviet military penetration, especially in the Arab world, proved far more fruitful than economic aid. The military role in education was enlarged, and the military view prevailed in literature. A group of high army and navy officers took a prominent part in a Conference of Young Writers in March, 1969.

The fading of ideological idealism and utopianism and the failure of Khrushchev's hopes for victory in peaceful economic competition made it logical that greater reliance should be placed in the army, and this seemed the readiest antidote for liberalization. It is clear, however, that the Soviet leadership wishes to use the military, not to share power with them. The parade of weaponry which formerly marked May Day has been dropped since 1969, and the military share of the November celebrations has been diminished. Military men were conspicuous at the republic congresses preceding the Twenty-Fourth Party Congress, but military representation on the Central Committee remained practically the same, 8%. In any case, the party and the army are not so much separate and potentially opposing institutions as different aspects of the basic Soviet pattern of rule by ideology, organization, and force.

The militant party is not far from a military organization. Despite its concessions to consultation below, it is, like armies everywhere and always, exclusive, elitist, and hierarchic. Its principles of obedience and loyalty are stern and militarily exacting. Discipline is its watchword in the everlasting war against

---

[34] The defense minister of Soviet bloc countries is regularly a soldier.

the class enemy. In his basic work, *What is to Be Done*, Lenin compared the party he wanted to an army, and the comparison has often been repeated. In 1904, one of Lenin's early supporters defected in disgust at the military spirit and language of the party.[35] In the civil war, the party was practically an army, as members were subject to assignment to the front or to whatever duty deemed most necessary.[36] Military terminology has continued to flavor the party's language, from Stalin's "comrades in arms" and "shockworkers" on the industrial or agricultural "front" down to the ever-recurrent insistence on "struggle." Peasants celebrate their "victory" in the "battle" to harvest the hay, and "fighting" ("boevoi"), with numerous derivatives, is one of the most common terms of the Soviet vocabulary. As a *Pravda* editorial begins, "The whole fighting course of our Communist party, founded and educated by V. I. Lenin, is a course of struggle and revolutionary building, of great achievements and historical victories."[37] The extensive use of uniforms and decorations is in the same spirit. Party duty is militarily stern. As a hero says, "Remember that even death is sometimes a party task."[38]

If the party as an organization is akin to the army, the latter shows few signs of philosophic disaffection. As in tsarist days, military leaders seem to be largely exempt from the doubts and dissidence of many intellectuals; to judge from the military press, they are at least as fundamentalist as the party leaders.[39] Some of the younger, more technically trained officers resented having to spend so much time on political indoctrination.[40] But the disagreement does not seem to have been deep, less between army and party than between technocrats and traditionalists within the army. The former expressed no different purpose but a feeling that they could serve better if less encumbered with affairs not germane to their specialties. The related semidebate over strategic emphasis has seemingly died down as the party has gone far toward giving satisfaction to both sides.

The aspect of Marxism-Leninism which might trouble the military is its equalitarianism, whereby the ordinary workers are the salt of the earth. The hierarchic and class separation of grades in the Soviet army is extreme, with differences of pay, accommodations, and social position about as marked as in any army in the world. A sailor is paid 5 rubles per month, a lieutenant 500, an admiral 2,000. The officers' corps may be becoming more castelike, as

---

[35] John S. Reshetar, *A Concise History of the Communist Party of the Soviet Union* (Praeger), New York, 1964, p. 43.

[36] Cf. Fainsod, *Smolensk*, p. 40.

[37] April 14, 1971, p. 1.

[38] *Pravda*, July 21, 1971, p. 3.

[39] Exceptionally, there were rumors in 1969 and 1970 of arrests in the Baltic fleet for political activity.

[40] Cf. Kolkowicz, op. cit., Chapter IX.

replacements are drawn from the service academies for officers' sons. The generals are a class apart, and each group has its special perquisites, down to the quality of tobacco furnished. This hinders the development of esprit de corps of the service as a whole; men and officers of different categories are semiequal comrades only in the framework of the party. The army reconciles real difference of privileges with the demands of ideology in much the same way the party does, by mixing pretensions of paternalistic and symbolic camaraderie with the realities of status; the ideal Soviet officer is stern but has a heart of gold.

Marxism-Leninism has much to commend it to men of arms. It provides them with a permanent enemy and a supreme mission of world order. They can gladly subscribe to a doctrine which elevates their peace and socialism against imperialism and capitalism. "The army of the socialist state is by its class character the army of the victorious proletariat, which most fully and consistently expresses the interests of all toiling masses. And as the workers of all countries are bound together by bonds of class brotherhood, they have common goals, and a single enemy, world imperialism; the socialist army is the army of proletarian internationalism. It cannot in reality be other than the defender of the interests of all toilers."[41]

The soldierly spirit is unfriendly to mercantile capitalism even without the benefit of Marxism; and so far as the army has a political purpose, it is identical with that of the party, the preservation of the united rulership of the Soviet domain, the multinational Soviet "family of nations" plus the satellites. The party and its ideology make the military domination of Eastern Europe practicable, while military force permits the party-ideological rule of the dominions. Party and army lean on each other in the repression of dissident movements and in the possible further spread of Soviet authority. Both dedicated to power, they equally desire discipline and loyalty. It is hard to guess how far the torrent of military indoctrination and propaganda is really designed to raise defensive capacities and how far it serves political aims; paramilitary organizations and training make a population not only better prepared to fight but easier to rule. "Heroism inspires," as Soviet propagandists write, and "The armed forces are a school for Soviet youth," nearly all of whom see themselves morally improved by military service.[42]

Military men plus the KGB are a substantial fraction of party membership, and the politicized military establishment is so intermeshed with the armylike party that the former cannot be considered really to form a separate organization. Rather, it is the adjunct of the party for custody of means of physical force and their possible use, in the same way that the trade union

[41] *Krasnaia zvezda*, July 30, 1970, p. 2.

[42] M. P. Shendrik, *Obshchenarodnoe gosudarstvo—novyi etap v razirtii sotsialisticheskoi gosudarstvennosti* (Izd. Lvovskogo universiteta), 1970.

system is the arm of the party for organization of workers and the Komsomol is the party's affiliate for mobilizing and directing youth.

If only Brezhnev and a few of his colleagues were replaced by professional military men, one could say that the party was serving the army instead of the reverse. But marshals in full power might do little differently. They already receive a large share of the national income; to burden the economy further would become counterproductive, inviting discontent and choking growth. They have a controlled society taught patriotism and worship of their uniforms; from the days of Sparta, few frankly military governments have gone so far in the ordering of society. They could hardly be more effective in stifling criticism of themselves and their ethos. If military men come to play a larger role in Soviet political life, it seems probable that this will be within, not against, the Soviet system. The party is as useful to the soldiers as they are to it.

There is no contradiction between militarism and socialism, *pace* Marx and thousands of pacific idealists, for whom standing armies and socialism were utterly incompatible. Military orders and armies incarnate authoritarian socialism, with purposeful command and the political will elevated over economic calculations and monetary relations. Socialism is the society of unified order and noncommercial values. Hitler was leader of the National Socialist German Workers' Party. Military leaders have ordinarily opposed socialism because of its plebeian airs and revolutionary aims abhorrent to the aristocrats who have generally manned officer corps. But military rulers of a number of dissatisfied countries of the underdeveloped world, especially in Africa, have turned to the left and adopted "socialistic" and pro-Soviet policies. As the Soviet system becomes more fixed and conservative, its authoritarianism appeals more and its revolutionary claims disturb the generals less.

Leninism has been successful not in the revolutionizing of developed countries but in the more or less military mobilization of less developed lands. Leninist patterns not only won against odds the civil war and the Great Patriotic War in the Soviet Union but have reaped spectacular victories against materially superior forces in Yugoslavia, China, and Vietnam. Communism has seemed to rise to its full potential when harnessed with militant nationalism.

READINGS

Est' stat' v stroi! (Izd. Molodaia gvardia), 1967.

Raymond L. Garthoff, *Soviet Military Policy* (Praeger), New York, 1966.

Kintner and Harriet F. Scott, *The Nuclear Revolution in Soviet Military Affairs* (University of Oklahoma Press), Norman, Okla., 1968.

Roman Kolkowicz, *The Soviet Military and the Communist Party* (Princeton University Press), Princeton, N. J., 1967.

Iu. P. Petrov, *Stroitelstvo politorganov, partiinykh i komsomolskikh organizatsii armii i flota (1918–1968)* (Voennoe izdatelstvo), Moscow, 1968.

Politodely (Voennoe izdatelstvo SSSR), Moscow, 1967.

The Soviet Military Technological Challenge (Center for Strategic Studies, Georgetown University), Washington, D. C., 1967.

12. National Minorities

The West thinks of the Soviet Union as "Russia," a state centered on Moscow and Leningrad, built by the Russian people, culturally and linguistically a Russian entity; and "Russian" is almost as a synonym of "Soviet." Yet one-half of the population is non-Russian. The multinational character of the Soviet state is often practically ignored even by careful students of Soviet politics; yet it is probably the most important determinant of the peculiarity of the Russian Revolution and the Soviet system.[1]

[1] Population figures for principal nationalities by the two last censuses are as follows: (in thousands)

	1959	1970
USSR	208,827	241,720
Russian	114,114	129,015
Ukrainian	37,253	40,753
Uzbek	6,015	9,195
Belorussian	7,913	9,052
Tatar	4,968	5,931
Kazakh	3,622	5,299
Azerbaidzhan	2,940	4,380
Armenian	2,787	3,559
Georgian	2,692	3,245
Moldavian	2,214	2,698
Lithuanian	2,326	2,665
Jewish	2,268	2,151
Tadzhik	1,397	2,136
German	1,620	1,846
Chuvash	1,470	1,694
Turkmen	1,002	1,525
Kirghiz	969	1,452
Latvian	1,400	1,430

The proportion of Russians is certainly overstated, as classification was by personal declaration only, and it is better to be a Russian than anything else. The decrease in the number of declared Jews from 2,268,000 to 2,151,000 is evidence of use of this option.

Nationality distinguishes the Soviet Union from all other powerful states. Of the world's great empires, it is the last and most dynamic; with the passing of nearly all of the colonial empires, the bulk of the world's nonindependent peoples are under Russian hegemony. The Russians themselves make much of this character of the state—and it is fair to speak of Russians in this context, as the leadership is either Russian or Russianized, Russian-speaking, and Russian-thinking. "The Soviet people is not some new nation, not a conglomerate of nations, but an international association of more than a hundred large and small nations and nationalities, free of social and national antagonisms, from mutual enmity and distrust built up over the ages by the exploiting classes."[2] "The Soviet people is simultaneously single and multi-national."[3] There is much play of national variety, costumes, and folk art in the "brotherhood of socialist nations," or the "unbreakable union of free republics," as the Soviet national anthem states in slight logical contradiction. It is the pride and the mission of the Communist Party and Soviet state to unite and thereby protect the peoples. National diversity is even at times exaggerated to exalt the success of unification in Soviet socialism.

In the official view, national friction develops because of the exploitation of weaker nations; this cannot occur under Soviet rule, therefore there can be no friction. There is no objective analysis in Soviet writings of the problems involved, even of practical questions of national psychology and the administrative complexities of dealing with people of diverse backgrounds and languages in the government or the army—all should simply enjoy the blessings of socialism. But the extreme frequency and emphasis with which Soviet ideologues recur to it indicates deep preoccupation, and from time to time Soviet organs point to the exceptional importance and dangers of nationalism as a live and present danger, far more critical than demands for freedom or democracy. It would be extraordinary if the Soviet Union had no grave problems of adjustment of peoples of different economic levels, cultural backgrounds, race, political traditions, and language.

Minority discontent has long been troublesome. It worried the tsarist empire, and Lenin correctly saw it as a potent revolutionary force. After achieving power, Lenin made concessions to minority feeling, not because he had any sympathy for it but because he appreciated its importance. In the Second World War, non-Russians evinced readiness to collaborate with the invading Germans almost everywhere that they could do so; and Stalin testified to anti-Soviet sentiments by his deportation of the Crimean Tatars and several small Caucasian peoples. After the war, anti-Soviet movements were active for several years in both the Ukraine and Baltic areas; even in victory, it was difficult to reassert Soviet authority.

[2] *Pravda*, November 26, 1968, p. 3.
[3] *Pravda*, July 16, 1971, p. 3.

In the following decades, Soviet authorities have from time to time indicated minority discontent by denouncing manifestations of "bourgeois nationalism." In recent years the problem has probably become more severe. In some ways, modernization tends to erode separatist feelings, by increasing travel, migration, the mixing of peoples, and spreading a blanket of uniform mass culture over inherited differences. But minorities also become more aware of what sets them apart, of real or fancied inequities, and of the promises of which they might demand fulfillment. Since the latter part of 1965 and especially since the aborted liberalization of Czechoslovakia, there have been numerous reports of repressions or signs of disaffection in minority areas. As *Pravda* stated frankly, "The national question is one of the most acute questions of social development. It has taken on special acuteness in the contemporary era, the era of struggle of socialism and capitalism. . . ."[4]

Soviet Response

Tsarist Russia handled the non-Russians in ways somewhat foreshadowing the nationality policies of the Leninist state. New dominions were allowed some autonomy for decades or generations. First there might be a merely personal union, the Russian tsar being recognized as the monarch of the newly affiliated territory, as Poland or Finland. Or a state might be given Russian protection, that is, become subject in foreign and defense affairs, but otherwise enjoy self-rule; parts of Central Asia were protectorates, not formally incorporated until Soviet times. As long as all went smoothly, the situation might remain hardly changed for long periods; and local rulers were kept in power so far as they were willing to cooperate. But the course was always toward assimilation and integration into the centralized bureaucratic political structure. Autonomy was sliced down, agreements were broken or ignored, and Russian settlers moved into outlying lands. Resistance hastened centralization, as those who showed themselves less cooperative had to be more closely controlled. Poland, for example, lost its standing as a semi-independent kingdom by the insurrections of 1830 and 1863 and became simply a part of the Russian state.

As the Soviet Union has emphasized the party and ideology, the tsarist government looked to the tsar and Orthodoxy to support its unity. The political disability of the minorities was mostly religious. Tatars, Poles, Balts, etc., had only to accept Orthodoxy and speak Russian in order to be fully accepted and eligible for high office; social or racial prejudice was slight. The Ukrainians in any case were hardly considered different from Russians; and their language, although as different from Russian as Spanish is from Italian, was held nonexistent. White Russians were not recognized as a nationality at all.

---

[4] November 26, 1968.

This approach to multinationalism might have remained successful if Russia had been able to isolate itself from the Western world. But tensions were slowly rising in the latter decades of the nineteenth century as the spirit of nationalism infiltrated from the bourgeois West. Earlier, tsars had often actually favored non-Russians as their servants; the feeling grew that Russians should enjoy more privileged status. Non-Russians, especially in the western border-lands, began to call for more consideration for native rights and cultures, although not ordinarily for independence. The tsarist government had no better answer than russification, thereby further raising tensions.

There was no workable solution within the conventional political framework. The conservatives could suggest only more of the old remedies. The liberals thought that the trouble was due to absolutism and would be solved by freedom. Leaders of the minorities were inclined to be leftists, because their opponent was a conservative rightist government; and they were favorable to Marxism, because they saw Russians as exploiters and capitalists. Hence the parties of the radical left proposed cultural autonomy and minority self-determination. But they shrank from drawing the logical conclusions of the break-up of the empire and, except for Lenin's Bolsheviks, failed to reach firm positions.

Lenin, who paid more attention to the nationality question than any other leader, evolved an apt position which became the conceptual basis of Soviet nationality policy. As a revolutionary, he was prepared to promise the minorities complete freedom. As a Marxist, he thought nationalism a backward and declining force and favored economic and political centralization. National-ism could be overcome by removing its primary cause, oppression, and particularly the policy of crude russification. At the same time, he insisted on the absolute unity of the party as the expression of the only legitimate political will. Therefore, in Lenin's view, he could harmlessly use nationalistic feelings against his enemies, ally himself with the banners of nationalistic revolt, and yet keep his movement united under the leadership of the supranational proletarian revolutionary party. In opposition to tsarist imperialism, Lenin recognized a right of secession; yet he claimed the right of his party to oppose separation because the movement demanded unity.[5] Bolsheviks felt free to encourage dissident minority peoples and to grant them formal freedom yet to demand real union; in the very message in which he recognized the independence of the

---

[5] In February, 1914, he wrote that the Russian proletariat had a twofold task, first, of recognizing the right of all nations to self-determination, and "second, precisely in the interests of the successful struggle against the nationalism of all nations, in all forms, it sets the task of preserving the unity of the proletarian struggle and of the proletarian organiza-tions, of amalgamating these organizations into an international community, in spite of the bourgeois strivings for national segregation." [V. I. Lenin, *Selected Works,* vol. 4 (Inter-national Publishers), New York, 1943, p. 293.]

Ukraine, Lenin insisted that it must be bolshevized. "Russia One and Indivisible" was the slogan of the Whites and the realization of the Reds.

This straddling of the issue helped to make the Revolution, win the civil war, and put together a state federal in form but centralist in content. When pro-Soviet forces overcame the separatist regimes in the Ukraine, White Russia, the Caucasus, and Central Asia, their territories were not annexed. But the Bolsheviks, carrying with them the laws and policies of the Russian center, established party-controlled governments wherever they could in non-Russian areas. It seemed at first unnecessary to set up a common government, because the victory of world revolution would erase all state boundaries. But effective union was arranged under special agreements and treaties of alliance; thus, military and economic affairs were placed under joint Russian-Ukrainian administration, while the Ukraine remained nominally independent in foreign relations. In 1922–1923, the several Soviet republics were officially joined in a multilateral treaty of formal equals to make the Soviet Union, proclaimed as a step toward the "World Soviet Socialist Republic."

Lenin was opposed to federalism in principle, as Marx and Engels had been; but it was acceptable as a transitional form with minimal content. Whereas Stalin wanted to override objections and centralize fully, Lenin favored a more patient policy; he was as much in favor of russianizing and integrating as anyone, but he wished it to come voluntarily. Consequently, while the new constitution gave the central government ample powers to do whatever it wished, it did not quite reduce the republics to administrative departments. They were left with jurisdiction (under party control) over such areas as education, social welfare, and most of the economy. There was even a little administrative autonomy for minority areas within the Russian republic set up as "autonomous republics." Russian chauvinism and discrimination against minorities were curbed as obstacles to true unity. Russian immigration to some minority areas was forbidden for a few years. It was attempted to recruit natives for the party and the government apparatus, replacing the ethnic Russians who were at one time a ruling caste in minority areas. Russianization was halted or reversed, and native languages and cultures were favored.

This policy permitted a bit of "national communism" and an upsurge of native culture, particularly in the Ukraine. But as the party saw it, the partial revival of capitalism in the NEP caused a relapse toward nationalism;[6] and the inclination from about 1926 was toward making firmer the "unity of self-governing peoples." As Stalin solidified his power, he identified Russian rule with Marxism-Leninism and began withdrawing the little autonomy previously permitted. Each of Stalin's great campaigns of the 1930's increased central

[6] *Istoria kommunisticheskoi partii sovetskogo soiuza* (Politizdat), Moscow, 1969, pp. 343–344.

control over the affairs of the non-Russian areas. Collectivization was more painful and disruptive for non-Russians than for Russians and had the effect of forcing all into a common mold under a single rule, from individualist Ukrainian peasants to oasis or pastoral farmers of Central Asia, even reindeer herders of the far north. Industrialization moved people around on a large scale and built up a single national economy under central planning and complete control of the ministries. The antireligious campaign struck harshly at a principal distinctiveness of the minorities. Control of the arts erased what little cultural independence had been tolerated. Registering these changes, the 1936 Stalinist Constitution gave less formal scope to the republics than its predecessor; its chief concession was the vaunted "right of secession." Finally, the Great Purges were even more savage in the Ukraine, Central Asia, etc., than in Russia proper. In the former, there was more genuine disaffection; and "bourgeois nationalism" and plots for separation of minority territories were a frequent charge in show trials. Stalin was always more assertive than Lenin of the absolute priority of the dictatorship of the proletariat, as he put it, over national feelings. Under his dictatorship, for a native bard to omit praise of Stalin in his poem or to fail to give Russia full credit for national liberation came to be enough to draw upon him the fatal accusation of "bourgeois nationalist."

It was some indication of tensions that after Stalin's death Beria saw the minorities as potential support for a bid for power. During the quarter of a year that he was influential, russification was reversed; after his demise he was accused of favoring national cadres against Russians and otherwise sowing discord. Khrushchev took various small measures to relieve pressure in 1956 and 1957: there was a slackening of cultural controls, and a few minority writers were rehabilitated; it was admitted that minority peoples might in some cases have been justified in fighting against tsarist oppressors; more management of cultural and economic enterprises was turned over to republic ministries, although central direction was never compromised; a good deal of the administration of justice was placed in the hands of the republics. There were even moves toward loosening central control in the party, allowing the republic parties some powers over their budgets and personnel. Stalin's special exaltation of the Russian people was left behind, and Russian preeminence was made less irritating.

Nevertheless, Khrushchev, as a good Communist, was a centralizer too; and in the latter years of his tenure the republics were again under pressure. Economic decentralization was largely undone. The Party Program of 1961 looked frankly to the "fusion" of the nationalities; boundaries should be obliterated in communism, to come some time after 1980. Fusion was assisted by Slavic migration to non-Slavic regions on a hitherto unknown scale. In this, White Russians and Ukrainians were enlisted as allies of the Great Russians; in Central Asia a Ukrainian became for all political effects a Russian and was so regarded by the natives.

After Khrushchev, there was a brief time of further relaxation in nationality affairs as in other fields. Leaders in various republics were able to evince public displeasure with russifying policies as they had not dared for thirty years. But the tide turned back in less than a year, and along with moderate re-Stalinization and pressures against the intellectuals came recentralization. The economic councils were dissolved for "localism"; justice and police were returned to central responsibility; education, once considered the most important prerogative of the republics, was brought under the direct rule of Moscow. The chorus of praise for the "socialist brotherhood of peoples" rose, with increased calls for economic and cultural merger.

Nonsovereign Republics

"The Union republic is the highest form of national statehood,"[7] but it is the most insubstantial. Civil liberties, for example, at least exist on paper, but the letter of the constitution leaves little self-government to the republics (see Federal Structure, Chapter 7).

It is a curious reversal that the two powers most strongly reserved to the federal regime in genuine federalisms, foreign affairs and defense, are nominally shared with the republics. The respective ministries are Union-Republican, and the republics are authorized (Articles 18 a and b) to conduct diplomatic relations and to maintain armed forces. The chief purpose of theoretical devolution of foreign affairs was to qualify Soviet republics for separate seats at the United Nations. No republic is permitted to have diplomatic relations with any country, despite the obvious utility for the Soviet image and possible expansion. In 1969, the Turkmen and Azerbaidzhan republics entered trade agreements with Iran, but such use is exceptional. As treated in Soviet writings, the "international relations" of a republic may consist of exchanges of cultural and civil delegations with foreign countries, the training of foreign students at its institutions, or the export of its products. The defense role of the republics is even less; there does not seem to exist any republic defense ministry, much less military formations. In the 1920's there were national detachments in the Soviet army, but these were all merged by 1939. In the fight for survival of the world war, national forces were again used; but since then the army seems to have been, in theory at least, wholly integrated. Much is made of the happy collaboration of men of all nationalities in the forces, and it may be assumed that two years' unrelieved exposure to Russian ways and language contributes to russification.

The republics lack an economic basis for autonomy. "Socialist property in the means of production is the economic basis of this union,"[8]

---

[7] *National naia gosudarstvennost soiuznykh respublik* (Izd. iurid. lit.), Moscow, 1968, p. 27.

[8] *Pravda*, November 26, 1968.

because all important property, including all land, belongs not to the republic but to the Union, which may permit the republic to administer some of it or may remove it from republican competence at will. Resources go to the center and are doled out to the republics. The latter only fill in details of their budgets, which must fit the central economic plan and must be ratified by Moscow. Only unimportant local industry is left to republican administration. Economic planning takes no account of republic boundaries and forwards russification through policies of specialization beyond or against strictly economic considerations. Industrial enterprises are so located as to require bringing in workers and materials from outside the republic.

Lenin's instrument of unity, the Communist Party, remains the most important of all. "Our party is the living incarnation of the unbreakable brotherhood of the peoples, of the ideas of socialist internationalism. There are represented in its ranks the best sons and daughters of more than a hundred and thirty nationalities and peoples, genuine internationalists, who have equal love and understanding for the interests of their own and any other socialist nation of our country. In the harmonic fusion of these interests under the leading role of the general interests of the united socialist fatherland lies the strength of Soviet patriotism."[9] All nationalities merge in the party "like the waters of the rivers in a mighty ocean."[10] Hence, although there are branches of the party corresponding to the minority republics, they do not have any of the nominal sovereignty conceded to the republics. The Ukrainian, Georgian, and other parties were never allowed to join the Comintern, and they send no delegations to world Communist conclaves. There are minor concessions to their dignity: they have "central committees" instead of simply "committees" as provincial and lesser party organizations enjoy, and they convoke "congresses" instead of "conferences." But they were wholly subject to the Russian Communist Party before the Soviet Union was set up, and they remain practically equivalent to oblast organizations under the Central Committee. The party rules deal with republic central committees alongside of and in the same way as regional, district, and city committees; and if the republic contains oblasts, obkoms may work directly with the Central Committee, by-passing the republic organization. Departments of the republic parties are directly subject to the departments of the Central Committee. And power at the summit is strictly Russian. Since 1964, all Secretaries of the Central Committee have been Russian.

The party thus rules the republics not only through the government apparatus but through the party machinery. The leading figures in the republic are not the chairmen of the council of ministers but the party secretaries. Even this organizational bond is not felt to be quite sufficient, as key positions in

[9] *Pravda*, March 9, 1969.
[10] *Partiinaia zhizn*, no. 21, November, 1970.

non-Russian republics are reserved for Russians or sometimes Ukrainians. Nationals of White Russia, Ukraine, Armenia, and Georgia are considered reliable enough largely to staff the higher ranks of their respective party apparatuses, but in the Baltic republics and especially in Central Asia, Russians occupy strategic posts. Frequently, the first secretary, presiding over the bureau of the central committee, is a native for appearances, while the second secretary, in charge of the secretariat and holder of the real power, is a Slav. (Correspondingly, in the government apparatus, the chairman of the republic supreme soviet, the chairman of the council of ministers, and most ministers are usually natives but are flanked by Russian or Ukrainian deputies, somewhat as native princes of tsarist days had Russian advisers. The supreme soviets have a native color, but the chief of the security forces and garrison commander are fairly sure to be Russian.[11])

Somewhat anomalously, although there are a Ukrainian party, an Uzbek party, etc., there is no Russian party, no Russian central committee, etc. This has historical reasons. The original party was called Russian, and the Ukrainian and other parties were set up as branches of it after the Revolution. When the Soviet Union was formed, the Russian became the Soviet party. To have kept it as the Russian branch of an all-Soviet party would have been in the logic of federalism, but it would have made the Russian party formally equal to the republic parties. At present, oblasts of the Russian republic, over one hundred in number, are practically equal in standing to non-Russian republics; if there were a Russian party, the all-Union party would be more like a federation. There is no need for a Russian party as pro forma concession to the Russians, who are aware of their superiority; and it might open the way to conflicts between the interests of the Russian and other national parties, or between the Russian party and the all-Union party, to the detriment of unity.

Antinational Ideology

The well-engineered political structure can work only thanks to ideological lubrication, or cement, reducing frictions and holding wills to common purpose. Marxism-Leninism justifies the domination of large and potentially independent lands from a distant and alien capital, excuses their incorporation into the Russian-dominated state, even palliates their one-time conquest by tsarist forces.

Marxism thrusts nationalism aside as something bourgeois and backward which has no legitimate place in Soviet society. "Bourgeois nationalism, an outgrowth of the system of private ownership, is a transient phenomenon. It grows on the class antagonisms of capitalist society. After the

[11] A. Avtorkhanov, *The Communist Party Apparatus* (Henry Regnery Co.), Chicago, 1966, p. 173.

liquidation of these antagonisms, national antagonisms will also gradually disappear."[12] "Under the flag of patriotism [the bourgeoisie] strives to build so-called 'national unity' to strengthen its domination of the toilers. . . ."[13] Therefore, so far as nationalism shows itself, it must be a result of Western or hostile class influences and should be banished.[14] It bespeaks individualism and struggle between peoples, narrowness, and hate. Soviet minority peoples can be nationalistic only in a limited sense, as Georgia, for example, takes pride in contributing to Soviet achievements. Nationalism is seen as old-fashioned, exemplified by peasant customs, perhaps quaint but tolerable only so far as unimportant. Minority writers are urged to look to things modern, that is, Soviet, or to the glorious common future, not to their peculiar past.

The valid unity is class unity; allegedly nonclass nationalism is held fraudulent, and the only acceptable struggle is the class struggle. In Western experience, the aristocrats have been the most internationalist class and the workers least so; but in the Marxist-Leninist canon, the workers are moved only by class, not by national will. Class interest required the Lithuanian working people, for example, to fight anti-Soviet Lithuanian guerrillas after the Second World War as a remnant of the exploiting classes. Hence, patriotism and internationalism can be called equivalent, and they epitomize the Russian-Soviet system. "In Soviet patriotism the national and international are united, since it does not divide nations but binds them into a single brotherly family. The internationalism of Soviet patriots shows itself both in the brotherly unity of the peoples of the USSR and in friendship with the toilers of other lands. . . ."[15]

It is the vocation of art to uplift Soviet multinationalism and brotherhood; and the happiness of the peoples, their equality, prosperity and freedom, and the firmness of their unity are perennial subjects. Antinationalism preempts the vocabulary of nationalism, promising freedom and equality of nations, much as Soviet party rule appropriates the language of democracy. The minority peoples frequently express their gratitude for liberation; it is typical that the Baltic states celebrate the anniversary of their incorporation into the Soviet Union. Stories carry the moral of brotherhood. For example, a suicidally dangerous mission in the world war was undertaken by a squad comprising men of eight nationalities. As the walls were crumbling under merciless shelling and only three heroes remained, a Kazakh rose to shout, "There are many nationalities in our country but only one Fatherland! And we are all its sons. We are fighting for our native land. Right, boys?"[16] A report tells of the

---

[12] *Pravda*, April 7, 1969.

[13] *Pravda*, January 8, 1971, p. 2.

[14] For reasons of foreign policy, nationalism abroad is usually considered good, and Communist parties regularly and successfully raise nationalistic banners.

[15] *Pravda*, November 26, 1968.

[16] *Pravda*, March 24, 1969.

establishment by Russians of a modern factory at an unnamed site, apparently in Central Asia. Russian workers help and train natives and make them good Communists. Along the wall there is a "red placard with marvelous words about the unbreakable holy friendship of the peoples of the Soviet Union. Perhaps this is why it is especially bright by the window."[17]

It is claimed that union of minority peoples with socialist Russia is indispensable to overcome their backwardness. By themselves the minority peoples would be too weak to progress or would be victims of Western imperialism. "The toilers of Armenia understand perfectly that [their successes] are only possible because the Armenian people live and toil in the brotherly family of the peoples of the Soviet Union. . . ."[18] The past is painted in similar terms. The Bolsheviks went into Central Asia in the civil war to save the peoples from British oppression, and much is made to this day of the brief British intervention and its brutalities. As seen by the Soviets, the so-called independence of Georgia and other regions was only disguised subjection to Western imperialism.

The treatment of conflicts between minority peoples and tsarist Russia and conquest by the latter has been more difficult. Until well into the 1930's the line followed was the Leninist one, that tsarist imperialism also was evil; but under Stalin the thesis was developed that annexation to tsarist Russia was good because it gave economic advantages and a settled peace and put the peoples on the path to eventual socialism. The recent position is that Russian expansion was progressive at all times; the enemies of the Muscovite power were always reactionaries. Tsarist occupation defended smaller peoples from worse exploiters. The present-day peoples of the Soviet Union are depicted as belonging together from the distant past. Central Asia and the Transcaucasus are treated in Soviet historiography as pertaining to Russia as far back as the thirteenth century, long before there was a united Russian state, much less a Russian empire impinging on their lands.

Marxist motifs are painted into the historical canvas. The common people of Russia and other nations desired unity, suffered together, and together, under the leadership of the Russians, opposed the feudal exploiters who stood in the way of their union.[19] Class struggle thus is presented as an adjunct of Russian expansion long before the Bolshevik Revolution. It even entered into the founding of the Russian autocracy, favoring unity of the people. "The class struggle accelerated the unification of the Russian lands and the establishment of organs of power and administration in a centralized

[17] *Pravda*, May 14, 1969.
[18] *Partiinaia zhizn*, no. 22, November, 1970, p. 19.
[19] Cf. Lowell Tillett, *The Great Friendship: Soviet Historians on the Non-Russian Nationalities* (University of North Carolina Press), Chapel Hill, N. C., 1969.

government."[20] Nationalism largely rests on shared history, but the history of minority peoples is rewritten to make association with Russia always beneficial and separatism as illegitimate.

Only Russian nationalism is consonant with Soviet patriotism and proletarian internationalism. Marxist proletarianism also favored and rationalized Russian domination because a majority of industrial workers were and still are of Russian nationality despite industrialization in minority regions. The proletarian vanguard was predominantly Russian, and the superiority of the proletariat over the peasantry was translatable into the superiority of urban Russians over villagers of other nationalities. The Russians form a large part of the population of the cities everywhere, providing an invaluable reservoir of recruits for the party in minority areas and giving a basis for hegemony without overt discrimination on the basis of nationality.

To rule soundly and well, an elite should have confidence in its unimpeachable cause, and Marxism gives the Russians an ideal reason for dominance. It helps Russians believe that the minorities are freely and voluntarily united for their own good and that only the misled or perverse could refuse to appreciate it. No exercise of Soviet power can be imperialism, and no advantages the Russians may receive from their situation can be exploitation, because in socialism these vices cannot exist. At the same time, it is easy for Russians to feel that something like "proletarian internationalism" is requisite for their empire.

Ideology makes subordination more bearable for the subordinated. It bespeaks equality of peoples, gives a basis for appeal by those who may feel wronged, and no doubt makes the conduct of many Russians in power less offensive, sometimes generous. It tells peoples that their inferior status is not a result of innate inferiority at all, as they need only dedicate themselves to the cause to be equals of the best. They are asked to bow not to a foreign nation but to an international and historically virtuous movement, a consolation for those who must accept their circumstances.

The Marxists are right in contending that nationalism is nothing inevitable and that it is tinged with irrationality. But it remains strong, and the Russians badly need something to offset it. A partial answer is voluminous political advertising and propaganda, to convince people that the Union is good and that they owe everything to it. The canonized Lenin is also used as a father-figure of the family of nations, not a Russian but a world figure. But for a philosophic answer, a simplist political Marxism serves fairly well to justify the single party rule for all the peoples. The Soviet state seems consequently tied to at least the basic idea of the priority of class interests until relations among the Soviet peoples have substantially changed.

[20] *Istoriia SSSR*, P. I. Kabanov and V. V. Mavrodin, eds., vol. 1 (Izd. Prosveshchenie), Moscow, 1966.

Assimilation

The Soviet state strives to solve the problem of national separatism by creating a homogeneous Soviet-Russian culture. It was Lenin's policy to remove the irritation of coercive russification and to encourage native languages and use them to carry the Bolshevik message to the people, proclaiming cultural autonomy coupled with political conformity. The motto was, "National in form but socialist in content." But Lenin took a narrow view of "national." As he said, "From each national culture we take only its democratic and socialist elements"; and he called cultural national autonomy "a thoroughly bourgeois and deceitful thought."[21] The "national" form came to mean very little. Literature in minority languages is as controlled as in Russian, so the productions of various Soviet peoples have come to be virtually indistinguishable. Minority languages are preferably used for political literature, Lenin's works and the like, less a means of national self-expression than of indoctrination of the non-Russian speaking population. Folklore and old songs have been reworked to bring in the party and the Soviet homeland. The most fostered aspect of national culture is folk dancing, of which more is made in the Soviet Union than in any other land. This is not only innocuous but associates national with peasant culture, making it more ornamental than serious.

Ostensibly there is no russification, only the development of common patterns. "Soviet people" has become a usual term since the latter 1930's, and the common pattern is called not Russian but Soviet, the Russian language happening to be useful merely as the lingua franca of the different peoples. Ukrainians and others should not necessarily become Russians but only embrace a common destiny with them. The literature studied in schools all over the Soviet Union is not "Russian" but "Soviet." A major duty of writers is to express the togetherness of the great "family of nations." Much is made of exchanges. "Preserving and developing the best national specialties and traditions, national cultures use creatively the achievements of the cultures of brother republics. This process is advanced by science days, weeks of literature and art, various festivals of culture, translations and editions of books, which have gained great acceptance among us."[22] Literature and arts of Baltic republics are promoted in Georgia, Armenians get a dose of Ukrainian culture, etc., a broadening which cannot be emotionally rejected as russification and which is flattering to the nationalities whose achievements are advertised. Yet the Uzbek sees Latvian culture as transmitted by Russians and in Russian translation.

Pressure against minority languages is excused on the grounds that, "The spread of the Russian language does not at all diminish the role and significance of national languages, but, on the contrary, facilitates their mutual

---

[21] Quoted by *Sovety deputatov trudiashchikhsia*, no. 1, January, 1969, p. 9.
[22] *Pravda*, February 7, 1970.

enrichment."[23] In the dialectical logic, the higher development of each is to bring all closer together. "The role of the Russian language in the cultural life of socialist society is great and noble. This role does not counter but, on the contrary, favors the development of national languages, the generalization of national cultures, their socialist unification and the flowering of their forms."[24] Association with Russian helps to perfect native cultures, and poets sing the praises of the Russian language, bond of the united Motherland, in their native tongues. But the "enrichment" of minority languages comes to resemble the sovereignty of the republics. More and more Russian terms are introduced into many languages, from "Moldavian"[25] to Central Asian dialects. The attack on the latter has been strongest. First, the Turkish speech of the area was artificially divided into several different "languages." Then they were shifted, in the late 1920's and early 1930's, from the Arabic to the Latin alphabet to isolate them from the Moslem world. In 1938–1940 the previously latinized alphabets were replaced by the Cyrillic used in Russian. Many old terms were banned in favor of Russian equivalents, which since 1953 have been spelled in the Russian manner. The Russian share of the vocabulary rises steadily; perhaps a third of the words in an ordinary newspaper in a Central Asian language are likely to be Russian. So far as new words are introduced they are from Russian or at least via Russian. The native language loses potency as a vehicle of national feeling.

Unofficially, Russians look down on minority languages and seldom take the trouble to learn them, even when in non-Russian republics. There is a great deal of attention to the teaching of Russian to non-Russians, almost none to the opposite endeavor; and according to the 1970 census only 3% of Russians know another language. The use of Russian is almost mandatory in administration and all economic matters beyond the strictly local. This should lead eventually to the disappearance of the minority language. "Thus there goes forward a shift not only from monolingualism to bilingualism but from the latter to monolingualism in the language of general communication among nationalities."[26]

About nine-tenths of Soviet magazines are published in Russian, and the percentage has long been rising. A large majority of journals published in the Ukraine, White Russia, and the five Central Asian republics are in the Russian language. (Those in the Caucasian republics, Georgia, Armenia, and Azerbaijan, are about three-fourths in the native language.[27]) Books printed in Russian in 1967 were over four-fifths of the total and eleven times the number in

---

[23] *Dialektika stroitel'stva kommunizma* (Izd. Mysl), Moscow, 1968, p. 243.

[24] *Pravda*, May 27, 1969.

[25] The Romanians living in Bessarabia are treated as a separate nationality, sufferers in the past from Romanian imperialism.

[26] *Sotsiologiia i ideologiia* (Izd. Nauka), Moscow, 1969, p. 443.

[27] *Narodnoe khoziastvo SSSR v 1969 g.*, Moscow, 1970, pp. 717–718.

Ukrainian, forty-two times the number in Uzbek, the nearest competitors. Publishing houses of non-Russian republics put out many books in the Russian language. Publications in many small languages, according to Soviet statistics, have been dropping, presumably indicating a gradual phasing out. The circulation of newspapers in minority languages has been somewhat better sustained, according to the figures. But where Russian and non-Russian papers exist in the same locality, they are to have (since 1963) a joint editorial board to improve the political level.

The broadcast media are probably more important for the spread of Russian language and culture. Radio Moscow is heard everywhere, rebroadcast by local stations. For example, listeners in Alma Ata are offered Radio Moscow programs and locally originated programs which are about half in Russian. Television stations in the Ukraine use much Russian in locally-originated programs, while many hours daily are relayed from the Russian network. Broadcasts of the Kiev TV center in 1969 were about one-fourth in Ukrainian and three-fourths in Russian. Latvian programs in December, 1968, were found to be about three-fourths in Russian on one channel and entirely in Russian on the other. In Uzbekistan and Azerbaidzhan the proportions were similar.[28] The centrally produced programs are technically superior and more attractive. Cinema is entirely Russian.

Education at first was left mostly to the jurisdiction of republic governments, in reaction against tsarist imposition of Russian schools; and much is still made of the freedom of education in the native tongue. But control of education through the party evidently was not enough. Step by step, administrative control, first of higher and then of general education, was gathered to Moscow. In 1966, an all-Union Ministry of Education was established to set uniform policies to be executed by republic ministries. In 1969, the Moscow Ministry of Education was given responsibility for all general schools, preschool institutions, and pedagogical training. The central ministry exercises a much closer control over teaching and content of courses than do local school boards in the United States.

The effect is to promote not only a strong ideological diet but the Russian language, the teaching of which is regarded as weakening "national prejudices." Russian was made obligatory in all schools in 1938, and it seems to be the language of instruction in a steadily growing proportion of the schools of the country. Parents are supposed to have free choice to send children to a Russian-language or minority-language school, but the former is probably better and is almost a necessity if children are to go on to higher education, which is largely in Russian. It may also help the political standing of a person of minority

---

[28] Wasil Veryha, "The Soviet TV Network—a Means of Russification of the Union Republics," paper for *Canadian Association of Slavists*, June 12, 1969.

nationality to give this token of loyalty. "It is a notable fact that Bashkirs, Tatars, and other nationalities of the Bashkir ASSR strongly desire to have their children educated in schools where classes are conducted in Russian, although we have enough schools in which children can be taught in Bashkir and other languages. This is fully understandable: knowledge of Russian gives better access to the great riches of Russian and world culture."[29] There may be little choice. For millions of persons living outside native republics, as numerous Ukrainians in the Russian republic and many Central Asians in mixed areas, there are no schools in their own language. In the upper grades of non-Russian schools, more time is given to Russian than to the native language and literature, while by a 1958 law, instruction in the minority language is no longer to be obligatory in Russian language schools in minority areas. Party, Soviet, and Komsomol organizations have been instructed to promote the study of the Russian language, "the common language of international cooperation among all the peoples of the Soviet Union."[30] In 1940, the percentage of school books in Russian was about the same as the percentage of Russians in the population; by 1965–1966, it had risen to 73%.[31]

Russian is much more dominant in higher schools, which are the gateway to a career. Apparently an overwhelming majority of higher educational textbooks are in Russian, and in minority areas much or most instruction is in Russian.[32] Stress is placed on the interrepublic exchange of staff (appointments being controlled by the ministry) and students, which requires that instruction be given in the common language.

Russians and Russian prevail in the modern economy and even in the administration of most of the republics. Promising men are likely to be posted outside their native republic, and one is likely to be given a coveted opportunity to advance himself in Moscow only if his mastery of Russian is complete. Persons frequently take Russian names, especially in Central Asia, to shed national identity. If writers are thoroughly conformist, they may be rewarded by translation into Russian; many seek a broader audience by writing in Russian.

Russification is also forwarded by the mixing of peoples. Stalin shipped many hundreds of thousands from the Baltic area and elsewhere to Siberia and Central Asia, and the large-scale movement of Slavs into non-Slav areas since his death has been mentioned. The Kazakhs and Kirghiz have become minorities in their own republics; and everywhere, at least in cities, there is a substantial Russian population to support the regime. Many non-Russians have

[29] *Partiinaia zhizn*, no. 6, March, 1969, p. 18.

[30] *Pravda*, February 13, 1969.

[31] John Kolasky, *Education in the Soviet Ukraine* (Peter Martin Associates), Toronto, 1968, p. 42.

[32] Cf. Yaroslav Bilinsky, "Education of the Non-Russian Peoples of the USSR, 1917–1967," *Slavic Review*, vol. 27, no. 3, September, 1968, p. 433.

also migrated, and they are especially subject to russification outside their areas. Graduates of higher educational institutions, who have to take assigned jobs for two years, are sent preferably out of their republic.[33] Army draftees ordinarily serve away from native republics and are encouraged to remain after their term is finished. Peasants are sometimes given free transportation and bonuses to move to distant regions. Baltic technicians are employed in Russia or Central Asia, Russian scientists in the Ukraine and vice versa; one can assume, from the extent of official concern, that political motives are mixed with economic.

That assimilation has had successes cannot be doubted. Many small nationalities have been absorbed, as Soviet writers note.[34] 196 nationalities were listed in 1926, 109 in 1957, and 91 by the 1970 census. Some larger ones seem to be fading. The nationalism of White Russia by some accounts is waning to a little local pride, as hardly anyone wants an education in the native tongue. Reportedly no schools in the capital use White Russian as the language of instruction.[35] Not much Ukrainian is to be heard on the streets of Kiev. More distinct nationalities, as Georgian and Armenian, are better able to retain independent identity. Mixed marriages, which are regarded with favor, seem to be increasing—one reason for opposition to religion is that it impedes this erosion of divisions. In another sense, assimilation is successful in that it has divided the minorities and deprived them of leadership; persons of talent are largely drawn into the service of the Soviet system. There is no organization around which discontents can coalesce, no visible alternative to the Russian-dominated order.

It is more necessary for persons of non-Russian nationality than for Russians to demonstrate their loyalty to the Soviet system and their repudiation of separatism. Those who seek to rise within the Soviet system may see in the minority nationalism a threat to the axioms of their careers and to the premises which enable them to better themselves; they may hence become superpatriots for the Soviet Union and prominent spokesmen of "proletarian international-ism." Many non-Russians, as Stalin, Dzerzhinsky, and Ordzhonikidze, have been ruthless in the suppression of minority nationalism. In 1968, such non-Russians as Mazurov and Shelest are said to have been most zealous that the Czech deviation should be crushed. At the 1971 Party Congress, leaders of all major minority nationalities made a point of decrying manifestations of nationalism by their own people, even calling for more "merging" of peoples and cultures. Thus, the Central Asian candidate member of the Politburo, Rashidov, said, "The enormous inclination of people of all nationalities for the study of the Russian language is persuasive evidence of the loyalty of the Soviet peoples to this union,

---

[33] Kolasky, *Education in Soviet Ukraine*, p. 136.
[34] *Dialektika stroitel'stva kommunizma* (Izd. Mysl), Moscow, 1968, p. 243.
[35] Kolasky, op. cit., p. 72.

of their affection and respect for their older brother. . . . The Russian language is the banner of the friendship and brotherhood of peoples. . . ."[36]

Problems

Conceivably the Soviet Union may one day become an essentially homogeneous state. But assimilative policies are party counterproductive. Integration of the economy makes independence difficult but causes resentments. As economic decisions are settled not by the impersonal mechanisms of the market but politically, there must be endless struggles behind the scenes to secure a larger slice of the pie, and both parties in conflicts of interest may feel wronged. Ukrainians complain that their resources are diverted to poorer areas, while more backward regions, as of Central Asia, can regard their poverty as proof of discrimination. Military training is a powerful blender, yet hundreds of thousands of youths must require a great deal of ceremonial and rhetoric to be convinced of the joy of serving in a semiforeign army. Non-national education erodes the traditional basis of nationalism at some cost in creating dissatisfactions. The mixing of peoples may give increased awareness of differences, and it is impossible to bring Russians into minority areas without causing resentments.

Probably for such reasons, there is a great deal of resistance to what would seem overwhelming pressures to become russified. In the period 1959–1970 not enough persons were converted to the Russian nationality to compensate for the lower birth rate of the Russians, and the proportion of the population calling themselves Russians dropped slightly to 53.5%. Significantly, the percentage of Russians shrank in all non-European republics. It is more remarkable that minority languages held their own. The percentage giving usual spoken language as the language of the nationality rose slightly, 1959–1970, for most of the major Asiatic and Caucasian languages; it dropped markedly only in the cases of the Germans, who were scattered, and the Jews, only 17.7% of whom were recorded as Yiddish-speaking in 1970.

The latter people illustrate that learning Russian, even forgetting the native tongue, by no means assures harmony. Soviet Jewry has no legal organization, there has been no schooling in Yiddish for decades, and publication in Yiddish is trivial. Approximately two and a half million Jews have only a handful of synagogues as centers. Yet numerous young people are demonstratively assertive of their Jewishness and many thousand Jews, despite harassment, probable loss of employment, abuse, and fees which may run to the equivalent of several thousand dollars, apply to emigrate to Israel.[37] Anti-Semitism smolders beneath the surface among the people and, although

---

[36] *Pravda*, April 2, 1971, p. 2; *Current Digest*, vol. 23, no. 14, p. 28.

[37] In 1971 about 13,000 Jews who ran the gauntlet of obstacles were allowed to leave, in an unprecedented liberalization of emigration.

officially denied and legally forbidden, infects official policy. Rolled together with anticapitalism and anti-Zionism, it is so consistent as to be almost part of Soviet ideology. History as published in the Soviet Union practically ignores anti-Semitism in tsarist history, Nazi persecutions, and the state of Israel. Jews are often accused of speculation or of being agents of a foreign power. There are quotas limiting Jewish entrants into the universities; and practically none are to be found in the higher brackets of the army, diplomatic service, and party apparatus. Jewish deputies in the Supreme Soviet, representation in which is centrally planned, are only five, the same number as of Karakalpaks, ten times less numerous. There is, apparently, unwillingness to see the Jews fully absorbed. Even if they would like to lose themselves in the Russian mass, they are marked by the obligatory designation of "Jew" in their passports, and applications, as for employment and housing, require statement of nationality.

If the superficial assimilation of the Jews does not preclude frictions, the same is true of more compact and numerous and less fully russified groups. "Naturally national prejudices, distrust and enmity, which were stirred up by the tsarist autocracy, do not disappear right away after the Revolution."[38] To the contrary, a Soviet study indicated that the most successful Tatars were the most nationalistic.[39] From time to time the Soviet press complains of efforts to impose the national language (that is, to check russification), overemphasis on tradition, or opposition to exchange of cadres (resentment against the influx of Russians in superior positions). The party must insist on selecting cadres on the basis of "political and practical qualifications,"[40] which probably favor Russians. *Pravda* warns of disguised nationalism: "Localism may look like an endeavor to strive for the flourishing of one's own republic, territory, or province . . . underestimation of contacts with fraternal people may be presented as a wish to make the most of one's own possibilities. . . ."[41] To combat such tendencies, there are occasional house cleanings in the leaderships of insufficiently vigilant party apparatuses in non-Russian republics, and in nearly all of them there have been repressions.

A worrisome area is the Ukraine. Ukrainians know that their country is amply large and prosperous enough to stand on its own, and they tend to regard themselves as more westernized, more civilized than the Muscovites. Proud of their productivity, they may feel somewhat exploited. On the surface, there is tranquillity; yet many Ukrainian intellectuals have been arrested. In 1969 there was founded a new Ukrainian Institute of State and Law for the stated purpose of combatting "bourgeois nationalist" views of Ukrainian

---

[38] *Partiinaia zhizn*, no. 21, November, 1970, p. 6.
[39] Zev Katz, "Sociology in the USSR," *Problems of Communism*, vol. XX, no. 3, May-June, 1971, p. 38.
[40] *Pravda*, July 16, 1971, p. 4.
[41] January 24, 1969.

"socialist statehood." A consolation for the Ukrainians is that they are junior Russians, "Little Russians," as they were formerly called, entrusted with a share in the management of the empire.

The Baltic states have less potential for self-reliance, but they have less in common with the Russians and more sense of belonging to the West. There has been much industrial construction; and thanks to good work habits, the standard of living seems to be higher than in central Russia. Some feeling simmers; as a Lithuanian leader wrote, "There are still people in our country who, while sharing the socialist ideology as a whole, continue to remain particularly under the influence of nationalist views and traditions on one question or another." These include some of the young, for "one does not necessarily have to be born into a bourgeois society in order to succumb to bourgeois-nationalist sentiments."[42] *Pravda* speaks of "the notorious myth that bourgeois Latvia was allegedly a land of general prosperity."[43] However, there has been a very large influx of Russians; Riga is a predominantly Russian city. Probably few of the new generation look to recovery of independence. Much the same may be true of the Georgians, who still have a special pride left over from Stalin's time. For Armenians, subordination to Russia is much better than historic subjection to Turkey. Theirs is the republic with the smallest percentage of Russians (2.7%), and they seem relatively satisfied.

Those who present by far the severest problem for the Soviet leadership are the underdeveloped nations within the Soviet Union, the Central Asians, peoples markedly different from Russians by language, culture, religion, and race. There was little integration of the Central Asian provinces and protectorates under the tsars, and an attempt to introduce compulsory service during the First World War provoked a massive rebellion. The Bolshevik reconquest of the area, carried out with the assistance of Russian colonists interested in maintaining their status, was difficult and bloody. For several years Central Asian states were kept as "People's Democracies," and artificial republics were set up to divide the essentially single Turkic people. In the Second World War, it was seen fit to mobilize less than 5% of the population, as opposed to 12% of Russians and 10% of Ukrainians, and numerous Asian nationalities were relegated to labor battalions.[44] There are now almost no Central Asians in the upper ranks of the armed forces, and very few are to be found in leading positions of government, economy, or party. Asians are conspicuous only in facade organs, as the Supreme Soviet.

Russification and Sovietization have not been very effective in Central Asia. The new industries are the province of the Russians, who have their

---

[42] *Pravda*, February 12, 1969.

[43] September 1, 1970, p. 3.

[44] Leo Heiman, "Russification of the Soviet Armed Forces," *Ukrainian Quarterly*, vol. 24, no. 1, Spring, 1968, p. 44.

own quarters of the cities. Collectivization was nominally imposed long ago, but pastoral nomadism is still common, and the new kolkhoz is a renamed kin-group. Islam remains strong, despite Soviet pressures. Asian mores are a sore point, as girls leave school early and, instead of seeking employment, marry and very likely use the veil. Of 12,700 higher students in Turkmenistan in 1969, only 429 were Turkmen girls.[45] Very few join the party or marry Russian men. The segregation of women and the veil have been reported actually spreading in recent years to groups previously without the tradition, and the new upper class of successful Communists and soviet and kolkhoz officials adopt polygamy as a status symbol.[46] "In the last ten years, the Central Committee of the Communist Party of Turkmenistan has taken up more than thirty times questions of the education and advancement of female workers, collective farmers, and representatives of the intelligentsia, matters of struggle against feudal survivals. City and district party committees regularly discuss these tasks. But it is one thing to talk about them and another to fulfill what is decided. Unfortunately, many a decision about work with women stays on paper. . . . The number of women in leading positions decreased. . . ."[47] In 1969, the Tadzhik central committee was berated for indiscipline, low yields, neglect, failure to increase investments, promoting unqualified men (presumably Tadzhiks instead of Russians), and related sins. To remedy all this, "Propaganda of the ideas of proletarian internationalism and the friendship of peoples and strengthening of fraternal bonds between Tadzhikistan's working people and all the peoples of the Soviet Union must be at the center of the attention of party, Soviet, trade union, and Komsomol bodies."[48] A year later there was a similar shake-up with similar accusations in Azerbaidzhan.[49]

The industrialization of Central Asia has been much celebrated, and the standard of living has been raised well above that of neighboring Iran or Afghanistan. But the new factories are largely an alien import, like modern establishments built by foreign capital in less developed lands of the non-Soviet world. Productivity remains low. Per capita incomes in the four Asian republics, Turkmenistan, Kirghizistan, Uzbekistan and Tadzhikistan, average not much more than half that of the Soviet Union, and that of the indigenous people must be substantially less if account is taken of the higher income of the Russian sector of the population.[50] The gap has been widening in recent years.[51]

[45] *Soviet Studies Information Bulletin*, no. 26, April, 1970, p. 63.

[46] Elizabeth E. Bacon, *Central Asians under Russian Rule* (Cornell University Press), Ithaca, N. Y., 1966, p. 172.

[47] *Pravda*, January 25, 1970.

[48] *Partiinaia zhizn*, no. 1, January, 1969, pp. 13–15.

[49] *Bakinskii rabochii*, March 22, 1970; *ABSEES*, July, 1970, p. 47.

[50] Alec Nove and J. A. Newth, *The Soviet Middle East* (Praeger), New York, 1967, p. 42.

[51] Ann Sheehy, "Equality of Nationalities in the USSR," *Mizan*, vol. XI, no. 3, May-June, 1969, p. 145.

The problem of underdevelopment is complicated in the Soviet Union, as elsewhere, by differential birth rates. In 1968, the birth rate in central Russia was recorded as 12.1 per thousand, and 14.9 in the Ukraine, as compared with 25.0 in Armenia, 32.3 in Azerbaijan, 35.0 in Uzbekistan, 37.3 in Tadzhikistan, and 36.2 in Turkmenistan;[52] and the Asiatic rates showed little decline over thirty years. The rural population of Central Asia and Azerbaidzhan increased one-third, 1959–1969, while in European parts of the USSR it markedly decreased.[53] Merely to keep the same distance, the Central Asians would have to manage an economic growth rate 2% higher than that of the Russian republic; in fact, their growth rate has usually been lower.

This does not necessarily imply that the Soviet regime intentionally discriminates against non-Russians. Although Soviet statistics indicate that smaller percentages of most non-Russian nationalities than of Russians obtain higher education, and the like, the evidence of injustice is not very strong, except in such cases as Crimean Tatars, Jews, and perhaps Germans. One can believe that the Soviet leadership would like to have all treated fairly and to see all equally contented beneath their aegis. What matters, however, is not justice or injustice as weighed by an outsider, but the perception of the peoples themselves. Minorities may be bitterly resentful while receiving what the ruling group regards as favors. Even if a nationality is overrepresented at the top, as the Ukrainians are with Politburo members, this does not alter the fact that the system is basically Russian or end the suspicion that it operates in favor of the Russians. Non-Russians may feel psychologically, if not materially, disadvantaged; and they inevitably chafe under orders from distant and alien decision-makers. What Russians are likely to see as simply failures of the regime, minorities can view as exploitation and oppression. Causes for dissatisfaction are more numerous as the government manages everything and is consequently to blame for everything. If meat is scarce or movies are dull, blame can be laid on the Russians.

Russians have good cause to accept the Soviet system and its imperfections because it is necessary for the integrity of the Russian sphere. Non-Russians are in the opposite condition, required to accept russification as well as bolshevization, and the system treats more severely those whose basic loyalty is questionable. If the leadership desires justice, administrators can be harsh. Russians look down on many non-Russians, for whom they have sundry deprecatory nicknames; Central Asians are particularly regarded as dirty. The designation of nationality in internal passports facilitates the discrimination to which the politically weaker minorities are vulnerable. Since Lenin, the emphasis has been entirely on combatting "bourgeois nationalism." Russian nationalism

[52] *Narodnoe khoziastvo SSSR v 1969 g.*, Moscow, 1970, p. 35.

[53] *Voprosy ekonomiki*, no. 9, September, 1970, pp. 34–43; *Current Digest*, vol. 23, no. 2, p. 1.

would seem almost as acceptable in practice, although not in theory, as before the Revolution.

While the Soviet state seems incapable of exploring new approaches, the problem threatens to become acute. Modernization and education raise sensitivities. It was easier for the Bolsheviks to rule in the first years because the non-Russian upper classes were wiped out. Now a new educated elite has been created. Most of these see the way to advancement in collaboration with the system, but some provide potential leadership of disaffection. The economic lag of some areas, especially Central Asia, must be increasingly obvious and irritating. As people rise above subsistence levels, political demands become more insistent.

The higher reproductive rate of the more disaffected areas not only checks economic development but poses political problems. The Asians may swell from under one-sixth of the total population to more than a quarter in a generation. Perhaps mostly for this reason, "To increase the birth rate is one of our country's urgent problems."[54] Yet another development which lends acuity to the nationalities question is the slowdown of the Soviet economy. Rapid growth legitimates the system, and complaints are buried in the euphoria of progress. But over the past decade, Soviet growth has become unexciting; the regime can no longer plausibly claim any wonderful solution to the problems of poverty and backwardness.

READINGS

Robert Conquest, ed., *Soviet Nationalities Policy in Practice* (Praeger), New York, 1967.

Walter Kolarz, *Russia and her Colonies* (Archon Books), New York, 1953.

Richard Pipes, *The Formation of the Soviet Union* (Harvard University Press), Cambridge, Mass., 1964.

Teresa Rakowska-Harmstone, *Russia and Nationalism in Central Asia* (Johns Hopkins University Press), Baltimore, 1970.

Robert S. Sullivant, *Soviet Politics and the Ukraine* (Columbia University Press), New York, 1962.

V. Stanley Vardys, *Lithuania under the Soviets* (Praeger), New York, 1965.

---

[54] *Literaturnaia gazeta*, April 21, 1971, p. 13; *Current Digest*, vol. 23, no. 15, p. 35.

13. Soviet Orbit

STATE UNBOUNDED

The tsarist empire flowed out from the Russian center and bound other peoples to the Russian-dominated state. Incorporation was gradual, and some areas were less completely amalgamated than others. On the eve of the First World War, Finland still had considerable autonomy; in Central Asia, Khiva and Bukhara were protectorates; Outer Mongolia and part of Persia were spheres of influence. As a result of revolution and war, Poland and Finland and some other areas were lost; but most of the empire was tightened and brought under firmer central control, even while the chief minority areas were organized as nominally sovereign states.

From victory in the Second World War there emerged an expanded Soviet polity. In 1939–1945 territories which had formerly belonged to the tsars were converted into Soviet republics, as Lithuania, Latvia, Estonia, and Bessarabia (Moldavia). Poland was not formally reincorporated but became subject to the hegemony of Moscow; along with other states of Eastern and Central Europe, it formed part of an enlarged entity, the "Socialist Commonwealth." The Soviet Russian political system is not strictly bounded but shades off in varying degrees of control and coordination.

Beyond the fourteen non-Russian Soviet republics, the oldest and most complete dependency of Moscow is the Mongolian People's Republic. Outer Mongolia came under Russian influence in 1911 as a result of political troubles of the Chinese empire, to which it belonged. It was separated during a few years of turmoil, but Bolshevik armies entered in 1921, and sovietization began immediately. The Soviet-controlled police gradually eliminated hostile elements. Soviet policies were faithfully echoed: economic relaxation of the 1920's, collectivization, the antireligious campaign, and the purges. The language has been written in the Russian (Cyrillic) alphabet since 1941, most teachers are trained in the Soviet Union, and the television tower in Ulan Bator retransmits Soviet programs. Party and government structures are copied after the Soviet, as is the organization of industry and agriculture.[1] Unlike Soviet republics, Mongolia carries on diplomatic relations. But its trade is with the Soviet Union or Soviet-managed; Soviet personnel, civilian and military, work freely in Mongolia; the railroad is operated by the Russians. The army is practically a division of the Soviet army. Graduation to the status of a Soviet republic would change little.

The Eastern European countries with Soviet forces in occupation, Hungary, Czechoslovakia, Poland, and Eastern Germany, have a little more latitude and individuality, but they are more thoroughly controlled, whatever their ostensible sovereignty, than India by Britain in the days of Queen Victoria. Their status is obscurely between that of a Soviet republic and that of an independent state. To them should be added Bulgaria, to which Soviet military and security forces seem to have free access. "We consider our army to be a part of the Soviet armed forces," the Bulgarian leader Zhivkov said in 1966; and the Soviet ambassador is practically a proconsul.[2]

In a gesture of liberalism doubtless regretted since, Khrushchev removed Soviet occupation forces from Romania in 1958. For a decade, the Romanian leadership edged toward greater independence, shifting some (eventually nearly half) of its foreign trade away from the Soviet bloc; but the limits of its freedom of action are only the limits of Soviet tolerance. These, as shown by the liquidation of "democratic communism" in Czechoslovakia in 1968, are not broad. While talking of sovereignty, the Romanian regime can institute no major changes of foreign or domestic policy without Soviet consent. It is not free to withdraw from military collaboration with the Soviet Union, and it must proclaim loyalty to "proletarian internationalism." It follows closely Soviet patterns in party, governmental, and economic organization, earning autonomy partly by orthodoxy. Romania acknowledges that the nations are eventually to be dissolved in a great Communist union, but it regards the prospect as distant and meanwhile desires as much freedom of action as feasible within the framework of the movement.

Romania belongs to the "Socialist Commonwealth," in which the Soviet Union has proclaimed the right of intervention in the name of the Communist movement, which is a "family of brotherly peoples," in the same terms used to describe the Soviet Union, and which *Pravda* has gone so far as to

---

[1] *Partiinaia zhizn*, no. 22, November, 1969. pp. 70–72, gives a detailed picture.
[2] Paul Lendvai, *Eagles in Cobwebs* (Doubleday), New York, 1969, pp. 206, 243.

call a single "Motherland" ("Rodina").[3] In regard to these states, the governing rules are not those of conventional international relations, but those of "proletarian internationalism" as interpreted by the Soviet Union. Within this sphere, all parties, under the Brezhnev doctrine, have the duty to help all others to maintain the correct social order and basic policies; in effect, loyalty to the Soviet Union.

It is not clear what other states are included in the "Socialist Commonwealth." Yugoslavia apparently belongs; the Russians have sometimes hinted the applicability to it of the right of socialist intervention. But only in a rather narrow juridical sense can it be said that the Soviet polity ends at the official Soviet boundaries; and in Soviet political affairs, as exemplified by constitutional rights, the conduct of elections, or the sovereignty of Soviet republics, the legal form is not of prime importance. The essence of Soviet socialism is claimed to be its international nature.[4] In the Soviet political philosophy there is no difference between Russians and Ukrainians, between these and Czechs, or between Slavs and Africans. "The goal of socialism is not only the liquidation of the fragmentation of mankind into little governments and of any sort of division of nations, it is not only the bringing together of nations but their merger."[5] If theory deviates from practice and outside observers are unclear as to how far to regard the Soviet system as an internationalist movement and how far as a state among states, the ruling party admits no doubt. Its rules, which have much more to do with political power than the official constitution, state that, "The Communist Party of the Soviet Union is an integral part of the international Communist and working class movement."

SIMILAR SATELLITES

In accordance with the philosophy of the Comintern, it was formerly assumed that any area which came under Soviet domination would automatically join the Soviet family of nations. However, Stalin declined to incorporate additional states, even when local leaders might have been willing, as were the Yugoslavs at one time. Reasons for the abstention seem to have been reluctance to exacerbate differences with Western powers and fear that too strong action in Eastern Europe would foreclose excellent chances for Communist victories elsewhere. Caring less for forms than the reality of rule,

[3] December 26, 1968, p. 1.
[4] *Sovetskoe slavianovedenie*, March, 1970, pp. 3–9; *ABSEES*, July, 1971, p. 34.
[5] V. I. Lenin, *Sochineniia*, 4th ed., vol. 22, Moscow, 1952, p. 135.

Stalin permitted more or less coalition governments with non-Communists and did not immediately and thoroughly sovietize Eastern European countries as he did the Baltic states taken in 1940. But he ruled firmly, at least after tensions between the Soviet Union and the West deteriorated in 1947. The most reliable executors of Stalin's will were always the Communists, so their role in the governments was increased by degrees to total domination. Institutions were squeezed more and more into the Soviet mold. After Stalin, there was some slackening, especially 1953–1956, and again (after a setback from the Hungarian uprising) for several years after 1961. But since 1965, especially since 1968, the reins have been pulled tighter.

The governments of satellites are only a degree less uniform than the Soviet republics. They are all party-states, in which policy-making is the province not of the official government but of the ruling party. In all, the party pyramid is structured in practically identical Soviet fashion.[6] The rules closely parallel those of the Soviet party, and they ordinarily include acknowledgment of obligations to "proletarian internationalism" or salute the CPSU as the vanguard of the world movement. For example, the constitution of the Hungarian Socialist Workers' Party begins, "The Hungarian Socialist Workers' Party is a Communist party, the revolutionary vanguard of the working class, an integral part of the international Communist and workers' movement. . . ." Party membership is from five to ten percent of the population. The primary party organization is usually on a production basis; it has, if large enough, committee, bureau, and secretary. There are periodic regional conferences, as in the Soviet Union, with respective committees, bureaus, and secretariats. At the center, there is held a party congress every few years, and it "forms" a central committee, which has its politburo and secretariat, flanked, as in the Soviet party, by a party control commission and an auditing commission. The top man is the General Secretary or First Secretary, who may be the same person as the chairman of the council of ministers. The Leninist principle of democratic centralism prevails. Party elections are largely a formality, although they may sometimes acquire reality, as when Gomulka was elected to leadership by secret ballot in 1956. There are youth organizations in the style of the Komsomol and other party-directed "mass organizations." The most obvious difference is that most of the countries—Bulgaria, Czechoslovakia, East Germany and Poland—do not insist on the formal monopoly of the Communists but have other "parties," with minor representation in the governments. These "parties" may be used to organize different sectors of the population; thus, Poland has a Peasant Party and a Democratic Party for the intellectuals alongside the ruling Workers' Party. They fully support the policies of the regime; the Christian Democratic Union of East Germany warns against pacifism as an "imperialist ideology."

[6] Cf. H. Gordon Skilling, *The Governments of Communist East Europe* (Thomas Y. Crowell Co.), New York, 1966, p. 58.

The satellite constitutions, like the Soviet, have impressive guarantees of rights, but they proclaim candidly the guiding role of the Communist Party. There are assemblies corresponding to the Supreme Soviet and at lower levels to local soviets. The Polish *Sejm* exceptionally recorded occasional negative votes or abstentions for a few years. As in the Soviet Union, there is a presidium vested with the assembly's authority in its absence; and legislation is largely by the cabinet, not the formal legislative body. Elections have served not to choose candidates but to demonstrate acceptance. As indicated by a Czech party directive, "Election preparations must proceed according to the Marxist-Leninist concept of the state. On no account can an election under socialism present itself as a rivalry or a political power struggle; only the organizations of the National Front can participate in elections."[7] There has been some experimentation, however, with permitting choice among a larger number of candidates than there are seats. In Poland, in 1957, more than a third of the candidates were surplus. Hungary has recently permitted some contests among party-approved candidates to enliven elections and improve relations with the people.

COORDINATION

It has been the unvarying Soviet policy to shape the areas which it controls into a single community, in foreign policy, production, and defense. Coordination has been most complete in foreign policy. On all major and nearly all minor issues, official positions are identical; there has hardly been a single divergent action of any of the delegations at the United Nations except as the result of a failure of communications or the misreading of a cue. Differences have been of emphasis; for example, Brezhnev at one time largely ignored West German "revanchism and neo-Nazism" when Walter Ulbricht was making much of it. This reflects different interests but does not necessarily imply an insurgency against Soviet policy, which may see utility in speaking with different voices. In principle there can be no difference, as all supposedly follow a single line dictated by "proletarian internationalism." There are frequent consultations, in which the views of satellite leaders may be taken into account, and the six East European regimes have sometimes made formal joint declarations on important questions. They have several times stated a common position on relations with West Germany and their claims against that country. On another occasion, the central committees and governments of the USSR and satellites solemnly expressed their support for the Arab cause in the Near East.[8]

[7] *Pravda*, June 4, 1969.
[8] *Pravda*, November 27, 1969.

Economic integration has proved more difficult, but it has shown that political drives can outweigh economic. Countries of Eastern Europe which before the Second World War had hardly any trade with Russia and little with their neighbors but a great deal with the Western industrial countries, have come into the opposite situation. From two-thirds (in the case of Poland) to four-fifths (in the cases of East Germany and Bulgaria) of their trade is within the Soviet bloc. Correspondingly, the Soviet Union carries on 70% of its trade with its satellites. It is indicative of the political direction of this commerce that Soviet exchanges with Bulgaria are four times those with one of its leading Western partners, Federal Germany.

The interchanges of the satellite countries and the Soviet Union were managed at first by bilateral agreements only. Over the years, there have been set up many and varied bilateral and multilateral organizations, from joint publishing enterprises to scientific coordination. A Joint Institute for Nuclear Research, for example, has charge of the nuclear development of the bloc. The overall organization for economic coordination is the Council of Mutual Economic Assistance, or Comecon, established in 1948 as an answer to the successful American-sponsored organization of Western Europe. This body at first remained feeble because of Stalin's distrust of any multilateral organization, concerning itself mostly with economic studies and standards. But from 1956 Comecon began synchronizing economic plans of satellites with the Soviet Union and setting targets for bloc trade.

In 1959, Comecon was given a charter, according to which members formally had equal representation. This meant that agreement could be assured only by Soviet economic, political, and ideological leverage; and the East European states showed more reluctance to give up control of their own economies than to subordinate themselves politically and militarily. It proved more difficult to integrate planned economies than market economies, because of the tendencies of planning units, like Soviet ministries and factories, to autarky, and because of the impossibility of agreeing on economic advantages in the face of artificial prices and exchange rates. To decide on specialization required secret political negotiations on literally thousands of products. Romania took advantage of its autonomy to stymie Khrushchev's scheme for welding all into a single economic unit. However, after 1963 draft plans of the several countries were partly coordinated. There also were a number of successful joint projects, as an electric grid covering Eastern Europe and the Ukraine, and a pool of railroad cars. Banking arrangements were made to facilitate multilateral exchanges, but the countries with export surpluses continued to be unable to convert their balances into hard currency. In 1971 it was necessary to postpone until 1980 the question of convertibility of members' currencies.

The goal of Comecon remained supranational economic planning, the achievement of which would deprive the satellite governments of their chief function; and presumably for this reason many local bosses resisted. But by promoting heavy industrialization, often uneconomical, the Soviet Union has tied East European states to itself as both source of raw materials and market for goods unsalable on the world market. This situation may be advantageous for at least some of the satellite lands, as they have a protected market over which they stand as more highly industrialized countries. At the beginning of this century, many Poles had concluded that independence was impractical because of the dependence of Polish industry on the Russian market; that dependence is much greater now.

Soviet expansion, like tsarist, has been political and military, not economic; and the basic means of holding the Soviet sphere is coercive power. Soviet security organs operate in the several states freely, although obscurely, acting with and through the local apparatus. Very prominent in Stalin's day, with extensive powers of administrative justice, they were somewhat checked in the years of liberalization but never removed from the scene. The security police of all satellite states is trained in the Soviet Union, and local forces work with if not under the KGB.

The Soviet army stands in the background. By formal agreement with Hungary, Poland, and Czechoslovakia, it is not to interfere in domestic affairs. When disturbances threatened Prague on the anniversary of the invasion, the city was occupied by Czech, not Soviet, forces; and Polish forces repressed the disturbances in the Baltic area in December, 1970. But the Soviet army remains prepared to crush resistance if necessary, as it did in Berlin in 1953, in Hungary in 1956, and in Czechoslovakia in 1968. The armies on the spot may be rather small, 70,000–80,000 in Hungary and a similar number in Czechoslovakia; and, to minimize friction, it is Soviet policy to keep their forces out of sight and to avoid unorganized mixing with the general population. They are effective because everyone knows that they will not hesitate to act ruthlessly if the power of the party is endangered. They are the guarantor of the system. In East Germany this is explicit: by treaty of 1959, the Soviet forces have the right to assume the government in case of a threat to security as judged by themselves. The Soviets often speak of their armed forces as guardians of the "Socialist Commonwealth," with the implication of an irrevocable duty to protect against any direct or indirect threat.

There are other political-military functions. Soviet soldiers are supposed to symbolize Communist brotherhood. In Czechoslovakia, Soviet soldiers after August, 1968, were given many missions of building good will; some helped farmers in the fields, while others went into factories to lend a hand and give an example. Being true workers and peasants, Soviet army men can represent only the positive political principle of socialism and anti-imperialism.

The national armies are auxiliaries to the Soviet forces. As organized under Stalin, they were formally independent but in practice not much different from sectors of the Soviet armed forces. Their organization was copied entirely after the Soviet; their arms and procedures were Soviet, with many Soviet advisers and some Soviet citizen officers in higher ranks. After the passing of the dictator, more need was felt for organizational links, and in 1955 the Warsaw Treaty was signed to tie together the satellite armies, including Romania. Despite this bond, the national armies became a little more distinct and autonomous. Uniforms deviated from the Soviet fashion in some countries, and Poland in 1956 was able to send home some thirty Soviet officers, including the defense chief, Marshal Rokossovsky. But there has been no evidence of any satellite military organization emerging as an independent force. There are party organizations in satellite armies very like those in the Soviet army, and there are many exchanges and conferences of political workers. Warsaw Treaty Organization (WTO) maneuvers have been held at least twice yearly since 1961, frankly for not only military but political purposes, to deepen the brotherhood of the armies and their "internationalist" spirit. The Brezhnev government has been more inclined than its predecessor to rely on military integration. The application of Soviet force with the (largely symbolic) cooperation of East Germany, Poland, Hungary, and Bulgaria against Czechoslovakia in August, 1968, greatly strengthened the organization and increased respect for it on both sides of the frontier. In October, 1970, for the first time, all WTO members participated in joint maneuvers.

Although the primary factor of unity is Soviet preponderance, the WTO is a rather potent organization. It has a Political Consultative Commission, composed of representatives of member countries, with a secretariat in Moscow, as a coordinating body. Its missions in the satellite states report to Moscow and amount to Soviet control personnel. The commander-in-chief is a Soviet marshal, and divisions are headed by Soviet officers. In January, 1970, it was reported that a joint force has been established in March of the previous year; but it was not clear how much this implied. Training under the aegis of the WTO is important; all higher officers of the East German army and an increasing proportion of those of other armies are said to have been trained in Soviet schools. Promotion may require the assent of a Soviet advisor.

The WTO also has a foreign policy role. By the Warsaw Treaty, the several states obliged themselves to consult on all important international questions, and WTO meetings are frequently considered suitable for making foreign policy declarations. Some are so brief as to suggest that consultation is pro forma only; for example, a WTO summit conference on August 20, 1970, lasted five hours. Soviet military dominance being uncontestable and unchallengeable, the satellite states seem to accept military integration with docility. It means, however, the effective nullification of sovereignty and gives substance to the conventional slogans of "unbreakable bonds of friendship."

PURSUIT OF ALLEGIANCE

Pan-Slavist Danilevsky, a century ago, thought that all the Slavs of Eastern Europe after their liberation by Mother Russia would rapidly and eagerly become Russian-speaking.[9] Having achieved that liberation, the Soviet Union is striving systematically to conquer minds as well as bodies. The Russians are not satisfied merely to be obeyed; they demand the love, or appearance of love, of their vassals; and they would assimilate all under their aegis to a common pattern. Cultural differences within the Socialist Commonwealth, they note, are meat for capitalist-imperialists and Maoists. At some remove, it is as within the Soviet Union: "Already there has been formed within the framework of the world socialist system an organic commonwealth of national cultures. . . . In the measure of their growing social uniformity, the socialist countries form an international culture which is varied in national forms and united in socialist content."[10]

Hence there are scores of organizations and programs and hundreds of conventions for cultural exchanges, cultural missions, institutes, and academies. Soviet-local friendship societies are politically important mass organizations. Propaganda not imported from the Soviet Union is produced locally under conditions not unlike those within the Soviet Union, although writers and artists are not quite so stringently controlled in most countries. From kindergarten on, the educational system is infused with Marxism-Leninism and "internationalism," the largest ingredient in which is love for the Soviet Union. Textbooks are copied from the Soviet, and study of the Russian language is mandatory from early grades to the top. As for the peoples of the Soviet Union, Russian is seen as the natural common language of the socialist nations.[11] For the political formation of the cadres, there are party schools on different levels, with Soviet-trained instructors.

Military indoctrination and paramilitary training are carried on in much the same fashion as in the Soviet Union. Societies akin to Dosaaf under military leadership teach shooting, gliding, communications technology, grenade-throwing, parachute-jumping, and the like, all under banners of class warfare and struggle against capitalist imperialism. As an East German pedagogical journal wrote, ". . . some teachers must finally free themselves from the idea that it is immoral to teach hatred."[12]

---

[9] Nikolai I. Danilevsky, *Russland und Europa* (O. Zeller), Osnabrück, 1965, p. 231.
[10] *Sovetskaia kultura*, September 9, 1971, pp. 1, 2.
[11] *Partiinaia zhizn*, no. 22, November, 1970, p. 73.
[12] *Die Zeit*, August 5, 1969, p. 2.

Polish boys and girls learn poems about Lenin and debated, in preparation for his hundredth birthday, topics such as "What it means to live and work in Lenin's way," and "Leninist convictions in the triumph of Communist ideals." East Germans are exhorted to raise their cultural level and develop their personalities; the way to do it is to read Lenin. Much is made of the virtues of the Soviet Union, its special place in the world, and the love of the workers for it. Marxism-Leninism is supposed to be a uniform truth, and the official doctrine in the vassal states closely follows the Soviet in nearly every realm. The satellite press waits for a Soviet lead before commenting on controversial events. Lysenkoism was obligatory for some years. Genghis Khan, whom the Russians dislike for purely nationalistic reasons, has been made a nonhero for the Mongolians.

The satellites follow the Soviet model or even surpass it in emphasis on discrediting the West and its political system. In East Germany, Poland, and to some extent Czechoslovakia, the theme of West German enmity or revanchism is played loudly. Troubles are blamed on Western aggression; because of the threat of imperialism Soviet protection must be extended over the land. In the battle between capitalism and socialism, neutrality is impossible, and the people must side with the Soviet toilers' state. Liberty and democracy are to be understood from a class point of view. In the East German motto, "Self-determination is a class question." As the government is a weapon of class interests, and the Czech or Polish workers can have no interests contradictory to those of their Soviet brothers, their government can have no purpose divergent from the other "socialist" countries.

Antinationalism is a major theme, nationalism being the chief danger to the Soviet position. As the commander of the WTO stated, "The Leninist principle of internationalism has special significance for the socialist education and consolidation of the armies of the Warsaw Treaty. Its essence is expressed in socialist cooperation and joint defense of revolutionary gains. It is one of the bases of the military doctrine of the governments belonging to the Warsaw Treaty. . . ."[13] In the words of a pro-Soviet Czech leader, "This principle [internationalism] is understood by every worker with class consciousness in distinction to the nationalistically inclined petty bourgeois."[14] Internationalism must not, of course, be taken as an excuse for cosmopolitanism, which is an insidious weapon of imperialism. It must never be forgotten that the world is torn by class struggle and divided into irreconcilable opposing camps. "National-ism under contemporary conditions is expressed above all in overlooking the basic contradiction of our epoch, the contradiction between socialism and capitalism, in the rejection of class positions . . . of the ideas of the unity of the

---

[13] S. Shtemenko in *Krasnaia zvezda*, May 14, 1969.
[14] L. Strougal in *Pravda*, April 23, 1969.

world revolutionary movement, and above all of the socialist countries in the struggle against the common enemy, imperialism."[15]

Supranationalism and the duty of all to come to the aid of "socialism" wherever endangered was used most strongly to justify military intervention in Czechoslovakia. The so-called Brezhnev Doctrine, alleging the superiority of the international (or Soviet) right over the national, was in essence as old as Lenin, but it had seemed qualified by many statements of respect for independence and sovereignty. In the Soviet interpretation, however, there is no contradiction between sovereignty and the right of intervention. "Aid to the toilers of the CSSR from the other socialist countries . . . is a practical struggle for the sovereignty of the Czechoslovak Socialist Republic. . . ."[16] "No one," Foreign Minister Gromyko said, "can deprive the people of the right of leaning on the help of friends who are true to their international duty and treaty obligations, and no one can deprive their friends of the right to help this people."[17]

Indoctrination does not seem to have been so effective as might be supposed. The Hungarians showed in 1956 how slight were the effects of a decade of Marxism-Leninism, and the Czechs were of less friendly disposition toward the Soviet big brother in 1968 than before a generation of propaganda. Indoctrination apparently can be shaken off when the power behind it recedes. But one must assume that it has at least the effect of making the present authority seem inevitable and resistance to it senseless. For the Communist elite, it serves as a rationalization of their antinational position while it supports their status. For those who must obey, it gives reasons for docility, a justification for apathy if not a cause for enthusiasm. The Russians hope that national independence will eventually fade, like a receding dream, for the people of their multinational domain, beyond as well as within the borders of the Soviet Union, in acceptance of the historic inevitability of Soviet power, the cardinal fact of the Marxist-Leninist universe.

CONFORMITY AND AUTONOMY

As long as essential loyalty is assured, with unconditional adherence to Soviet foreign policy and defense arrangements, the Soviet leadership may permit a certain autonomy in internal affairs. Behind a conformist front, the satellite world is variegated, and life is much less Sovietized than political institutions. Pressure toward conformism in Soviet patterns encounters the drive

[15] *Pravda*, January 15, 1969.
[16] *Pravda*, September 26, 1968.
[17] *Pravda*, July 11, 1969.

toward distinctiveness, and at various times and places it seems that one or the other is gaining.

In Hungary, after the Russians put Kadar in power following the 1956 insurrection, he sought to reduce tensions by a policy of conciliation. Some gestures were made to the Catholic Church, and writers were given more leeway than their Soviet counterparts on condition only of refraining from criticism. Ideology fell somewhat into the background, and the people were permitted a degree of frivolity unlike the mandatory seriousness of the Russian way. Trade and cultural contacts with the West were modestly developed. Hungary embarked on the most extensive economic reform of the "Socialist Commonwealth" (Yugoslavia excluded). Prices were partly freed of controls, enterprises were authorized to contract among themselves on the basis of demand, wages were made negotiable, and planning authorities drew back from management to general direction and regulation of the economy. Collective farms were allowed to sell their produce freely. A healthy private sector, entrepreneurs being permitted as many as ten employees, did much to brighten the face of socialism, as in Russia in the 1920's. Good restaurants and night clubs made Budapest the Paris of the Communist world. This economic liberalization has been followed by some political relaxation. Rights of party members have been broadened; higher party bodies must give reasons if they annul decisions of lower ones. The bounds of Hungarian autonomy were made clear in 1968. Kadar was able to evince coolness toward the coercion of Czechoslovakia but not to refrain from participation.

By defying Khrushchev in 1956 and at the same time convincing him of their trustworthiness, Poland's Gomulka and his colleagues earned a degree of internal autonomy then unprecedented. A general relaxation gave the regime some popularity and permitted a revival of intellectual life. The parliament acquired some reality as a national forum, elections offered a little choice, and police powers were checked. But probably because of Soviet military and economic leverage and pressures behind the scenes, there began an uneven countertrend after the latter 1950's. The workers' councils were subordinated to the government, economic reforms were allowed to wither, and strikes were again made illegal. Religious education in the schools was gradually terminated; the Catholic Church was subjected to sundry restrictions designed to wear it down. Deviant publications were closed. Protest in 1964 brought intensified repression. When Polish students, inspired by Czech liberalization, rioted in March, 1968, the response of the authorities was forceful suppression and expulsion. There followed a campaign against Jews and liberal intellectuals. In August the Polish regime participated willingly in the "normalization" of Czechoslovakia.

As a satellite, Poland is seriously backward in failure to subjugate the church and to collectivize agriculture. In all other bloc countries 90% of the farmland was collectivized, as against 15% in Poland. Perhaps because a substantial sector of the economy remained outside state management, by 1970 Poland was showing some revival of the spirit of 1956. In December, workers struck in several Baltic ports against increases in food prices. The intellectuals seemed to have been so domesticated since 1956 that they remained quiet, and the workers' movement found little resonance in higher party circles. It became so menacing, however, that Gomulka and nearly half the Polish Politburo and Secretariat were hastily replaced; nonetheless, protests and slowdowns continued for two months, a novelty in Communist history. The new Gierek showed itself much friendlier but seemed unable or unwilling to undertake real change.

The Russians learned in Czechoslovakia in 1968 that it was not sufficient that a country be ruled by a Communist party and have Soviet-like economic and political institutions; control required Soviet power on the spot. After the invasion of August, 1968, the Russians at first kept in charge the reformist leader, Alexander Dubček, in whose name calls were made for calm and order. A treaty with his government gave legal cover for the presence of Soviet troops, and full control was step by step affirmed. Censorship was reinstated, and journalists were purged. The controlled media all hammered the themes of party discipline, proletarian brotherhood, and the need to cooperate with the Russians. Organizations were cleansed; some that refused to bow, as the students' union, were dissolved and replaced. The labor unions, which had been in the forefront of change, were brought back to subservience. The economic reform was turned back, reform-minded managers were purged, and trade with the West was downgraded.

As a result of anti-Soviet disturbances of April, 1969, and a threat of renewed Soviet occupation of the cities, Dubček was replaced by a more "conservative" leader, Gustav Husak. The army was made reliable, until by the first anniversary of the invasion it could be used to suppress anti-Soviet demonstrations. The security forces were rebuilt and were given powers to detain and punish anyone who "fails to do his duty in accordance with socialist ideals." By the first part of 1970, none of the reformist leaders remained; of the party membership, a third had resigned, while the remainder were subjected to individual scrutiny. In May, 1970, a new treaty was signed binding Czechoslovakia more explicitly to the Soviet system, obligating Czech forces to fight anywhere for the Soviet Union. It became official doctrine that the Soviet and WTO forces did a right and necessary action in entering the country, and that the proponents of "Democratic Communism" in the spring of 1968 were practically traitors, called upon to repent and retract. Czech leaders expressed their gratitude for Soviet intervention. In January, 1971, a poll allegedly showed that the people approved the invasion and occupation of their country.

The German Democratic Republic showed how a small but dedicated minority, armed with the traditional Soviet means of rule and backed by unchallengeable force, could make an unwilling population into an efficient state. This was not possible until the erection of the Berlin Wall, August, 1961, cutting the citizens off from the prospect of fairly easy escape to the West. But thereafter, the East German regime was able to make their state the second industrial power of the "Socialist Commonwealth," the largest trade partner of the Soviet Union and its principal supplier of machinery. Ulbricht is said to have been as influential in Moscow as the best of viceroys; the basic policy of the leadership is not to claim autonomy but to make itself valuable.

Lacking legitimacy as German leaders, the East German rulership rest their claims on the superiority of class to nation. They are the most dogmatic of the Soviet sphere. They are also the most militaristic, emphasizing soldierly duties and virtues and spending twice as large a proportion of the national income on defense as the West German state which they daily brand as militaristic. Soviet domination of Eastern Europe is more essential for them than it is for the Soviet rulers themselves. They were perhaps most threatened by the liberal movement in Czechoslovakia, and they were most pleased to see it stamped out. But no satellite is nearly so productive and technologically advanced, and none is better organized, whatever the masses feel about the division of Germany or their subordination to a foreign power. Perhaps better than any other Soviet satellite the German Democratic Republic could appeal to the pride of its citizens in their economic achievements and offer them a rising standard of living, although the gap in productivity between East and West Germany increased slightly, 1960–1970.[18]

RUSSIA AND THE EMPIRE

The government of the Soviet empire is as difficult to understand as that of the non-Russian areas of the Union. In the external realm even more than within Soviet borders, it is essential to maintain maximum appearances of freedom and equality while governing as securely as possible peoples with strong national aspirations. There is no apparent wish to follow the Leninist course of welcoming the subject states into the Soviet family of nations as Soviet republics. It would damage Soviet external relations; it would be possibly disastrous for the world Communist movement and prospects of further expansion. East Europeans would be discordant in the Soviet system, at least until their reeducation has progressed more. Bureaucratic conservatism stands in the way; a radical change of status would disturb a thousand settled operational modes. Bringing in more developed people as Poles, East Germans, and Czechs would dilute the essentially Russian power. It would not be easy to deny the most productive sectors of the Soviet population representation at the top, and

---

[18] *Die Zeit*, January 29, 1971, p. 3.

such a large proportion of non-Russians might well turn Soviet federalism into a reality.

Neither is there any prospect of willing surrender of any part of the dominions. "The Leninist principle of the unity of patriotism and internationalism is incompatible with the least weakening of bonds of any brother country with its natural and reliable allies, the socialist countries and Marxist-Leninist parties. . . ."[19] Khrushchev was prepared to loosen up in order, he hoped, to rule better; but there never was any idea of relinquishing Eastern Europe. Whenever a will to independence asserted itself, it had to be cut down. Withdrawal would belie the ideological image of inexorable historical advance. It would be far worse to count Czechoslovakia in the camp and then to lose it than never to have claimed it. As the satellites are part of the Soviet system, weakening of control in them, as anywhere else, would threaten further loss. Why, Ukrainians asked, should they not have the same rights as the "socialist sisters, Russia, Poland, and Czechoslovakia?"[20] Fear of repercussions among non-Russians most probably moved the otherwise indecisive and conservative Politburo to action in 1968.

There are numerous pressures tending to weaken Soviet control of the satellites. The peoples involved, probably even a good many of the party leadership, would like better relations with Western Europe, with which they feel more affinity than with Russia. Many of them regard themselves as superior to the Russians, and this feeling is reinforced by higher productivity and living standards in the more advanced countries. They need more trade with the West; and they have opened their lands to tourism to a degree hardly conceivable for Russia, risking political weakening in return for hard currency. They need economic liberalization to raise the productivity which contributes to their usefulness to the Soviet Union, and economic liberalization practically entails some political liberalization. One may assume that satellite leaders are continually trying to secure a shade more freedom of action for themselves, fuller recognition of their spheres of autonomy, especially economic and cultural, even while protesting loyalty. They already have apparently attained some security in office, as the Soviet Union seems to have largely lost since the 1950's the ability or will to make changes in the top ranks of its vassals. If the Soviet leadership becomes less vigorous, it will be difficult to resist such erosion of their effective control.

There are on the other hand pressures toward greater unification. In the nineteenth century a contiguous Russian-controlled territory was certain to be joined to the body of the empire; and the aspirations of Soviet Russia are no more modest than those of tsarist Russia. The way of the Soviet republics has been mostly toward closer approximation, with a goal, as has been stressed at

[19] *Pravda*, January 8, 1971, p. 3.
[20] *The Ukrainian Quarterly*, vol. 24, no. 1, 1968, p. 15.

times, of complete fusion; there is no clear reason that lands which did not happen to be part of the old empire should be allotted a different future. The countries of Eastern Europe are slowly being formed in a common mould of Marxist-Leninist education and Soviet-style institutions. Even though the populations may not be brought to love the Russians, they may come to see their situation as improvable only within and through the system. Supranational institutions and arrangements grow ceaselessly. Administrative convenience and logic dictates dealing with all alike, putting the Ukraine on the same footing as Poland, etc.

Institutional amalgamation might also help to solve some problems of management. The less tightly controlled East European satellites are channels for the flow of Western influence into the Soviet Union. Soviet citizens visit and work there in large numbers, and any minor freedoms of Hungary or others may be cited as ideologically acceptable since they are permitted in orthodox "socialist" countries. The relative independence of satellites is at least potentially embarrassing in comparison with the limited rights of Soviet republics, and it might be a basis to claim more. If they can follow even slightly different roads to socialism, there is no reason why Soviet republics should not have similar latitude. It is ideologically anomalous that there should be a closely guarded border, with strict controls over movement of persons and goods, between the Soviet Union and fellow Marxist-Leninist states.

The ideology and the entire outlook of the Soviet system are universalist and bespeak a single political order. Soviet means "international."[21] The purpose of Soviet universalism is primarily to maintain the realm, only secondarily to expand it; and the present rather immobile leadership would seem inclined to avoid overt changes as long as calm prevails. The future of the Soviet empire, whether disintegrative or integrative tendencies are to prevail, depends on the evolution of the world scene; and it is no more predictable. But it is of immense economic, strategic, and political importance for the Soviet state. If it were lost, the party could hardly sustain the ideological image of leadership in a great universal movement, an image which is essential for the party and the Soviet system. Russians are justly proud of it; it is part of the mystique. "Hearing the declarations of their foreign friends and brothers, Soviet Communists with new force felt themselves an indivisible part of the great international movement dedicated to remaking the world. . . ."[22] Likewise, hegemony over many peoples prevents relaxation either of ideology or of political controls, and the "class" approach of Marxism becomes the more necessary as national self-awareness grows. The system is artificial and vulnerable, but the Russians have acquired an empire and they cannot let it go.

[21] *Sovetskaia kultura*, July 6, 1971, p. 1.
[22] *Pravda* editorial, April 13, 1971.

READINGS

Vaclav Benes, *Eastern European Government and Politics* (Harper & Row), New York, 1966.

James F. Brown, *The New Eastern Europe* (Praeger), New York, 1966.

Paul Lendvai, *Eagles in Cobwebs* (Doubleday & Co., Inc.), New York, 1969.

Ghita Ionescu, *The Politics of the European Communist States* (Praeger), New York, 1967.

Harold G. Skilling, *The Governments of Communist East Europe* (Crowell), New York, 1966.

Richard F. Staar, *The Communist Regimes in Eastern Europe: An Introduction* (Hoover Institution), Stanford, Calif., 1967.

14. Change and Prospects

MODERNIZATION

The Soviet state has been exceptionally stable for nearly forty years. Since Stalin carried out his second revolution from above, its institutions and the style and language of its politics are superficially very like those of a previous generation. But beneath this surface, change goes forward in the Soviet Union as everywhere, and particularly as in other lands wherein conditions of life are being rapidly altered. This kind of change, of content and practice, is obscure, shielded from public view, and difficult to analyze.

The most obvious cause for political change is that the Soviet Union is materially another country from that of the latter 1920's, when Stalin was moving toward dictatorial power; and it cannot be governed in the same way. The Soviet Union was then a peasant land, four-fifths rural, largely illiterate, and with only a handful of persons of higher education. Now it is industrialized, with urban population approaching three-fifths, with literacy as high as almost anywhere and with the world's largest number of highly trained professionals. The family, basis of the social order, has been altered beyond recognition, as the birth rate has dropped from that of a peasant country (44.3 per 1,000 in 1928) to that of Western Europe and the United States, 14.2 in the Russian republic in 1969.[1] The divorce rate has shot up from 0.4 per 1,000 in 1950 to 2.6 in 1969. The content of politics, the range of problems with which the state deals, has

[1] *Narodnoe khoziastvo SSSR v. 1969 g.*, Moscow, 1970, p. 35.

been transformed as in any state evolving from an agricultural to an industrial economy; and after change of content there must predictably come change of form.

From our own experience, we may formulate some idea of the effects of education and modernization on political life. Modern communications and education increase people's awareness of themselves and their affinities and the rights they may claim, especially when these rights are written into legal instruments. The educated are less easily satisfied with dogmatic simplifications, and they often look down on political leaders whose knowledge is inferior to their own. Technocratic attitudes are contrary to ideology and arbitrary power. The advanced industrial economy outgrows crude political controls, and it requires many persons of special skills, whom political leaders must take into account. Force and coercion become less effective means of government; the regime must rely more on incentives, which raise the standing of the recipients. The very fact that people are urbanized makes them harder to govern than landbound and immobile peasants. The city permits the individual to lose himself in anonymous masses; it gives choice of occupations and associations. The metropolis, a meeting place of ideas, has always been a breeding ground of heterodoxy, if not opposition. With increasing mobility people can become politically more active; doubtless because of awareness that the automobile multiplies problems of control the regime has been reluctant to bring Russia into the automotive age. But the demand grows ever stronger. The growth of international trade and contacts undermines opinion controls. The more complex society raises innumerable questions hard to decide by political means. Modernization seems to mean political pluralism.

Some evidence of the pressure against political controls in the Soviet Union has been presented in connection with economic problems and the intellectual opposition. Truth-seekers and efficiency-seekers challenge the system in different ways.[2] Ideas press forward against the curtain of censorship; artists who strive to be modern and original inevitably clash with controls, as do scientists who wish to participate fully in world developments of knowledge. Modern devices help the spread of information. A good many persons can listen to foreign broadcasts; some can put together their own transmitters. When everyone has a telephone, the KGB cannot possibly listen in on any considerable fraction. If photocopiers become widely available, censorship is diluted. The economy becomes too complicated for politicians to claim competence over all its aspects.

Highly qualified specialists require some security and self-respect if they are to fulfill their tasks efficiently. Education may be the chief generator of

---

[2] As noted by Zbigniew Brzezinski, *Between Two Ages* (Viking Press), New York, 1970, p. 80.

discontent of minority nationalities; most of the Ukrainian dissidents who have come to the attention of the West, for example, are intellectuals or students. Educated or semieducated young people in the major cities are bored with ideology and official art and are curious about the outside world and eager to travel. The intelligentsia becomes too numerous to keep under any sort of surveillance. Censorship becomes a problem with larger numbers of more technical publications. The Soviet Union desires to strengthen its place in the world, but a large merchant marine means exposing many persons to the outside and giving opportunities for defection. The teaching of foreign languages opens to subversive influences. Many thousand Soviet citizens have close contacts with foreigners, and many thousand foreigners are brought into the Soviet Union for business needs. Tourism, although unauthorized contacts are minimized, entails some opening, while it means a little leak in the foreign trade monopoly and nourishes a small class of independent traders ("speculators"). The recognized importance of science encourages a critical and rationalistic approach. As *Izvestia* put it, the goal of teachers must be "the process of endlessly deepening awareness, of ceaseless search for truth and means of applying truth to human affairs."[3]

Perhaps most critical is the mentality of the children of the elite, who must one day inherit power or wrest it from their fathers if these are unwilling to let it go. They grow up in a universe so different from that in which the present rulership was formed that the values of many of them and their character must be deeply set in new directions. They cannot be cut off effectively from foreign influences; they wish to be modern and are resistant to indoctrination with the old myths. Yet if they become a ferment in Soviet society, they cannot be crushed as the kulaks were crushed. Perhaps the most likely spark for radical change in Soviet society would be riots at the elite universities, which could not be controlled because they were led by children of the apparatchiks, if not of the Politburo.

We cannot really assess, however, the political consequences of modernization, and may be led astray by drawing analogies with American developments. The example of the Germany of the 1930's shows that an educated and industrialized modern nation, one with some experience with democracy and great respect for the legal order, can become totalitarian if political conditions are favorable. Education, as in Confucianist China, may lead away from the modern Western style of society;[4] and the Soviet Government seems confident that its education increases conformism. It is a desirable thing, in the Soviet view, if half the party secretaries have a higher education.[5] The

[3] January 16, 1971, p. 3.
[4] George Fischer, *The Soviet System and Modern Society* (Atherton Press), New York, 1969, p. 142.
[5] *Bakinskii rabochii*, October 24, 1970.

most advanced and educated of the satellites, East Germany and Czechoslovakia, are among the most dogmatic and conformist in their different ways. Those trained to a narrow specialty while subjected to lengthy indoctrination may be satisfied to leave political questions to the party. If a regime can point to rising material standards and achievements in material security and cultural amenities, as the Soviet has been able to do, people may for a long time accept this as adequate evidence of the superior knowledge of the elite and their right to rule. The complication of the modern society requires leaving more and more decisions to experts and specialists; by implication, political decisions also are for the political leaders, and ordinary folk need not concern themselves. The need for state controls, the desirability of planning not only the economy but many aspects of life becomes more apparent; and it is easier for the human lost in the complexity of the modern universe to retreat to the shelter of the all-powerful paternalistic state.

Moreover, if politically different societies face similar problems, their responses may be opposite. Student unrest in the United States has led not only to modifications of curricula but in many places to bringing students into the governing process of the universities. In the Soviet Union, the dominant reaction has been firmer discipline, more careful screening, and increased indoctrination. Television in the United States has become a powerful medium of criticism, in the Soviet Union of education and conformity. Apparently for such reasons, the United States and the Soviet Union have visibly diverged in the half dozen years after the Khrushchev period, when the two industrial societies were apparently heading in similar directions. The United States has seen social protest and a ferment of debate as seldom to be found in history, while the Soviet Union has retreated toward ideological fundamentalism and neo-Stalinism.

It is consequently impossible to foresee, especially where our information is so incomplete as in the Soviet case, just what results are to be expected from computerology, cybernetics, education, mobility, higher material standards, modern communications, and the complexity, promise, and problems of industrial civilization. In some ways, this development is libertarian. In others, it may lead to more sophisticated, possibly more effective controls; the regime is consciously trying to develop a science of political management. In some ways, it is equalitarian, as old distinctions lose meaning and all are integrated into the dynamic society; it is elitist in raising the importance of special skills, training, and background, as well as giving further advantages to organizational forces.

AGING REVOLUTION

It is also unclear to what extent changes observable in Soviet political life are attributable to modernization. If the Soviet Union becomes less extreme, less concerned with dogma, more critical, and in various ways more like conventional Western societies, if life becomes more livable and secure and less exciting, if there is more corruption, more laziness, less enthusiasm, and less hatred, all this may be largely because its Revolution is becoming ever more remote. The Soviet Union came out of a deep social revolution, and it would necessarily be changing even if technology were static because it is leaving its galvanizing political origin behind. To an unmeasurable extent, the Soviet Union owes the vigor it has displayed to the shake-up of society which attended its formation; no matter which side won the civil war, Russia might well have seen dramatic progress.

The Revolution and attendant struggles brought forward a new and energetic elite constrained to justify itself by its contribution to social purposes. It wiped out special privileges and swept away outworn structures. It permitted institutional renovation. The new social order, coupled with the reinforced sense of Russian destiny, gave large numbers of persons a profound sense of importance and purpose. It opened the way for exceptionally capable, energetic and dedicated men to assume leadership. The Bolsheviks, feeling that they had something to live and die for, set about realizing the potentials of Russia. It was a bright new dawning after a long darkness of disappointments and defeats. Victory in the civil war, in which the Bolsheviks felt they had turned back the united forces of world capitalism, deepened convictions of glorious destiny.

Such feelings could not last indefinitely, and they receded as the men who made the Revolution left the scene. The inauguration of the five-year plans, a great novelty at the time, helped rejuvenate the Revolution; but the Soviet system was showing signs of decadence by the beginning of the Second World War. This appears from the unbelievably poor showing of the Red Army against Finland, the self-deception of the top leadership and its deafness to all warnings, the sluggishness with which the government reacted to invasion, and the incapacity of the military forces in the first weeks. But Nazi brutality and the threat to Russian national existence restored the feeling for reality. Capable generals replaced intriguers and bootlickers. The common purpose of people and government was reborn. National character was reshaped in the crucible of a glorious struggle, the importance of which is shown by the large role it is given in the literature and entertainment media to this day. A result of high national morale was the very rapid growth of the first postwar years.

The searing and inspiring experiences, from the storming of the Winter Palace to the capture of Berlin, are now history to a majority of the Soviet population. As a Soviet writer puts it, "present-day youth has not gone through the vital school of revolutionary class struggle, in which the convictions and the class awareness of the older generation were formed."[6] The excitement is past, revolutionary promises, whether realized or failed, have lost relevance.

[6] *Kommunist*, no. 8, August, 1970, p. 29.

The general and ideal have yielded to the particular interest. The elite is no longer remaking society but has become self-preserving, fixed, and satisfied. The new political system has become ingrown. It values stability rather than change. It is somewhat as in the history of imperial China: the remoralization and renovation of a new dynasty in a few generations gave way to weariness and a return to the old court politics.

The ideology with which the Revolution was made loses relevance not only because it has less appeal for the better educated younger generation and less application to modern society, but also because the Soviet Union has long ceased to be a revolutionary society. It becomes ever more difficult for the elite to identify themselves with anything like a proletariat. It is idle that Soviet commentators reiterate that "the scientific-technical revolution not only does not do away with the contradictions between the two systems but on the contrary sharpens them."[7] Nowadays, to be revolutionary means to stand against the present regime, and Marxism may sharpen awareness of class differences in Soviet society. Young Russians can find in Lenin inspiration to struggle against a powerful establishment as he did. One remedy is to turn attention to the world arena, in which the ideology remains more applicable and cogent; but here, too, Soviet diplomatic interests contradict any consistent Marxist-Leninist approach. Another partial remedy is to stress nationalist-patriotic and military themes.

Khrushchev sought to revive ideology, but on a basis less of moral conviction than of what he saw as Soviet material success. Since Khrushchev, the feeling of being in the vanguard of social change may have dimmed further, despite the fact that the present leaders treat ideology as absolutely vital. It is a sign of reduced seriousness of the faith that writers are hardly attacked on ideological grounds but are mostly accused of lack of patriotism. The children of the highest ranks turn away from politics and assure their futures with a technical education.[8] Soviet youth may be fully as concerned as American with things material. As a letter-writer in *Sovetskaia kultura* put it, "With what interest, practically passion, [the girls] assess the new leather skirt Ira wore today, or Nina's 'sharp' shoes . . ."—while making fun of good students.[9] It is probably harder for Soviet leaders to believe in their own doctrines; they use quotations from Lenin rather cynically with little concern for Lenin's meaning.[10] Communist leaders seem fairly frank among themselves that their system is designed to protect their power.[11] The good apparatchik regards

---

[7] *Kommunist*, no. 7, July, 1970, p. 78.

[8] Svetlana Alliluyeva, *Only One Year* (Harper & Row), New York, 1969, p. 419.

[9] August 3, 1971, p. 2.

[10] Günther Wagenlehner, "Ideologische Verwirrung im Lenin-Jahr," *Osteuropa*, vol. 20, no. 12, December, 1970, pp. 866–878.

[11] For expressions of Eastern European leaders, see Edwin Weit, *Ostblock intern* (Hoffman u. Campe), Hamburg, 1970.

politics as something of a game, in which idealism and enthusiasm are means to be manipulated.[12]

The succession of generations also has meant a change of quality of leadership; each change has been a step away from revolutionary beginnings. Lenin was a revolutionary intellectual; Stalin was a machine politician. Lenin was a thinker and political analyst; Stalin was relatively crude and afraid of the competition of more sophisticated Marxists. Still, Stalin was a man of parts who earned the respect of the world; and his writings, at least up to the time of his absolutism, were often to the point, fairly well reasoned, and quotable. Khrushchev was a less impressive leader with few pretensions to ideological authority. The collective leaders seem to lack even Khrushchev's peasant flair and limited idealism, although they are more methodical and careful.

If the party does not advance the most dynamic men to the top, this accords with timeless political principles. Those on top have chosen their own lieutenants, and the leader who has more position than security does not want next to him persons who may threaten his standing. Lenin surrounded himself with men willing to defer entirely to him; there was no room for outstanding minds at his side, although he permitted some intellectual independence to persons of his trust, as Bukharin. Stalin, a dictator without dictatorial office or legitimacy, was inordinately suspicious of anyone who seemed to offer a possible alternative to his leadership. This may have been a motive for the murder of the popular Kirov, and it played a major part in the purges; for a political figure to display independent intelligence was practically equivalent to a sentence of death. Some capable men, as Malenkov, Molotov, and Khrushchev, managed to survive around Stalin only by submerging their own personalities. Khrushchev in turn sought to get rid of the more self-assertive of his associates, and one can assume that he endeavored to fill the top echelon with people whom he saw as innocuous. The present leadership seems reluctant to advance anyone.

The aging of the Revolution has entailed the aging of the leadership. Lenin, at forty-seven, was the oldest important member of the first Soviet government; the average age of the Politburo in 1917 was thirty-six. Since then it has tended irregularly upwards, checked by Stalin's replacement of older revolutionaries by younger adherents in the latter 1920's and early 1930's, and by Khrushchev's replacement of rivals in the latter 1950's; the average age of the Politburo (full members, as enlarged at the Twenty-Fourth Congress) in 1971 was sixty-one. Now there is no one strong enough to force retirement of any, and none has withdrawn voluntarily since Mikoyan departed in health in 1965. From 1967–1968, when Secretary Andropov (police chief) joined the Politburo and Katushev entered the Secretariat, there has not been a single demotion, retirement, or addition to the little group composed of Central Committee Secretaries and full and candidate members of the Politburo.

[12] Wolfgang Leonhard, *Die Revolution entlässt ihre Kinder* (Ullstein Bücher), Frankfurt, 1961, p. 468.

Senescence seems rather general in the upper levels of Soviet organizations, perhaps in part because it is harder to get rid of the superannuated; purge being excluded, there is nowhere for them to go, no private sector to which a political leader can usefully and honorably withdraw. Old men usually reign even in scientific institutions where youthful creativity and receptivity have most to recommend them. Four of the five top military men, Yakubovsky, Grechko, Yepishev, and Shtemenko, were born 1903–1908. For marshals, as for Politburo members, there is no fixed retirement age, although generals step down at sixty. Very few persons, except athletes, attain eminence in the Soviet Union short of their fiftieth birthday. The party ages, too. In 1966, the age for admission to the party was raised from twenty-one to twenty-four. In 1927, 14% of its membership was over forty; by 1967, 48%.[13]

As the Revolution has thus grown old, it has ceased to be revolutionary. Stalin made little alteration in formal party institutions shaped by Lenin, but he somewhat modified the state structure by his 1936 constitution, introduced significant amendments to ideology, and transformed the industrial and agricultural basis. Khrushchev made changes mostly in the name of going back to Leninism. His grand schemes added up to little more than an extension of basic policies, as in the amalgamation of the kolkhozes. When he tampered with the party, dividing it into local and provincial sections for agriculture and industry, the apparatus rose in revolt. Changes instituted by the post-Khrushchev government were mostly reversions to Stalinism. It was their height of boldness to alter criteria in planning to give more weight to profits, but even this has been largely nullified.

Soviet society has correspondingly become more traditional, less Communist and more Russian. It has rediscovered the past on a large scale. Soviet writers speak of a general revival of old customs; it is even urged that Soviet intellectuals steep themselves in Russia's historical past, not the "nihilism" of the 1920's.[14] The collection of icons and peasant art is very fashionable, and antiques are in high demand. Russians flock to listen to choral music and to view old churches and architectural monuments, and the government spends enormous sums and employs many thousand craftsmen to restore antiquities. Every town is to have its museum of local, especially military, history. The worker entering a factory receives a booklet recounting its past. Collective farms write up chronicles of their history, build monuments to heroes who fell in the Revolution and the wars, and study regional history. They revive traditional celebrations and develop new ones to commemorate the

[13] T. H. Rigby, *Communist Party Membership in the USSR* (Princeton University Press), Princeton, 1968, p. 354.

[14] *Nash sovremmenik*, January, 1970, pp. 101–107; *ABSEES*, July, 1970, p. 91; *Molodaia gvardiia*, July, 1970, pp. 308–320; *ABSEES*, January, 1971, p. 3.

induction of new members, marriages, births, the send-off of recruits to the army, the first furrow of spring, and the completion of the harvest.[15] "Today we consecrate Volodia Brovar as a wheatgrower. Volodia, serve your dear kolkhoz as your father did."[16] Numerous books have been published about the new Soviet ceremonies, not only the Soviet versions of traditional rites as marriage and death but new ones such as receiving a passport or entering a factory work force. It is required that registering authorities make marriage (with the consent of the partners) an appropriate ceremony, and each village soviet should have a commission for promoting the new rituals and old ones so far as suitable.[17] No country is fonder of distinctions, awards, etc.; the ordinary Soviet general sports dozens of medals. Soviet public life is protocol and status-conscious, and status is widely underlined by uniforms. There seems to be much more attention to etiquette than in the United States; slight infractions are damned as "nekulturny." In the ordinary manner of conservative regimes, there is increasing reliance on the family as the "primary organization of Soviet society." Mothers of many children are recognized and rewarded heroines. "It is a high party duty to strengthen the family, to help it raise up a younger generation of undaunted patriots to carry forward the great cause of communism."[18]

As the structure becomes more fixed, those in positions of authority increasingly form a new elite, the new owners of the state. These political specialists and managers are truly, as Djilas stressed, a new class in the Marxian sense, by their control of the means of production as well as of the means of force. Engels once remarked that a revolutionary leader might become something very different: "He is compelled to represent not his party or his class, but the class for whom conditions are ripe for domination. In the interest of the movement itself, he is compelled to defend the interests of an alien class and to feed his own class with phrases and promises."[19] The successors of those who made the Revolution in the name of the proletariat have become not a new bourgeoisie but a service nobility, with position dependent not on possession but on political relations and loyalty to their superiors. Party work is a profession, the highest of professions.[20] "We often speak of the special ability of the

---

[15] *Selskaia zhizn*, October 22, 1969.

[16] *Pravda*, June 12, 1971, p. 6.

[17] *Sovety deputatov trudiashchikhsia*, no. 2, 1971, p. 85.

[18] *Pravda*, July 26, 1970.

[19] Quoted by Robert V. Daniels, *The Nature of Communism* (Random House), New York, 1962, p. 60.

[20] It is not an acknowledged aspiration, however. When secondary school students were queried regarding preferences among seventy-four occupations, there was no mention of party or government work, except municipal service personnel. (Murray Yanowitch and Norton T. Dodge, "The Social Evaluation of Occupations in the Soviet Union," *Slavic Review*, vol. 28, no. 4, December, 1969, pp. 617–641.)

musician or architect, but to be a leader of men it is also necessary to have one's special ability."[21] Professionalization increases. At the 1965 elections, 25% of judges were new, implying an average tenure of twenty years; in 1970, only 17% were new, implying an average thirty years' tenure.[22] In 1967, only 9% of workers in production, but 21% of those in the administrative apparatus had held their jobs over twenty-five years.[23] It is frankly regarded as a good thing that secretaries remain in their positions.[24]

The separation of official and unofficial society is reinforced by secrecy. Those on the inside have access to knowledge denied the public; and data to which one has access widens as one's responsibilities grow. Special knowledge thus reinforces the claim to decide for and to stand over the masses. Leaders live secluded lives and are "public servants and anointed gods."[25]

Status implies material privileges; the times when high Bolsheviks lived modestly and received a worker's pay are long past. Inequality of incomes has been mentioned, but the compensation for the work and responsibilities of leadership is much less in income than in perquisites. A Komsomol chief in a small republic may make only about four times as much as an ordinary worker, so that he can hardly afford a car; but he is furnished a chauffeured limousine. The state or party provides apartments, dachas, servants, travel, expense accounts, banquets, and entertainment. A form of wealth is the prerogative of buying in special shops, where one may get foreign wares or off-season fruits and vegetables at modest prices, or in foreign currency shops. Officers' wives have first call on scarce goods at army posts.[26] A growing part of the Soviet elite shows fondness for Western styles and amenities, in the manner of their tsarist predecessors. The Ministry of Agriculture raises race horses for the Soviet Ascot set.[27] The elect hunt in reservations closed to ordinary people and sun themselves on private beaches. If ill, they go to their own hospitals. It is not remarkable that power should serve itself, and that special advantages should be used to bind the elite at different levels, rewarding and distinguishing those who have earned confidence. It is more remarkable, considering the ease with which successful revolutionaries have turned sybaritic in the past, that top Soviet leaders still live rather modestly, and the privileges of the elite have been kept inconspicuous.

Unlike Lenin, Soviet leaders who call on the people to put in an extra day's work for a "Communist Saturday" do not deign to turn out to lay a

---

[21] *Pravda*, November 11, 1970, p. 3.

[22] *Sotsialisticheskaia zakonnost*, March, 1971, p. 4; *ABSEES*, July, 1971, p. 35.

[23] Shendrik, *Obshchenarodnoe gosudarstvo*, p. 135.

[24] *Bakinskii rabochii*, October 24, 1970.

[25] *Message from Moscow* (Jonathan Cape), London, 1970.

[26] *Krasnaia zvezda*, August 1, 1969.

[27] Some details are given by *Pravda*, August 11, 1970, p. 61.

symbolic brick. It is held important to "maintain the dignity of a Soviet functionary." Distance between teacher and students should be maintained. When a teacher told his pupils, "You should prepare your lesson carefully. I also prepare every day, because I am no god and can't know everything," he was chided for reducing the magisterial authority.[28] The young people of today, moreover, need more work, less book learning.[29] Ordinary farm workers take off their hats to the brigade leader.[30] The horror of an educated family that the son should marry a slightly less educated girl was recently subject of a successful drama in Moscow.[31]

It would seem unavoidable in these circumstances that status should become partly hereditary. Industrialization of itself brings social mobility, but the upheaval of the first years and the First Five-Year Plan is finished. The gateway to advancement is increasingly higher education, not only in professional and technical specialties but in politics. Four-fifths or more of chairmen of city soviets and raion executive committees were reported (as of 1967) to have a higher education, a qualification much less common in the Soviet Union than in the United States.[32] In 1970, 87% of the rather lowly party group organizers in Kharkov had a secondary or higher education, an increase of 6% from a year before.[33] Men with higher education should be favored as party secretaries and kept in office even though subject to criticism.[34] As in other settled societies, those who are well placed can undoubtedly do much, legally or not, to give their children a head start, to improve their preparation, to ease their way past (largely oral) examinations, and to secure the political recommendations which are a major criterion.

There is some hereditary professionalism, as sons of military men are favored for military academies, sons of railroad workers for railroad training schools, and so forth. Parentage undoubtedly also plays a role in entry into the party, not only because the party cannot easily deny membership to its scions but also because those of the right family background are felt to be most assuredly loyal, and no other criterion is so important. So far, sons of the Politburo have not apparently become crown princes. However, few questions are more important for the future of the Soviet system than the degree to which the rulership may become hereditary privilege. Probably because of its political significance, there is practically no information.

[28] *Sovetskaia Estonia*, October 28, 1970, p. 3.

[29] *Izvestia*, December 18, 1970, p. 4.

[30] *Pravda*, May 25, 1970, p. 4.

[31] "Unequal Marriage," by V. Konstantinov and B. Ratser.

[32] *Nauchnye osnovy gosudarstvennogo upravleniia v SSSR* (Akademia Nauk), Moscow, 1968, p. 304.

[33] *Partiinaia zhizn*, no. 22, November, 1970, p. 53.

[34] *Partiinaia zhizn*, no. 15, August, 1970, pp. 23–24.

COLLECTIVE OR ONE-MAN RULE

A much discussed issue of Soviet politics is whether the country is to have collective leadership, with implications of potential pluralism, regularization of power, and semidemocratic development, or to revert to the mastery of a single individual, with implications of dictatorship and arbitrary power. If one can judge by the past, the answer is neither, permanently. The Soviet Union may be said to have had single leadership roughly 1917–1922, 1929–1953, and 1957–1964, or thirty-six of fifty-four years. No one held dictatorial powers, although one man has nearly always been clearly in front of his peers, during 1922–1929, 1953–1957, and 1964–1971, or eighteen of the Soviet years.

After the departure of each leader, the Politburo has apparently firmly resolved to carry on an indefinite collective rulership, which for all but one of them would be more advantageous than permitting a single individual to become the master. The process of gathering up dictatorial power has been long and difficult. Stalin was potentially in first place from his assumption of the post of General Secretary of the party in April, 1922, but he forwarded himself to a large extent as the modest man in the middle, one not to be feared; and he had to split off and discredit successively various sectors of the party to leave a core wholly loyal to himself—a process which has become difficult if not impossible. He was unable freely to exercise his sole will until 1929, and he could gain complete control only by practically destroying the party in the purges. In the last part of his life, Stalin's grip again seems to have been weakening despite his immense stature as genius-leader to victory and the custom of decades of deference.

After Stalin, there was an apparently fervent call for collective leadership; and the front-runner, Malenkov, was probably forced to relinquish his party secretaryship because of anxieties that he might step into Stalin's shoes. He could never gather the reins of power into his hands. Khrushchev could not take the premiership for several years after ousting Malenkov; and he was able to remove his principal rivals from the Presidium (Politburo) in June, 1957, only by rather fortuitous circumstances. With less legitimacy than Stalin, little military aura, and no association with Lenin and the Revolution, Khrushchev was unable to build himself up impressively. He had no weapon of terror but at all times had to reckon with his colleagues in the leadership. He never built up a loyal personal following.

Since Khrushchev, collectivity was for a long time sufficiently effective that outsiders had to guess whether Leonid Brezhnev was substantially weightier than his fellow Politburo members. At one time, Stalin's daughter judged Suslov to be the most influential, and the trekking of nearly the entire Politburo to negotiate in 1968 with the Czechs might indicate a group of mutually distrustful men unable to agree on any one or several of their number to conduct the discussions. Not until the Lenin celebrations in April, 1970, did publicity suggest much preeminence for the General Secretary. During and after the Twenty-Fourth Congress Brezhnev strongly held the limelight. He was sometimes referred to as "head" of the Politburo, much more often by the formal title, General Secretary of the CC of the CPSU—Stalin was ordinarily simply "Comrade Stalin." But there was no indication that he was strong enough to remove anyone from Politburo or Secretariat; at best he could advance some of his friends to full membership in the former.

There are numerous reasons why it is difficult to assert dictatorial power in the Soviet system.[35] One reason is the fear of the oligarchs of a boss capable of hurting them. Stalin actually used this fear against the most prominent of Lenin's heirs, Trotsky. Subsequently, Trotsky and Stalin's former allies tried to get together to stop the ambitious General Secretary, but it was then too late. Fear of a single rulership clearly worked in 1953 against Malenkov; Khrushchev seemed less dangerous at the time. Collective leadership spells general security; a political fight is dangerous for all, and a new dictator must inevitably wish to be rid of those who were formerly on a level with himself.

It has always been difficult to expel men near the top. One cannot go outside the party for support, and the inner circle hangs together. Stalin had to meet enemies on the Politburo long after he had raised himself over them. Thus, Trotsky remained a member until October, 1926. Khrushchev had great difficulty in securing removal of his enemies, even near the height of his power in 1961.[36] If no one has been forced out at the top since Mikoyan in 1965, this can hardly be because the General Secretary would not like to replace anyone.

It is harder for anyone to make himself dictator because there is no monarchic office. The position of General Secretary gives no publicly acknowledged powers; and, so far as is known, there is not even an official chairman of the Politburo. The principle of collegiality has always been rather strong in the Soviet system; it is not so much a hierarchy of leaders as of committees with bureaus and secretariats, with decision-making groups typically of about a dozen men, as the Politburo. There has never been an overt leadership principle. When Stalin stood at his acme of despotism, he did *not* decree in the imperial manner, "We Joseph Stalin, Leader of the Soviet Party and People," but in the name of the Central Committee, J. V. Stalin signing as General Secretary. The ideology proclaims the rights of the working class and secondarily the party which claims to represent it, and Marxism plays down the individual's role in history. The party, the Central Committee, and the image of Lenin serve as symbols of state unity, as does also the Politburo, which has become something of a representative body with members of the principal national groups.

[35] Cf. T. H. Rigby, "The Soviet Leadership: Towards a Self-Stabilizing Oligarchy?" *Soviet Studies*, vol. XXII, no. 2, October, 1970, pp. 167–190.

[36] Michel Tatu, *Power in the Kremlin* (Viking Press), New York, 1969, p. 169.

It has probably become more difficult as the system has matured and settled down for anyone to pull himself up to supremacy. As terror is excluded and officials become more habitually fixed in tenure, it is harder to eliminate opponents and build up a personal following. It is harder to divide and discredit a section of the party in Stalin's manner, because there are no more grand issues of social transformation, political form, or ideology. Stalin had the fundamental questions of reconstruction; for Khrushchev, there were still important matters, as de-Stalinization and economic reform. But today differences among the leaders are entirely muted. This may be partly attributed to the long and very thorough "political education" of high party men in a settled and accepted doctrine. "Genuine collectivity is inconceivable without ideological steadfastness, without the strongest discipline."[37] The oligarchs have as complete and as uniform an indoctrination as can be achieved, and they seem entirely agreed on the need of maintaining their and the party's power and on the general means of doing so.

All this means that dictatorial power is personal, identified with an individual, and dependent upon his capabilities and upon the following which he can secure. For Stalin to assert sole power he had to claim unique qualities as supreme genius, supported by his contributions to theory and his special leadership in collectivization and industrialization, later by his wartime role. Probably Khrushchev felt driven to putting forward one grandiose scheme after another to justify his own preeminence, and he was driven from power when he no longer had much success to his credit. It becomes increasingly difficult for the aging managers of a staid social order to make themselves indispensable. A new dictatorship would probably be more qualified and unstable than Khrushchev's.

Yet the Soviet system has repeatedly tended toward one-man leadership. If there is no fixed office for the ruler, who must be rather a tyrant than a king in the ancient Greek terminology, there is no fixed allocation of power among members of the central rulership. Without such constitutional support, oligarchy is unstable; it must rest on agreement among the oligarchs and can last only so long as they agree on the need to check potential tyranny of any one of their own. Historically, there have been very few enduring oligarchies, and none in big empires. All previous great authoritarian states have had a single leader as at least the symbolic head and ultimate decider of the allocation of power. Chinese emperors or Turkish sultans did not usually manage their government, but they stood as legitimizing figures in whose name power was exercised, naming and dismissing the head of the administration. The usual form of all Marxist-Leninist states likewise has been single-dictatorial, from Castro's Cuba to Mao's China. There seemingly is a deep political need for a final, single

[37] *Partiinaia zhizn*, February 3, 1969, p. 18; *Current Digest*, vol. 21, no. 7, p. 3.

decisive authority both in the revolutionary situation and in the established one-party state.

Lack of constitutional restraints means that it is impossible for the oligarchs to prevent a gradual accumulation of power by one of their number—particularly the one who, as chief figure in the party apparatus, has most power to reward or punish. There may be pressure to look to a leader to get decisions; an eleven or fifteen man committee is too cumbersome to act as effective head of state. It is particularly incapable of movement and renovation; Politburo members must be aware that the fixed oligarchy, incapable both of removing the old and bringing in new blood, is too stiff to be a permanently viable form of government. Only a single leadership can inject new life and dynamism into the system.

It may be concluded that both oligarchy and dictatorship are somewhat unstable in the Soviet system, and that the future, like the past, will probably see an alternation between them, although no one can repeat Stalin's long tenure because men no longer reach the summit before ripe middle age. The system needs a strong leader, yet it has no regular place for one or means of selecting him, and is prevented from doing so by its ideology and pretenses. In reality, it does not seem to have usually made a great deal of difference. A committee cannot carry out drastic measures, and it may be expected generally to give a relatively rational and careful administration. On the other hand, collective leadership is more subject to decadence, as it loses the ability to innovate. But under both, party rule has ordinarily proceeded in much the same manner, and it probably has not mattered much for the average apparatchik whether Stalin (after the war), Malenkov, Khrushchev, or the Brezhnev-led Politburo was in charge.

STRENGTHS

The Soviet system is stable because of its strengths, which are not less real if they are somewhat different from those usually emphasized by the Soviet Union and its foreign admirers. The Soviet state has at least outwardly a coherent social order which elevates public purpose. Resources are concentrated, in theory strongly, upon social needs and improving the capacities of the collectivity. There is certainly much less production of frivolous, useless, or harmful goods than in more disjointed societies. The attitude that, "The People's Health is the Nation's Wealth"[38] is somewhat instrumentalist but sound in effect. The directedness of society gives economic and psychological security.

[38] *Pravda*, March 16, 1971, p. 3.

Life is fairly simple and assured for ordinary Soviet youth. If one conforms (as nearly all do), studies, and works, he can get ahead supposedly to the limit of his talents and perhaps carve out a little autonomy for himself according to the status he attains. He can be sure of finding a job when he finishes school; he has studied for an occupation deemed necessary by the state. Thereafter his employment is fairly secure, as are treatment in illness, maintenance in disability, and retirement in age. There is little need to save money; life is less nervous and competitive than in the West.

Unlike old-style autocracy, the Soviet state does not ignore the common man but offers him a role in the apparatus of control and administration. It plays up to him at least verbally, tries to give him a feeling that what he has to do has some superior value, and insists that his is an equalitarian society. People are invited to join some aktiv or to become local deputies with some appearances of authority, or to be controllers of some kind, with a socially useful and undeniably important purpose. There is no room for individualism; the Russian language even lacks a word for "privacy." People are less alone than in Western society, but are practically compelled to integrate themselves into the collective of mutual responsibility. Thanks to the sense of belonging, many favor the system who do not care about ideology.

From birth to death, the average Soviet citizen has to make few independent choices. He is hardly troubled by electives in school. After having picked his professional specialization and institute, his course is fixed. Upon finishing, he has a limited choice of positions, and thereafter he is seldom expected to show initiative. Soviet émigrés find it oppressive to have to decide countless matters such as where they will live and when they will take vacations.

The state also relieves of moral and philosophic uncertainty. There are no problems of values to perplex Soviet man, no reason to stand in awe of the mysterious universe or to try in vain to make an older ethics fit a distraught modernity. Even if the answers given by the all-knowing party are not very good, they may be more satisfying than the doubtful or contradictory answers which confuse Western society. Most people are content to let someone take charge; doubt and controversy become hateful. A Soviet television commentator in the United States stated that an effort to present a discussion on Soviet television was a failure. "We organized a round-table discussion by five experts. And we got thousands of letters complaining about the program and telling us it was shameful to see five grown men arguing on television."[39]

The party's interpretation of universal purpose and the direction of history is agreeable for Soviet people, in its updated version of the old Russian vision of universal order and salvation. It is self-congratulatory, an always comfortable although sometimes unproductive approach. American futurology is

---

[39] *International Herald Tribune*, February 8, 1971, p. 7.

apt to be gloomy, and American science fiction envisions bizarre misapplications of technology. Soviet writers look ahead with obligatory optimism in the planned course of affairs and the unquestionable beneficence of science.

The Soviet system represents, at least outwardly, direction and order in a world that often seems directionless and disorderly. Its patriotism is uncomplicated, of unqualified right and duty. Its art is simple and its values straightforward. Soviet citizens are shielded from what they are taught to regard as the depravity and decadence of the West—amorality, class, social and racial conflict, and petty squabbling among nations. If capitalism is unstable, the "socialist" system offers, at least in theory, harmony and stability. Boys happily "grow up in awareness of our rightness on earth."[40] Life is serious and healthily directed. Sociologists found out that, at Soviet parties, 37% of talk was of work, 24.1% of things political, 19% of books, films, and plays, 16.6% of friends and acquaintances, 3.3% of other subjects.[41] People are given firmly to understand that they are happy, and if they are not, they must be wrong-minded, whereas in the West people are encouraged always to demand more. Anyone who compares the didactic severity of Soviet cinema and television with the diet of violence, frivolity, and sex of Western productions must question whether the former may not have survival value in a competitive world. If pornography is bad, the Russians can congratulate themselves on freedom from it. Their literature and press are uplifting, glorifying good deeds, heroism, and self-sacrifice.

It is the principle of the state that Soviet citizens are to be made good. The moral ethos and the endless inculcation of civic virtue, dedication to peace and brotherhood as defined by the party, cannot be dismissed as idle. Brezhnev told the 1970 Komsomol congress that Soviet youth was marching forward in step while Western youth was caught up in stormy crises. "Our youth," the Komsomol secretary reported, "is firm in its ideals, politically tempered, an active creative force of Soviet society, boundlessly faithful to the teachings of the great Lenin and our beloved Communist Party."[42]

The Soviet state is so gargantuan and all encompassing that it requires extraordinary independence for a citizen to stand against it. It constructs magnificent monuments; it plans cities and projects the transformation of geography, as the diversion of giant rivers from Siberia to Central Asia. It claims, and logically should have, more technocratic rationality than possible in the societies of the West. Its very self-righteousness as sole possessor of truth and the assurance with which it suppresses the opposition make efforts to think against it seem futile. To brand dissidents as insane is not merely sardonic; it is impractical if not irrational for an individual to set himself against the mighty party.

---

[40] *Pravda*, May 1, 1971, p. 6.
[41] *Cina*, February 4, 1970; *ABSEES*, July, 1970, pp. 60–61.
[42] *Pravda*, May 27, 1970, p. 2.

More important than the fact that the Soviet system carries conviction for most of the people is the fact that it suits the elite very well; a small minority can comfortably rule a discontented majority if the rulers remain united and determined. For this the Soviet system of successively narrower and more privileged circles is admirably fashioned; all parts share a broad interest in the maintenance of the apparatus. To rise politically, people must invest in a training which fits them only for the party career, and the farther people rise in various sectors the more their interests converge. The party puts in positions of power those best equipped to fortify it, as the way to advance is primarily to manage others for the benefit of the party.

Everyone in a position of authority has a vested interest in the supremacy of the party, and the party is not only an organization but a moral value. It is the unifier of the tremendous realm, and this is the basic justification for everything else which comprises the Soviet way, planned economy, police controls, sham elections and elected bodies, censorship, official creed, and monopoly of organization. No other way is apparent that the hundred-odd nationalities on one-sixth of the earth's surface could be held together. The party does all in its power, furthermore, to exclude any alternative by the repression of all other political groups and tendencies; any unofficial or spontaneous political activity is a danger to the system, no matter what its goals. The Soviet Union remains totalitarian in that the citizen can look to no independent organization for support. The alternative to the party is anarchy, the ultimate evil. Even if one should hate it, one can hardly contemplate its overthrow, much as the Germans remained obedient to Hitler even when they knew the war was lost, because he had removed all other institutions of leadership. Likewise, victims of the purges would uphold to the end their loyalty to the party which was persecuting them. To be against the party is to oppose the entire order of society. The safety of the state has always been the supreme law. Once this required the burghers to prostrate themselves before the despot of Muscovy; now it requires or seems to require the apparatus of the Soviet state.

WEAKNESSES

Enough has been written in previous chapters of the inefficiencies of the Soviet system and the difficulty of securing efficiency, creativity, and innovation under political controls. But these are due not merely to the youthful clumsiness of socialism; the Soviet government has become not more but less effective in imposing its will. There has been little progress toward Khrushchev's goal of making Soviet toilers as dutiful and disciplined in communism as bees in a hive.[43]

[43] *Pravda*, November 18, 1959.

The best dictator is frustrated by his own people. Stalin was angered that his servants had made themselves into a high caste with special rights and luxuries, but he felt unable to do anything about it.[44] The immense administrative machinery built up to carry out the central will develops its own ways, interests, and interrelations. As the original drive becomes diffuse and revolutionary purposes become irrelevant, powerholders at all levels use their power for their own, as well as governmental, purposes. Becoming bureaucratic, rule-bound, more or less corrupt, and self-seeking, the leadership loses the ability to move the apparatus, and the apparatus to move the people.

How far this process of decadence has proceeded in the Soviet Union one can only guess. But it is clear that orders do not count as they once did. A Ukrainian raikom in 1969 took up the work of a chemical factory seven times, passed appropriate resolutions, and changed nothing.[45] Novosibirsk University prepared 150 teachers for rural schools, but only eight showed up for work.[46] In 1970 the Soviet press complained several times about "pirates" on the air, breaking the official monopoly of broadcasting, even hampering communications at Moscow's main airport. In some places in Siberia almost all the fur trade is in the hands of illegal dealers, and the only remedy suggested was to raise state prices.[47] In the Ukraine in 1970, 4,500 drivers were cited for using state vehicles illegally; apparently not one was prosecuted.[48] The unregulated and more or less illegal sector of the economy may be growing more rapidly than the controlled sector; street selling is reported to be ever more massive in Baku.[49] A school director had to get private contractors to construct a school building.[50] Of 107 garages built in Moscow, 70 were designed privately by employees of the State Architectural Planning Agency, contrary to explicit regulations, for 10,000–20,000 rubles each.[51] Restaurant musicians get twice as much in tips as in salary.[52] De facto private landholding seems to be growing, at least in the countryside. City dwellers buy peasant homes as summer houses. Of 2,700 families living on a kolkhoz near Samarkand, only 676 belonged to the collective.[53] To avoid controls and because "Not months but years would pass in finding a suitable Ministry, interesting it, settling the budget, getting official acknowledgment . . ." innovative enterprises are formed irregularly under the aegis of Komsomol bodies, Trade Unions, etc. Despite emphasis on preventive

---

[44] Svetlana Alliluyeva, *Twenty Letters to a Friend* (Harper & Row), New York, 1967, p. 166.

[45] *Partiinaia zhizn*, no. 22, November, 1970, p. 5.

[46] *Sovetskaia Rossia*, November 14, 1970, p. 2.

[47] *Sovetskaia Rossia*, January 31, 1971, p. 2.

[48] *Radianska Ukraina*, March 5, 1971, p. 4; *ABSEES*, July, 1971, p. 36.

[49] *Bakinskii rabochii*, February 18, 1971, p. 4.

[50] *Pravda*, September 10, 1971, p. 3.

[51] *Pravda*, August 6, 1970, p. 3.

[52] *Sovetskaia kultura*, June 17, 1971, p. 3.

[53] *Pravda*, July 7, 1970, p. 2.

medicine, there was an epidemic of cholera in southern Russia in 1970, a disease usually associated with underdeveloped countries.

The Soviet state is no more successful than Western ones in battling alcoholism; narcotic use is a rising problem. Central coordination may fail; in one case, there were severe losses because the Ministry of Agricultural Construction and the Ministry of Industrial Construction could not agree on procedures, and no solution was envisaged.[54] Socialist firms, like capitalist ones, may refuse to pay their bills; creditors dun, but nothing is done.[55] There has been much lyrical propaganda about the development of Western Siberia, the Soviet storehouse of raw materials, but population growth there was only 8% from 1959–1970, against 16% for the country as a whole. The cultivated area of the largest Siberian district, Yakutia, decreased from 137,700 hectares in the early 1950's to 62,000 in 1969.[56] The party seems to have given up, as the 1971–1975 plan turned back to developing the established centers.

Sovietization has failed to advance in Central Asia, perhaps has been reversed. East Europe has become increasingly difficult to manage, or the means of managing it have weakened. In 1968, it became necessary to send an army into Czechoslovakia, previously a faithful satellite under merely party controls, to keep it obedient. Some liberalization in the bloc was tolerated under Khrushchev, sometimes even pushed by Moscow, for the sake of modernization; now it seems to be tolerated because of the difficulty of repressing it.

The economy responds sluggishly to the stimulants perpetually applied, and exhortation and concentration of resources on productivity bring minimal results. The Soviet share of world trade (including exchanges with the bloc) decreased from 4.3% in 1960 to 4.0% in 1969, and the Soviet share of world industrial production remained stable during that period. There is perhaps less likelihood of quickly overtaking the United States than of being surpassed by Japan. It is anomalous that a modern industrial power should have a large number of shops in which its currency is not acceptable and in which choice Soviet goods are four or five times cheaper than in open stores. Despite campaigns, control commissions, tinkering with planning devices, and even substantial investment, agricultural output has been painfully sluggish since 1958; factor productivity has grown hardly at all. Despite larger investments, a growth of only 20%–22% is foreseen for 1971–1975. The ratio of output to capital in industry has declined over almost all of Soviet history, whereas elsewhere it has regularly risen because improved technology makes capital more productive.[57] In the First Five-Year Plan, workers pressed forward or were

---

[54] *Pravda*, April 29, 1970.

[55] *Pravda*, November 12, 1970, p. 3.

[56] *Selskaia zhizn*, December 25, 1969.

[57] S. Cohn in G. Treml, *The Development of the Soviet Economy* (Praeger), New York, 1969, p. 36.

pushed with eagerness and enthusiasm, and they secured rather rapid growth despite bungling and mismanagement. Now, in normal circumstances, under sophisticated management, and with much ampler material rewards, workers loaf. As noted in Chapter 8, in the 1960's the Soviet Union reverted to the import of Western factories and technicians to run them, as in the 1930's, despite the large political cost. Not only leading industrial powers are called upon to help; the Finns build a hotel in Tallinn; the Yugoslavs give technical assistance on cattle feeding equipment. A decade ago it seemed that Soviet science was rapidly on the way to surpassing American; it has now fallen farther behind. More education is apparently not seen as the answer; while nearly everywhere in the developed world the university population has been expanding, in the Soviet Union it has been a slightly declining percentage of the population since 1966–1967.

Increasing numbers of persons have become able to challenge the regime. In the 1930's, the government could squeeze the Church practically out of organized existence. New weapons have been added to the legal arsenal, and the official position opposing religion is unchanged, but growing numbers ignore or defy the will of the party. Jews protest, sometimes even taunt the police, and demand to emigrate. Public demonstrations against official policies have been on a small scale, but such lapses would have been inconceivable in Stalin's time and unthinkable in Khrushchev's. Important scientists can make public, in a discreet way, their nonconformity with Soviet policy. Most writers continue to be entirely conformist, and censorship goes on; but critical writers attacked by the party have ceased to recant and do public penance. Instead, they may virtually challenge the regime, as when Solzhenitsyn called the Soviet Union "our seriously sick society" in a fierce protest against his exclusion from the Writers' Union. Modern painters and sculptors go on producing unapproved works and selling them in private. The growth of an underground literature, with regular publications and apparently access to police records, shows both the audacity of many writers and readers and the weakening of the will of the police to repress it. The dissent is numerically small, but it may become fashionable, as it was in tsarist Russia and as it is in most of the world today. The Soviet state has lost the fervor to effectively persecute heretics within its ranks.

The police are less zealous in enforcing the dictates of the rulers, and it is rumored that they may close their eyes for a material consideration and that prisoners may buy the way to freedom. Corruption is an age-old softener of dictatorship; and it is unavoidable, perhaps in the long run uncontrollable, in a closed society without strong idealism. Countless persons are in a position to be helpful to others by stretching or violating rules, or simply by exercising options, and they are more likely to expect material compensation as the system loses dynamism and officials gain more security. It is apparently common, if not customary, to require extra payment for such routine services as entering a freight shipment, issuing a bill of health, or assigning living space. Or a bank, before finalizing a building loan, demands the assignment of several future apartments to its own staff.[58] When a girl in a dry cleaning shop gets a job done on time, the supervisor assumes a palm-greasing.[59] In Moscow, ten times more cars are transferred by fraudulent gift certificates than by sale through legal channels.[60] "A recent checkup by employees of a supervisory board showed that the 'advanced workers' sent by collective and state farms to a medical institute were all, with few exceptions, frauds!"[61] Among the most indoctrinated and presumably best motivated, ethics are questionable. Cribbing is a problem in examinations at cadet schools.[62]

There is much sympathy and understanding for well-placed malefactors and incompetents, although in the older Bolshevik ethos standards were supposed to apply more strictly to them than to ordinary folk. Traffic police look the other way when party men commit violations. For more serious offenses, it is evidently up to the party organization to decide whether a transgressor should be tried in court or be subjected to party discipline only. When the manager of a truck depot loaned some trucks to an enterprise in return for cash, he was given a "severe reprimand."[63] About the same time, a bookkeeper who assigned an apartment for a bribe was sentenced to four years.[64] Both cases were reported as correct procedure. Numerous such cases are reported in the Soviet press. A university prorector in Sverdlovsk appropriated from university resources building materials and labor to build himself a solid private house. He apparently would not have been bothered if he had done a good job as prorector, and he would be properly forgiven if he expressed repentance.[65] A party man who sold privately goods produced in his factory was not even removed from the buro of his party organization.[66] A fairly well placed poacher seems to be able to carry on a large scale business with practical impunity.[67] The real wealth, however, is political position, so the real and invisible corruption is the improper securing or dealing in status.

So far as power is arbitrary, its abuse is unavoidable; and the basic weakness of the Soviet system is that the Leninists have never devised regular and acceptable ways of allocating power. The resolution of conflicts between

[58] *Pravda*, February 18, 1970, and January 29, 1971, p. 6.

[59] *Pravda*, August 27, 1971, p. 6.

[60] *Izvestia*, March 10, 1971, p. 4; *Current Digest*, vol. 23, no. 10, p. 34.

[61] *Izvestia*, February 24, 1971, p. 4; *Current Digest*, vol. 23, no. 9, p. 26.

[62] *Krasnaia zvezda*, September 28, 1969.

[63] *Pravda*, August 11, 1969; *Current Digest*, vol. 21, no. 32, p. 21.

[64] *Pravda*, August 13, 1969; *Current Digest*, vol. 21, no. 33, p. 4.

[65] *Pravda*, August 7, 1970, p. 2.

[66] *Pravda*, January 20, 1970.

[67] *Pravda*, August 14, 1969.

individual and collective, between groups and the entirety, which is the essence of political order, requires suitable procedures for selecting leaders and defining authority. Only the ideology assures that the party has a right to rule, and the myth that leaders are selected by a regular and democratic process of election within the party is very hollow. The principle of cooption, whereby those who got to the top remain there indefinitely and choose their successors, is not a system of permanent vigor. The Leninists have not found a solution for the problem of power, which has sooner or later led all previous authoritarian systems to decay.

It would be remarkable if they had done so, because they have never openly confronted the problem. Lenin and his followers sought first to gain power and then to use and strengthen it, while trying to cloak it in acceptable appearances of participation; but they gave no thought to limiting it. As embittered refugees of a semibackward empire, narrowly educated in history and politics, they were in no position to do so. They had a nineteenth-century mentality and were well versed only in a simplist and already outdated analysis of society. Deeply imbued with Russian attitudes, they were obsessed with revolution in their particular country, not with fundamentals of government.

In the Marxist outlook there was no problem, since government was by classes and intrinsically dictatorial, and the way to end tyranny was by giving power to the workers. The ostensible object of the Revolution was to usher in a society of no government. Like most Russian radicals, the Bolsheviks thought not in terms of restraining the state but of putting it to proper uses and then seeing it vanish. As dedicated revolutionaries and masters of socialism, they assumed that their intentions could only be perfect.

Lenin, forced into inactivity by illness, came to some perception that Bolshevik party members and "socialist" government could commit sins like those of the tsarist bureaucracy, but deep inquiry would have implied a reversal of his lifelong way of thought. He could propose nothing more helpful than bringing new blood into the Central Committee and having Stalin replaced as Secretary General. Stalin used the first to advance his acolytes and his own power, and Lenin was unable to suggest either how Stalin should be removed or how the authority of the Secretary General might be curbed.

Since then, the Soviets have shown little awareness of the dangers of unbridled power. Exceptionally, Khrushchev devised some rotation of cadres and stressed, at the Twenty-Second Congress, the advisability of "systematic renewal of elected organs." But his reforms, which were hardly put into effect, did not touch the top leaders and may have been designed only to make more effective the rule of the center. The entire subject is tabu; if Soviet leaders are driven to think about it or discuss it privately, they have the benefit of no informed Soviet writing. Nor are there any independent groups which could press their views upon the leadership. Soviet Russia is in this regard worse off than tsarist Russia, which could fairly freely discuss causes of failures.

The problem may be insoluble, even if leaders were prepared to give it their fullest attention. It is difficult to imagine any means whereby those on top could be compelled to timely retirement or to provide for their own replacement without fundamentally dividing power. But the concentration of power is the essence of the Soviet system. Any splitting of sovereignty in the empire would be a crack that might open to a chasm, leading to controversy and division and—it would be feared—to anarchy in the society that has to be tightly bound together.

PROSPECTS

There is no reason to suppose that the Soviet system cannot continue for a long time more or less as it has in the past decades. So much is hidden from view that no one should be surprised if there were sudden changes of leadership; but it would seem likely that, even if a new group should come to power, most things would continue with little change: rule by party elite, political controls with concessions to democratic appearances, censorship, and the monopoly of the official creed. Although pressures may be accumulating, the intellectual opposition is apparently at least as thin as it was in the 1870's, and the masses as passive. It should not be difficult to keep police and army loyal; if ferment threatens from below, the leadership may well prefer to strengthen controls rather than relax them, meanwhile perhaps conciliating the public by turning more resources to consumer goods. Even if the leadership continues to age and becomes much weaker than at present, there is no force in view which seems capable of replacing them, no organizational alternative to the party, no real intellectual challenge to Marxism-Leninism. The Soviet leaders have made themselves essential to the integrity of the state.

The greatest stimulus for change for the Soviet state, as once for the tsarist, is the competition of the West and the need to keep up with the advancing world of science and industry. This drive may be more compelling in one sense than it was before the Revolution because the world is more integrated and awareness of foreign ideas and achievements cannot be excluded. In another sense, however, it is weaker. The most convincing reason for improvement is not rivalry in economic or cultural spheres but feelings of insecurity, and the Soviet Union has achieved a degree of security in the nuclear balance that the tsars could not hope to attain. Now, as never before, minimal exertions should suffice to deter attack, particularly because the outside world can be kept in uncertainty regarding Soviet destructive capabilities. Defeats from time to time spurred the tsarist empire to reform and renewal, but no such stimulus is in prospect for its Soviet successor.

For the same reason, it seems unlikely that future economic shortcomings could badly shake the regime as long as it fulfills its internal political functions. If modernization lags somewhat, this is no great threat to security; and production suffices to provide necessities for all and luxuries to some. Communism was originally, and can be in the future, more a moral-religious (or political) vocation than an economic promise. Smaller authoritarian regimes in Africa and Latin America, with much weaker economies and less well organized regimes, have been able to manage their people for long periods. The Soviet citizens are deprived, as completely as the party is able, of means of exerting pressure from below. If Russian workers should try to press demands they would have, as the Polish workers, only the party and party-run unions to turn to; they would be in a worse position, as opposition to the Marxist-Leninist state would represent not a national but an antinational cause. The measures of liberalization which have been taken have come from the top and have been revocable by the top, as in the case of Khrushchev's reforms. These were consequently superficial. There was an intellectual opening, which the leadership deemed necessary, and it went far; for example, in 1962, Harvard Professor Harold Berman was invited to give a lecture series at Moscow University. But while Khrushchev was permitting intellectual relaxation and freer exchange of views, he was closing many churches Stalin had permitted to remain open, applying the death penalty for economic crimes, and exiling urban "parasites" to dismal regions. In spite of this, his successors found Khrushchev's loosening too dangerous.

Contact with the West has historically stimulated ferment in Russian society and created a potential for change, and this contact cannot be excluded because isolation means backwardness. But if Western influences seem to be eroding the foundations of Soviet society, barriers can be raised against them. This has been done to some extent. Hence the emphasis on ideological truculence and the rejection of any compromise which would seem to offer fissures for the penetration of liberal ideas. Trade is necessary and useful, but it can be handled through government agencies by persons whose interests largely coincide with those of the Politburo; and trade properly used reduces the need for economic liberalization at home. Insistence from the very beginning on the total state monopoly of foreign trade is intended not only to protect the controlled economy but to insulate from erosive political influences. The plan for 1971–1975 contemplates an increase of 32%–35% of foreign trade, most of it with satellites, against an increase of industrial production of 42%–46%, at a time when in most of the developed world foreign commerce grows more rapidly than production.

Tourism is an excellent means of garnering foreign exchange, but in the last several years, while tourism has leaped forward elsewhere, it has hardly increased in the Soviet Union. In 1969, the Soviet Union had fewer visitors (1.8 million, 62.6% of them from Eastern Europe) than Romania or Poland, less than one-third as many as Hungary.[68] Foreign reporters have in the last few years been shut off from all but the most perfunctory contact with Soviet citizens. Senior Western diplomats may spend years in Moscow without ever talking informally with any high-ranking Soviet official. Soviet tourism outside the bloc has not followed up the beginnings of a decade ago and remains trivial. Politburo members give a good example by rarely travelling outside the bloc and client states. It is a psychological handicap for the Soviet government to have to confine its citizens, but the East German resists quite successfully pressures many times stronger. It may be enough for the Soviet Union to permit the departure of a very few at the price of renouncing possessions and citizenship.

The difficulty of securing publications from abroad has been increased; they are to be only for those who show professional need. Non-Communist foreign newspapers are practically unobtainable even for tourists. The information furnished the Soviet citizen is most carefully filtered and selected; the neo-Stalinist secrecy with which the regime has tightly wrapped itself impedes comparison and makes criticism difficult. Knowledge is kept largely for those called upon to use it for proper purposes, even in realms of little direct political significance. Jurists and police supposedly know the real situation about criminality; outsiders have no basis for talking. Unauthorized persons cannot speak intelligently about the costs of the space program; much less can they say anything about the way questions are decided in the party or government or compare with foreign practices. Unless technology should leap over borders, as in some means whereby Soviet viewers could receive Western television programs, there seems no reason that, at an economic price, the Soviet Union should not be able to keep direct external influences manageable.

Change in the Soviet system is probably also impeded by the fear that it is dangerous, that yielding anything might lead to increased pressures, that any crack in the structure of authority could lead to grave fissures. Economic relaxation might lead to political relaxation. Permitting a contest in some elections could raise demands for freedom of political agitation and real elections everywhere. Giving any reality to representative institutions would provide a forum and a focus for discontents and divisions which are now kept out of sight and out of mind for the majority. In tsarist times, the feeble and unrepresentative Duma contributed to the growth of nationality feelings; in the Supreme Soviet, minority deputies would only have to ask for the realization of

---

[68] *New York Times*, January 5, 1971.

the promises of independence and autonomy so generously given. It is difficult to imagine what would happen in a democratic Russia, with its tensions and authoritarian mentality. Few seem to try to imagine, but repeat the common phrase, "The people need a leader."

Concessions to the national minorities would be especially perilous. Given a modicum of autonomy, the republics might become effective pressure groups working for ever more autonomy. Anything yielded to one republic would become harder to deny to others. One of the first demands would be relief from censorship and permission for national self-expression; this would release national consciousness. Literary gatherings easily become political manifestations. To devolve management of the economy would be to give a firmer basis for demands for autonomy. Such a feeble decentralization as Khrushchev's opened the door to protection of local interests. If the republics could bargain with central authorities, overall planning would become very difficult. Planned economies strongly tend toward autarky; the reconciliation of countless conflicts of interest would overload political capacities. "National communisms" would develop, and ideological divergency would call into question the legitimacy of the whole order.

Consequently, the task of the party may be summarized as controlling change to keep modernization consonant with the rule of the Soviet domain. For this purpose, it seeks to make its own jurisdiction as complete as possible, to keep alive as much as possible of its fading sense of mission, and to make the party so far as possible the sole intellectual as well as political leadership. It tries to bring all professions within its web, even scientists and artists, by its control of rewards and by reserving to itself the right to decide the big questions, leaving them only the minimum freedom necessary for their work. "It is very important that the agronomist or engineer should not be shut up in the confines of his professional duties but should be a fighter in the realm of ideas and take part in educational work."[69] But to bring modernization into concord with political immobility on the basis of a largely obsolete ideology is not easy.

The Soviet system has achieved much, but it cannot be counted a permanent success unless or until it can find means for the regular renewal of leadership. Many persons long thought that the Bolshevik experiment must fail because it was excessively radical and unconventional. This was an error. Its successes came primarily because it could, to a degree, make new beginnings; so far as it is incompetent and unsuccessful, this is rather because it is basically conservative and too much like authoritarian systems of the past.

[69] *Pravda*, December 26, 1970.

READINGS

Zbigniew Brzezinski, ed., *Dilemmas of Change in Soviet Politics* (Columbia University Press), New York, 1969.

R. Barry Farrell, ed., *Political Leadership in Eastern Europe and the Soviet Union* (Aldine Publishing Co.), Chicago, 1970.

Myron Rush, *Political Succession in the USSR* (Columbia University Press), New York, 1965.

APPENDIX

Rules of the Communist Party of The Soviet Union[1]

I.   PARTY MEMBERS, THEIR DUTIES AND RIGHTS

1.   Membership of the CPSU is open to any citizen of the Soviet Union who accepts the Program and the Rules of the Party, takes an active part in communist construction, works in one of the Party organizations, carries out all Party decisions, and pays membership dues.

2.   It is the duty of a Party member:

a) To work for the creation of the material and technical basis of communism; to serve as an example of the communist attitude towards labor; to raise labor productivity; to display the initiative in all that is new and progressive; to support and propagate advanced methods; to master techniques, to improve his skill; to protect and increase public socialist property, the mainstay of the might and prosperity of the Soviet country;

b) To put Party decisions firmly and steadfastly into effect; to explain the policy of the Party to the masses; to help strengthen and multiply the Party's bonds with the people; to be considerate and attentive to people; to respond promptly to the needs and requirements of the working people;

c) To take an active part in the political life of the country, in the administration of state affairs, and in economic and cultural development; to set an example in the fulfillment of his public duty; to assist in developing and strengthening communist social relations;

d) To master Marxist-Leninist theory, to improve his ideological knowledge, and to contribute to the molding and education of the man of communist society; to combat vigorously all manifestations of bourgeois ideology, remnants of a private-property psychology, religious prejudices, and other survivals of the past; to observe the principles of communist morality, and place public interests above his own;

[1] Adopted by the Twenty-second Congress of the CPSU, as amended by the Twenty-third Congress in 1966 and the Twenty-fourth Congress in 1971.

e) To be an active proponent of the ideas of socialist internationalism and Soviet patriotism among the masses of the working people; to combat survivals of nationalism and chauvinism; to contribute by word and by deed to the consolidation of the friendship of the peoples of the USSR and the fraternal bonds linking the Soviet people with the peoples of the countries of the socialist camp, with the proletarians and other working people in all countries;

f) To strengthen to the utmost the ideological and organizational unity of the Party; to safeguard the Party against the infiltration of people unworthy of the lofty name of Communist; to be truthful and honest with the Party and the people; to display vigilance; to guard Party and state secrets;

g) To develop criticism and self-criticism, boldly lay bare shortcomings and strive for their removal; to combat ostentation, conceit, complacency, and parochial tendencies; to rebuff firmly all attempts at suppressing criticism; to resist all actions injurious to the Party and the state, and to give information of them to Party bodies, up to and including the CC CPSU;

h) To implement undeviatingly the Party's policy with regard to the proper selection of personnel according to their political qualifications and personal qualities; to be uncompromising whenever the Leninist principles of the selection and education of personnel are infringed;

i) To observe Party and state discipline, which is equally binding on all Party members. The Party has one discipline, one law, for all Communists, irrespective of their past services or the positions they occupy;

j) To help, in every possible way, to strengthen the defense potential of the USSR; to wage an unflagging struggle for peace and friendship among nations.

3.   A Party member has the right:

a) To elect and be elected to Party bodies;

b) To discuss freely questions of the Party's policies and practical activities at Party meetings, conferences and congresses, at the meetings of Party committees and in the Party press; to table motions; openly to express and uphold his opinion as long as the Party organization concerned has not adopted a decision;

c) To criticize any Communist, irrespective of the position he holds, at Party meetings, conferences and congresses, and at the plenary meetings of Party committees. Those who commit the offense of suppressing criticism or victimizing anyone for criticism are responsible to and will be penalized by the Party, to the point of expulsion from the CPSU;

d) To attend in person all Party meetings and all bureau and committee meetings that discuss his activities or conduct;

e) To address any question, statement or proposal to any Party body, up to and including the CC CPSU, and to demand an answer on the substance of his address.

4. Applicants are admitted to Party membership only individually. Membership of the Party is open to politically conscious and active workers, peasants and representatives of the intelligentsia, devoted to the communist cause. New members are admitted from among the candidate members who have passed through the established probationary period.

Persons may join the Party on attaining the age of eighteen. Young people up to the age of twenty-three may join the Party only through the Leninist Young Communist League of the Soviet Union (YCL).

The procedure for the admission of candidate members to full Party membership is as follows:

a) Applicants for Party membership must submit recommendations from three members of the CPSU who have a Party standing of not less than five years and who know the applicants from having worked with them, professionally and socially, for not less than one year.

Note 1. Members of the YCL who join the party shall submit a recommendation of the district or city committee of the YCL, which is the equivalent of the recommendation of one party member.

Note 2. Members and alternate members of the CC CPSU shall refrain from giving recommendations.

b) Applications for Party membership are discussed and a decision is taken by the general meeting of the primary Party organization; the decision is considered adopted if voted by no less than two thirds of the party members at the meeting, and takes effect after endorsement by the district Party committee, or by the city Party committee in cities with no district divisions.

The presence of those who have recommended an applicant for Party membership at the discussion of the application concerned is optional.

c) Citizens of the USSR who formerly belonged to the Communist or Workers' Party of another country are admitted to membership of the Communist Party of the Soviet Union in conformity with the rules established by the CC CPSU.

Former members of other parties are admitted to membership of the CPSU in conformity with the regular procedure, except that their admission must be endorsed by a regional or territorial committee or the CC of the Communist Party of a Union Republic.

5. Communists recommending applicants for Party membership are responsible to Party organizations for the impartiality of their description of the moral qualities and professional and political qualifications of those they recommend.

6. The Party standing of those admitted to membership dates from the day when the general meeting of the primary Party organization decides to accept them as full members.

7. The procedure of registering members and candidate members of the

Party, and their transfer from one organization to another is determined by the appropriate instructions of the CC CPSU.

8. If a Party member or candidate member fails to pay membership dues for three months in succession without sufficient reason, the matter shall be discussed by the primary Party organization. If it is revealed as a result that the Party member or candidate member in question has virtually lost contact with the Party organization, he shall be regarded as having ceased to be a member of the Party; the primary Party organization shall pass a decision thereon and submit it to the district or city committee of the Party for endorsement.

9. A Party member or candidate member who fails to fulfill his duties as laid down in the Rules, or commits other offenses, shall be called to account, and may be subjected to the penalty of admonition, reprimand (severe reprimand), or reprimand (severe reprimand) with entry in the registration card. The highest Party penalty is expulsion from the Party.

In the case of insignificant offenses, measures of Party education and influence should be applied—in the form of comradely criticism, Party censure, warning, or reproof.

When the question of expelling a member from the Party is discussed, the maximum attention must be shown, and the grounds for the charges preferred against him must be thoroughly investigated.

10. The decision to expel a Communist from the Party is made by the general meeting of a primary Party organization. The decision of the primary Party organization expelling a member is regarded as adopted if not less than two thirds of the Party members attending the meeting have voted for it, and takes effect after endorsement by the district or city Party committee.

Until such time as the decision to expel him is endorsed by a district or city Party committee, the Party member or candidate member retains his membership card and is entitled to attend closed Party meetings.

An expelled Party member retains the right to appeal, within the period of two months, to the higher Party bodies, up to and including the CC CPSU.

11. The question of calling a member or alternate member of the CC of the Communist Party of a Union Republic, of a territorial, regional, area, city or district Party committee, as well as a member of an auditing commission, to account before the Party is discussed by primary Party organizations.

Party organizations pass decisions imposing penalties on members or alternate members of the said Party committees, or on members of auditing commissions, in conformity with the regular procedure.

A Party organization which proposes expelling a Communist from the CPSU communicates its proposal to the Party committee of which he is a member. A decision expelling from the Party a member or alternate member of the CC of the Communist Party of a Union Republic or a territorial, regional, area, city or district Party committee, or a member of an auditing commission, is taken at the plenary meeting of the committee concerned by a majority of two thirds of the membership.

The decision to expel from the Party a member or alternate member of the Central Committee of the CPSU, or a member of the Central Auditing Commission, is made by the Party congress, and in the interval between two congresses, by a plenary meeting of the Central Committee, by a majority of two thirds of its members.

12. Should a Party member commit an indictable offense, he shall be expelled from the Party and prosecuted in conformity with the law.

13. Appeals against expulsion from the Party or against the imposition of a penalty, as well as the decisions of Party organizations on expulsion from the Party shall be examined by the appropriate Party bodies within not more than one month from the date of their receipt.

II.   CANDIDATE MEMBERS

14. All persons joining the Party must pass through a probationary period as candidate members in order to more thoroughly familiarize themselves with the Program and the Rules of the CPSU and prepare for admission to full membership of the Party. Party organizations must assist candidates to prepare for admission to full membership of the Party, and test their personal qualities.

The period of probationary membership shall be one year.

15. The procedure for the admission of candidate members (individual admission, submission of recommendations, decision of the primary organization as to admission, and its endorsement) is identical with the procedure for the admission of Party members.

16. On the expiration of a candidate member's probationary period the primary Party organization discusses and passes a decision on his admission to full membership. Should a candidate member fail, in the course of his probationary period, to prove his worthiness, and should his personal traits make it evident that he cannot be admitted to membership of the CPSU, the Party organization shall pass a decision rejecting his admission to membership of the Party; after endorsement of that decision by the district or city Party committee, he shall cease to be considered a candidate member of the CPSU.

17. Candidate members of the Party participate in all the activities of their Party organizations; they shall have a consultative voice at Party meetings. They may not be elected to any leading Party body, nor may they be elected delegates to a Party conference or congress.

18. Candidate members of the CPSU pay membership dues at the same rate as full members.

III. ORGANIZATIONAL STRUCTURE OF THE PARTY INNER-PARTY DEMOCRACY

19. The guiding principle of the organizational structure of the Party is democratic centralism, which signifies:

a) Election of all leading Party bodies, from the lowest to the highest;

b) Periodical reports of Party bodies to their Party organizations and to higher bodies;

c) Strict Party discipline and subordination of the minority to the majority;

d) The decisions of higher bodies are obligatory for lower bodies.

20. The Party is built on the territorial-and-production principle: primary organizations are established wherever Communists are employed, and are associated territorially in district, city, etc., organizations. An organization serving a given area is higher than any Party organization serving part of that area.

21. All Party organizations are autonomous in the decision of local questions, unless their decisions conflict with Party policy.

22. The highest leading body of a Party organization is the general meeting (in the case of primary organizations), conference (in the case of district, city, area, regional or territorial organizations), or congress (in the case of the Communist Parties of the Union Republics and the Communist Party of the Soviet Union).

23. The general meeting, conference or congress, elects a bureau or committee which acts as its executive body and directs all the current work of the Party organization.

24. The election of Party bodies shall be effected by secret ballot. In an election, all Party members have the unlimited right to challenge candidates and to criticize them. Each candidate shall be voted upon separately. A candidate is considered elected if more than one half those attending the meeting, conference, or congress have voted for him. At elections of all party organs—from primary organizations to the Central Committee of the CPSU—the principle of systematic renewal of their staff and continuity of leadership will be observed.

25. A member or alternate member of the CC CPSU must by his entire activity justify the great trust placed in him by the Party. A member or alternate member of the CC CPSU who degrades his honor and dignity may not remain on

the Central Committee. The question of the removal of a member or alternate member of the CC CPSU from that body shall be decided by a plenary meeting of the Central Committee by secret ballot. The decision is regarded as adopted if not less than two thirds of the membership of the CC CPSU vote for it.

The question of the removal of a member or alternate member of the CC of the Communist Party of a Union Republic, or of a territorial, regional, area, city or district Party committee from the Party body concerned is decided by a plenary meeting of that body. The decision is regarded as adopted if not less than two thirds of the membership of the committee in question vote for it by secret ballot.

A member of the Central Auditing Commission who does not justify the great trust placed in him by the Party shall be removed from that body. This question shall be decided by a meeting of the Central Auditing Commission. The decision is regarded as adopted if not less than two thirds of the membership of the Central Auditing Commission vote by secret ballot for the removal of the member concerned from that body.

The question of the removal of a member from the auditing commission of a republican, territorial, regional, area, city or district Party organization shall be decided by a meeting of the appropriate commission according to the procedure established for members and alternate members of Party committees.

26. The free and businesslike discussion of questions of Party policy in individual Party organizations or in the Party as a whole is the inalienable right of every Party member and an important principle of inner-Party democracy. Only on the basis of inner-Party democracy is it possible to develop criticism and self-criticism and to strengthen Party discipline, which must be conscious and not mechanical.

Discussion of controversial or insufficiently clear issues may be held within the framework of individual organizations or the Party as a whole.

Partywide discussion is necessary:

a) If the necessity is recognized by several Party organizations at regional or republican level;

b) If there is not a sufficiently solid majority in the Central Committee on major questions of Party policy;

c) If the CC CPSU considers it necessary to consult the Party as a whole on any particular question of policy.

Wide discussion, especially discussion on a countrywide scale, of questions of Party policy must be so held as to ensure for Party members the free expression of their views and preclude attempts to form factional groupings destroying Party unity, attempts to split the Party.

27. The supreme principle of Party leadership is collective leadership, which is an absolute requisite for the normal functioning of Party organizations,

the proper education of cadres, and the promotion of the activity and initiative of Communists. The cult of the individual and the violations of inner-Party democracy resulting from it must not be tolerated in the Party; they are incompatible with the Leninist principles of Party life.

Collective leadership does not exempt individuals in office from personal responsibility for the job entrusted to them.

28. The Central Committees of the Communist Parties of the Union Republics, and territorial, regional, area, city and district Party committees shall systematically inform Party organizations of their work in the interim between congresses and conferences.

29. Meetings of the aktif of district, city, area, regional and territorial Party organizations and of the Communist Parties of the Union Republics shall be held to discuss major decisions of the Party and to work out measures for their execution, as well as to examine questions of local significance.

IV.   HIGHER PARTY ORGANS

30. The supreme organ of the Communist Party of the Soviet Union is the Party Congress. Congresses are convened by the Central Committee at least once in five years. The convocation of a Party Congress and its agenda shall be announced at least six weeks before the Congress. Extraordinary congresses are convened by the Central Committee of the Party on its own initiative or on the demand of not less than one third of the total membership represented at the preceding Party Congress. Extraordinary congresses shall be convened within two months. A congress is considered properly constituted if not less than one half of the total Party membership is represented at it.

The rates of representation at a Party Congress are determined by the Central Committee.

31. Should the Central Committee of the Party fail to convene an extraordinary congress within the period specified in Article 30, the organizations which demanded it have the right to form an Organizing Committee which shall enjoy the powers of the Central Committee of the Party in respect of the convocation of the extraordinary congress.

32. The Congress:

a) Hears and approves the reports of the Central Committee, of the Central Auditing Commission, and of the other central organizations;

b) Reviews, amends and endorses the Program and the Rules of the Party;

c) Determines the line of the Party in matters of home and foreign policy, and examines and decides the most important questions of communist construction;

d) Elects the Central Committee and the Central Auditing Commission.

33. The number of members to be elected to the Central Committee and to the Central Auditing Commission is determined by the Congress. In the event of vacancies occurring in the Central Committee, they are filled from among the alternate members of the CC CPSU elected by the Congress.

34. Between Congresses, the Central Committee of the Communist Party of the Soviet Union directs the activities of the Party, the local Party bodies, selects and appoints leading functionaries, directs the work of central government bodies and public organizations of working people through the Party groups in them, sets up various Party organs, institutions and enterprises and directs their activities, appoints the editors of the central newspapers and journals operating under its control, and distributes the funds of the Party budget and controls its execution.

The Central Committee represents the CPSU in its relations with other parties.

35. The CC CPSU shall keep the Party organizations regularly informed of its work.

36. The Central Auditing Commission of the CPSU supervises the expeditious and proper handling of affairs by the central bodies of the Party, and audits the accounts of the treasury and the enterprises of the Central Committee of the CPSU.

37. The CC CPSU shall hold not less than one plenary meeting every six months. Alternate members of the Central Committee shall attend its plenary meetings with consultative voice.

38. The Central Committee of the Communist Party of the Soviet Union elects a Politburo to direct the work of the Party between plenary meetings and a Secretariat to direct current work, chiefly the selection of cadres and the verification of the fulfillment of Party decisions. The Central Committee elects a General Secretary of the CC CPSU.

39. The Central Committee of the Communist Party of the Soviet Union organizes the Party Control Committee of the CC.

The Party Control Committee of the CC CPSU:

a) Verifies the observance of Party discipline by members and candidate members of the CPSU, and takes action against Communists who violate the Program and the Rules of the Party and Party or state discipline, and against violators of Party ethics;

b) Considers appeals against decisions of Central Committees of the Communist Parties of the Union Republics or of territorial and regional Party committees to expel members from the Party or impose Party penalties upon them.

40. In the period between congresses of the party, the Central Committee of the CPSU may as necessary convene All-Union party conferences for discussion of urgent questions of party policy. The procedure for conducting an All-Union party conference is determined by the CC CPSU.

V. REPUBLICAN, TERRITORIAL, REGIONAL, AREA, CITY AND DISTRICT ORGANIZATIONS OF THE PARTY

41. The republican, territorial, regional, area, city and district Party organizations and their committees take guidance in their activities from the Program and the Rules of the CPSU, conduct all work for the implementation of Party policy and organize the fulfillment of the directives of the CC CPSU within the republics, territories, regions, areas, cities and districts concerned.

42. The basic duties of republican, territorial, regional, area, city and district Party organizations, and of their leading bodies, are:

a) Political and organizational work among the masses, mobilization of the masses for the fulfillment of the tasks of communist construction, for the maximum development of industrial and agricultural production, for the fulfillment and overfulfillment of state plans; solicitude for the steady improvement of the material and cultural standards of the working people;

b) Organization of ideological work, propaganda of Marxism-Leninism, promotion of the communist awareness of the working people, guidance of the local press, radio and television, and control over the activities of cultural and educational institutions;

c) Guidance of Soviets, trade unions, the YCL, the cooperatives and other public organizations through the Party groups in them, and increasingly broader enlistment of working people in the activities of these organizations, development of the initiative and activity of the masses as an essential condition for the gradual transition from socialist statehood to public self-government under communism.

Party organizations must not act in place of government, trade union, cooperative or other public organizations of the working people; they must not allow either the merging of the functions of Party and other bodies or undue parallelism in work;

d) Selection and appointment of leading personnel, their education in the spirit of communist ideas, honesty and truthfulness, and a high sense of responsibility to the Party and the people for the work entrusted to them;

e) Large-scale enlistment of Communists in the conduct of Party activities as nonstaff workers, as a form of social work;

f) Organization of various institutions and enterprises of the Party within the bounds of their republic, territory, region, area, city or district, and guidance of their activities; distribution of Party funds within the given organization; systematic information of the higher Party body and accountability to it for their work.

Leading Bodies of Republican, Territorial and Regional Party Organizations

43. The highest body of regional, territorial and republican Party organizations is the respective regional or territorial Party conference or the congress of the Communist Party of the Union Republic, and in the interim between them the regional committee, territorial committee or the Central Committee of the Communist Party of the Union Republic.

44. Regular regional and territorial Party conferences are convened by the respective regional or territorial committees once every two or three years. Regular congresses of the Communist Parties of the Union Republics are convened by the CC of the Communist Party at least once in every five years. Extraordinary conferences and congresses are convened by decision of regional or territorial committees, or the CC of the Communist Parties of the Union or on the demand of one third of the total membership of the organizations belonging to the regional, territorial or republican Party organization.

The rates of representation at regional and territorial conferences and at congresses of the Communist Parties of the Union Republics are determined by the respective Party committees.

Regional and territorial conferences, and congresses of the Communist Parties of the Union Republics, hear the reports of the respective regional or territorial committees, or the Central Committee of the Communist Party of the Union Republic, and of the auditing commission; discuss at their own discretion other matters of Party, economic and cultural development, and elect the regional or territorial committee, the Central Committee of the Union Republic, the auditing commission and the delegates to the Congress of the CPSU.

In the period between congresses of the Communist Parties of the Union Republics, for discussion of important questions for action by the party organization, the CC of the Communist Party can as necessary convene republic Party conferences. The procedure for conducting republic Party conferences shall be determined by the CC of the Communist Party of the Union Republic.

45. The regional and territorial committees and the Central Committees of the Communist Parties of the Union Republics elect bureaus, which also include secretaries of the committees. The secretaries must have a Party standing of not less than five years. The plenary meetings of the committees also confirm the chairmen of Party commissions, heads of departments of these committees, editors of Party newspapers and journals.

Regional and territorial committees and the Central Committees of the Communist Parties of the Union Republics may set up secretariats to examine current business and verify the execution of decisions.

46. The plenary meetings of regional and territorial committees and the Central Committees of the Communist Parties of the Union Republics shall be convened at least once every four months.

47. The regional and territorial committees and the Central Committees of the Communist Parties of the Union Republics direct the area, city and district Party organizations, inspect their work and regularly hear reports of area, city and district Party committees.

Party organizations in Autonomous Republics, and in autonomous and other regions forming part of a territory or a Union Republic, function under the guidance of the respective territorial committees or Central Committees of the Communist Parties of the Union Republics.

Leading Bodies of Area, City and District (Urban and Rural) Party Organizations

48. The highest body of an area, city or district Party organization is the area, city and district Party conference or the general meeting of Communists convened by the area, city or district committee every two or three years, and the extraordinary conference convened by decision of the respective committee or on the demand of one third of the total membership of the Party organization concerned.

The area, city or district conference (general meeting) hears reports of the committee and auditing commission, discusses at its own discretion other questions of Party, economic and cultural development, and elects the area, city and district committee, the auditing commission and delegates to the regional and territorial conference or the congress of the Communist Party of the Union Republic.

The quota of representation to the area, city or district conference are established by the respective Party committee.

49. The area, city or district committee elects a bureau, including the committee secretaries, and confirms the appointment of heads of committee departments and newspaper editors. The secretaries of the area, city and district committees must have a Party standing of at least three years. The committee secretaries are confirmed by the respective regional or territorial committee, or the Central Committee of the Communist Party of the Union Republic.

50. The area, city and district committee organizes and confirms the primary Party organizations, directs their work, regularly hears reports concerning the work of Party organizations, and keeps a register of Communists.

51. The plenary meeting of the area, city and district committee is convened at least once in three months.

52. The area, city and district committee has nonstaff functionaries, sets up standing and *ad hoc* commissions on various aspects of Party work and uses

other ways to draw Communists into the activities of the Party committee on social lines.

VI. PRIMARY PARTY ORGANIZATIONS

53. The Primary Party organizations are the basis of the Party.

Primary Party organizations are formed at the places of work of Party members—in factories, state farms and other enterprises, collective farms, units of the Soviet Army, offices, educational establishments, etc., wherever there are not less than three Party members. Primary Party organizations may also be organized on the residential principle in villages and at house administrations.

In individual cases, with the permission of the oblast committee, the krai committee, or the Central Committee of the Communist Party of a Union Republic, primary party organizations may be established in the framework of several enterprises forming part of a production combine and located, as a rule, on the territory of one raion or several city raions.

54. At enterprises, collective farms and institutions with over 50 Party members and candidate members, shop, sectional, farm, team, departmental, etc., Party organizations may be formed as units of the general primary Party organizations with the sanction of the district, city or area committee.

Within shop, sectional, etc., organizations, and also within primary Party organizations having less than 50 members and candidate members, Party groups may be formed in the teams and other production units.

55. The highest organ of the primary Party organization is the Party meeting, which is convened at least once a month. In Party organizations having shop organizations, a general Party meeting is conducted at least once every two months.

In large Party organizations with a membership of more than 300 Communists, a general Party meeting is convened when necessary at times fixed by the Party committee or on the demand of a number of shop or departmental Party organizations.

56. For the conduct of current business and primary, shop or departmental Party organizations elects a bureau for the term of one year. The number of its members is fixed by the Party meeting. Primary, shop and departmental Party organizations with less than 15 Party members do not elect a bureau. Instead, they elect a secretary and deputy secretary of the Party organization.

Secretaries of primary, shop and departmental Party organizations must have a Party standing of at least one year.

Primary Party organizations with less than 150 Party members shall have, as a rule, no salaried functionaries released from their regular work.

57. In large factories and offices with more than 300 members and candidate members of the Party, and in exceptional cases in factories and offices with over 100 Communists by virtue of special production conditions and territorial dispersion, subject to the approval of the regional committee, territorial committee or Central Committee of the Communist Party of the Union Republic, Party committees may be formed, the shop and departmental Party organizations at these factories and offices being granted the status of primary Party organizations.

The Party organizations of collective and state farms may set up Party committees if they have a minimum of 50 Communists.

In Party organizations with more than 500 Communists, with the permission of the oblast committee, the krai committee, or the Central Committee of the Communist Party of a Union Republic, Party committees can be formed in large shops, and the rights of a primary Party organization can be extended to Party organizations of production divisions.

The Party committees are elected for a term of two or three years. Their numerical composition is fixed by the general Party meeting or conference.

58. Party committees of primary organizations having more than 1,000 Communists, with the permission of the CC of the Union Republic Communist Party, may be granted the rights of a district Party committee regarding questions of acceptance into Party membership and on registering regular and candidate members and on examination of personal cases of Communists.

59. Party committees which have been granted the rights of district Party committees are elected for a two-year term.

In its activities the primary Party organization takes guidance from the Program and the Rules of the CPSU. It conducts its work directly among the working people, rallies them around the Communist Party of the Soviet Union, organizes the masses to carry out the Party policy and to work for the building of communism.

The primary Party organization:

a) Admits new members to the CPSU;

b) Educates Communists in a spirit of loyalty to the Party cause, ideological staunchness and communist ethics;

c) Organizes the study by Communists of Marxist-Leninist theory in close connection with the practice of communist construction and opposes all attempts at revisionist distortions of Marxism-Leninism and its dogmatic interpretation;

d) Ensures the vanguard of Communists in the sphere of labor and in the sociopolitical and economic activities of enterprises, collective farms, institutions, educational establishments, etc.;

e) Acts as the organizer of the working people for the performance of the current tasks of communist construction, heads the socialist emulation movement for the fulfillment of state plans and undertakings of the working people, rallies the masses to disclose and make the best use of untapped resources at enterprises and collective farms, and to apply in production on a broad scale the achievements of science, engineering and the experience of front-rankers; works for the strengthening of labor discipline, the steady increase of labor productivity and improvement of the quality of production, and shows concern for the protection and increase of social wealth at enterprises, state farms and collective farms;

f) Conducts agitational and propaganda work among the masses, educates them in the communist spirit, helps the working people to acquire proficiency in administering state and social affairs;

g) On the basis of extensive criticism and self-criticism, combats cases of bureaucracy, parochialism, and violations of state discipline, thwarts attempts to deceive the state, acts against negligence, waste and extravagance at enterprises, collective farms and offices;

h) Assists the area, city and district committees in their activities and is accountable to them for its work.

The Party organization must see to it that every Communist should observe in his own life and cultivate among working people the moral principles set forth in the Program of the CPSU, in the moral code of the builder of communism:

Loyalty to the communist cause, love of his own socialist country, and of other socialist countries;

Conscientious labor for the benefit of society, for he who does not work, neither shall he eat;

Concern on everyone's part for the protection and increase of social wealth;

Lofty sense of public duty, intolerance of violations of public interests;

Collectivism and comradely mutual assistance: one for all, and all for one;

Humane relations and mutual respect among people; man is to man a friend, comrade and brother;

Honesty and truthfulness, moral purity, unpretentiousness and modesty in public and personal life;

Mutual respect in the family circle and concern for the upbringing of children;

Intolerance of injustice, parasitism, dishonesty, careerism and moneygrubbing;

Friendship and fraternity among all peoples of the USSR, intolerance of national and racial hostility;

Intolerance of the enemies of communism, the enemies of peace and those who oppose the freedom of the peoples;

Fraternal solidarity with the working people of all countries, with all peoples.

60. Primary Party organizations of enterprises in industry, transportation, communications, construction, material-technical provision, trade, meal service, services to the public, collective farms, state farms and other agricultural enterprises, projection organizations, construction bureaus, scientific-research institutes, educational institutions, cultural and health establishments have the right of control of administration.

Party organizations in Ministries, State Committees, and other central and local soviet and economic establishments and offices carry on control of the work of the apparatus in the fulfillment of directives of the Party and the government and the observance of Soviet laws. They must actively promote improvement of the apparatus, cultivate among the personnel a high sense of responsibility for work entrusted to them, promote state discipline and the better servicing of the population, firmly combat bureaucracy and red tape, inform the appropriate Party bodies in good time on shortcomings in the work of the respective offices and individuals, regardless of what posts the latter may occupy.

VII. THE PARTY AND THE YCL

61. The Leninist Young Communist League of the Soviet Union is an independently acting social organization of young people, an active helper and reserve of the Party. The YCL helps the Party educate the youth in the communist spirit, draw it into the work of building a new society, train a rising generation of harmoniously developed people who will live and work and administer public affairs under communism.

62. YCL organizations enjoy the right of broad initiative in discussing and submitting to the appropriate Party organizations questions related to the work of enterprises, collective farms and offices. They must be active levers in the implementation of Party directives in all spheres of communist construction, especially where there are no primary Party organizations.

63. The YCL conducts its activities under the guidance of the Communist Party of the Soviet Union. The work of the local YCL organizations is directed and controlled by the appropriate republican, territorial, regional, area, city and district Party organizations.

In their communist educational work among the youth, local Party bodies and primary Party organizations rely on the support of the YCL organizations, and uphold and promote their useful undertakings.

64. Members of the YCL who have been admitted into the CPSU cease to belong to the YCL the moment they join the Party, provided they do not hold leading posts in YCL organizations.

VIII. PARTY ORGANIZATIONS IN THE SOVIET ARMY

65. Party organizations in the Soviet Army take guidance in their work from the Program and the Rules of the CPSU and operate on the basis of instructions issued by the Central Committee.

The Party organizations of the Soviet Army carry through the policy of the Party in the Armed Forces, rally servicemen round the Communist Party, educate them in the spirit of Marxism-Leninism and boundless loyalty to the socialist homeland, actively further the unity of the army and the people, work for the strengthening of military discipline, rally servicemen to carry out the tasks of military and political training and acquire skill in the use of new technique and weapons, and to irreproachably perform their military duty and the orders and instructions of the command.

66. The guidance of Party work in the Armed Forces is exercised by the Central Committee of the CPSU through the Chief Political Administration of the Soviet Army and Navy, which functions as a department of the CC CPSU.

The chiefs of the political administrations of military areas and fleets, and chiefs of the political administrations of armies must be Party members of five years' standing, and the chiefs of political departments of military formations must be Party members of three years' standing.

67. The Party organizations and political bodies of the Soviet Army maintain close contact with local Party committees, and keep them informed about political work in the military units. The secretaries of military Party organizations and chiefs of political bodies participate in the work of local Party committees.

IX.   PARTY GROUPS IN NON-PARTY ORGANIZATIONS

68. At congresses, conferences and meetings and in the elective bodies of Soviets, trade unions, cooperatives and other mass organizations of the working people having at least three Party members, Party groups are formed for the purpose of strengthening the influence of the Party in every way and carrying out Party policy among non-Party people, strengthening Party and state discipline, combating bureaucracy, and verifying the fulfillment of Party and government directives.

69. The Party groups are subordinate to the appropriate Party bodies: the Central Committee of the Communist Party of the Soviet Union, the Central

Committees of the Communist Parties of the Union Republics, territorial, regional, area, city or district Party committees.

In all matters the groups must strictly and unswervingly abide by decisions of the leading Party bodies.

X. PARTY FUNDS

70. The funds of the Party and its organizations are derived from membership dues, incomes from Party enterprises and other revenue.

71. The monthly membership dues for Party members and candidate members are as follows:

Monthly earnings	*Dues*	
up to 50 rubles	10 kopeks	
from 51 to 100 rubles	0.5%	
from 101 to 150 rubles	1.0	of the
from 151 to 200 rubles	1.5	monthly
from 201 to 250 rubles	2.0	earnings
from 251 to 300 rubles	2.5	
over 300 rubles	3.0	

72. An entrance fee of 2 percent of monthly earnings is paid on admission to the Party as a candidate member.

Index